ure **&**
ture DUNDEE

ship
council

ary

INDUSTRIAL ARCHAEOLOGY:
A HANDBOOK

INDUSTRIAL ARCHAEOLOGY: A HANDBOOK

Marilyn Palmer, Michael Nevell
and Mark Sissons

CBA Practical Handbook No. 21
Council for British Archaeology 2012

Published in 2012 by the Council for British Archaeology
St Mary's House, 66 Bootham, York, YO30 7BZ

British Library cataloguing in Publication Data
A catalogue record for this book is available from the British Library
ISBN 978-1-902771-92-2

Typeset by Carnegie Book Production
Printed and bound by Henry Ling Ltd

The publisher acknowledges with gratitude a grant from English Heritage towards the
cost of publication

Front cover: Excavation of 19th-century housing at Hungate, York, in the shadow of
Leetham's Flour Warehouse (© York Archaeological Trust)
Back cover: Furnaces at the Blaenavon World Heritage Site, South Wales (© Marilyn
Palmer); Scotland's Industrial Souvenir, 1905 (courtesy of Dundee City Archives);
Lathom Junction locks, Leeds and Liverpool Canal (© Michael Nevell)

Contents

List of illustrations

Acknowledgements

The origins of this book

This book is the outcome of a series of eleven day schools run between September 2008 and February 2011 by the Association for Industrial Archaeology (AIA) in conjunction with the Council for British Archaeology, with funding from English Heritage's National Capacity Building Programme. Two national pilot days were run in Manchester and Bristol, followed by nine other day schools in each of the English Heritage regions. Their purpose was to train volunteers in the identification of significant features of industrial buildings and to enable them to make informed comment in the planning context. Fact sheets were provided by speakers at the day schools, and these were initially used in planning this book, although considerable additional material was written by the three editors. Since delegates from professional archaeological contract units and local authorities also attended the day schools, it was decided to include sections in the book not just on industrial buildings but also on excavated sites, since in recent years brownfield archaeology has demonstrated the importance of excavation for understanding the scale of industrial activity in Britain. As is often the case, this book has grown in the writing and now offers the most recent assessment of the origins, scope and impact of industrial archaeology in Britain, as well as extensive guides to Further Reading and suggestions for places to visit.

The following are thanked for their help in numerous ways: Lynne Walker, formerly of the Council for British Archaeology (CBA), and Brian Grimsditch of the Centre for Applied Archaeology (CfAA), University of Salford, for all their work in organising the day schools.

Tony Crosby, former Chairman of AIA, Bruce Hedge, Treasurer of AIA, and Peter Olver, Finance Director of CBA, for their help with the financial arrangements for the day schools and the book.

Catrina Appleby, Frances Mee and Gill Chitty at the CBA for all their help, guidance and encouragement for writing this book.

Keith Falconer of English Heritage for reviewing the first draft of the book and making many helpful suggestions, and Simon Thurley, Chief Executive of English Heritage for writing the Foreword.

The following are thanked for their particular help with sections of the book: Amber Patrick (AIA); Gill Chitty (CBA); David George (Manchester Regional Industrial Archaeology Society); Helen Gomersall (AIA); Shane Gould and Martin Newman (English Heritage); Miles Oglethorpe and Mark Watson (Historic Scotland); and Ian West (University of Leicester and AIA).

Organisers of the day schools, apart from the editors, were David Alderton (AIA) at Ipswich, Ian Ayris (Tyne and Wear Specialist Conservation Team) at Newcastle, Mike Bone (AIA and Bristol Industrial Archaeology Society) at Bristol, Robert Carr (AIA and Greater London Industrial Archaeology Society) at London, Glenys and Alan Crocker (AIA and Surrey Industrial History Group) at Chilworth, David de Haan (Programme Director, Ironbridge Gorge Museum Trust and AIA) at Ironbridge, Peter Stanier (AIA) at Exeter, and Lynne Walker (CBA) at York. Most of the organisers also contributed fact sheets. Other contributors to the day schools and providers of fact sheets included David Calow, Paul Collins, David Cranstone, Nigel Crowe, Andrew Davison, Bill Fawcett, Ian Gibson, Roger Holden, Bob Maltster, Chris Matcham, Richard Newman, Andrew Norris, Keith Reedman, George Sheeran, Tim Smith, Paul Sowan, Barrie Trinder, Malcolm Tucker, Geoff Timmins, Martin Watts, Mark Watson and John Yates.

The Editors

The Editors are all Council members of the Association for Industrial Archaeology (AIA). **Marilyn Palmer** is Emeritus Professor of Industrial Archaeology in the University of Leicester, whose mission has been to ensure the academic acceptance of industrial archaeology in higher education while not losing sight of its roots in the voluntary sector. A former Chairman of AIA and co-editor of *Industrial Archaeology Review,* she is currently its President. She was a Commissioner with the Royal Commission on the Historical Monuments of England from 1993 until its amalgamation with English Heritage in 1999, and now serves on various national committees concerned with archaeology and industrial archaeology for English Heritage and the National Trust as well as being a Trustee and a Vice-President of the CBA. **Michael Nevell** is Head of the Centre for Applied Archaeology at Salford University and has done important work to ensure that industrial archaeology is taken seriously by professional archaeologists and is also Chairman of the Buildings Archaeology Group of the Institute for Archaeologists. His research interests include the origins and development of industrialisation and its impact on contemporary society in Britain and Europe, and the landscape and social impact of the textile industry. He is currently co-editor of *Industrial Archaeology Review.* **Mark Sissons** trained in textile technology and worked in many different managerial roles in the hosiery and knitwear industries. In retirement in North Yorkshire, he is archivist to, and a director of, the North Yorkshire Moors Railway and sits on the North York Moors National Park Archaeological Advisory Committee. A previous secretary of the Council for British Archaeology's Industrial Archaeological Committee, he is currently Chairman of AIA and has particular interests in the continuing role of the volunteer in industrial archaeology.

The editors are very grateful to all contributors for permission to make use of their material but errors of fact and interpretation remain with the editors. The way the book has been written means that there are some differences in style between the sections.

Images

Many of the images are those from the editors' own collections: those credited to Michael Nevell are copyright of the Centre for Applied Archaeology, University of Salford. Figures 2.5, 2.6, 3.3, 3.6, 3.8, 4.3 and 4.16 were drawn with the assistance of the late Peter Neaverson and Deborah Miles-Williams at the University of Leicester. Other images and permissions for use were kindly provided by Ian Miller (Oxford Archaeology); Martin Railton (North Pennines Archaeology); Andy Chopping (Museum of London Archaeology Services); Northern Counties Archaeology Services; Weald and Downland Museum; Mike Hardy (National Trust); Ian Shipley (www.isphotographic.co.uk); Phil Newman, (NAMHO); Allen Adams (English Heritage); Paul Barnwell (Oxford University Centre for Continuing Education); Kathleen Elkin (Leicestershire Museums Service); Paul Collins (South Staffordshire Council); Suzanne Lilley (University of York); Colin Ray; Angus Buchanan (University of Bath); Gary Campion (University of Northampton); Tim Smith (GLIAS); Wiltshire and Swindon Archives; Birmingham City Libraries and Archives.

Notes on Further Reading

Chapter One, an analysis of the origins and scope of industrial archaeology, is fully referenced and a bibliography can be found in section 1.5. For the other chapters, notes on further reading can be found after each of the sections, with suggestions about where to start on each subject.

Many references are included to *Industrial Archaeology Review*, the UK's leading journal on the subject. Published by Maney of Leeds, all issues since the journal's inception in 1976 are available on-line: see http://maney.co.uk/index.php/journals/iar/. Individual articles can be purchased as downloads, or full access is available by joining the Association for Industrial Archaeology: see http://www.industrial-archaeology.org/.

Many of the technical terms used in this book are explained, often with useful diagrams, in the *Dictionary of Industrial Archaeology* by William Jones (Sutton Publishing, 2nd edn, 2006).

The data from the original site cards from the National Record of Industrial Monuments originally located at the University of Bath are being made available by English Heritage and many can already be accessed via PastScape: see http://www.pastscape.org.uk/. The complete Step One MPP reports are being digitised and will also shortly be available on-line from English Heritage. The Step Three reports are in the English Heritage Library (formerly the National Monuments Record) in the Engine House, Fire Fly Avenue, Swindon SN2 2EH which is open to the public each weekday except Mondays, as well as in the Library of the Ironbridge Institute in Shropshire and the offices of the Council for British Archaeology in York. Many of the sites included in the Step Three MPP reports have been added to the National Record of the Historic Environment, also available through PastScape. English Heritage has also put together a guide to its collections of historic industrial photographs: see http://www. englishheritagearchives.org.uk/Catalogues/Default.aspx.

Some grey literature reports on industrial sites are available through the Archaeology Data Service: see http://archaeologydataservice.ac.uk/ as well as in individual HERs.

Foreword

Understanding and valuing our industrial past is one of the great challenges of modern-day heritage management. This year's English Heritage *Heritage at Risk* programme focused on the threats facing industrial heritage, which is disproportionately more likely to experience both neglect and heritage crime than any other type of heritage. Yet industrial remains are some of the most striking, and most loved, of all. From the volunteers who keep the machinery running at collieries and lighthouses, to the archaeologists who help us learn more about a rapidly vanishing past, the appeal and the importance of industrial heritage is clear.

The CBA has been at the forefront of campaigning for industrial heritage, indeed it even has a claim for its invention. In this exciting new volume, which English Heritage is extremely pleased to be funding, the CBA has brought together renowned experts to present an up-to-date and comprehensive introduction to an area of archaeology many may be unfamiliar with. From the remains of manufacturing industries ranging from aeroplanes to lace, to studies of how workforces were housed and provided for, this book is seminal in looking across the breadth of the subject, including studies of previously excavated sites.

I encourage anyone with an interest in our past to take a glance through the chapters of this book, and familiarise themselves with what industrial archaeology encompasses, and why we should all care what happens to it.

Dr Simon Thurley
Chief Executive, English Heritage

Industrial archaeology: an overview

1.1 The origins, development and scope of industrial archaeology

The archaeological study of the physical evidence of recent industrial activity has been one of the most important developments in archaeology, at least in Britain, in the second half of the 20th century. Industrial archaeology has been transformed from a fringe activity in the 1950s to an internationally recognised element of the discipline of archaeology, demonstrated by the large number of cultural landscapes designated as World Heritage sites by UNESCO which have industrial activity at their heart. In this, however, lies the dichotomy of industrial archaeology – it is both an archaeological study of the ways in which people lived and worked in the past through the physical remains which survive into the present and at the same time a conservation movement to protect and interpret those remains. Obviously, the two aspects come together: it is impossible to interpret industrial sites and monuments unless they are understood through archaeological and historical study. Yet the popular and even the professional conception of industrial archaeology has tended to adopt its meaning as a movement to conserve the industrial past, which would be better termed 'industrial heritage', rather than its meaning as the study of the ways in which people worked in the past. Undoubtedly, the conservation movement in the early days of industrial archaeology looked to preserve key machines and technologies from those classic industries and transport networks of the Industrial Revolution then in decline: canals, coal mining, engineering, iron working, railways, ship building, and textiles (Palmer 2010). This led to the establishment of national, regional and local industrial archaeology museums, many of which survive today and act as an important archive for understanding the technological and scientific development of specific industries long gone.

However, the increasing involvement of archaeologists in both the academic and public arenas as well as the numbers of professional archaeologists dealing with brownfield sites as part of developer-funded archaeology has begun to redress this balance; in the first decade of the 21st century, roughly 30% of all professional archaeology done in Britain has examined archaeological deposits that include material from the classic period of industrialisation. This work has demonstrated just how much can be learnt from the physical remains of past industrial activity, even in the more recent past, and this has also found its way into more university-based courses rather than only into adult and continuing education where it was first taught.

Origins: the role of the Council for British Archaeology (CBA)

Industrial archaeology originated in Britain in the 1950s, after the post-war preoccupation with renewal had led to the destruction of much of the landscape associated with early industrialisation. It is generally agreed that the term was first used in print by Michael Rix, Staff Tutor in Architectural History in the University of Birmingham's Department of Extramural Studies, who was running extramural classes in the Black Country; both he and his students became aware of the destruction of the landscape going on around them. Rix wrote an article in *The Amateur Historian* in 1955, which concluded that 'there are still many monuments to be scheduled, many books to be written and much fieldwork to be done before industrial archaeology can take its rightful place among the studies of these islands' (Rix 1955, 228). In the same year, W G Hoskins brought out his seminal *The Making of the English Landscape* (Hoskins 1955), which prompted those interested in local studies to take more note of the landscape and buildings around them, not just through documentary sources, and undoubtedly helped to create an atmosphere conducive to the development of a new discipline which also considered surviving physical evidence in the modern landscape. Rix wrote a longer piece about industrial archaeology in a Historical Association pamphlet, *Industrial Archaeology*, in 1967, in which he reiterated the importance of an archaeological approach to industrial sites: 'the prime task of the industrial archaeologist at the moment is an archaeological one and that is in fieldwork'. He also posed a challenge to the archaeological community: 'industrial archaeology serves as a useful reminder to the whole archaeological world that the *terminus post quem* of archaeological research is not 55 BC nor AD 410. The *terminus post quem* of archaeological research is today' (Rix 1967, 18).

The CBA had been founded in 1944 in response to war-time devastation and had established its role as a forum for representing the views, ideas and policies of British archaeology to government, the media, and the public. The organisation has always been quick to respond to new developments in archaeology and was ready to champion the new discipline. A well-attended conference was organised in 1959, the outcome of which was to throw the problem back to the CBA and urge that the organisation should seek to persuade both central and local authorities to formulate a policy for recording and preserving industrial monuments. The CBA set up an Industrial Archaeology Research Committee, with a membership which encompassed various eminent scholars from all aspects of the discipline including Professor W F Grimes, the eminent prehistorian and successively Secretary and President of the CBA. This group made an important decision which was to influence the future direction of industrial archaeology by insisting that 'the subject should be considered for practical purposes as post-medieval, but so as

Figure 1.1 Beatrice de Cardi *c* 1966 as Assistant Secretary to the CBA (courtesy of CBA)

to include all interested in the field, the term industrial archaeology was adopted rather than the archaeology of the industrial age which would have confined it to a definite period'. This was a highly significant decision which has enabled industrial archaeologists to study and research sites where phases of development often extend back well beyond the classic period of industrialisation (Palmer 2010).

The CBA, especially its hard-working Assistant Secretary, Beatrice de Cardi (Fig 1.1), did its best to obtain official support for an extensive survey of surviving industrial sites in Britain but met with lukewarm responses from the various Royal Commissions on Historical Monuments and from the then Ministry of Public Buildings and Works (MPBW), the predecessor of English Heritage. Forced to depend on its own resources including its affiliated groups, the CBA took a tremendous step forward by devising a basic Record Card for Industrial Monuments which was to be produced and paid for by the local groups who wanted copies. In 1962 the CBA persuaded the MPBW to provide a small sum to employ someone for a couple of years to coordinate the activities of local groups and so provide some sort of direction for this *ad hoc* survey of existing industrial sites. Rex Wailes, already well known for his pioneering work on windmills, was appointed on a part-time basis and travelled round the country advising volunteers on the best ways to carry out regional surveys and to fill in the cards as well as make sketches and take photographs. The first survey of industrial monuments in Great Britain was, then, undertaken entirely by volunteers, the only exception being in Northern Ireland where the Ancient Monuments Board of the Ministry of Finance commissioned a survey of the industrial monuments of County Down from Dr E R R Green as early as 1956 and then appointed Dr W A McCutcheon to follow this up by undertaking a similar survey of the whole of Northern Ireland from the 1960s onwards (Green 1963; McCutcheon 1980).

Arrangements for the central deposition of all the record cards being filled in by English volunteers did not work very well until, in 1965, Dr Angus Buchanan at Bath University of Technology (or Bristol College of Science and Technology as it then was) undertook the creation of a central, classified, record from these cards, the National Record of Industrial Monuments (NRIM). Then, in 1971, Keith Falconer was appointed by MPBW as the first full-time Survey Officer to the Industrial Monuments Survey in succession to Rex Wailes; he worked mainly with Dr Buchanan in the University of Bath, although he acted as Secretary to the CBA's Industrial Archaeology Committee. An Advisory Panel from within this Committee had been set up in 1967 to oversee the work of the Survey and to make recommendations for statutory designation, recording or preservation by museums (see 1.3 below). In 1981, the NRIM and the Industrial Monuments

Survey were transferred from Bath to the National Monuments Record (NMR) of the Royal Commission on the Historical Monuments of England (RCHME) (Newman 2009, 2010). Keith Falconer became Head of Industrial Archaeology within RCHME in 1986 and continued in that capacity after RCHME was amalgamated with English Heritage in 1999. English Heritage has continued to enhance the national record of industrial sites as part of the NMR but the original survey was undoubtedly a CBA initiative and the means of carrying it out was very much in line with CBA policy of encouraging the work of volunteers. Many industrial sites would have disappeared completely unrecorded had it not been for the work of volunteer groups as well as the CBA's Industrial Archaeology Committee, which in 1981 produced a useful review of the Recording of Industrial Sites, detailing what was being done in both England and Scotland at that time (Falconer & Hay 1981).

The CBA Industrial Archaeology Committee also tried from the very beginning to produce a *Handbook on Industrial Archaeology* which would supplement its 'Hints to Reporters' and be of help to volunteer fieldworkers. This was eventually produced not by the CBA itself but by Kenneth Hudson, a member of the Research Committee and Industrial Correspondent for the BBC West region based in Bristol (Hudson 1963, 1967). The CBA never did produce a Handbook of Industrial Archaeology itself at the time of its initial involvement in the championship of the discipline, and the present book has been written to commemorate those efforts 50 years on.

Growth and development

The CBA's encouragement of the completion of its record cards by local volunteers also led to the formation of many county-based specialist groups, one of the earliest being the Bristol Industrial Archaeology Society in 1967. Of course, special interest groups of this kind had existed earlier, notably the Sheffield Trades Historical Society, dating back to 1918 and seeking to conserve both the tools and skills of the Sheffield metal-working trades, and the Cornish Engines Preservation Committee, founded in 1935 to try to ensure the preservation in their original houses of some of the steam pumping and winding engines from the declining metal mining industry; the Trevithick Society is its successor. The difference in the new groups was their concern to make a record of the whole range of industrial sites and structures which still existed in their localities, since these were not then included on county Sites and Monuments Records (SMRs) (now Historic Environment Records, HERs), and so not monitored in local planning processes. The problem was to translate these local studies into some kind of national understanding of the extent of survival of the remains of past industrial activity in the United Kingdom. A series of national conferences, first organised in Bath by Dr Angus Buchanan (Fig 1.2), eventually led to the formation in 1973 of a national organisation, the Association for Industrial Archaeology (Buchanan 2000). Through its affiliated societies scheme, this organisation provided a focus for many of the volunteer groups throughout the United Kingdom and went on to found its own journal, *Industrial Archaeology*

Review, in 1976, which eventually superseded *The Journal of Industrial Archaeology*, initially edited by Kenneth Hudson and published by David & Charles of Newton Abbot in Devon from 1964 to 1983.

Various publishers now began to take industrial archaeology seriously. Angus Buchanan's seminal *Industrial Archaeology in Britain* (Buchanan 1972), together with Arthur Raistrick's *Industrial Archaeology: an Historical Survey* (Raistrick 1972) and Neil Cossons' *The BP Book of Industrial Archaeology* (Cossons 1975), stimulated discussion about the scope of industrial archaeology (see below). Numerous regional gazetteers of sites were also a feature of the 1960s to the 1980s, when discoveries of industrial sites were being made throughout the UK by volunteers and professionals alike. The series *The Industrial Archaeology of the British Isles*, published by David & Charles and edited by Dr E R R Green, began with Kenneth Hudson's *Southern England* (Hudson 1965) and David Smith's *East Midlands* (Smith 1965). These followed a similar format, with introductory chapters on the industries of the region preceding a substantial gazetteer of sites. Nearly twenty such volumes were published between 1965 and 1975, together with companion volumes like Jennifer Tann's *Gloucestershire Woollen Mills* (Tann 1967). Other publishers then took up the baton, notably Batsford with its regrettably short-lived *The Industrial Archaeology of the British Isles*, edited by Keith Falconer and including his influential nationwide *Guide to England's Industrial Heritage* (Falconer 1980). This series tackled important areas not covered by David & Charles such as the West Midlands (Brook 1977), East Anglia (Alderton & Booker 1980), central-southern England (C A & R A Buchanan 1980) and Scotland (Hume 1976 and 1977).

By the 1980s, it had become impossible for volunteer organisations to keep pace with the rapid decline of many of the classic 18th- and 19th-century industries, when whole classes of monuments such as textile mills, iron works and coal mines

Figure 1.2 Bath Industrial Archaeology Conference, 1968. Examining the Griffin gas engine from Bowler's workshop in Bath (now in Bath Museum of Work), from left to right, are Neil Cossons, Michael Rix, Angus Buchanan, Frank Atkinson, Robert Vogel (USA), and Marie Nisser (Sweden) (© *Bath Chronicle*, courtesy of Professor Angus Buchanan)

Figure 1.3 Boiler
bases in Bradford
Iron Works,
East Manchester.
Established in 1813,
the firm subsequently
became Richard
Johnson and Nephew;
it manufactured every
kind of steel and iron
wire, rope, copper
wire and drawn
copper bars, and
famously supplied the
sheathing wire for the
first trans-Atlantic
cable. The image
captures the housings
for a row of three
Lancashire boilers
(the ironworks housed
a total 20 boilers),
with the remains
of a regenerative
furnace and its
associated arched-
capped flue visible
in the background
(© Oxford
Archaeology Ltd)

became redundant within a very short period. This led to a significant shift towards thematic rather than regional studies of monument types, led by the Royal Commissions on Historic Monuments in Scotland, England and Wales (see eg Hay & Stell 1986). This was a major methodological leap for industrial archaeology, as the technique involved understanding the development of an industrial building type from its size and building materials, power systems and machinery, and landscape context. Industrial buildings studied in this way since the 1980s include the textile mills of Cheshire, Greater Manchester and Yorkshire (Calladine & Fricker 1993; Giles & Goodall 1992; Williams with Farnie 1992), the planned farmsteads of England (Barnwell & Giles 1997), buildings of the Northamptonshire boot and shoe industry (Morrisson & Bond 2004), hospitals (Richardson 1998), workhouses (Morrisson 2000), and warehousing (Taylor, Cooper & Barnwell 2002). Similar work was carried out on the coal industry by the statutory organisations in England, Scotland and Wales (Thornes 1994; Hughes *et al* 1995: Oglethorpe 2006), while Stephen Hughes' magisterial study for the Welsh Royal Commission of the threatened landscape of 'Copperopolis', the lower Swansea Valley in south Wales, set new standards for the recording of industrial buildings in their cultural context (Hughes 2000). English Heritage continued to fund studies of industry as part of its Monuments Protection Programme (MPP) (see below and 1.3), and a series of *Informed Conservation Studies* of significant industrial areas in England has been produced. The end of the Cold War has also resulted in a series of studies of military sites, including a large-scale survey of the Royal Gunpowder Factory at Waltham Abbey as well as other surveys of the defence estate (Cocroft 2000). This thematic approach remains one of the key ways of studying industrial-period monuments.

However, this techno-centric approach to individual industries or structures, with a consequent lack of synthesis, meant that the contribution of archaeologists to the debate on the validity and origins of the Industrial Revolution as a concept had not been as great as perhaps it should have been. Industrial archaeology, with its focus on standing structures rather than artefacts and excavated sites, tended to result in an archaeology of production rather than consumption, and there was little discussion about the consequences of industrialisation, such as the rapid shift from a rural to an urban-based society. From the 1990s, however, a new generation of industrial archaeologists, many now professionally involved in either academic, contract or public archaeology, moved the debate forwards and put the role played by industrialisation, its social consequences and the changes in the landscape at the heart of their research (Campion 1996, 2001; Palmer & Neaverson 1998, 2005; Rynne 1999, 2006; Casella & Symonds 2005; Nevell 2003, 2006; Gwyn 2006). In part this was spurred on by the revival of large-scale urban excavations, particularly on brownfield sites in cities such as Birmingham, London, Manchester, Sheffield, and York, where these sites have often included both the remains of manufacturing processes and workers' housing from the 18th and 19th centuries (Fig 1.3). Industrial archaeology has slowly established itself as a discipline within its own right, with its own methodologies, theoretical framework and research agenda, and has come a very long way from its origins over half a century ago.

Definitions and scope

Some early practitioners of industrial archaeology argued that the discipline was a thematic rather than a chronological one and could range from the prehistoric to the modern period, notably Arthur Raistrick in his *Industrial Archaeology: an Historical Survey* (Raistrick 1972). However, as discussed above, the decline of many of the classic 18th- and 19th-century industries and the growing recognition of the historic value of textile mills, iron works, and transport networks has led to a general acceptance that industrial archaeology involves the systematic study of standing as well as sub-surface structures of the classic period of industrialisation from the early modern and modern periods, mainly the early 18th to the 20th century. What characterises this period is capital investment on a large scale in both buildings and equipment and the organisation of the labour force to maximise production. It is with this development that industrial archaeology is largely concerned, although it must be recognised firstly that 'industrialisation', in this sense, began earlier in some industries than others and that therefore an interpretation of a particular site or industry may need to go back to the 16th century or earlier. Secondly, it is clear that the domestic or home-based method of production continued to co-exist with large-scale factory-type production well into the 19th century, albeit with many changes in the lifestyle of the workforce (Barnwell, Palmer & Airs 2004).

Industrial archaeology, then, is generally concerned with the evidence for people at work and so defines a type of human activity rather than just a type of site, since 'work', even after the so-called 'Industrial Revolution', could be based in domestic as well as non-domestic locations. The purpose of industrial archaeology is to contribute towards a greater understanding of the causes and consequences of the process of industrialisation by, to paraphrase Charles Orser, 'digging locally and thinking globally'. One of the outcomes of developer-funded archaeology has been the fragmentation of archaeological study and the consequent lack of synthesis for many periods, a notable exception being Richard Bradley's *The Prehistory of Britain and Ireland* (Cambridge World Archaeology, 2007) which made substantial use of recent material derived from developer-funded excavations. It was partly to combat this fragmentation and to provide local authority archaeologists with a framework for making judgements about the relative importance of the sites on which work was being undertaken that English Heritage began in the 1990s to encourage the provision of both national research frameworks put forward by the various period-based societies as well as regional ones. Firstly, for industrial archaeology, the Association for Industrial Archaeology (AIA) followed up its 1991 publication of research priorities, *Industrial Archaeology: Working for the Future* (Palmer 1991), with a framework for research in industrial archaeology, *Understanding the Workplace: a Research Framework for Industrial Archaeology in Britain* (Gwyn & Palmer 2005), which considered a range of approaches to the study of industrial sites and structures and also proposed a list of questions which might be considered when such sites are treated archaeologically to help further our understanding of the process of industrialisation. The Historical Metallurgy Society produced a research framework in 2008 (Bayley, Crossley & Ponting 2008), whilst English Heritage has published its own thematic research strategy for the Historic Industrial Environment (Falconer 2010). The National Association of Mining History Organisations (NAMHO) is working on a comprehensive research framework for the extractive industries (NAMHO 2010). Secondly, in England, a series of regional research frameworks has been published in one- or two-volume studies. These have provided a synthesis of the known work on the archaeological and historic environment, and crucially included chapters on the post-medieval and industrial archaeology of each area. Published regional research frameworks include those for the eastern counties (Glazebrook 1997), East Midlands (Cooper 2006), London (Nixon, McAdam, Tomber & Swain 2002), north-east England (Petts & Gerrard 2006), north-west England (Brennand with Chitty & Nevell 2006), south-west England (Webster 2008), West Midlands (Watt 2011), and Yorkshire (Ottaway, Manby & Moorhouse 2003). They provide a rich source of background material for the future study of the industrialisation process in these regions.

This new way of looking at industrial archaeology is therefore rooted firmly in the survey and excavation techniques of British archaeology. It thus emphasises the primary nature of archaeological evidence drawn from monument types and material culture, whilst relating these back to the contemporary documentary, photographic and oral evidence; the production, consumption and urbanisation aspects of post-1500 archaeology in Britain are thus reunited. Industrial archaeologists can now demonstrate the great change in both the material culture remains and the range of monument and landscape types associated with the industrial transition from the early 18th century onwards, which ranks as one of the major changes in human evolution alongside the development of language, agriculture and urbanism. The landscape and social processes involved in this transition demand a coherent period approach from archaeologists, and are best articulated by those archaeologists dealing directly with these issues: in other words, industrial archaeologists. We may ultimately come to see both post-medieval archaeology and industrial archaeology as distinctive stages within the emerging concept of global historical archaeology, but for the moment industrial archaeology is recognised as a period discipline within its own right and this Handbook is intended to assist both professionals and volunteers who deal on the ground with the physical remains of past industrial activity in Great Britain.

1.2 Models, methodology and fieldwork

Introduction

The modern generation of industrial archaeologists have developed a variety of approaches that provide a research toolkit, a set of archaeological methodologies and theoretical approaches that can be applied to the archaeology of industrialisation across four broad areas of study:

- technological and economic understanding;
- social and landscape approaches;
- industry-specific studies;
- site-specific surveys.

Some of these approaches concentrate wholly upon the recording of technology, others upon the landscape changes and social context. All seek to explore and understand from an archaeological perspective the origins, course and consequences of industrialisation. None is exclusive of the other; indeed, they work best when these issues are considered together. In practice this requires the student of the industrial period to be familiar with archaeological techniques such as landscape surveying, artefact recognition, measured survey and recording techniques. These are all data-gathering techniques common to any archaeologist and there are many good introductory text books available on basic archaeological field techniques (eg Grant, Gorin & Fleming 2002; Green & Moore 2010; Renfrew & Bahn 2008), while the specific recording of industrial sites and structures was described in Pannell 1974, Bodey & Hallas 1978, and Major 1975. However, as Palmer and Neaverson pointed out in their key text in 1998 (Palmer & Neaverson 1998, 3–8), industrial archaeology has its own needs and skills driven by the material culture of the industrial period. These include the need to understand the technology and science of the period; an understanding of the contemporary documentary material available to augment archaeological fieldwork; and the recognition that rural and urban landscapes were shaped by the processes of industrialisation. The following section sets out to review those aspects of archaeological fieldwork that are particular to industrial archaeology, from making sense of the mass of data available, through understanding the technology of the period and the documentary material available, to specific skills required to record standing industrial structures and excavate industrial sites.

Making sense of the data

One of the chief problems faced by any archaeologist studying the industrial period is the mass of new data available, partly because of the considerable survival of evidence from the post-1550 era but also from the increasing amount of developer-funded work undertaken on sites of this period. For instance, the Greater Manchester Historic Environment Record had, at the end of 2010, 17,116 entries, of which more than half were below-ground monuments, buildings, and listed structures from the industrial period. Furthermore, in the year 2009–10, the volume of developer-funded archaeological work in Greater Manchester amounted to 84 pieces of fieldwork, more than three-quarters involving post-1550 landscapes and buildings. How this mass of data can be used to aid our understanding of the process of industrialisation has been the subject of study since the 1990s. In that time two research methods have emerged that are beginning to provide an overview of this process and contribute to the increased understanding of both the landscape and social archaeology of the period.

Firstly, the 'Manchester Methodology' was developed in the late 1990s and early 2000s in the Manchester city region as a research tool to aid the understanding of the rate at which the new industrial-period monument types were introduced into any given area and their impact on local communities (Nevell & Walker 1999; 2004). Two adjacent Pennine parishes, Ashton-under-Lyne and Mottram-in-Longdendale, were chosen for the pilot study area and a broad date range for the project was established, from 1348 to 1870. The rate of archaeological change in these two parishes was studied through the temporal occurrence of sites as defined in English Heritage's *Thesaurus of Archaeological Monument Types* (English Heritage 1997). The decade during which each monument type was first recorded was noted and a cumulative graph produced of the 101 monument types identified. The shape of the resultant graph was then studied to assess how and when the new sites were introduced. The analysis of this data was taken a step further by putting each of the monument types identified in their social context through assigning their ownership or authorship to one of three contemporary social groupings: lords, freeholders, or tenants. The types of site associated with each social group were then further studied. The validity of the method has been tested elsewhere in north-west England (Nevell 2005) and in northern Wales (Gwyn 2005) and southern Ireland (Nevell 2005). Unsurprisingly each area produced slightly different results, but in each case the method of charting the growth of new monument types was shown to work, whilst the different social backgrounds in each area produced radically different results – which themselves emphasised the localised nature of the social context of industrialisation. The 'Manchester Methodology' was thus intended to provide, firstly, a way of charting archaeologically the impact of new industrial-period monument types on a given piece of landscape; and, secondly, to explore the relationship of these new monuments with the contemporary local social structure. One of the consequences of using this methodology is that it allows a greater understanding of the nature and causes of industrialisation in specific localities and the linkage of that phenomenon to mass production. This can be done by breaking down the archaeological database of any given rural or urban area into these separate monument types and then looking at their spatial and social distribution. In this way the chronology and nature of the phenomenon of industrialisation can be traced archaeologically in the new hamlets, villages and towns of the industrial transition.

Secondly, the technique of Historic Landscape Characterisation (HLC) is increasingly being used to study how the landscape was changed by industrialisation at a county or regional level. This technique, and that of the Extensive Urban Survey which was also developed in the 1990s but has since been incorporated within the HLC methodology for areas such as Greater Manchester, Lancashire and the Black Country, was developed by English Heritage in the early 1990s primarily as a conservation and planning tool (Rippon 2004). The HLC methodology embraces a series of approaches that focus upon how the rural and urban landscapes came into being, integrating a wide range of source material in order to understand the processes of landscape change. A combination of five elements distinguishes this approach: the use of the physical remains of the historic landscape as a data source; the inclusion of all the historic elements of a given zone, from modern and ancient features to semi-natural; a focus on the period depth of the surviving elements of the landscape; a county or regional approach in order to observe landscape changes on the macro-level; and the grouping of land-form elements into a series of *generic* types based on their morphology and/ or character. In practice the large amount of information thus generated has to be recorded on a Geographical Information System (GIS) as a series of polygonal data-sets which can be assigned one of many different characteristics. HLC provides archaeologists with a powerful research tool that can be used to study the ways in which the transition towards an industrial society is reflected in the landscape. When allied to the Manchester Methodology it should be possible to chart the physical changes of the industrialisation process in immense detail and on a highly local basis, whilst setting them in their social context.

These landscape archaeology methodologies provide possibly the most useful routes into studying the industrialisation process from an archaeological viewpoint at a regional level. The last 20 years have also seen a number of other approaches explored on a more local level. Firstly, Trinder's study of the spatial and social archaeology of 18th- and 19th-century market towns (Trinder 2002) sought to bring order to the mass of data from these lesser urban centres (from documents to buildings and excavated material) by a methodology that allows the comparison of small town development to be measured against the key changes in the townscape and industry of the larger 18th- and 19th-century industrial cities. This approach aims to highlight the social context of industrialisation in these smaller settlements. In the same year, ARCUS (Archaeological Research and Consultancy at the University of Sheffield) published its study of the historical archaeology of the cutlery industry, stressing the individuality of the Sheffield-based workers in comparison with their counterparts in Europe and Germany (Symonds 2002). The growing study of linear monuments of the industrial period, already shown in the work by Stephen Hughes on the Montgomery and Swansea Canals (Hughes 1979–80, 1988), has been further developed by the comprehensive survey of the Welsh section of Thomas Telford's London to Holyhead turnpike road (Quartermaine, Trinder & Turner 2003). All of these approaches have sought to push the study of industrial archaeology and the archaeology of industrialisation into the areas of landscape and social change by building models and testing them against the archaeological data.

Technology, documents and industrial archaeology

An understanding of the technology and economic background of particular industries is necessary in order both to make an adequate record of a given industrial site and also to understand its particular impact. This involves two quite different skill-sets: a knowledge of the technological development of a given industrial process or technique; and a familiarity with the available documentary material.

Technological and scientific development is at the heart of the industrialisation process, a point repeatedly stressed by David Cranstone (Cranstone 1989; 2004, 316) and Roger Holden (Holden 2009). The archaeological approach has been to record particular machines and processes either in the field or later in museum collections. Michael Bailey and John Glithero's study of the engineering history, archaeological integrity, and conservation of Stephenson's *Rocket* is an exemplar of how a piece of machinery should be studied as an archaeological artefact, bringing together two characteristic strands of industrial archaeology research: detailed technological recording and analysis, and the setting of that record against the context derived from the contemporary documents (Bailey & Glithero 2000). Roger Holden's work on water supplies for steam-powered textile mills in the Manchester city region (Holden 1999) reminds the student of industrial archaeology that the location of industrial sites is dependent upon the needs of technology as much as on the topographical context, even when advances in power technology seemingly free an industry from its traditional geographical location. In this case an understanding of the thermo-dynamic properties of engine condensers for later steam engines was used to explain the continuing bias in the distribution of textile mills towards waterside locations in the late 19th and early 20th centuries. Equally, his understanding of loom technology has enabled him to demonstrate how the increasing speeds of a weaving loom in the 19th century must have had significant effects on the ways in which the workforce operated (Holden 2009).

Figure 1.4 The remains of the arsenic calciner at Botallack Mine, West Cornwall, part of the Cornwall and West Devon Mining Landscape World Heritage Site (© Marilyn Palmer)

Past archaeological research is an important source of material when studying a particular industry or landscape, although sometimes it can be difficult to find a summary of the mass of fieldwork available. A useful source of synthetic material that provides historical and technological overviews of some of the key industries of the period is the archive of the Monuments Protection Programme (MPP), held by English Heritage in the National Monuments Record (NMR) at Swindon, with copies also held by the Ironbridge Institute and by the CBA in York (see 1.3 below). The lack of industrial sites in SMRs, together with the absence of many detailed monument class descriptions for industrial sites and structures, led to particular concentration on industrial archaeology. The AIA's project, The Index Record for Industrial Sites (IRIS), was intended to encourage local groups to help enhance local SMRs, and *inter alia* developed class and site/component terms to enable the computerisation of forms submitted to the SMRs. This project contributed to the English Heritage *Thesaurus of Monument Types*, which resulted in the construction of detailed monument class descriptions for many new types of site, including industrial sites and, within the MPP project, the identification of large numbers of sites which had not previously been recorded. The Industrial MPP also produced detailed reports on the history and technology of 23 industrial monument types and industries from the gas, electricity, and water and sewage industries, to the clay, iron, lead, lime and salt industries (English Heritage 2006a, 31). Whilst the archive is only England-focused, most of the industrial processes recorded can be found throughout the British Isles and in many cases it remains the best introduction to understanding the history and technology of these industries (Stratton 1990; Cherry & Chitty 2009; Newman 2009, 2010).

The national and regional archaeological research frameworks (see above) are also a useful source of data, as are the Nomination Documents for World

Heritage Sites in the UK, which often go beyond the immediate site being considered as the nomination process requires a justification of outstanding universal value. Consequently, for example, the Nomination Documents for New Lanark, The Derwent Valley of Derbyshire, and Saltaire (all 2000) include a great deal of information on the textile industries, while that for the Cornwall and West Devon Mining Landscape (2004) provides considerable insight into the landscape, settlement and technology of tin, copper, and arsenic mining (Fig 1.4). The Nomination Document for the Pontcysyllte Canal and Aqueduct (2008) deals not just with canals and outstanding engineering structures but also with the concept of monumentality in a 'Picturesque' landscape, something which could well be considered in relation to many other industrial monuments.

Working within the industrial period enables the archaeologist to make use of an additional source of information: documentary material (Palmer & Neaverson 1998, 105–28; English Heritage 2006a, 22–5). This comes in a variety of forms from probate material and parish and estate records, through trade directories, census returns, rate books, paintings, photographs, and historical maps, and to legal records such as business, probate, and tax archives (Fig 1.5). Such primary material can be found in public records (local studies libraries, county

Figure 1.5 The limestone quarries and lead mines at Dimminsdale, Leicestershire, c 1850, showing the two Newcomen engines which kept the quarry dry (© Leicestershire Museums Service)

records offices and the national archives), private records, and in contemporary publications (catalogues, memoirs, technical handbooks, and publications). The use of this material needs to be handled with care by the industrial archaeologist, since such documentary material contains its own bias. Trade directories were commercial ventures with each entry paid for; census returns gathered social data on population size, density and character within contemporary local government units but there was no consistency in the identification of occupations, making it difficult to use them to trace particular trades over time (Palmer & Neaverson 2004, 40–55). Historical maps only show landscape features thought relevant or important by the map makers or their sponsors, and descriptions of mining ventures in the pages of technical journals were often only intended to impress potential shareholders rather than being accurate accounts of discoveries made. It is not, however, the purpose of this handbook to describe the value and pitfalls of the evidence from these related areas when so many good sources already exist.

However, the emergence of the desk-based assessment as one of the most important archaeological planning tools of the last 20 years has meant that the idea of studying this range of documentary material, familiar to the first industrial archaeologists of the 1950s and 1960s, has become embedded in developer-funded archaeological projects. Of central importance to the desk-based assessment is the concept of the compilation of a historic map sequence, or regression, providing one of the most important additional sources of information for the late 18th-, 19th- and 20th-century industrial landscape. This technique allows the changes in a local landscape to be charted through a detailed analysis of the map evidence and at its most comprehensive uses all the available map data from estate maps and private maps commissioned to illustrate trade directories, to the scaled and triangulated maps of the Ordnance Survey. A feature of the technique is to enlarge to the same scale all the available maps of a given research area, highlighting the boundary of the area under study, and then, using map overlays, to highlight on a master plan all the landscape features identified over the time-frame of the maps analysed, from field boundaries and roads to pits, buildings, and transport routes. In this way macro- and micro-changes to the landscape can be observed, from the introduction of the first canal, railway or engineering works to the identification of steam engine and boiler houses, wheelpits, and slag heaps. It is even possible, using the largest-scale urban mapping, to record the location of cellar dwellings and the plan of back-to-back houses and courts.

Yet, although this documentary material is a vital additional information source to the traditional ways of gathering archaeological data (the landscape survey or excavation), the industrial archaeological perspective must always be allowed to take precedence. An archaeological viewpoint should be the aim of such documentary and map research, and archaeological research priorities should drive the use of such additional source material. After all, theories about how a landscape, townscape or building developed and its impact on the area or region derived solely from the documentary or map evidence always change once archaeological fieldwork is undertaken on these sites, since archaeological fieldwork provides a unique source of data.

Excavating a revolution

As seen earlier, industrial archaeology began as a campaign for the selective preservation of surviving sites and structures from the industrial period. Angus Buchanan, in his *Industrial Archaeology in Britain* in 1972, saw the discipline as an historical one and thought that it was 'archaeological' in so far as it dealt with physical objects and required fieldwork, even if the excavatory techniques of the classical archaeologist were not often applicable. The lack of standard archaeological practices used in excavation and the classification and interpretation of recovered artefacts was pointed out back in 1968 by David Crossley, who stated in a review of Michael Rix's Historical Association pamphlet on *Industrial Archaeology* in 1968 that 'there is a growing feeling that much is being lost in industrial studies by the inability or unwillingness of industrial archaeologists to appreciate the benefits that a training in excavation techniques would bring them'. In Britain and Europe, though, above-ground remains undoubtedly formed the basis of most industrial archaeology in the first half-century of its existence as a discipline and the material culture of the workforce, which might have been obtained through systematic excavation, was neglected.

This all changed with the advent of developer-funded archaeology in the 1990s. Some industrial archaeologists had long advocated the need for excavation, particularly on mining sites where so much was being lost by site clearance (Palmer 1983; Palmer & Neaverson 1987; Palmer & Neaverson 1989; Cranstone 1989). Much of the work previously undertaken by volunteers was taken over by professional archaeological units, and in fact volunteers could never have coped with the large-scale urban excavations which became widespread from the late 1990s onwards in cities such as Manchester, Sheffield, and York. For professional archaeologists, the core of the subject is excavation: the systematic recording through hand-digging, photography, and measured survey of below-ground remains. There are, though, several problems that distinguish the excavation of historic-period industry from earlier industries and landscapes: namely the scale of such sites, the formation processes involved, the contamination encountered, and the presence of standing buildings (see below).

The scale of the original industrial activities and the size of the archaeological excavations needed to understand such sites are frequently huge. English Heritage's guidance paper on excavating and analysing industrial-period sites, *Science for Historic Industries: Guidelines for the investigation of 17th- to 19th-century industries*, has illustrated this by showing how the development of the furnace in the iron and steel industry grew enormously over several centuries (English Heritage 2006a, 9). Equally, process structures could evolve even more rapidly during the industrial period. Arkwright's early water-powered cotton spinning mill, which housed his water-frames of 1771 design, was 30ft wide (*c* 10m) and 60ft long (*c* 20m) with three storeys. In the 1820s the steam-powered cotton spinning mill, filled with automatic mule spinners, was *c* 60m long and *c* 25m wide and five or six storeys high, with an end or projecting engine house. By the 1890s the introduction of steel, concrete, and high-pressure steam meant that new mills were often seven or eight storeys high

Figure 1.6 An aerial view of the 2011 area excavations at Oak Mill, Spencer Street, Oldham, by the Centre for Applied Archaeology at the University of Salford. This complex was founded in the 1870s as a steam-powered cotton spinning mill and expanded in the 1870s by the addition of a second spinning block. The excavations show the 1870s' power systems including the boiler house for four Lancashire boilers, flue system and chimney base, and the site of the northern engine house which housed a horizontal steam engine (courtesy Suave Air Photos, © copyright CfAA, University of Salford)

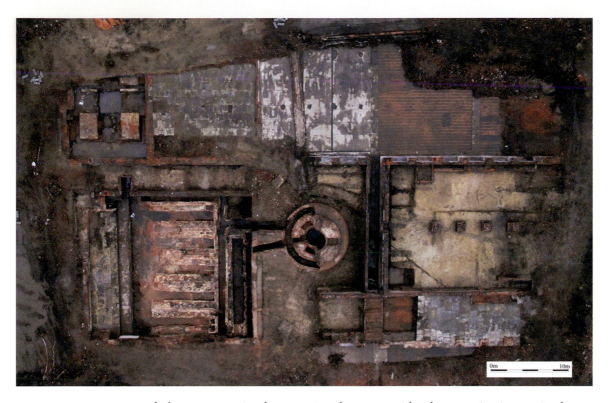

0m   10m

and almost square in plan, at *c* 60m by *c* 50m with a large projecting engine house and separate boiler house. The use of small evaluation trenches on such sites is pointless since they could end up being wholly within one room of the building or structure, so larger trial trenches and area excavations are needed that are targeted to specific parts of the site, such as the main processing area or the power systems (Nevell 2010) (Fig 1.6).

The typical large-scale manufacturing processes of the Industrial Revolution, engineering, iron and steel, pottery, and textiles, have all left substantial foundations of the process buildings involved. These contained working floors, furnaces, and kiln bases, and substantial foundations for power systems such as wheelpits, engine houses, boilers, and flues. Any or all of these features could be found on a single industrial manufacturing site, although the risk of encountering unknown large-scale processes can be minimised by the use of documentary and map evidence as a broad predictor of these features and as an aid to interpretation of the site (see above). The excavation of such sites frequently produces large quantities of 'process residues': raw materials such as limestone, ore, and sand; deposits of process residues from such features as crucibles, drains, flues, and furnaces; and large-scale waste products such as clinker, hammer-scale, and slag. These deposits can be bulk-sampled for scientific analysis as part of a programme of research that answers questions about the date, origin, and use of such materials and by implication the nature of the activity from the sample area (English Heritage 2006a, 13–15). The wider landscape context of the manufacturing site also needs to be considered by the industrial archaeologist.

Ancillary features such as transport links (road, canal, and rail), warehouses, gas supply, water supply (leats and reservoirs), and domestic buildings for the owner and workforce are also very common and provide not only evidence for the scale of landscape change wrought by these industries but also the social archaeology of industrialisation (Palmer & Neaverson 1994, 1–17).

The availability of labour and the arrival of steam-powered and later combustion engine-powered earth-moving machinery meant that many industrial-period manufacturing sites saw extensive earth-moving (Hughes 2000; Gwyn 2006; English Heritage 2006a, 11). Dumping, levelling, quarrying, and terracing activities radically changed the look of many pre-industrial landscapes at the site level and often these changes can only be recorded by combining landscape survey data with the excavation evidence. A problem on many industrial sites is thus establishing the undisturbed natural deposits and the potential for sealed earlier land-surfaces and structures. This is one of the reasons why the extensive use of machine excavation is so important, although its use needs careful monitoring. The industrial archaeologist also needs to be aware of the potential absence of some dumping and process residue deposits. Ore and metal processing, mining, and quarrying resulted in extensive waste products which on many sites have disappeared (Palmer & Neaverson 1987; Jones, Walters & Frost 2004). Some of this material was removed at the time and sold as make-up material for other construction sites or was even recycled as building materials; the presence in local buildings of slag bricks may be the only indication of a local metal processing industry, as in the dock walls of Hayle in Cornwall, site of foundries making steam engines for the world market. Slag heaps and quarry spoil were also removed by landscaping during the 20th century, leaving only a truncated range of processes on the industrial site under investigation. Thus the sampling of such residues on site during the excavation may be the only way to assess the exact range of processes originally present on the site. Large-scale earth moving was not confined to manufacturing sites but could also be found on linear transport monuments such as canals, railways, and turnpikes, where study of the landforms can reveal the construction processes, as in the case of tunnels.

A major health and safety concern on excavations involving historic industries is contamination. Whilst taking many forms, the two most commonly encountered are heavy metals and organic compounds (English Heritage 2006a, 11). Such contamination is often found in drains, engine beds, furnaces, and flues, but can also be encountered on any processing surface or surviving machinery. Such contamination can be broadly anticipated from documentary research but inevitably excavation will reveal unexpected material and suitable precautions need to be taken as part of a risk assessment.

Recording industrial structures

Standing structures are frequently found on historic-period manufacturing sites and the study and understanding of the buildings of industry have formed a central feature of industrial archaeology since the inception of the subject

(Hudson 1963; Major 1975; Palmer & Neaverson 1998). Indeed, the experience of recording in detail industrial buildings and their surviving machinery was an important development in the emerging archaeological sub-discipline of historic building recording (Wood 1994), with its focus on the form, fabric, and function of a structure (Morriss 2000). In the mid-20th century RCHME developed a series of standards for recording buildings depending upon the level of detail required and this approach now forms the core of English Heritage's 2006 guidance paper on *Understanding Historic Buildings. A guide to good recording practice* (English Heritage 2006b). Ranging from a brief photographic record (Level 1), through a basic visual record involving a measured ground plan (Level 2), to the more detailed analytical record using both plans, sections and brief documentary research (Level 3) and the comprehensive analytical record (Level 4) which involves three-dimensional recording and detailed historical analysis, these standards form the basis for most historic building recording programmes undertaken through the planning process.

Whilst building recording is by no means a feature unique to industrial archaeology, the comparatively high number of surviving industrial buildings and structures from the industrial period means that they are regularly encountered on manufacturing sites and even if absent, surviving examples elsewhere provide comparators for the excavated evidence. In the early 21st century most surviving historic industrial buildings no longer contain much in the way of machinery and are seldom complete in terms of their structures; many, too, lack their original topographical context because of urban redevelopment or land clearance.

Recording the buildings of industry has, like excavation, its own unique features. Firstly, there are likely to be buildings and process structures spread over a large area and it would be easy to get lost in the detail of the individual buildings. It is thus necessary to identify the types of buildings surviving on a site (processing, power, transport, office, warehousing structures etc), and to prioritise the recording appropriately. Supplying the context for an industrial building or complex can be approached in several ways: checking to see if the site comes under one of the 23 industry types covered by the Monuments Protection Programme is one, and looking at the industry-specific thematic buildings surveys undertaken by the Royal Commissions in the 1980s and 1990s and continued since by English Heritage and Historic Scotland is another (see above).

Secondly, whilst process and power machinery are now seldom found within an industrial structure, the remains of the fixtures and fittings of such items are frequently encountered. These remains take the form of brackets for line shafting and hoists, wall fixtures and arches for power transmission, machine, boiler, and engine beds that can be in stone, brick or concrete, notches and fixing points for machinery on original floors, and the bases of chimneys which are often the only hint of a nearby furnace or boiler house. Examples of recording the ghosts of long-lost machinery include the detailed recording of steam engine houses in Cornwall (Cornwall Archaeological Unit 1992), Murray's Mill in Manchester (Miller & Wild 2007), and the Stone Dam Mill Engine House (Fitzgerald 2007b). Many local industrial archaeology groups have also carried out such detailed building recording, notably the recipients of the AIA's Fieldwork and Recording Award, and a search of the on-line indexes of *Industrial Archaeology Review* provides a good starting point (http://www.industrial-archaeology.org/apubls.htm).

Finally, to enable the understanding of process-flow within individual buildings, the concept of access analysis (Campion 1996, 2001; Mellor 2005; Symonds 2002) and activity analysis (Hayman 1997; Badcock & Malaws 2004) has been tried for small-scale and, more rarely, for large-scale industrial buildings. Both techniques seek to reconstruct spatial patterns of domestic and work use within standing structures, access analysis looking at the relationship of room spaces to one another and activity analysis mapping the way in which workers interacted with their machinery. There are several problems with these approaches, aside from the fact that 20th-century working practices may already have been recorded on film or as oral history. Firstly, activity analysis is based upon parallels with current working historic industries and these examples may not be based in a contemporary building and will only reflect later working practices. Thus, a study of the last working felt hat works in Stockport, Christy's on Hillgate which did not close until the end of the 1990s (McKnight 1996), showed the relationship of the workforce to later 20th-century felt hatting machinery but not to the semi-mechanised production process of the 19th century nor the relationship of the workspace to the original building since the hat works had been set up in a converted cotton spinning mill. Secondly, access analysis has the same pitfall plus the added problem of recording the access to an industrial building in its final phase. To get back to any earlier layout involves further interpretation, although this can be very revealing. At 1–5 Kelvin Street in Manchester, for instance, a set of three fustian weavers' cottages built in 1772–73, access analysis of the final plan form revealed how the row of three buildings had been converted into three tenement blocks in the 1890s and later used as commercial premises. Yet, a reconstruction of their original form revealed how the attic rooms were all linked to one another as a series of workshops and that there was a single taking-in door to the rear (Nevell 2008). Nevertheless, such techniques allow archaeology to begin to reconstruct the work experience from the physical evidence, taking into account the likelihood that individual workers were creatively involved in the way in which goods were manufactured.

Another technique which tries to reconstruct the work-flow within industrial buildings is that of process recording, carried out in buildings where work still continues in order to gain an understanding of the physical operation of a site in terms of both people and processes which can then be utilised at redundant sites. It has been successfully applied to a large-scale 20th-century industry, the manufacture of Shredded Wheat at Welwyn Garden City (Butterfield 1994), and then by RCAHMW at Taff Merthyr Colliery during its efforts to record the rapidly declining Welsh coal industry (Malaws 1997; Badcock & Malaws 2004). Both projects ensured that the processes taking place were fully recorded alongside the architectural and engineering aspects of a building or structure. Full process recording, as at the colliery site, also involved understanding how buildings related to each other in the work-flow, taking into account the various changes of use which buildings can go through over time. The importance of doing this was pointed out by RCHME when undertaking surveys of large-scale industrial sites such as that of the extensive Royal Ordnance Factory at Waltham Abbey (Everson 1995; Cocroft 2000), and on the layout of planned farmsteads (Barnwell & Giles 1997). The siting of buildings in the landscape in relation to their topography is often very important in determining process-flow, since natural slopes facilitated, for example, the charging of lime kilns and iron furnaces, the processing of minerals, and the provision of power and transport (Palmer & Neaverson 1998, 16–19).

Industrial archaeology fieldwork in the 21st century

Some criticism has persisted that industrial archaeology concentrates on the recording and conservation of technology, that it lacks any coherent methodology, and is devoid of any understanding of the landscape and social context of the changes brought about by this technology (Darvill 2003; Fitzgerald 2007a, 51; Clark 1999, 296, sadly repeated in the second edition, Clark & Casella 2009, 368). If these comments are at all applicable, at best they might relate to the discipline before the 1990s; they do not reflect the industrial archaeology of the early 21st century. Fifty years on from its inception, industrial archaeology has crystallised into a distinctive way of studying the physical remains of industrialisation, as much concerned with the social and landscape origins and impact of the Industrial Revolution as with charting, recording, and understanding the technological innovations that made the period possible. Since industrialisation has developed into a world-wide phenomenon not particular to a century, or indeed country, it is vital for archaeologists to provide a distinct view of the origins, course, and consequence of this process of technological change at a regional, national, and international level. The models, methodologies, and fieldwork practices reviewed here provide that distinctive viewpoint.

1.3   Protection of the industrial heritage and its archaeology

Introduction

In Britain industrial heritage is protected using the same legislation and conservation management principles as apply to the protection of the historic environment in general. Individual industrial sites, historic buildings and landscapes also benefit from guardianship and preservation in the hands of government heritage agencies and independent trusts.

Statutory protection – through designation by scheduling, listing and in the various national registers – recognises the significance of sites, buildings, and landscapes for their historic, archaeological, architectural, and artistic interest and is used to manage changes that affect them. The list of World Heritage Sites (WHS), which includes many industrial heritage sites, is maintained by UNESCO and inscription for 'outstanding universal significance' requires governments to have in place a conservation management plan and protective measures for WHS. More generally the land-use planning system in the UK provides an effective mechanism for managing changes to heritage assets through a local plan and development management system. Devolution means that planning policy and guidance for the historic environment is set by a variety of governmental bodies in the UK: the Westminster Parliament for England, the Northern Ireland Assembly, the Scottish Parliament, and the Welsh Assembly.

In the countryside, protected areas such as National Parks, National Nature Reserves, and Areas of Outstanding Natural Beauty provide care for the rural industrial legacy which often requires a landscape-scale approach to conservation. Some nature conservation designations also benefit the care of industrial sites, where historic extraction, processing, and manufacture have created environments with distinctive ecologies that are rich in biodiversity. Woodland management, historically a key factor for supplying fuel for industry, also plays a part in the conservation of former industrial landscapes that include, or have been colonised by, woodland.

These conservation measures have grown up piecemeal, as different legislation and approaches to protection have evolved, and are equally applicable to every aspect of the historic environment. However, the sheer scale of some historic industrial processes, such as mining, quarrying, and mass production, can be a conservation challenge in itself. Specific technical issues – such as the toxicity of process residues, structural failure of mass construction, instability of materials, maintenance of historic machinery and plant – can also demand particular approaches to applying conservation principles in practice. The discussion below considers the history of and current practice in protecting the industrial heritage in the UK.

Guardianship and industrial heritage trusts

Some of the earliest measures for the protection of historic industrial sites were through independent local organisations that acquired properties in order to preserve them. Bodies such as the Sheffield Trades Historical Society and the Cornish Engines Preservation Committee (see 1.1. above) were ahead of their time in recognising the national significance of industrial sites long before government agencies began to consider designation of industrial heritage seriously. Like the early statutory protection for ancient monuments, under which the state simply relieved the owner of responsibility for taking care of nationally important sites, in the mid-20th century it was independent heritage trusts and local authorities which stepped forward to provide this protection for the industrial heritage. Many of these early initiatives developed into museums of industrial history, both independent and local authority, often with an emphasis on the history of technology rather than on the wider significance of industrialisation in the

Figure 1.7 A view of the scaffolding and access stairway on the pumping engine house at Old Engine Shaft, Trewavas Head, West Cornwall. The adits from this copper mine of the mid-19th century reached out under the sea (© Mike Hardy: National Trust)

historic environment. National museums also played a major part in preserving both the sites and the structures of early technology and industries, such as the National Museum of Wales for the slate quarries at Dinorwic, north Wales, and coal mining at Big Pit, Blaenafon.

State guardianship of industrial monuments began from the mid-20th century in a minor way with the Iron Bridge, Shropshire, in 1934 and the Berney Arms and Saxted Green windmills, both gifted into state guardianship in 1951. Although today the national agencies all include some industrial sites in their guardianship – Cadw managing Blaenafon ironworks, for example, and Historic Scotland, Stanley Mills – the representation of the industrial heritage in the 'national collections' of monuments in care is relatively poor across the whole of the UK. Fewer than a dozen industrial sites form part of English Heritage's portfolio of over 400 properties in care, although it is notable that among the most recent properties taken into their ownership have been two nationally and internationally important industrial sites: Ditherington Flax Mill, Shropshire (freehold acquired in 2005), and J W Evans silver works, Birmingham (2008). However, it is the larger national conservation trusts, such as the National Trust, Railway Heritage Trust, and Waterways Trust, and a myriad of local heritage and building preservation trusts that have been instrumental in taking on the management of the conservation challenges that many of these problematic sites present (Fig 1.7).

Industrial sites represent some of the most significant heritage conservation issues for the 21st century, as does the sustainability of the voluntary groups and trusts which have ensured a future for many of the best-preserved sites. As Sir Neil Cossons remarked in a recent study for English Heritage:

> The achievements of the – largely voluntary – bodies who pioneered industrial heritage preservation over the last forty years have been prodigious and outstanding. Today, with ageing volunteers, often in diminishing numbers, and with preservation standards and public expectations rising, the condition of many of these important sites is problematic and their future prospects often fragile (Cossons 2008, 13).

Statutory protection: scheduling and listing

The first statutory protection for archaeological sites and monuments was provided by the Ancient Monuments Protection Act of 1882, the result of a sustained campaign by Sir John Lubbock. Despite being resisted as an assault on the rights of private property owners, the Act established the principle of state responsibility for preservation of sites of national importance. Successive Acts widened the definition of monuments and made provisions for public access but the legislation remained permissive (ie owners had no responsibility for maintenance or repair and only needed to notify their intention to carry out changes) until the 1979 Ancient Monuments and Archaeological Areas Act. This introduced a formal consent procedure for works to scheduled monuments, parallel to the planning consent system under the Town and Country Planning Acts. A monument, for the purposes of scheduling, may not be occupied for residential use and is defined as a 'building or structure, cave or excavation which is above or below the surface of the land; or on / under the sea bed within UK territorial waters (or a site that contains the remains of one)' and 'a site comprising any vehicle, vessel, aircraft or other moveable structure (or contains the remains of one)'. This broad definition allowed protection to be extended to industrial sites and machinery.

The idea of including historic buildings in the planning system emerged in the inter-war period, with the Housing Acts which gave ministers powers to draw up town planning schemes that would preserve the character and setting (then called the 'space about buildings') of 'the special architectural, historic or artistic interest attaching to a locality ... with a view to preserving the existing features of the locality'. Although there had long been talk of compiling 'lists', the first national survey to list buildings of special architectural and historic interest began in 1947. The initial 'lists' were drawn up during World War II as a means of controlling works to important historic buildings during and after the wartime bombing. The 1944 Act introduced controls over alterations and additions and made unauthorised works a criminal offence; the successive Acts for England and Wales, and for Scotland, in 1947 introduced the duty to draw up a list of buildings 'of architectural and historic importance' (see Delafons 1997; Cherry *et al* 2010, 13). In England and Wales, consolidation of town and country planning legislation and measures for the protection of listed buildings were included in the Planning (Listed Buildings and Conservation Areas) Act 1990, and its equivalent in Scotland and Northern Ireland. This remains the primary legislation, supported by Circulars and planning guidance. Buildings are graded against selected criteria designating them as Grade I, Grade II* and Grade II (Grade III was abandoned in 1970).

The history of these two strands of legislation is significant because the statutory framework for protecting individual industrial sites and buildings has developed around the distinction between ancient monuments and historic buildings. Scheduling has been used selectively for protecting a relatively small number of nationally important sites (in 2011 around 19,700 were designated in England, *c* 1800 in Northern Ireland, *c* 8000 in Scotland and *c* 4000 in Wales) for which unchanged preservation is the priority. It introduces a high degree of control over all works, even minor repairs, and includes machinery, plant, and fixtures. Where refurbishment or adaptive reuse could compromise the significance of a nationally important industrial building, scheduling will normally be preferred, to preserve the building and its plant in a low-intensity use consistent with its vulnerable character. Scheduling has been used extensively to provide comprehensive protection for industrial heritage. Decisions on consent for works to scheduled monuments are taken by the Department for Culture, Media and Sport in England, Cadw, Historic Scotland, and the Department of Environment NI.

Listing is normally preferred to scheduling for industrial buildings where continuing use, adaptation or conversion is considered to be the most beneficial management and a way of keeping a traditional working enterprise in the building or encouraging suitable alternative uses. In essence, protection by scheduling is intended to preserve sites unaltered with minimal necessary change, while listing is designed to manage essential and appropriate adaptation of buildings in use. Consent for works to listed buildings is managed through the local planning authority with advice from English Heritage, Historic Scotland, Cadw and DOE NI.

The choice between applying scheduling and listing appears straightforward but in the case of the industrial heritage this distinction has not always been so clear cut. Many industrial sites are both listed and scheduled, and in this situation the scheduling protection takes precedence, removing the consent process from the local planning authority's control and direct involvement of local communities in decisions. Despite the close controls that scheduling provides over all works to a monument, it does not prevent an owner neglecting a site and wilfully allowing it to fall into disrepair and dereliction. Scheduling affords no powers for local authorities or national agencies to intervene (as there are for listed buildings), except to take the site compulsorily into guardianship or undertake compulsory repairs, both at the expense of the public purse. The use of scheduling to protect the industrial heritage at risk has therefore not been very effective without public resources to support it. One of the earliest structures scheduled specifically for its industrial significance was the Iron Bridge, Shropshire, in 1934.

Selective listing and scheduling of industrial sites began in the 1960s as awareness of the significance of this part of the UK's heritage increased and the first listing resurvey began in 1966. Large numbers of early industrial sites were in fact already protected by virtue of being included in the scheduling of prehistoric, Romano-British, and medieval sites. Examples include early glass making at Monkwearmouth and Glastonbury Abbey, pottery kilns associated with Roman and medieval suburbs, early aqueducts and water supply systems in Roman forts and cities such as Bath and Lincoln, lime kilns with medieval castle and manorial sites, and early bloomeries with monastic estates.

A comprehensive programme of listing resurvey was embarked upon from the mid-1960s, with the impetus of the landmark demolition of Philip Hardwick's Euston Arch (1961) and the increasing impact of intensive urban redevelopment in Britain's Victorian towns. The campaigning of the recently founded Victorian Society and of the CBA ensured that 19th-century industrial and commercial buildings began – very gradually – to be considered seriously for protection. The rate of listing was slow, however, and coverage was still very incomplete when the demolition of the Art Deco Firestone Factory in Brentford in 1980 (knocked down over a Bank Holiday weekend and due to be protected by listing) raised a storm of protest. The result was the so-called 'accelerated resurvey' which aimed to cover the whole of rural England and most smaller towns over the next decade, and the urban list review which followed from 1989. Similar survey programmes followed in Scotland and Wales.

During the same period scheduling of industrial sites also gradually increased but it was not until the Monuments Protection Programme (MPP) was initiated by English Heritage that progress in England accelerated. Between 1986 and 2004, English Heritage's MPP developed a systematic approach for classifying, evaluating, and selecting industrial sites for protection by scheduling and through other forms of management. The initial rapid assessment of archaeological resources had shown that existing research and records for industrial archaeology varied widely in depth and consistency, while the high numbers of surviving sites posed a further challenge for understanding and evaluation (HBMCE 1984). The MPP returned to first principles and 'adopted an approach aimed at creating an ordered sequence of data-gathering, synthesis and peer-aided judgement' (Schofield 2000, 6). This staged approach for evaluation and selection of industrial monuments for statutory protection proceeded through a series of 'Steps' and included consultation with SMRs, specialist groups and experts at several stages (Stocker 1995). The programme was based on Arthur Raistrick's classification of industry by material and process (Raistrick 1972) as the structure for systematic evaluation: extractive industries; inorganic manufacturing; agricultural (organic) processing and manufacture; power and utilities; transport and communications.

The MPP programme remains the most detailed and comprehensive survey of historic industries undertaken for designation purposes, albeit that it was never completed. It introduced the concept of an integrated approach to designation which considered a range of conservation options from scheduling through to local listing and land management regimes. When the MPP programme was halted in 2004, Step 1 'characterisation' reports had been produced on 33 industries, and nearly 5000 sites and buildings had been evaluated in the field, with recommendations for over 1000 new Scheduled Ancient Monument (SAM) designations and over 350 candidates for listing (Cherry & Chitty 2009, 13–14). It has been estimated that there are currently around 1800 industrial sites scheduled as ancient monuments and 38,000 industrial listed buildings, representing around 9% and 10% respectively of the total designated stock of heritage assets in England (Cossons 2008, 16–17). In Scotland and Wales, thematic studies of particular industries and their buildings (collieries, textile mills, mining and metal industries) have been led by the Royal Commissions.

The Heritage Protection Bill, introduced in 2009, aimed to modernise the framework for heritage protection in England and Wales and to resolve the anomalies which have developed from the use of two parallel sets of legislation. The government indicated 'its intention of integrating the currently separate systems of listing buildings, scheduling monuments and archaeological sites and registering historic parks, gardens and battlefields into a unified heritage protection system' (English Heritage, DCMS 2005). In pilot work to develop the new unified designation, Darnall Steel works in Sheffield was used as an exemplar of how industrial heritage could benefit from the approach. Regrettably, parliamentary time for the passage of the Bill was not secured and the designation systems in the UK still remain separate, though reformed for Scotland in 2010. However, the principles of a unified approach and a common vocabulary for all designated 'heritage assets' is gradually being established though national planning and heritage policy guidance. There is now a single National Heritage List for England which includes all designated sites, buildings and areas. Statutory management agreements also now provide a framework for the conservation of complex historic industrial sites with a mix of designated and undesignated, scheduled and listed structures. The move towards an integrated approach is one that will benefit and enhance the conservation of industrial heritage assets in the future.

Other heritage designations and non-statutory protection

The designation by local planning authorities of Conservation Areas can also provide a framework for the conservation of large complexes of industrial buildings and for the physical context and setting of individual scheduled or listed buildings. Conservation Areas have a special historic character which it is considered desirable to preserve and enhance. Within them there are controls on demolition; planning policies are normally used explicitly to prevent harmful land-use changes. This form of local designation has not been employed widely

Figure 1.8 Papplewick Pumping Station, Nottinghamshire, built between 1882 and 1884 to supplement the water supply for the growing city of Nottingham. In the main building there are two massive beam pumping engines, thought to be the last built by the firm of James Watt & Co. of Soho Works, Birmingham and London. The interior is furnished with lavishly ornamented pillars, delicate metalwork and stained glass featuring water motifs (© Marilyn Palmer)

to protect industrial quarters and large-scale complexes and there is potential to make much wider use of it. Conservation Areas such as the Birmingham Jewellery Quarter, the Longton Conservation Area in the Potteries, and in Bridport and West Bay for the flax and hemp industry, show the value of these designations in practice for conserving not just individual structures but also the character, group value and streetscape of specific industries and their communities.

The Registers of Historic Parks and Gardens, and in Wales the Register of Historic Landscapes, also deserve a mention as a mechanism for ensuring that changes affecting important landscapes are fully integrated in planning and land management. Many designed elements of industrial sites and mining landscapes benefit from this non-statutory protection. The grounds of Papplewick pumping station, Nottinghamshire, for example, are registered as an historic designed landscape and include important plant collections and an original garden layout as well as the cooling pond, covered reservoir, and remains of the tramway for transporting coal (Fig 1.8). Registered parks and gardens around large country houses often preserve innovative, early schemes for power generation. The Welsh Historic Landscape Register includes outstandingly important industrial landscapes such as Parys Mountain (Mynydd Parys) copper mines (see Fig 4.14).

World Heritage Site (WHS) status, like the non-statutory registers, confers no additional requirement for planning consent, but highlights the international importance of outstanding sites as a key material consideration for planning authorities. The international significance of the UK's industrial heritage is reflected in the relatively high proportion of such sites inscribed as World Heritage Sites: Blaenafon industrial landscape, Cornwall and West Devon mining landscape, Derwent Valley mills, Ironbridge Gorge, the Port of Liverpool, New Lanark, Pontcysyllte aqueduct and canal, and Saltaire. In all these extensive urban and rural landscapes, WHS inscription provides a defined context and a strong incentive for integrated conservation management to protect the industrial character of an extensive area.

Turning to wider conservation interest, abandoned industrial remains of mining and mineral processing can have special geological or ecological interest in addition to their archaeological interest. Protection may be afforded to these by their inclusion in National Nature Reserves (NNR) or Sites of Special Scientific Interest (SSSI) under the 1983 Wildlife and Countryside Act. This requires that permission is sought from Natural England or the relevant national agencies for potentially damaging operations. The protection afforded by SSSI status also enables nature conservation agencies to enter into management agreements with applicants if permission for an operation is withheld and provides the basis for agreeing management that protects the historic as well as the natural environment. Crown Field shaft mounds, Kent, has exceptional preservation of dated Iron Age mining remains and is protected as part of the Wye and Crandale Downs SSSI. Ore Pit Holes, Durham, another iron mining site, is an example of medieval, rake-type working with bloomeries nearby, which is also protected as part of a NNR and SSSI.

For the majority of industrial monuments, however, designation of one kind or another may not offer the best management option or is simply not appropriate. Even statutory protection is not necessarily a sustainable option in the case of large complexes of disused industrial buildings and plant where no positive conservation regime exists, and where investment of the substantial resources required for conservation cannot be assured in the long term. It is sometimes necessary to accept that historic assets cannot be physically retained or conserved, as for example in the case of a heavily polluted or substantially damaged or unstable site. Assessment and evaluation of the site's significance and a programme of recording prior to redevelopment or reclamation is essential, however, so its archaeological and historical value can be realised in other ways, through creating new knowledge and understanding, involving local communities in the process of investigation, and through public interpretation and publication.

Generally speaking the planning system is well suited for managing the conservation of industrial buildings when continuing or adaptive reuse is the preferred option (see 1.4 below). Where a programme of research and recording is an acceptable alternative to offset the loss of long-term preservation, development management can ensure that the significance of the site is properly understood and that there are proportionate requirements for investigation and public availability of the findings. Protection of the historic environment through the planning system is guided by national planning policy, issued by government, and at the local level through individual local development plans produced by local planning authorities.

The new emphasis on neighbourhood planning and the recognition of locally significant heritage in the character of an area is likely to increase the importance of locally listed heritage assets. Local lists (some based on former Grade III lists), compiled by local authorities in conjunction with neighbourhood and community groups, will become increasingly important for conservation of more commonplace buildings and features of local industrial history. Around 50% of local authorities currently maintain local lists in some form. While these do not bring any additional planning consent requirements, local designation does mean that the contribution which a building makes to the character of the area can be a material consideration in planning decisions.

Industrial archaeology is an important element in urban archaeology and has been a particularly formative influence on the character of urban development over the last three centuries. It is an integral part of the urban historic fabric, both built and buried, and its management is most effective where it is fully integrated with urban conservation and design. Preservation has to be finely balanced with other conservation needs in historic urban centres and with the wider imperative to ensure they continue, or are regenerated, as viable social and economic centres. In urban contexts, therefore, it has been more effective to consider industrial archaeology within the non-statutory framework of national planning guidance, as outlined above, than in the context of scheduling with its emphasis on physical preservation in preference to adaptation or reuse.

Assessment surveys of the urban industrial resource are a valuable tool, in conjunction with regional research frameworks, for developing conservation and planning strategies. Programmes of extensive urban surveys and detailed urban archaeology database projects, for example, form the basis for assessment of current knowledge and understanding of the overall archaeological resource in historic centres; they can be linked to strategic policies for urban archaeology suitable for adoption as Supplementary Planning Documents in the Local Plan. These, together with historic area surveys, developed in partnership with local planning authorities, provide a framework for the assessment of historic industrial quarters and centres in an urban context. This type of survey-based approach with strategic planning objectives is particularly appropriate as a means to identify the distinctive contribution of historic industrial areas to the urban scene and as a means of integrating the industrial heritage in conservation planning and urban design. Increasingly the use of urban characterisation programmes provides a comprehensive mapping of historic urban character within which specific industrial attributes can be identified for their local relevance and contextualised (English Heritage 2005a; Quigley 2010; English Heritage 2010).

Industrial landscapes and rural conservation

The wider recognition of historic landscape character has been developed through the work of Natural England's Countryside Character Programme, the Countryside Council for Wales, Scottish Natural Heritage, and a well-established programme of historic landscape characterisation supported by

English Heritage, Cadw, and Historic Scotland (Clark, Darlington & Fairclough 2004; English Heritage 2005b) The inclusion of historic character areas in landscape assessments is an important mechanism for integrating conservation management for industrial heritage on the extensive scale found in the extractive and manufacturing industries. Characterisation programmes can also be linked to supplementary planning guidance, to designation within local plans, and to the identification of zones of distinctive or vulnerable landscape character with special conservation and management needs.

Scheduling or listing is used to protect core areas or compact groups of industrial remains but in general the historic interest of an extensive industrial landscape is likely to be managed most effectively for its overall contribution to landscape character through wider countryside and land management regimes. These include those implemented through the conservation strategies and management plans of National Parks; of local authority countryside services; and under other measures such as the agri-environment schemes administered by government through DEFRA and other departments. In most cases, there will be other conservation interests to be considered, for example for wildlife and biodiversity, and geological interest. In such cases it will be necessary to ensure that the importance of the cultural component of these landscapes is recognised but these other frameworks for protecting landscape provide perfectly appropriate means for managing the historic environment component.

In rural areas, industrial archaeology can benefit from the protection and conservation management agreements offered under agri-environment schemes and LEADER programmes, currently supported through the European Rural Development Fund. These are employed proactively to enhance, protect, and increase public access to, and enjoyment of, industrial landscapes and sites whether designated or not. Locally negotiated management agreements under the aegis of local authority and National Park conservation strategies can be equally effective in achieving positive protection measures alongside, or in place of, the need for statutory protection. Local nature conservation interests often coincide with historic mineral extraction and working areas. For example, Kilton Hill Mine, Redcar & Cleveland, recognised as a nationally important site with a rare intact conical spoil heap forming a striking landscape feature, is also designated as a local nature reserve. Irchester country park, Northamptonshire, preserves a nationally important landscape of 20th-century open-cast quarrying, rare because not reinstated, and is managed locally as a landscape feature within the County Council's country park.

The management of woodland is a significant conservation issue for some areas of early mining and also for the historic coppiced woodlands formerly managed to supply fuel, for example, for the early iron industry. It is often the case that abandoned mining sites are colonised by woodland, or subsequently deliberately planted. Local authority archaeology services are now routinely consulted on forestry and woodland grant schemes where there is an opportunity to design planting that is sensitive to landscape and archaeological constraints. Survey work in advance of tree-planting proposals, such as that carried out for the Exmoor National Park, has both improved understanding of the archaeology and provided a basis for selective planting and protection of vulnerable areas of early industry. Recommendations for management of the 'scowles' of the Forest of Dean, based on the recent ALSF-funded study, emphasise the need for integrated conservation approaches led by the local authority which involve all the nature conservation agencies.

The CBA and industrial archaeology

The Council for British Archaeology has been involved with the identification and protection of industrial archaeological sites since it was founded in 1944: it created the first Industrial Archaeology Research Committee in 1959 (above 1.1). In its statutory role within the planning system as a national amenity society, it has advised on numerous listed building applications for conversions of industrial buildings, from the internationally significant Ditherington Flax Mill, Shrewsbury, to the locally significant domestic loomshop. It has campaigned against senseless demolition, the loss of machinery and plant from interiors, insensitive brownfield development, and worked with the Association for Industrial Archaeology to further understanding and appreciation of industrial sites, particularly their wider context, and their beneficial reuse, particularly in the series of day schools 2008–11 which gave rise to this book.

The CBA has an inclusive approach to protecting the industrial heritage as part of the historic environment which fits well with the changing, integrated approaches to heritage protection that are developing in public policy, breaking down the artificial barriers between listed buildings and scheduled sites, designated and undesignated sites. This is part of the ongoing realisation that heritage is not just individual monuments or a listed building but what surrounds us – the terraced houses that many of us live in, the buildings that we work in, the streetscapes that are the legacy of industrialised society. It is the evolved historic landscapes – the locally listed structure and the undesignated site or building – that are of interest to the community. The more holistic approach now being adopted combines both expert knowledge, informed by research and study such as characterisation studies and historic area appraisals, and local views on the significance in individual neighbourhoods and landscapes.

Heritage organisations

Many organisations campaign and care for the historic environment. Advisers to Government include English Heritage, Cadw, Historic Scotland, and Department of the Environment Northern Ireland (DOE NI). The national amenity societies, listed below, are statutorily notified of listed building applications and advise on a wide range of aspects of industrial heritage and its conservation. The Garden History Society and SAVE Britain's Heritage are also involved as heritage organisations with industrial heritage. The Association for Industrial Archaeology is the specialist association covering the UK.

National heritage agencies and departments

Cadw www.cadw.wales.gov.uk
English Heritage www.english-heritage.org.uk
Historic Scotland www.historic-scotland.gov.uk
DOE Northern Ireland www.doeni.gov.uk

National amenity societies

Ancient Monuments Society www.ancientmonumentssociety.org.uk
Council for British Archaeology www.britarch.ac.uk
Georgian Group www.georgiangroup.org.uk
Society for the Protection of Ancient Buildings (SPAB) www.spab.org.uk
Twentieth Century Society www.c20society.org.uk
Victorian Society www.victoriansociety.org.uk
SAVE Britain's Heritage www.savebritainsheritage.org
Garden History Society www.gardenhistory.org
Civic Voice www.civicvoice.org.uk

Specialist industrial archaeology and heritage organisations

Association for Industrial Archaeology www.industrial-archaeology.org.uk
SPAB Mills Section www.spab.org.uk/spab-mills/
National Association of Mining History Organisations www.vmine.net/namho-2010/
Mills Research Group www.millsresearch.org.uk/
Gunpowder and Explosives History Group www.royalgunpowdermills.com/history-and-heritage/gunpowder-and-explosives-history-group/
Society for Post-Medieval Archaeology www.spma.org.uk
Welsh Mines Society www.welshmines.org/

1.4 Adaptive reuse of industrial buildings

Introduction

Changes in the patterns of industry and commerce in recent years have produced significant numbers of buildings which are no longer needed by industry but are suited to reuse. Both the transfer of manufacturing overseas and businesses moving to more modern premises has produced a stock of redundant buildings. Despite their age and frequently run-down condition, many of these buildings are soundly built and employ traditional constructional methods which render them eminently suitable for conversion and reuse. A building that is not in use and not maintained is potentially a building under threat, while the decline of individual buildings can rapidly drag down whole areas. Deterioration of the fabric of a disused building is almost inevitable, coupled with a high risk of vandalism and fire damage. The practice of comprehensive redevelopment of entire areas, which was undertaken in the UK in the 1960s and 1970s, often led to the destruction of long-established communities. Rehabilitation of areas and adaptive reuse of some or all of the building stock within the area, as opposed to total demolition, can be seen to have both sociological and environmental advantages through the maintenance of communities.

The best use for a building is generally the one for which it was originally designed, but changing needs mean that this may no longer be possible or reasonable. If the building is listed or lies within a conservation area, then demolition should not be an option but any conversion of a building will almost certainly require alterations and it is critical that these are of such a nature as to preserve its original character and any distinctive features related to the original use of the building. The use of careful techniques for conservation and restoration can bring even apparently seriously derelict buildings back to a useful life.

It is often assumed that the conversion of industrial buildings for residential use and other types of adaptive reuse is a phenomenon of the last few decades of the 20th century. It is probably true to say that landmark conversions, like that of the old Covent Garden fruit and vegetable market, opened up a far greater public understanding of the scope offered by the creative reuse of old industrial buildings that have outlived their originally designed use, as opposed to their demolition and replacement with new ones. In fact, the conversion of industrial buildings and adaptive reuse goes back very nearly as long as the factory building itself. Many fledgling industries have started up in buildings discarded by other industries which had vacated the building because of changing needs or for financial reasons. For instance, Bage's Flax Mill of 1797, the country's earliest cast-iron-framed building, was converted for use as a maltings in 1896. Many early textile spinning mills had a relatively short life in their original usage due to the rapid increase in size and power consumption of machinery, while most early car factories were adaptations of other buildings.

As well as the historical, heritage, and aesthetic considerations, the economic and environmental benefit of reuse is a major consideration. Unless the building requires major structural modification, reuse may well cost less and be quicker than demolition and rebuilding. Further benefits can be found in a lower carbon footprint driven through the reuse and conservation of existing materials when compared with a new build. Many traditional industrial buildings were over-built, in the sense that they used constructional techniques and materials of greater strength or in greater quantity than would be deemed necessary under modern building regulations. There is also benefit in the continuance of the techniques and skills of craftsmen derived from the reuse of old buildings. However, on occasions, the scale of alteration renders the existing building unrecognisable and destroys the original form. Excessive rebuilding, the removal of many original features and the insertion of inappropriate new features can contribute to an unsatisfactory conversion, whereas in a successful conversion the original form and use of the building is still clearly apparent. It is also important to consider the

Figure 1.9 The Albert Dock, Liverpool, designed by Jesse Hartley and Philip Hardwick in 1846, and built of cast iron, brick and stone, with no wood in its construction. It was converted for museum, retail and residential use in the late 20th century (© Marilyn Palmer)

context of a building conversion; if it is located in an area in which other buildings have architectural merit, this may increase the appeal of the building. Conversely inappropriate conversion of the building may detract from the architectural integrity and character of adjacent buildings and the area.

Conversion for domestic use raises many issues. Old water mills, oast houses, barns, and similar buildings have a very long history of domestic conversion. They fulfil many of the necessary criteria: they are not too big, do not have excessively wide floor spaces and are frequently in picturesque locations. Thus a disproportionate number of remote rural industrial premises have seen conversion into domestic properties. Many later industrial buildings, though, raise significant problems. In general the larger the building the greater will be the problems encountered. This is further compounded by issues such as of the age of the building, the method of construction, ceiling heights, fenestration, width of the building, and the number of floors. Thus, for instance, first-generation cotton spinning mills on a number of sites have been successfully converted for both domestic and commercial use. They are relatively narrow and are usually around four storeys high. The second generation of cotton spinning mills with artificial lighting and built to accommodate far larger machines are frequently unsuitable for conversion other than for use as warehousing or for light industrial processes. This can be very clearly seen in locations in the Derwent Valley in Derbyshire where first- and second-generation mills stand alongside each other at Belper and Matlock Bath.

The importance of location cannot be underplayed. Thus, buildings located in urban, intensively industrial, and frequently run down areas, often with many similar types of buildings, are usually much harder to generate any interest in conversion for reuse. The exception to this is where the industrial area is subject to wholesale redevelopment or is immediately adjacent to a major commercial area. However current trends in local and central government do favour brownfield developments. Many former industrial buildings in Greater London have been successfully converted due to their proximity to commercial centres. Leeds and Manchester, to name two other cities, have seen a similar trend. Buildings in waterside locations also have a major aesthetic advantage. Canalside, riverside and former dockland areas have all proved much more of a draw for investment in adaptive reuse than have many former industrial areas. Albert Dock in Liverpool (Fig 1.9) and some areas of the banks of the River Aire in Leeds are excellent examples. Buildings that stand in an isolated rural location, such as mills and farm buildings, or ones that stand in an area that has subsequently been redeveloped as a mainly residential area, have a far better chance of successful conversion.

Reuse of old industrial and commercial buildings should not be seen as being limited to 19th-century and earlier structures. Recently there has been a significant increase in the interest in the preservation of 20th-century buildings. This has been driven by a reassessment of familiar buildings which, with the passing of time and with a growing awareness of architecture and the built environment, can now be seen as having historical merit.

Proposals for adaptive reuse

Legislation Protection: PPS 5 sets out guidelines for the handling of listed and scheduled structures in the planning process and defines a heritage asset as 'a building, monument, site, place, area or landscape positively identified as having a degree of significance meriting consideration in planning decisions' which has value to this and future generations. Such assets do not have to be officially designated: they include 'assets identified by the local planning authority during the process of decision making or through the plan making process, including local listing' (see 1.3 above).

Any proposal for conversion should, therefore, demonstrate that the developer clearly understands the history of the building and its significance, in both a local and national context. An appraisal of the building should highlight original features that survive. The nature of the original industry, as well as defining many of the characteristics of the building, will also determine other problems that may arise when the building is considered for redevelopment. Contamination of the building and its adjacent grounds can be a major problem, both the obvious areas of contamination such as asbestos and the less obvious ones such as heavy metal contamination of adjacent soil. Engineering works, metal processing sites and chemical works can be particularly difficult in this respect. The desire to retain original features which are mentioned in the listing of some building types can render adaptive reuse problematical; the Grimsby fish docks ice factory graphically illustrates this problem (see Fig 2.11).

Retention of original features: When reviewing any proposal for conversion for either domestic or commercial use there are several factors that should be considered. The principal question is whether the conversion maintains the character of the building and key features of the building's past. Changes that alter fenestration significantly, both in terms of location and the type of windows and framing used, should be avoided. Changes to the location of doorways and principal means of access to a building can frequently make the historical usage of the building harder to understand and thereby compromise the reasons for conserving the building. Conversions that change roof lines or add extra storeys can similarly change the building out of all recognition. The addition of inappropriate roof lights and dormer windows to roofs needs to be considered carefully. Removal of external features such as ironmongery and hoists can dilute the integrity of the converted building.

Internal alterations: The internal conversion of a building should respect surviving traditional features and be in keeping with key elements of the original purpose. The inappropriate insertion of partition walls and ceilings can obscure and/or destroy the original spatial qualities of the building. Thus conversion of a building for residential use which requires relatively small internal rooms to conform to the demands of modern living can be more damaging to the internal character of a building than a commercial use which permits bigger internal spaces. The resiting of staircases and insertion of new staircases, lift shafts and service ducting all need careful consideration. Wherever possible, original surfaces should be retained.

Additions: A development which proposes significant areas of new build adjacent to the converted structure raises several dilemmas. Should the new build portion be in keeping with the original building in architectural style or should it introduce a complete contrast so that the changes and additions are obvious? Period pastiches frequently fail to be aesthetically satisfactory. The scale and proportions of the new build should neither dwarf nor adversely affect the setting of the original building. Choice of building materials is also important as in some cases a blend of modern and traditional elements can show what is new and old. In other cases the more traditional structure and interior finishes are left in place and contribute to a warm, comfortable and aged residential quality. The siting of any additional structures such as walls, fences, parking areas, garages, service and storage areas should also be carefully considered, as inappropriate handling of these external features can have an adverse effect on the setting of the building.

Partial demolition: Where this is part of the planning proposal, it is critical that the relationship to the core building of the parts of the building proposed for demolition is understood, in terms both of dating and function. Careful selective demolition of inappropriate later additions to a building may enhance the original building and can reveal previously hidden original features. However the removal of adjacent buildings that have a key functional relationship to the main building can have a detrimental effect on both the setting and the understanding of the main building.

Dismantling and resiting: This should always be viewed as an action of last resort. The relocation of a building introduces major problems, the biggest of which is the fundamental issue of whether they actually do get rebuilt on a new site: there are many such buildings in so-called temporary storage. Even a successful rebuild means that the original context and any subterranean archaeology will be permanently lost. In the process of dismantling it is frequently only the external walls which are retained and most, if not all, original internal detailing is lost and layouts are frequently changed. The dismantling and subsequent storage of the bomb-damaged Baltic Exchange Building in St Mary Axe, London, is an illustration of this problem.

Case studies

Dewar's Lane Granary, Berwick-upon-Tweed

Built in 1769, the former granary of Dewar and Carmichael, corn and iron merchants, was empty for more than 20 years before it was successfully converted to new uses that included a youth hostel, meeting/conference rooms and exhibition space at a cost of £4.7 million. The partnership scheme involved The Berwick Preservation Trust, English Heritage, Heritage Lottery Fund (HLF) and Berwick-upon-Tweed Borough Council.

The successful conversion necessitated the recording and removal of internal timber framing and stabilising the six-storey structure, which had previously leaned over, with an internal steel frame which, in places, still allows the dramatic spaces within the structure to be appreciated. The interior was reconfigured and although floor levels were altered, external openings remained unchanged, with window apertures retaining their wooden shutters and fasteners and some fixtures and fittings left on display.

Modern extensions housing staircases are plain and in character with the functional former industrial building and allow traces of extant timber framing to be seen. A new walkway connects Berwick's quay wall to the second-floor gallery via a glass pavilion allowing new circulation routes and connectivity. Interpretative panels tell the story of the building and its significance to Berwick's industrial, economic and social history. Popular with the people of Berwick and visitors alike, new life has been breathed into a redundant and challenging building. Further information can be found at www.berwick-pt.co.uk.

Cricklepit Mill, Exeter

Flour has been milled on the site since the 13th century but the extant watermill appears to date mainly from the 19th century. A fire in the 1990s badly damaged the roof and first floor but, internally, gearing and the oak main shaft survived, as did two of the three water wheels. The machinery has been retained and there are operating days when the internal wheel grinds flour; the external wheel was brought back into use generating electricity in 2010.

The mill now houses the headquarters of the Devon Wildlife Trust whose offices are in a new build by architects Gillespie and Yunni, which hosts many sustainable new features designed to reduce its carbon footprint. It includes a timber frame, wooden window shutters that control heat and light, toilets which use 'grey water' from the leat, and where possible materials have been sourced locally. It has a hardy sedum roof which acts as insulation and reduces the amount of run-off water. This lessens the burden on sewerage systems and reduces the risk of pollutants being washed into local water courses causing harm to wildlife.

Weaving sheds, Higherford Mill, Lancashire

Higherford Mill is a former textile mill built *c* 1824, with subsequent additions. The site contains offices, warehouse, engine and boiler house, weaving sheds, sluices and headrace. It was a substantially complete example of a first-generation purpose-built spinning mill with single-storey weaving sheds.

Weaving sheds are an important element (historically and visually) within north-east Lancashire (see Chapter 5). The area became a specialist power loom weaving district, and this site retains a 17-bay weaving shed built in two phases. As single-storey buildings, these sheds have a large footprint and their form is distinctive with saw-tooth rooflines and north-facing roof lights. The shed roofs are carried on rows of cast-iron columns with integral brackets to carry line-shafting. Such buildings have engendered a myth that their reuse is difficult, making them vulnerable to demolition and replacement with more cost-effective multi-storeyed buildings. At Higherford Mill, which was proposed for demolition in 1994, the Heritage Trust North West, as part of the refurbishment of the wider site, is creating a centre for the creative industries in east Lancashire. It has used the weaving sheds to create studio space for local artists at affordable rents.

For further information see *Northern Lights: Finding a Future for the Weaving Sheds of Pennine Lancashire*, www.burnley.gov.uk/site/scripts/download. php?fileID=3279, an excellent study on reuse.

Stanley Mills, Perth

This complex stands on the banks of the River Tay in Perthshire. Built from 1787 onwards, Stanley Mills was one of the earliest mills in Scotland to develop cotton spinning using Arkwright's system. The three major mill buildings form a U-shape. The oldest mill is the Bell Mill of 13 bays and 5 storeys built of brick on a stone base. The 20-bay East Mill of *c* 1840 is built in rubble blocks and is linked to the East Mill by the 22-bay Mid Mill which was rebuilt *c* 1850 after a fire. There are several ancillary buildings on the site including the remains of a gas works. Power was derived from a lade running though a tunnel to exploit the 21ft (6.4m) fall in the River Tay, which runs in a tight loop around the site. Water wheels were superseded by turbines and then a hydro-electric scheme; the mills were never steam-powered. After several changes of ownership and clever product diversification into webbing, belting and specialised tapes for cigarette manufacturing, the production of all products including spun yarns ended in 1989. In 1995 Historic Scotland purchased the derelict site. The East Mill and

part of the Mid Mill have since been converted to housing, and in early 2008 parts of the Bell Mill and Mid Mill were opened as a visitor attraction, interpreting the story of the mills and the people who worked there (Fig 1.10).

The conversion has preserved the ambience of the entire mill complex and at the same time provides good interpretation of the process which took place and the power sources used. Most of the ancillary buildings have survived, including some which will never generate revenue such as the remains of the gas works. Minimal additions have been made to the exterior of the whole complex and very little new building carried out. The whole development is in sympathy with the site.

Figure 1.10 Stanley Mills stands on the banks of the River Tay in Perthshire. An outstanding example of an early cotton spinning complex, the picture shows to the right, Bell Mill of 1787 and, to the left, Mid Mill rebuilt after a fire in 1850. The gas works chimney is encased in scaffolding (© Mark Sissons)

Derby Roundhouse

This spectacular building opposite Derby Railway Station was built by the North Midland Railway in 1839. It was part of a complex of several buildings, including the circular locomotive and rolling stock repair building, probably the world's oldest surviving building of its type, a carriage shop, engine shop, and an office complex. The buildings ceased to have an active use in the 1980s, and although the Roundhouse was listed Grade II*, it took over 20 years to find a sustainable use and the complex was placed on the Buildings at Risk Register.

The site was eventually purchased by Derby College, and using contractors Bowmer and Kirkland, the buildings were converted at a cost of £48m to form its main campus, opening in September 2009. The buildings had many large-span, open sheds, which perfectly matched the spatial demands of the college. The central space in the Roundhouse serves as a social area and refectory for students and considerable effort was made to retain existing features such as the radiating turntable lines which have been covered with varnished timber, one being covered with glass so that its original function can be seen, as well as some of the gearing (Fig 1.11). The open spaces in the carriage shop have been equally well utilised as the College Library. The original cast-iron window frames have been retained wherever possible, and the main doors feature a glass etching of an original Midland Railway engine waiting to depart.

The Roundhouse has been linked to the former Engine Shop by an equally spectacular glass-fronted new build which changes colour and complements the redeveloped site. Situated between the railway and bus stations, the College encourages the use of environmentally friendly transport and so has turned its location to its advantage. The complex has a public restaurant as well as being available for conference and public events, and has played a significant role in the regeneration of this part of Derby.

1.5 References and Bibliography for Chapter 1

Alderton, D & Booker, J, 1980 *The Batsford Guide to the Industrial Archaeology of East Anglia*. London: Batsford

Badcock, A & Malaws, B A, 2004 Recording People and Processes at Large Industrial Structures, in Barker and Cranstone 2004, 269–89

Bailey, M R & Glithero, J P, 2000 *The Engineering and History of Rocket*. York: National Railway Museum

Barker, D & Cranstone, D, 2004 *The Archaeology of Industrialization*, Association for Industrial Archaeology and the Society for Post-Medieval Archaeology. Leeds: Maney

Barnwell, P S & Giles, C, 1997 *English Farmsteads 1750–1914*. Royal Commission on the Historical Monuments of England

Barnwell, P S, Palmer, M & Airs, M, 2004 *The Vernacular Workshop*, CBA Res Rep **140**. York: Council for British Archaeology

Bayley, J, Crossley, D & Ponting, M, 2010 *Metals and Metalworking: a research strategy for archaeometallurgy*, Historical Metallurgy Society Occasional Publication **6**

Belford, P, Palmer, M & White, R (eds), 2010 *Footprints of Industry Papers from the 300th anniversary conference at Coalbrookdale, 3–7 June 2009*, BAR Brit Ser **523**. Oxford: BAR, 153–6

Bodey, H & Hallas, M, 1978 *Elementary Surveying for Industrial Archaeologists*. Princes Risborough: Shire

Brennand, M, with Chitty, G & Nevell, M (eds), 2006 *The Archaeology of North West England. An Archaeological Research Framework for North West England: Vol 1. Resource Assessment*, Archaeology North West Vol 8. The Association of Local Government Archaeological Officers and English Heritage with The Council for British Archaeology North West

Buchanan, C A & Buchanan, R A, 1980 *The Batsford Guide to the Industrial Archaeology of Central Southern England*. London: Batsford

Buchanan, R A, 1972 *Industrial Archaeology in Britain*. London: Pelican

Buchanan, R A, 2000 The Origins of Industrial Archaeology, in Cossons (ed) 2000, 18–39

Butterfield, R J, 1994 The Industrial Archaeology of the Twentieth Century: the Shredded Wheat Factory at Welwyn Garden City, *Industrial Archaeology Review* **16**:1, 196–215

Calladine, A & Fricker, J, 1993 *East Cheshire Textile Mills*. Royal Commission on the Historical Monuments of England

Campion, G, 1996 People, process and the poverty pew: a functional analysis of mundane buildings in the Nottinghamshire framework-knitting industry, *Antiquity* **70**, 847–80

Campion, G, 2001 People, Process and the Place: an Archaeology of Control in East Midlands Outworking, 1820–1900, in Palmer & Neaverson 2001, 75–84

Casella, E C & Symonds, J, 2005 *Industrial Archaeology: Future Directions*. New York: Springer

Cherry, M & Chitty, G, 2009 Heritage Protection Reform implementation – Strategic designation: Review of past and present thematic programmes, October 2009 (report for English Heritage) http://www.english-heritage.org.uk/content/imported-docs/p-t/NHPP-draft-review-thematic (accessed 15 July 2011)

Cherry, M, Chitty, G, Cox, J, & Edwards, R, 2010 'Heritage Protection Reform: statutory lists review of quality and coverage', July 2010 (report for English Heritage) http://www.english-heritage.org.uk/content/imported-docs/p-t/statutory-lists-review-of-quality-and-coverage-2010.pdf (accessed 15 July 2011)

Clark, J, Darlington, J, & Fairclough, G, 2004 *Using Historic Landscape Characterisation*. English Heritage and Lancashire County Council

Clark, K, 1999 The Workshop of the World: the Industrial Revolution, in J Hunter & I Ralston (eds), *The Archaeology of Britain: an Introduction from the Palaeolithic to the Industrial Revolution*. London: Routledge, 280–96

Clark, K & Casella, E C, 2010 The Workshop of the World: the Industrial Revolution, in J Hunter & I Ralston (eds), *The Archaeology of Britain: an Introduction from the Palaeolithic to the Industrial Revolution*, 2nd edn. London: Routledge, 368–89

Cocroft, W D, 2000 *Dangerous Energy: the archaeology of gunpowder and military explosives manufacture*. London: English Heritage

Cooper, N, 2006 *The Archaeology of the East Midlands: an Archaeological Resource Assessment and Research Agenda*. Leicester: Leicester University Press

Cornwall Archaeology Unit, 1992 *Engine House Assessment – Mineral Tramways Project*.Truro: Cornwall County Council

Cossons, N, 1975 *The BP Book of Industrial Archaeology*. Newton Abbot: David & Charles (3rd edn 1993)

Cossons, N (ed), 2000 *Perspectives on Industrial Archaeology*. London: Science Museum

Cossons, N, 2008 Sustaining England's Industrial Heritage: A future for preserved industrial sites in England (unpublished report for English Heritage)

Cranstone, D, 1989 The Archaeology of Washing Floors: problems, potentials and priorities, *Industrial Archaeology Review* **12**:1, 40–9

Cranstone, D, 2004 The archaeology of industrialisation – new directions, in Barker & Cranstone 2004, 313–20

Darvill, T, 2003 *The Concise Oxford Dictionary of Archaeology*. London

Delafons, J, 1997 *Politics and Preservation Policy 1882–1996*. London: Taylor & Francis

English Heritage, 1997 *Thesaurus of Archaeological Monument Types*. See http://thesaurus.english-heritage.org.uk/. For industrial monument types, see http://thesaurus.english-heritage.org.uk/class_list.asp?class_no=132062&thes_no=1&class_name=INDUSTRIAL

English Heritage, DCMS, 2005 *Listing is Changing*. English Heritage

English Heritage, 2005a Urban Characterisation: Improving methodologies, *Conservation Bulletin* **47**, 11–17

English Heritage, 2005b Historic Landscape Characterisation: A national programme, *Conservation Bulletin* **47**, 20–2

English Heritage, 2006a (Dungworth, D & Paynter, S) *Science for Historic Industries; guidelines for the investigation of 17th- to 19th-century industries*, http://www.helm.org.uk/upload/pdf/Science-Historic-Industries.pdf

English Heritage, 2006b (Menuge, A) *Understanding Historic Buildings: a guide to good recording practice*, http://www.helm.org.uk/upload/pdf/Understanding_Historic_Buildings_1.pdf

English Heritage, 2007 *Industrial Buildings Selection Guide*, http://www.english-heritage.org.uk/publications/industrial/industrialselectionguide.pdf

English Heritage, 2010. *Understanding Place. Historic Area Assessment: Principles and Practice*, http://www.english-heritage.org.uk/content/publications/docs/understanding-place-haa.pdf

Everson, P, 1995 The survey of complex industrial landscapes, in Palmer & Neaverson 1995, 21–8

Falconer, K, 1980 *Guide to England's Industrial Heritage*. London: Batsford

Falconer, K, 2000 Not a bad record? Changing perspectives in recording, in Cossons (ed) 2000, 57–85 [this contains a very useful bibliography of industrial and related publications by the three Royal Commissions and English Heritage]

Falconer, K, 2010 *English Heritage Thematic Research Strategies. A Thematic Research Strategy for the Industrial Historic Environment*. English Heritage http://www.english-heritage.org.uk/content/imported-docs/f-j/industrial-research-strategy.pdf

Falconer, K & Hay, G, 1981 *The Recording of Industrial Sites: a Review*, CBA Occasional Paper, http://archaeologydataservice.ac.uk/archives/view/cba_op/op13.cfm

Fitzgerald, R, 2007a Historic building record and the Halifax Borough Market Doors, *Industrial Archaeology Review* **29**:1, 51–74

Fitzgerald, R, 2007b The Stone Dam Mill engine house, *Industrial Archaeology Review* **29**:2, 115–31

Giles, C & Goodall, I H, 1992 *Yorkshire Textile Mills. The Buildings of the Yorkshire Textile Industry 1770–1930*. Royal Commission on the Historical Monuments of England

Glazebrook, J (ed), 1997 *Research and Archaeology: a Framework for the Eastern Counties 1*, East Anglian Archaeology Occasional Paper **3**

Grant, J, Gorin, S & Fleming, N, 2002 *The Archaeology Coursebook. An Introduction to Study Skills, Topics and Methods*. London & New York: Routledge

Green, E R R, 1963 *The Industrial Archaeology of County Down*. Belfast: HMSO

Green, K & Moore, T, 2010 *Archaeology: An Introduction* (5th edn). London & New York: Routledge

Gwyn, D, 2005 The Landscape Archaeology of the Vale of Ffestiniog, in Gwyn & Palmer 2005, 97–104

Gwyn, D, 2006 *Gwynedd: inheriting a Revolution: the archaeology of industrialisation in north-west Wales*. Chichester: Phillimore

Gwyn, D & Palmer, M (eds), 2005 Understanding the Workplace. A Research Framework for Industrial Archaeology in Britain, *Industrial Archaeology Review* **27**:1

Hay, G D, & Stell, G P, 1986 *Monuments of Industry: an illustrated historical record*. Edinburgh: RCAHMS

Hayman, R, 1997 The Archaeologist as Witness: Matthew Harvey's Glebeland Works, Walsall, *Industrial Archaeology Review* **19**:1, 61–74

HBMCE, 1984 *England's archaeological resource*. London: Historic Buildings and Monuments Commission

Holden, R, 1999 Water supplies for steam-powered textile mills, *Industrial Archaeology Review* **21**:1, 41–51

Holden, R, 2009 Lancashire Cotton Mills and Power, in A Horning & M Palmer (eds), *Crossing Paths or Sharing Tracks? Future directions in the archaeological study of post-1550 Britain and Ireland*, Society for Post-Medieval Archaeology Monograph Series. London: Boydell Press, 261–72

Hoskins, W G, 1955 *The Making of the English Landscape*. London: Hodder & Stoughton

Hudson, K, 1963 *Industrial Archaeology: An Introduction*. London: John Baker

Hudson, K, 1965 *The Industrial Archaeology of Southern England*. Dawlish: David & Charles

Hudson, K, 1967 *Handbook for Industrial Archaeologists*. London: John Baker

Hughes, S, 1979–80 The Swansea Canal: Navigation and Power Supplier, *Industrial Archaeology Review* **4**:1, 51–69

Hughes, S, 1998 *The Archaeology of the Montgomery Canal*. Aberystwyth: RCAHMW

Hughes, S, 2000 *Copperopolis: Landscapes of the early industrial period in Swansea*. Aberystwyth: RCAHMW

Hughes, S, Malaws, B, Parry, M & Wakelin, P, 1995 *Collieries in Wales: Engineering and Architecture*. Aberystwyth: RCAHMW

Hume, J R, 1976 *The Industrial Archaeology of Scotland 1. The Lowlands and Borders*. London: Batsford

Hume, J R, 1977 *The Industrial Archaeology of Scotland 2. The Highlands and Islands*. London: Batsford

Jones, N, Walters, M & Frost P, 2004 *Mountains and Orefield: metal mining landscapes of mid- and north-east Wales*, CBA Res Rep **142.** York: Council for British Archaeology

Major, J K, 1975 *Fieldwork in Industrial Archaeology*. London: Batsford

Malaws, B A, 1997 Process Recording at Industrial Sites, *Industrial Archaeology Review* **19**:1, 75–99

McCutcheon, W A, 1980 *The Industrial Archaeology of Northern Ireland*. Belfast: HMSO

McKnight, P, 1996 Christy's Hat Works, Stockport: the site, buildings and industrial processes from 1742 to 1996. Unpublished MSocSc thesis, Ironbridge Institute, University of Birmingham

Mellor, I, 2005 Space, Society and the Textile mill, in Gwyn & Palmer (eds) 2005, 49–56

Miller, I & Wild, C, 2007 *A & G Murray and the Cotton Mills of Ancoats*. Lancaster Imprints **13**. Lancaster: Oxford Archaeology North

Morriss, R K, 2000 *The Archaeology of Buildings*. Stroud: Tempus

Morrisson, K A, 2000 *The Workhouse. A Study of Poor-Law Buildings in England*. London: English Heritage

Morrisson, K A & Bond, A, 2004 *Built to Last? The Buildings of the Northamptonshire Boot and Shoe Industry*. London: English Heritage

NAMHO, 2010 Archaeology of Extractive Industries (http://www.vmine.net/namho-2010/research.asp) (accessed 16 January 2012)

Nevell, M (ed), 2003 *From Farmer to Factory Owner: Models, Methodology and Industrialisation. The Archaeology of the Industrial Revolution in North-West England*, Archaeology North-West **6**. Council for British Archaeology North-West

Nevell, M, 2005 Industrialisation, ownership, and the Manchester Methodology: the role of the contemporary social structure during industrialisation, 1600–1900, in Gwyn & Palmer (eds) 2005, 87–96

Nevell, M, 2006 The 2005 Rolt Memorial Lecture: Industrial archaeology or the archaeology of the industrial period? Models, methodology and the future of industrial archaeology, *Industrial Archaeology Review* **28**:1, 3–16

Nevell, M, 2008 *Manchester. The Hidden History*. Stroud: The History Press

Nevell, M, 2010 Excavating the cotton mill: towards a research framework for the below-ground remains of the textile industry, in Belford, Palmer & White 2010

Nevell, M & Walker, J, 1999 *A History and Archaeology of Tameside. Volume 7. Tameside in Transition 1642–1870*. Tameside Metropolitan Borough Council with the University of Manchester Archaeological Unit

Nevell, M & Walker, J, 2004 Lands and Lordships; the role of the Landlord, Freeholder and Tenant in the Industrialisation of the Manchester Area, 1600–1900, in Barker & Cranstone 2004, 53–78

Newman, M, 2009 Industrial archaeology and the National Inventory: enhancement and access, *Industrial Archaeology News*, **148**, 6–7

Newman, M, 2010 New life for old industrial archaeology records, in Belford, Palmer & White 2010, 247–51

Nixon, T, McAdam, E, Tomber, R & Swain, H, 2002 *A Research Framework for London Archaeology*. London: Museum of London

Oglethorpe, M K, 2006 *Scottish Collieries*. Edinburgh: RCAHMS

Ottaway, P, Manby, T G & Moorhouse, S, 2003 *The Archaeology of Yorkshire: an Assessment at the Beginning of the 21st Century*. Yorkshire Archaeological Society Occasional Paper **3**

Palmer, M, 1983 *The Richest in All Wales!: the Welsh Potosi or Esgair His and Esgair Fraith Lead and Copper Mines of Cardiganshire*, Chesterfield: Northern Mine Research Society Monograph **22**

Palmer, M, 1991 Industrial Archaeology: Working for the Future, *Industrial Archaeology Review* **16**:1, 17–32

Palmer, M, 2010 Industrial Archaeology and the Archaeological Community: Fifty Years On, *Industrial Archaeology Review* **32**:1, 5–20

Palmer, M & Neaverson, P A, 1987 *The Basset Mines of Cornwall; their History and Industrial Archaeology*, Chesterfield: Northern Mine Research Society Monograph **32**

Palmer, M & Neaverson, P A, 1989 Nineteenth-century Tin and Lead Dressing: a Comparative Study of the Field Evidence, *Industrial Archaeology Review* **12**:1, 9–39

Palmer, M & Neaverson, P A, 1994 *Industry in the Landscape, 1700–1900*. London: Routledge

Palmer, M & Neaverson, P A, 1995 *Managing the Industrial Heritage; its identification, recording and management*, University of Leicester Archaeology Monograph **2**

Palmer, M & Neaverson, P A, 1998 *Industrial Archaeology: Principles and Practice*. London & New York: Routledge

Palmer, M & Neaverson, P A, 2001 *From Industrial Revolution to Consumer Revolution: Transactions of the Millennium Congress of the International Committee for the Conservation of the Industrial Heritage*. Leeds: Association for Industrial Archaeology, English Heritage, National Museum of Science & Industry

Palmer, M & Neaverson, P A, 2004 Home as Workplace in nineteenth-century Wiltshire and Gloucestershire, *Textile History* **35** (1), 27–57

Palmer, M & Neaverson, P A, 2005 *The Textile Industry of South-West England: a Social Archaeology*. Stroud: Tempus

Pannell, J P M, 1974 (2nd edn edited by K Major) *The techniques of Industrial Archaeology*. Newton Abbot: David & Charles

Petts, D & Gerrard, C, 2006 *Shared Visions: the North East Regional Research Framework for the Historic Environment*. Durham: Durham County Council

Quigley, P, 2010 *The Legacy of Factory Buildings in the Black Country*. http://archaeologydataservice.ac.uk/catalogue/adsdata/arch-939-1/dissemination/pdf/LegacyofFactoryBuildings.pdf). Accessed 19/09/2011

Quartermaine, J, Trinder, B & Turner, R, 2003 *Thomas Telford's Holyhead Road*. CBA Res Rep **135**. York: Council for British Archaeology

Raistrick, A, 1972 *Industrial Archaeology: an Historical Survey*. London: Eyre Methuen

Renfrew, C & Bahn, P, 2008 *Archaeology: Theories, Methods and Practice*. London: Thames & Hudson

Richardson, H, 1998 *English Hospitals 1660–1948. A Survey of their Architectural Design*. London: English Heritage

Rippon, S, 2004 *Historic Landscape Analysis: Deciphering the Countryside*. CBA Practical Handbooks in Archaeology **16**. York: Council for British Archaeology

Rix, M, 1955 Industrial Archaeology, *The Amateur Historian* **2**:8, 228

Rix, M, 1967 *Industrial Archaeology*. London: The Historical Association

Rynne, C, 1999 *The industrial archaeology of Cork city and its environs*. Dublin: Stationery Office

Rynne, C, 2006 *Industrial Ireland 1750–1930: An Archaeology*. Cork: The Collins Press

Schofield, J, 2000 *MPP 2000: A Review of the Monuments Protection Programme, 1986–2000*. London: English Heritage

Smith, D, 1965 *The Industrial Archaeology of the East Midlands*. Dawlish: David & Charles

Stocker, D, 1995 Industrial archaeology and the Monuments Protection Programme in England, in Palmer & Neaverson (eds) 1995, 105–13

Stratton, M, 1990 Industrial Monuments: a Protection Programme, *Industrial Archaeology Review* **13**:1, 35–49

Symonds, J (ed), 2002 *The Historical Archaeology of the Sheffield Cutlery and Tableware Industry 1750–1900*. Arcus Studies in Historical Archaeology **1**. Sheffield: Sheffield University

Tann, J, 1967 *Gloucestershire Woollen Mills*. Newton Abbot: David & Charles

Taylor, S, Cooper, M & Barnwell, P S, 2002 *Manchester. The Warehouse legacy. An Introduction and Guide*. London: English Heritage

Thornes, R, 1994 *Images of Industry: Coal*. London: RCHME

Trinder, B, 2002 18th- and 19th-Century Market Town Industry: An analytical model, *Industrial Archaeology Review* **24**:2, 75–90

Watt, S (ed), 2011 *The Archaeology of the West Midlands: A Framework for Research*. Oxford: Oxbow Books

Webster, C J (ed), 2008 *The Archaeology of South West England. South West Archaeological Research Framework: Resource Assessment and Research Agenda*. Taunton: Somerset County Council

Williams, M with Farnie, D, 1992 *Cotton Mills in Greater Manchester*. Preston: Carnegie Press

Wood, J (ed), 1994 *Buildings Archaeology: Papers Given at the Institute of Field Archaeologists Buildings Special Interest Group Symposium, January 1993*. London: Oxbow Archaeological Monographs

CHAPTER TWO

Processing the products of agriculture

2.1 Introduction

Buildings concerned with processing the products of agriculture have not always figured largely in studies of industrial archaeology, yet without the intensification of agricultural production, industrial activity in the early modern period could never have been sustained. In the course of the 18th century, the growth and redistribution of population was accompanied by increased efficiency in agriculture which ensured that town dwellers and full-time industrial workers could be fed. The number of people living in England and Wales rose from the 5.5 million estimated by Gregory King in 1688 to nearly 9 million by the time of the first census in 1801 and to 32.5 million in 1901. In 1851 the number of people living in towns was for the first time equal to the number of rural inhabitants, but by 1901 the proportion had increased to three to one. While the number of non-growers increased rapidly, by dint of improving agricultural productivity and food processing, as well as some imports, there were no real food shortages in Britain.

This section considers buildings constructed to enable food to be produced more efficiently as well as to process and store it for human consumption.

2.2 Land drainage structures and pumping plant

One of the ways in which agricultural productivity was increased in the early modern period was by bringing what had previously been waste land into cultivation. The enclosure of the wastes and commons had been in progress since the 16th century, but from the early 17th century onwards, greater efforts were made to drain waterlogged land. However, across many areas of the country, agricultural land drainage does not exhibit a dominant presence. Large numbers of clay pipes were installed below ground and ditches alongside fields flow quietly into streams by gravity, and then onwards into river channels. It tends to be only in extensive areas of low-lying lands, such as the Fens of Cambridgeshire and Lincolnshire, Romney Marshes, and the Somerset Levels, that more visible land drainage structures are to be seen. These can be broadly grouped into:

- gates and sluices to direct flow by gravity in drainage channels (which may include major rivers), and to restrict the entry of coastal sea water into inland river systems;
- pumping machinery and the buildings within which that machinery is (or has been) sited.

Key elements and plan forms

Gates and sluices

These controlled gravity flow, and, although locally important for flood control, are often small and inconspicuous. The use of sluices dates back to the Middle Ages, with wooden designs being progressively replaced by those of iron and steel. The largest sluice structures are often sited on rivers at tidal limits, where they control the risk of coastal flooding from the sea. Some pairs of 'pointing doors' survive, which when closed form a 'V', pointing outwards into the tidal waters. As the tidal water level falls below that of the water stored on the inland side of the doors, the pointing doors open to allow outward flow. As the tide rises above the level of the outward flow, the doors are closed by tidal water pressure, preventing further flow of sea water into the inland river system. The 1930s saw the construction (often by Ransomes and Rapier of Ipswich) of a number of very large 'guillotine' (vertically lifting) gate structures for flood control, both along major rivers and at tidal limits. The gates are raised and lowered vertically by electric motors to control the flow. More recent structures have included the Thames Barrier (opened in 1984) and the Jubilee River (designed to divert flood flows from the Thames in the area around Windsor), which was opened in 2002.

Pumping plant

This proved necessary where surplus water could not be drained from farm land by gravity. The drainage of peaty areas was made difficult as the more water was removed, the more the surface level of the reclaimed peaty soils sank. Initially wind power was used extensively, as in the Netherlands, but only very few wind pumps remain. A mechanism very similar to that of a wind mill for grinding corn was used, but the final drive was to a horizontal shaft on which paddle blades were fixed to form a scoop wheel. The turning of the mill rotated the blades, which dipped into water in a low-lying drain, and propelled the water upwards to spill over a raised cill into an upper drainage channel.

The early steam-powered pumps employed the same principle of the scoop wheel, the small engine being sited next to the wheel with an adjacent boiler house and chimney. An alternative design, used especially on the Somerset Levels, combined a steam engine, a vertical drive shaft and an impeller in one unit. As the impeller rotated, water was lifted vertically. By combining all components on one frame, the problem of differential sinking – which could occur with the steam engine mounted separately from the pump wheel – was much reduced.

Figure 2.1 Berney Arms High Mill, Reedham, Norfolk, built *c* 1865 to grind cement clinker but from 1886 serving to drain the surrounding marshes until the 1940s; the large scoop wheel is evidence of this use. It was restored by the Ministry of Public Buildings and Works in 1965 and is now in the care of English Heritage (© Marilyn Palmer)

The coming of diesel engines (especially after World War I) often resulted in the steam engine houses being reused, either with diesel engines alone, or with steam plant maintained as 'back up'. With the risk of sudden flood flows, older pumping plant has often been retained over the years to help cope with emergencies. The coming of electrical plant (often driving submersible pumps which could be lowered into position down access holes) resulted in the demolition of many old steam-era pumping stations and their replacement by small, undistinguished box-like electric engine houses. Even today, however, some diesel engine units are maintained for use in emergencies.

Organisation

Responsibility for structures and pumping plant is currently divided mainly between the Environment Agency (EA), which manages the major river and channel systems, and Internal Drainage Boards (IDBs), which cover local areas. The Boards are partially funded by charges linked to properties within their boundaries. IDBs, although most common in areas where low-lying land predominates, can be found in other areas of England and Wales, where local areas of farm land (and adjacent properties) need protection against flooding. They have a strong interest in history and in almost any pumping station you will see one or more plaques commemorating the opening of different stages of the development of the station.

Key sites

Large flood-control structures, linked to land drainage control include:

Denver Sluice: a complex of sluice gates and locks controlling flow in the Great Ouse River (http://www.lapollo.net/denver_sluice.htm)

Holme Sluices, Colwick, which control flooding around Nottingham on the River Trent (http://www.geograph.org.uk/photo/651485)

Marsh Road Sluice, Spalding: interesting 'flap gates' at the seaward end of the Coronation flood relief channel (http://www.geograph.org.uk/search. php?i=19016318)

Thames Barrier: by far the largest flood-control structure in the UK (http://www.environment-agency.gov.uk/homeandleisure/floods/38353.aspx)

Land drainage pumping plant:

Wind power is represented by *Berney Arms Drainage Mill* (Fig 2.1), Norfolk and *Wicken Fen*, Cambridgeshire (http://www.wicken.org.uk/visit/windpump.pdf)

Steam-pumping stations can be seen at *Dogdyke Engine*, Lincolnshire (http://www.dogdyke.com/); *Pinchbeck Engine*, Lincolnshire; *Stretham Old Engine*, Cambridgeshire (http://www.strethamoldengine.org.uk/history.htm); *Westonzoyland Pumping Station Museum*, Somerset (http://www.wzlet.org/); *Pode Hole*, Lincolnshire (scoop wheel no longer present).

Working diesel engines can be seen at *Prickwillow Museum*, Cambridgeshire – see (http://www.prickwillow-engine-museum.co.uk/). In addition, some smaller old diesel engines and land drainage pumps are preserved, especially in Lincolnshire.

Further reading

H C Darby, *The Draining of the Fens* (Cambridge University Press, 2nd edn, 1956) is the classic work on Fenland drainage, while M Williams, *The Draining of the Somerset Levels* (Cambridge University Press, 1970) provides useful historical background on that region.

The following provide more technical details, both published by Landmark Publishing of Ashbourne: R L Hills, *The Drainage of the Fens* (2008) and K S G Hinde, *Fenland Pumping Engines* (2006).

For historical background, S Tarlow, *The Archaeology of Improvement: Britain 1750–1850* (Cambridge University Press, 2006), deals with the historical archaeology of land improvement.

2.3   Farm buildings and mechanisation

There is now quite a large body of information on farm buildings, both published and in the form of unpublished reports in the National Monuments Records and in local Historic Environment Records, but there is much to learn about how such buildings can help us to understand the means by which food production was intensified to enable the growing population of Britain to be fed.

Barns

The barn is normally the oldest as well as largest surviving building on a farmstead, identifiable by its opposing double doors. Often considered as a warehouse, a place in which crops were stored, most surviving barns should also be seen as factories where raw materials were processed into finished products and stored only temporarily, except in certain cases such as *tithe barns*. The process of hand threshing with a flail needed an open space with a through draught provided by the opposing doors so that the chaff winnowed from the ears of corn could be blown away. This was a slow and laborious process but it provided employment for labourers when they could not work in the fields and also the fodder and litter needed by the farm animals. The majority of early barns were timber-framed and are often superb examples of the carpenter's art, but some were of stone or brick where these materials were more readily available than timber. Barns might be ventilated below the eaves, but generally had few or no windows at all, since light for threshing was provided through the doors; this characteristic can present problems in modern conversions for other uses.

The increase of grain production in the late 18th century led to a great increase in the number of barns built, particularly in the east of England. At the same time, Andrew Meikle's invention of the threshing machine around 1786 began the elimination of hand-threshing. Power for the machine could be provided by water or, more rarely, wind, but the most commonly used form of power was the horse gin. This could take two forms: the sweep, in which the horses stepped over the drive shaft, or the overhead gearing in which the horses trod a circular route underneath a crown wheel and pinion gear serving a horizontal drive shaft. The former type was often in the open air and can be identified from a depression in the ground where the bearing used to be, while the latter was usually housed in a single-storey building. Many examples of circular or multi-angular buildings housing horse gins can still be found, together with engine houses where steam power replaced horse power. These engines could also power other devices such as root and chaff cutters.

Other barns may be found out in the field rather than in the farmstead, and these served several purposes such as the storage of hay for feeding animals, together with carts for transporting it, as well as shelter for the animals. The *bank barn* or *field barn* made use of a natural slope: at the lower level, there was often access to a cart shed and stalls for animals, while at the upper level a ramp on the opposite side of the building led through a large door into a storage barn from which fodder could be dropped down into the mangers in the lower level. Such barns have often been converted as bunk barns for walkers, but their distribution across the landscape in northern England is very characteristic of the mixed type of farming practised there, and they should be retained if at all possible.

Other farm buildings

Cow houses were provided on most farms to shelter valuable animals in bad weather; these generally had stalls with a central feeding passage at the lower level and a hay loft above with a regular series of pitching eyes for the hay facing the yard. Stables for horses were usually more elaborate than cow houses, although usually the interiors were similar with hay lofts above and stalls below, except that these tended to be larger and often more ornate with a manger at horse height on the wall. On country estates, many stables were architect-designed and situated away from the home farm. A granary was intended principally for the storage of

threshed grain away from the depredations of vermin, and small granaries could
be of timber, brick or stone and placed on *staddle stones* to raise them above
ground level. Many farms made use of the space below granaries by turning
these into open-fronted cart sheds, often with brick, stone or cast-iron pillars
to support the granary, which was accessed by an external stair. Pig sties were
another distinctive farm building, comprising a covered shelter, possibly with a
hen house in the loft, and a walled yard, usually split into separate compartments.
Pigs could be dangerous animals and elaborate iron feeding troughs were devised
to keep them away from the farmhands who fed them; these are well worth
recording.

Model farms

Many new farms, particularly on large estates, were built on the 'model farm'
principle in which, as in a factory, each function had its particular space, logically
arranged within a single integrated complex so as to facilitate the flow of processes
and to ensure maximum efficiency (Fig 2.2). In other cases, farmers added these
new types of buildings and tried to rationalise the processes of the farmyard as
best they could. There is a rich field of study here for industrial archaeologists,
since much of what has previously been written has concentrated more on the
vernacular styles of farm buildings than their functions as part of what was by
the 19th century a well-integrated industrial activity.

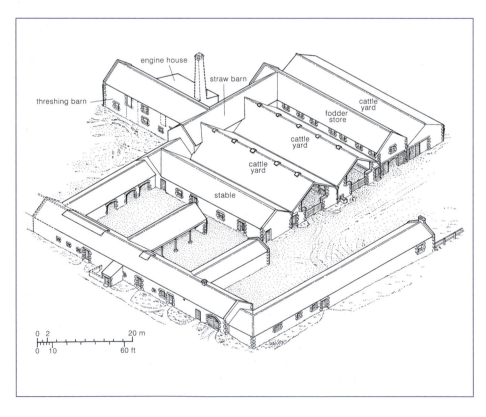

Figure 2.2 Crookham
Westfield Farm, Ford,
Northumberland. A
large mixed farmstead
built in the late 19th
century (© Crown
Copyright. NMR)

Key sites

Most farm buildings are privately owned, but examples of individual structures can be seen in various open air museums such as the *Avoncroft Museum of Buildings*, Worcestershire; *Weald and Downland Open Air Museum*, West Sussex; *St Fagans National History Museum*, Cardiff. Some of the great tithe barns are open to the public, such as those at *Bradford-on-Avon* in Wiltshire and *Great Coxwell* in Oxfordshire. The National Trust and other landowners have also opened estate farms to the public, as at *Shugborough* in Staffordshire, *Wimpole Hall* in Cambridgeshire, and *Holkham Hall* in Norfolk.

Further reading

A good starting point is R W Brunskill, *Traditional Farm Buildings of Britain and their conservation* (Yale University Press in association with Peter Crawley, 2007). Also useful here are P Barnwell & C Giles, *English Farmsteads 1750–1914* (RCHME, 1997) which has detailed studies of specific regions and is well illustrated, and P S Barnwell, 'Farm Buildings and the Industrial Age' (*Industrial Archaeology Review* 27:2, 2005, 113–20). J Woodforde, *Farm Buildings in England and Wales* (Routledge & Kegan Paul, 1983), has some very useful drawings.

For model farms, the standard work is S Wade-Martins, *The English Model Farm: Building the Agricultural Ideal, 1770–1914* (Windgather Press, 2002).

Good regional studies include I L Donnachie, *The Industrial Archaeology of Galloway* (David & Charles, 1971) (farm horse gin houses); T Jordan, *Cotswold Barns* (Tempus, 2006); E William, *The Historical Farm Buildings of Wales* (John Donald, 1986).

The large number of farm buildings owned by the National Trust are reviewed by D Thackray in 'The Industrial Archaeology of Agriculture: Rural Life Collections and the National Trust' (*Industrial Archaeology Review* 18:1, 1995, 117–31).

Between 1986 and 2003 the Historic Farm Buildings Group produced an annual Journal, with many articles on farm buildings. See http://www.hfbg.org.uk/texts/publications_main_text.php?id=2 (accessed August 2011).

2.4 Dovecots

Domestic pigeons were an important source of fresh meat for the household from Norman times onwards, particularly in the winter months when most other meat was salted or smoked following the autumn slaughter of animals because of the lack of winter fodder. At first a jealously guarded feudal right, restricted to lords of the manor and to abbeys and monasteries, building sanctions were relaxed from the 16th century onwards and by the 18th century few farms were without one. Pigeon farming declined after the improvements in animal breeding and new fodder crops from the late 18th century onwards, but many survived for decorative purposes

to house ring doves and even racing pigeons. Pigeon dung was also an important source of saltpetre, an ingredient of gunpowder, and in the early modern period the saltpetre men had the right to dig up pigeon droppings from dovecots and other farm buildings, often causing considerable damage to property.

Key elements and plan forms

Dovecots (*doocots* in Scotland) are important vernacular structures which usually reflect the use of local building materials including wood, stone, and brick. They could be circular, rectangular, square or even octagonal in shape, topped by a cupola or lantern to create an entrance for the birds but also to keep rain out of the interior (Fig 2.3). Some barns and even houses incorporated nesting places for pigeons which can be identified from rows of holes usually in the upper storeys of buildings. The walls inside a dovecot are lined with rows of nest holes, sometimes numbering a thousand or more (Fig 2.4). These often start at a metre or so above the floor in an effort to prevent rats reaching the nests. The *squabs*, as the young birds were known, were collected by means of a *potence*, a central stout wooden pole pivoted above and below to allow it to rotate, with ladders attached to the lateral arms to provide access to the nest holes.

Figure 2.4 A sketch
of the nesting boxes
built into the wall
inside a square
dovecot (© Colin
Ray)

Dovecots are therefore one of the earliest structures whose function was a form of factory farming, replicated in more recent times by poultry battery houses. Their attractive form has, however, meant that many are listed structures and therefore available for inspection and study. The use of the upper storeys of houses and farm buildings to house pigeons is frequently neglected, however, and should always be recorded.

Key sites

Dovecots can be seen on many National Trust and other properties open to the public, including *Felbrigg Hall*, Norfolk; *Erdigg*, Clwyd; *Cotehele House*, Cornwall; *Dunster*, Somerset; *Minster Lovell*, Oxfordshire; *Painswick Rococo Garden*, Gloucestershire; *Phantassie Doocot*, Preston Mill, East Lothian; *Finavon Doocot*, Angus. See http://www.photographers-resource.co.uk/A_heritage/Dovecots/Lists/Dovecots/ (accessed 19/01/2011) for lists of dovecots which can be photographed in England, Wales, and Scotland.

Further reading

P & J Hansell, *Dovecots* (Shire Publications, 1988), is a good starting point, together with their *A Dovecote Heritage* (Millstream Books, 1992). For Scotland, see T Buxbaum, *Scottish Doocots* (Shire Publications, 1987). An older useful book is available on-line: A O Cooke, *A Book of Dovecotes* (T N Foulis, 1920, http://openlibrary.org/books/OL23282176M/A_book_of_dovecotes).

See also K Spandl, *MPP: Dovecotes Step 1 Report*, Report for English Heritage (Oxford Archaeology, 1995) and K Spandl, *MPP: Dovecotes Step 3 Report, Sections 1–4*, Report for English Heritage (Oxford Archaeology, 1995).

There are also many regional studies of dovecots, mostly about their vernacular architecture. See, for example, P Ariss, 'The Dovecotes of Gloucestershire' in the *Journal of the Historic Farm Buildings Group* **6**, 1992, 3–34 (http://www.hfbg.org. uk/downloads/dovecotes_of_gloucestershire_philip_ariss.pdf).

A useful documentary source for the existence of dovecotes is discussed in J McCann, 'Engravings as evidence of dovecotes', *Vernacular Architecture*, **42**, 2011, 36–52.

2.5 Corn milling

For the majority of people in Britain in 1700, bread was the staple food and continued to be such until well into the 19th century. This is reflected in the number of corn mills, both water and wind powered, which have survived in most parishes, at least in England. Water mills were first introduced into Britain by the Romans during the 1st century AD, and over 6000 mills (presumed to be water mills) were recorded in Domesday Book in 1086. Wind mills were first introduced in the late 12th century, but generally water mills have probably outnumbered wind mills by about two to one.

Key elements and plan forms

(Water and wind power are dealt with in more detail in Chapter 3.)

In parts of Scotland, particularly the crofting communities of the islands, small corn mills using a horizontal water-wheel, the form first adopted by the Greeks but often called Norse mills, remained in operation into the 20th century as they were ideally suited to the individual hamlets and farms which were the characteristic settlements of the area. These usually had a single pair of stones fed by grain from a hopper on the floor above the pit in which the wheel was situated. Where nucleated settlement predominated, as in Lowland Scotland and much of England, the village or manorial mill served the community.

The vertical wheel used in these mills transmitted the drive through a series of gears to the millstones. Higher speeds and increased power meant that several sets of stones could be driven from one wheel, resulting in a greater output of meal or flour. In most mills, the corn was taken to the top floor by means of a sack hoist worked from the water wheel and descended down through the stones by gravity (Fig 2.5). Most cereal mills had a set of both French burr and Derbyshire Peak stones, the latter being used for coarse flour and animal feed and the burrs for fine white flour. Larger cereal mills would also incorporate other flour-processing machinery such as boulters (sieves), and small electric or diesel motors for providing auxiliary power when the water levels were low can still be

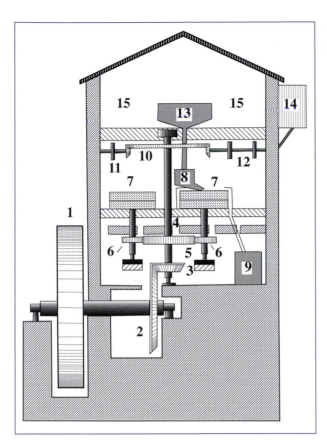

Figure 2.5 Diagrammatical section of water-powered corn mill with a vertical wheel driving several pairs of stones and auxiliary machinery via gearing. 1, waterwheel; 2, pit wheel; 3, wallower; 4, main shaft; 5, great spur wheel; 6, stone nuts; 7, millstones; 8, grain hopper and feed shoe; 9, meal bin; 10, crown wheel; 11, auxiliary machine drive pulley; 12, sack hoist and auxiliary machine drive pulleys; 13, grain bin; 14, lucam; 15, grain storage (© Marilyn Palmer)

found. Some mills, particularly in Scotland and Ireland, had adjacent kilns for drying wet grain before processing, and most also had a nearby miller's house. Where a suitable tidal range and long coastal inlet coincided, *tide mills* making use of the rise and fall of the tide could be built. Of all industrial buildings, water mills are probably the best indicators of the vernacular building tradition since many of those surviving were built before canal or railway transport enabled the widespread distribution of alternative building materials.

The types of wind mill used for corn grinding are described in Chapter 3. Early post mills could not house more than two pairs of millstones, and so their milling capacity was limited. By the end of the 18th century, they were being replaced by the sturdier brick- or stone-built tower mill, often with multiple sails which gave greater power than the four sails of the post mill. The increased space and height available made multiple floors possible, which enabled more sets of millstones to be introduced, while the lower floors could be used for storage.

By the 19th century, many steam-powered mills were being built in towns or alongside canals and railways, usually constructed of brick and not of local materials. They supplemented rather than replaced earlier types of mill as coal had to be purchased, whereas water and wind were free, albeit not so reliable. Sometimes they were built close to earlier mills to 'help out' when natural power was unobtainable. Late in the century, the introduction of the technique of roller milling proved particularly suitable for the processing of the hard wheat being imported from America and eastern Europe after the repeal of the Corn Laws in 1849. The process of gradual reduction using rollers produced much more white flour than the single passage through stones of a traditional corn mill, and this was in great demand by consumers. Some rural mills, even water-powered ones, converted to roller-milling, but huge mills were also built at ports to process imported grain.

Corn mills, despite their often attractive appearance, are functional, working buildings which were frequently rebuilt and their machinery and equipment modernised. It is important to remember that a mill is a complex cross between a building and a machine and that the structure and the mechanism or process are closely interdependent. While this is particularly apparent with wind mills, it is less obvious with water mills, so an understanding of this interdependence is necessary to help analyse and interpret remains and also to enable decisions to be made about the value of recording and retaining mill buildings with their machinery and equipment.

Assessment of sites

+ Topographic setting: region, environment, geology; river systems and catchment areas.
+ Landscape setting: related to settlement, agriculture and land use; access by land and water.
+ Hydraulic infrastructure: weirs, leats, ponds, sluices, spillways, wheel pits, penstocks, launders, tailraces; fresh and salt water supply.
+ Buildings: form, construction, materials; vernacular and designed.
+ Machinery: waterwheels, turbines, gearing/drives, millstones, machines; local and regional mill wrighting and engineering traditions in design, layout, and construction.
+ Functions: as well as corn milling, water mills and, to a lesser extent, wind mills, were also used for fulling and other textile processes, metal working, water pumping, paper and gunpowder manufacture, timber sawing, mining and quarrying, water supply, electricity generation, etc. Once a good water-power site was utilised, it tended to be reused over and over again for different processes as the need changed.
+ History: historical descent; ownership of mill and milling rights; manorial mill or 19th-century agricultural installation; social and family history.
+ Associated buildings and structures, such as drying kilns, storage buildings, living accommodation.
+ Existing repair and restoration, together with previous recording.
+ Conversion and re-use.

Key sites

Wind mills and water mills are among the most common industrial structures, but many have been converted for residential accommodation. Some water mills are on National Trust properties, such as *Cotehele* in Cornwall, *Stainsby Mill* on the Hardwick Estate in Derbyshire, and *Preston Mill*, East Linton in Scotland, or open to the public through English Heritage, Cadw or Historic Scotland (see Chapter 3). *Dounby Mill* on the Mainland island of Orkney is a surviving example of a Norse mill, while tide mills can still be seen at *Carew Castle* in Pembrokeshire and *Woodbridge* in Suffolk. Others are run by private trusts and groups of volunteers, such as the Norfolk Windmills Trust. The Society for the Protection of Ancient Buildings (SPAB) has had a Mills Section since 1929, and protects large numbers each year from damage or demolition. They also coordinate the National Mills Weekend each May and details can be found on http://www.spab.org.uk/spab-mills. *Caudwell's Mill* at Rowsley in Derbyshire is a good example of a small water mill converted to roller milling in 1885. Many of the later roller mills in ports have been demolished.

Further reading (see also wind and water power in Chapter 3)

R Holt, *The Mills of Medieval England* (Blackwell, 1988), deals with both wind and water mills in the manorial economy, as does J Langdon, *Mills in the Medieval Economy: England 1300–1540* (Oxford University Press, 2004).

A good starting point for corn milling are books by M Watts, specifically *Water and Wind Power* (Shire Publications, 2nd edn, 2005); *The Archaeology of Mills and Milling* (Tempus, 2002); *Watermills* (Shire Publications, 2006) and *Corn Milling* (Shire Publications, 2008).

For Scotland, see E Gauldie, *The Scottish Country Miller, 1700–1900; A History of Water-Powered Meal Milling in Scotland.* (John Donald, 1981), and for Ireland see A Bielenberg (ed), *Irish Flour Milling: A Thousand Years History* (Dublin: the Lilliput Press, 2004).

On the introduction of roller milling, see J Tann & R Glyn Jones, 'Technology and Transformation: the Diffusion of the Roller Mill in the British Flour Milling Industry, 1870–1907', *Technology & Culture*, **37**:1, 36– 69 (1996), while for an archaeological study of a large roller mill, see J Clarke, 'Remnants of a Revolution: Mumford's flour mill, Greenwich' (*Industrial Archaeology Review* **24**:1, 2002, 37–55).

Regional studies and guides to individual mills vary greatly in quality and content. Some useful ones are: J Goodchild & S Wrathmell, *The King's Mills, Leeds. The History and Archaeology of the Manorial Water-powered Corn Mills* (Leeds Philosophical and Literary Society, 2002); A Graham, J Draper & M Watts, *The Town Mill, Lyme Regis. Archaeology and History AD 1340–2000* (Lyme Regis: The Town Mill Trust, 2005); J K Harrison, *Eight Centuries of Milling in North East Yorkshire* (Helmsley: North York Moors National Park Authority, 2001); A Stoyel, *Memories of Kentish Watermills* (Landmark Publishing, 2008), a personal view of water mills on the rivers Cray and Darent which existed 50 years ago, with pertinent comment on the value of fieldwork and recording.

2.6 Oast houses

Oast houses are used for processing hops for the manufacture of beer. They are generally part of a complex of farm buildings in a rural setting or on the edge of a village rather than in a town. Hops were grown in England from the 16th century and were cultivated in a number of counties including Essex, Oxfordshire, and Nottinghamshire as well as their current regional distribution of the counties of Kent, Sussex, Hampshire, and Hereford and Worcester. Hop fields always had a characteristic appearance with the hop bines trained up tall chestnut poles, about 4000 to the acre; only in the late 19th century were permanent wirework support systems introduced. Hop picking was always done by hand until the 1930s and was a traditional summer holiday for Londoners.

The green hops were dried in kilns, known as oasts in south-east England but simply called hop kilns in the West Midlands. The kiln was fired, generally with charcoal, at ground-floor level with the drying floor directly above. The drying floors were of two types: either of woven wire in iron joists or a woven horse hair, which could be rolled up, on timber joists with cross-bracing underneath. The steep pitched roof channelled the hot air through the hops to the top, where a cowl or vane pivoted to control the air extraction and stop rain getting in. Attached to the kiln was the stowage, which had a cooling floor and press at first floor and storage area at ground floor. The dried hops were taken from the drying floor to cool and then to be packed using a hop press. This compressed hops in a large sack called a 'pocket', suspended to the ground floor, where the filled pockets were stored to await collection.

There are four main types of oasts. Originally the kilns were built in the centre of adapted barns, with a kiln in the centre. As these were usually constructed of timber, many burnt down or were replaced with purpose-built oasts in the late 18th century. The kilns were usually square in section at first, but circular-section kilns were introduced in the 19th century as they were thought to be more efficient in heat dispersal. Nevertheless, the square kiln survived and became much larger later in the 19th century in response to the large demand for hops, and economy of scale. It was down to the preference of the farmer or architect whether they chose a square or round kiln, and there are many round-kilned oast houses with additional square kilns added. Large square oasts are particularly prevalent in east Kent as by the latter part of the hop-producing years east Kent was a driving force in the industry. More recent, 20th-century oasts have a ridge-ventilated system.

Small farms often had one or two kilns attached to them, some of which can still be seen although many have been converted for other purposes. As with maltings, brewers invested in hop-growing by the 19th century and built large kiln complexes for their benefit. Hops, like malt, were subject to excise duty from 1710 to 1862 and were marketed through special exchanges and warehouses. The most impressive of these was the Hop Exchange in Southwark with its large dealing floor, and the Hop Market and several warehouses in Worcester.

Key sites

Farm-based examples can still be seen on farms in the south-east and West Midlands. The largest surviving group of oasts is at *Beltring*, Kent, which was built for Whitbreads in the early 20th century and is now a theme park.

Further reading

A useful starting point is R Filmer, *Hops and Hop-Picking* (Shire Publications, 1982). Other studies tend to be regional, such as A Cronk, 'Oasts in Kent and East Sussex: parts 1 & 2' (*Archaeologia Cantiana* **94**, 1978, 99–110, and **95**, 1979, 241–54) which provide a good introduction to the 17th- and 18th-century process, whilst J Bell & G Jones, 'Getting to the truth: recording and interpreting a farm building: Turks Farm Oast, Mayfield, East Sussex', *Journal of the Historic Farm*

Buildings Group **2** (1988) 3–14 is a good small-scale study of a very rare square kiln (http://www.hfbg.org.uk/downloads/Turks_farm_Oast_Mayfield_Gwen_Jones_John_Bell.pdf (accessed August 2011). The Brewery History Society has also produced some useful articles: see I P Peaty, *Essex Brewers and the Malting and Hop Industries of the County* (Brewery History Society, 1992); P Tann, 'A brief history of the hop industry in Kent', *Brewery History* **118,** 21–6 (2005), and S Humphrey, 'The hop trade in Southwark', *Brewery History* **123,** 5–13 (2006). This journal has many other articles on hops, maltings, and breweries and an index can be found at http://www.breweryhistory.com/journal/archive/index.html). See also their catalogue at http://www.breweryhistory.com/ArchiveCatalogue_0809_copy2.pdf) (accessed 07/02/2011).

2.7   Maltings

Malt is artificially germinated grain (usually barley) used in the brewing process. Many villages had a malt house during the 18th century which supplied malt to local publicans, estate and domestic brewers, whereas during the 19th century, in order to supply brewing companies, large malt houses were frequently built adjacent to railway lines in both rural and urban locations. There are three distinct stages in malting: steeping (soaking the grain), germination, and kilning. The process created a functional building whose characteristics can usually be recognised, even after conversion to other purposes. The most common type of maltings in England were floor maltings; pneumatic maltings, popular on the Continent, were never widely adopted in England and very few have survived.

Key elements and plan forms

Malt houses are usually long in relation to their width, and have low storeys; as the grain was laid out no more than 8in (203mm) deep, the height of each storey had only to be that of the man who turned the barley by hand. Since light was not essential for the germinating grain, windows were often smallish and placed in every other bay, while the even temperature required could be achieved with the use of louvres in the windows. The imposition of the malt tax led to the addition of iron bars on many windows to prevent theft. Apart from lucams or hoists, the most distinctive external feature of a maltings is usually the kiln although before the mid-19th century it was not uncommon for the kiln roof to be completely hidden within the ordinary roof structure of the building. Like water mills, malt houses often reflect the local vernacular tradition in building materials.

It is a common misconception that because there is nothing in a malt house except large open spaces that all the machinery that must once have existed has been removed. In fact, relatively little machinery was ever found in a malt house. The large open floor areas were an essential feature of floor maltings, and the storage of both barley and malt also required space. In later maltings, the storage

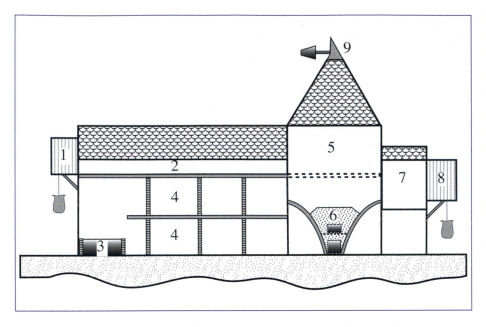

Figure 2.6
Diagrammatical
section of a three-
storey floor maltings
with two growing
floors. 1, barley intake
hoist in lucam;
2, barley store and
screens; 3, steeping
cistern; 4, growing
floors; 5, kiln floor;
6, kiln furnace;
7, malt store; 8, malt
delivery lucam and
hoist; 9, cowl for
air flow (© Marilyn
Palmer)

area was divided into wooden boxes, sometimes hopper bottomed and/or zinc
lined. The most modern storage is to be found in concrete silos which also have
hopper bottoms.

The grain was soaked before germination in a steep or cistern, which was
generally constructed of large stone slabs, or of rendered brick, for waterproofing.
Until the repeal of the malt tax in 1880, both this and the adjacent couch had
to be flat-bottomed to enable the excise officer to gauge the grain. Its former
position may be indicated by slotted or flat-faced columns, grooves in the floor
or raised plasterwork on the walls. After 1880, hopper-bottomed steeps could be
used, which were often made of cast iron, and some flat-bottomed cast-iron steeps
with bottom and side unloading hatches were also used. These could be found on
the mezzanine or first floor, whereas all earlier steeps were on the ground floor.
The floor surfaces on which the grain germinated could be made of quarry tiles,
pamments (hand-made floor tiles), bricks, stone or slate slabs, cement screed or
gypsum plaster, but never wooden boards. The weight of the damp grain meant
that the upper floors had to be supported on cast-iron or timber columns.

Finally, the kiln consisted of a furnace at ground or basement level and a kiln
drying floor at an upper-floor level (Fig 2.6). The furnace in an older maltings
was usually fairly squat and even in a stone building was often constructed of
brick, although stone ones are known. The bottom part of the furnace shaft has
four vertical sides, which rise to the walls of the room in the form of barrel-
vaulted arches. These brick stacks are nearly always well built with fine pointing
and often appear to be of a better quality of construction than the rest of the
building. The furnace consisted of fire bars which were sometimes enclosed
by doors. It is rare to find two early furnaces that are of the same design. By
the last quarter of the 19th century, patent kiln furnaces were in use, although
older types sometimes survived until the mid-20th century. Patent kilns were

manufactured by H J H King of Nailsworth, Gloucestershire, Robert Boby of Bury St Edmunds, and less frequently by Robert Free of Mistley, Essex. All these furnaces have doors as well as ventilators and heat regulators. Maltings which operated from the 1960s onwards usually had Suxé anthracite furnaces.

The kiln drying floors were in the majority of cases of perforated ceramic tiles. These range from single holers to multi-holers patented by Fisons, Stanley Bros of Nuneaton, and various firms in Bridgwater (Somerset), although there were also locally produced ceramic tiles. A few cast-iron tiles were also manufactured although their survival *in situ* is rare. The supports for these tiles were of stone or brick in early malt houses but in the later and larger malt houses, narrow iron beams supported on iron or even brick columns were used. In the last quarter of the 19th century the use of wedge wire floors became more common, although woven wire floors were used from the 1830s.

In all malt houses it was necessary to move grain around the building and as a result a malt house always has a variety of hatches and chutes in it as well as elevators and the motors necessary to drive them. The original power source may have been a steam engine, gas or more recently electricity. Grain cleaning machinery may survive in a maltings.

Conversion of maltings

It is rare for a maltings to be converted solely to commercial or retail use, although there are some examples. The most frequent conversion of a maltings is to residential use, which is undoubtedly the most secure but it can also be the most intrusive. The malting process did not require light but houses or

Figure 2.7 The enormous malting complex built in the first decade of the 20th century for Bass, Ratcliff and Gretton at Sleaford, taking advantage of locally grown barley and water from an artesian well. It ceased production in 1959, was used as a chicken farm and was listed Grade II in 1974. It is now subject to planning proposals for residential conversion (© Marilyn Palmer)

apartments do. In many conversions, additional windows are inserted in the blank bays between original windows, which can make the maltings look like a textile mill. Roof lights are also often installed. Internally the most difficult features to retain in conversion are steeps and kiln furnaces, although in small malt houses it may be possible to retain the latter. Every effort should be made to retain small features such as hatches, chutes, and shutters, even if they do not function. The cast-iron columns should be retained, as well as the perforated kiln tiles, which can be made a feature in a suitable location. The conversion should ensure that the building retains sufficient features both internally and externally to enable it to be clearly recognised as a former malt house. If there are to be major changes it is essential that they are obvious so that the original building can be 'read', and any particularly important features should be identified so that they can be included in a recording condition.

Key sites

Malt houses were particularly common in the east of England. The largest surviving are the former Bass maltings at *Sleaford*, Lincolnshire (Fig 2.7), while other large ones, some converted to flats, are in *Ware, Stanstead Abbots* and *Sawbridgeworth* in Hertfordshire, *Newark* in Nottinghamshire, and *Mistley Maltings* in Manningtree, Essex. Many small conversions survive, such as *Burwell Maltings* in Cambridgeshire, while *Boyes Croft Maltings* in Great Dunmow, Essex, and *Tucker's Maltings*, Newton Abbot, Devon, can be visited. The best-known conversion is probably *Snape Maltings* concert hall near Southwold in Norfolk.

Further reading

Historical background is provided in J Brown, *Steeped in Tradition, The malting industry in England since the railway age* (University of Reading, 1983) and C Clark, *The British Malting Industry since 1830* (Hambledon, 1988).

A Patrick's studies of the building features of maltings are invaluable: see her 'Establishing a Typology for the Buildings of the Floor Malting Industry' (*Industrial Archaeology Review* **18**:2, 1996, 180–200), and 'Victorian Maltings in England', 1837–1914 (*Brewery History; the journal of the Brewery History Society* **123**, 2006, 14–34). She was also the author of English Heritage's State of the Historic Environment Report (SHIER) on maltings (Parts 1 and 2) which has some excellent illustrations (http://www.english-heritage.org.uk/publications/ maltings/maltings-pt1.pdf and http://www.english-heritage.org.uk/publications/ maltings/maltings-pt2.pdf).

Good regional studies are: T Crosby, 'The Development of Malthouses around the Hertfordshire-Essex border' (*Industrial Archaeology Review* **22**:1, 2000, 39–53), and R Appel, *The Malt-Stars of Warminster: the remarkable survival of Britain's oldest maltings* (Warminster Maltings, 2010).

2.8 Breweries

Before 1800, domestic brewing was predominant, carried out in the home, on the farm or on the landed estate; the latter often had large breweries depending on the size of the household. Some publicans brewed for their own sales, while others were supplied by the common brewer who came to dominate the trade by the end of the 19th century. Ports such as Liverpool, King's Lynn, and Workington established breweries because of the ease of transporting beer by water, but London dominated the coastwise trade as well as serving a vast urban market. The growth of the canal network, and later the railways, enabled towns like Burton-on-Trent, with its excellent water supply from artesian wells, to become important. Changes in taste, particularly the demand for lighter beers, led to the large London companies constructing new breweries, particularly in Burton-on-Trent, in the second half of the 19th century.

Key elements and plan forms

The characteristic form of the brewery was dictated by the nature of the process. This made use of gravity to transfer the liquid or wort from one vessel to the next, starting with the mash tun near the top of the building and descending to the copper where the wort was boiled with hops in a fermenting vessel at the lowest level, from which the beer was drawn off into casks. Estate breweries were usually two-storey buildings with louvred windows to provide ventilation, the copper often being supported on a mezzanine floor. Small breweries can sometimes still be recognised at the rear of public houses.

Figure 2.8 Castle Brewery, Newark, in 1991, now converted for residential use. Note the louvred windows in the top storey (© Marilyn Palmer)

The tower brewery reflects a larger scale of production, with a malt store and mill at the top and several floors for duplicate sets of vessels (Fig 2.8). Steam engines were used to pump water to the top of the tower and to power the machinery. Louvred windows allowed ventilation at all levels of the building. The characteristic profile of a tower brewery dominated many urban landscapes until recently and their facades were frequently ornamented with terracotta and other forms of decoration. By the 20th century, pumping by electricity meant that the gravity system was no longer necessary as the wort could be pumped between vessels on the same level and tower breweries gave way to large, rectangular brick structures whose functional appearance was often relieved by blind arcading. The union system of fermentation was developed in

Burton-on-Trent, in which the fermenting process was completed in long ranges of barrels, sometime numbering over 2000 150-gallon casks in a single system, accommodated in large single-storey buildings.

Many other buildings were necessary for a brewery, including cooperages for barrel-making, bottling stores, stabling for the dray horses, wagon sheds and often its own maltings. A water tower was frequently a prominent feature of the site, and many of the breweries built by major companies were architect-designed and highly ornamented. The brewery became a large complex, with buildings grouped around a courtyard and usually containing buildings of different dates. It is necessary to establish the process-flow around the site at any one period in its history when trying to record such a site. Brewers were also dependent on transport networks for exporting their product to the wider market, and so means of transport must also be taken into account, as well as housing for the workforce which was often adjacent to the brewery itself. The great cellars of St Pancras station were partly built to house large hogsheads of beer from Burton-on-Trent.

Assessment of sites

+ Regional factors – scale of production, vernacular style/construction of early breweries and continued use of local materials by national architects into the later 19th century. Process variation: fermentation systems differ across the UK.
+ Integrated sites – completeness: rural breweries sometimes had farms and their own maltings, but city-centre sites often brought in malt. Wholesale alteration of parts of a site can damage its essential character.
+ Architecture and process – plan: enclosed sites with buildings grouped around a yard. Survival of buildings for different processes. Architectural style increasingly important in later 19th century with rise of the brewery architect.
+ Technological innovation – eg first use of steam power in the town; new building techniques; new processes, eg trial of continuous fermentation or early lager brewing.
+ Historic interest – significant links with history of trade, such as pioneering 'lighter' beer styles, or link with noted brewer/chemist/architect, writer, etc.
+ Rebuilding and repair – a case can often be made for changes on a site as evidence for necessary evolution/adaptation, eg growth in size/capacity, end of lengthy storage of ales/porters, rise of bottling/conditioning in inter-war years.

Key sites

Good estate breweries can be seen on National Trust properties such as *Shugborough* in Staffordshire and *Calke Abbey* in Derbyshire. The *National Brewery Centre* in Burton-on-Trent provides an insight into the process, although the town does not boast as many breweries as once it did. The *Anglo-Bavarian Brewery* in Shepton Mallet in Somerset brewed German-style lager from the 1870s and is finding new uses as part of a trading estate. *John Smith's Brewery* in Tadcaster, North Yorkshire, has maintained its fine set of stone buildings dating from 1884. Small micro-breweries are increasingly found adjacent to public houses, but rarely seem to reuse former buildings.

Further reading

R Putman's *Beers and Breweries of Britain* (Shire Publications, 2004) is a good starting point.

For small-scale brewing see I P Peaty, *You Brew Good Ale: a history of small-scale brewing* (Sutton Publishing, 1997), and P Sambrook, *Country Home Brewing in England, 1500–1900* (Hambledon Press, 1996).

For brewery architecture, see L Pearson, *British Breweries: an architectural history* (Hambledon Press, 1999). This includes a directory of brewers' architects (1780–1939) and a summary of brewery construction by town (1865–1906), the great period of brewery building. L Pearson was also the author of the English Heritage SHIER on brewing, http://www.english-heritage.org.uk/publications/brewing-industry/bhs-brewing-ind-shier.pdf, which has excellent illustrations.

All of the above feature buildings and plant. For readable economic history, see two classic works: P Mathias, *The Brewing Industry in England, 1700–1830* (Cambridge University Press, 1959), and T R Gourvish & R G Wilson, *The British Brewing Industry, 1830–1980* (Cambridge University Press, 1994). Both have been reprinted. Two more straightforward books are H S Corran, *A History of Brewing* (David & Charles, 1975), and I Donnachie, *A History of the Brewing Industry in Scotland* (John Donald, 1998). I Richmond & A Turton (eds), *The Brewing Industry: a Guide to historical records* (Manchester University Press, 1990), is useful for research although a little dated because of all the later mergers of companies.

The Brewery History Society journal, dating back to 1973, has some very useful articles: see http://www.breweryhistory.com/journal/archive/index.html.

2.9 Distilleries

Distilling is the process whereby an alcoholic beverage is further concentrated to produce a stronger spirit or liqueur. This is traditionally carried out in an *alembic* or *still*, a copper vessel of distinctive shape which is heated to vaporise the contents. When condensed, the resulting liquor has a higher concentration of alcohol than the original liquid. The best known spirits produced in the UK are whisky and gin, the former characteristic of Scotland and Ireland, the latter of England, especially London.

Scotch whisky distilleries

Whisky distilleries are one of the most distinctive and attractive industrial building types in Scotland. The oldest and most traditional form of their product is *single malt* whisky, which is made from malted barley in a process which closely resembles the brewing of beer, but with the addition of subsequent distillation and maturation. A *single malt* is a whisky derived exclusively from one distillery, and is produced in copper pot stills of a design and shape particular to that distillery. By far the largest quantities of Scotch whisky are, however, produced in grain distilleries using continuous distillation processes in a column still. Most *grain* whisky is blended with single malt whiskies to produce a *blended* whisky, which accounts for up to 90% of the whisky industry's output.

Whisky is an essential part of Scottish life and culture, and has become an important element within Scotland's national identity. The first documented references to whisky distilling in Scotland were in the 15th century, when it was known in Gaelic as *Uise-beatha*, the 'water of life'. Whisky was soon perceived to be a potentially rich source of government revenue, and enforced licensing and increasing taxes on producers led to the growth of a large illegal industry in the form of illicit stills. Production grew massively during the 19th century, driven in particular by the introduction of continuous or column stills, which led to the production of grain whisky on a huge scale. The outbreak of disease caused by the Phylloxera insect across Europe in the 1880s destroyed cognac production, and whisky was able to fill the gap in the spirits market. This led to the establishment of over 30 new distilleries by 1899. Amongst these are some of Scotland's most famous and distinctive distilleries, many being designed by the architect Charles Doig (1855–1918).

The production process

Wort from the brewing process which had been fermented in tanks known as washbacks was passed through two or more copper pot stills to produce whisky. The stills are now almost always heated by steam coils from steam generated in an adjacent boiler house, but many were heated by direct coal fires until the second half of the 20th century. After leaving the still, the whisky must be matured in wooden casks for at least three years to become whisky, and can then be bottled and sold either as a single malt or mixed with grain whisky to form a blend. Grain distilleries were similar in principle, but are much bigger in scale, the washbacks constantly feeding one or more continuous column stills.

Distilleries in the landscape

With the exception of a small number of Lowland malt whisky distilleries, the largest concentrations of distilleries can be found on the island of Islay and on Speyside, with smaller groups elsewhere in the Highlands. Many are situated not far from the arable farms from which they acquire their barley, and need to be close to rivers from which they can draw their water. In contrast, grain distilleries are much larger in scale but fewer in number, making less of a collective impact on both the rural and urban landscapes of which they are a part.

Many of Charles Doig's malt whisky distilleries, which were stone-built with slate roofs, form a classic traditional pattern which is linear, frequently running alongside a railway, whose origin lies in the growth of the whisky industry. The sequence of buildings usually commences with the maltings and kiln blocks, and the mill house, the mash house, the tun room (containing the washbacks), and the still house. The requirement for a long maturation period results in most distilleries being dominated by large warehouse blocks where the barrels of ageing whisky are stored. Many also had cooperages for making and repairing casks and barrels, but this work is now centralised at a few large coopering yards.

Irish whiskey distilleries

As in Scotland, whiskey distilleries were an important building type in Ireland but, on the whole, these were urban in distribution rather than rural as in Scotland, and many of them continued to use the pot still rather than the more productive column still (Fig 2.9). Now only three legal distilleries remain, but many distillery buildings survive in other uses and can still be identified.

Figure 2.9 Midleton Distillery, Cork, Ireland, established in 1825 in a former woollen mill of 1793. Other buildings were added in the 1830s and one of the copper pot stills can be seen outside what is now a Visitor Centre (© Marilyn Palmer)

Gin distilleries

Gin is a grain-derived spirit whose distinctive flavour is largely derived from juniper berries. It had been imported from Holland since the 17th century, but small distilleries in the UK making use of inferior grain resulted in a cheap product which led to the Gin Craze of the early 18th century, as portrayed by cartoonists such as William Hogarth, and subsequent attempts at regulation. London dry gin appeared soon after the column or continuous still was invented in 1831. This new still made a purer spirit possible as well as a higher alcohol concentration, and the product was usually flavoured with other 'botanicals', as they are known, such as citrus peel or coriander seed.

Key sites

In Scotland, over 90 malt distilleries and five grain distilleries are still in operation. The best examples of still floor malting are *Laphroaig* and *Bowmore* on Islay, and *Springbank* in Campbeltown. Especially good architectural examples of distilleries include *Balvenie* in Dufftown, and *Longmorn* near Elgin (both in Moray), *Ardmore* at Kennethmont, and *Glengarrioch* at Old Meldrum in Aberdeenshire. *Dallas Dhu Distillery* near Forres produced malt whisky from 1889 to 1993 and is now managed by Historic Scotland as an historic site with good surviving buildings and plant. There are many whisky trails and visitor centres worthy of a visit, especially on a rainy day.

In Ireland, the three surviving distilleries are *Bushmills* in County Antrim, the *Midleton Distillery* in County Cork (Fig 2.9), both of which also have museums attached, and the *Cooley Distillery* in County Louth. Two distillery museums exist on the sites of former working distilleries, *Jameson's Old Bow Street Distillery* in Dublin and *Locke's Distillery Museum* in Kilbeggan, County Westmeath. The *Midleton Distillery* is the source of most Irish whisky today and retains some interesting buildings, including a converted woollen mill of 1793. It retains the largest pot still in the world.

In England, *Three Mills* on the River Lea in Newham, London, were corn mills which were used for distilling from the 18th century onwards. The distillery itself retains 19th-century stills. The *Plymouth Gin distillery*, opened in 1793 and housed in a former friary in the Barbican, supplied the Navy and subsequently built up a world trade. Gin is still made there and guided tours are available.

Further reading

For Scotland, A Barnard, *The Whisky Distilleries of the United Kingdom*, is a reprint (by Birlinn Limited, Edinburgh, 2008) of the original of 1887. M S Moss & J R Hume, *The Making of Scotch Whisky: A History of the Scotch Whisky Distilling Industry* (2nd revised edition 2000, Canongate Books, Edinburgh), is a readable account, while G D Hay & G P Stell, *Monuments of Industry: An Illustrated Historical Record* (HMSO, Edinburgh, 1986, pp 31–62), is an excellent record of some of the buildings. R B Weir, *The History of the Distillers Company, 1877–1939: Diversification and Growth in Whisky and Chemicals* (Clarendon Press, 1995), is a business history of one of the major distillers.

Less has been written on the buildings for the distillation of spirits, except for the social impact of gin, for which see P Dillon, *The much-lamented death of Madame Geneva: the eighteenth-century gin craze* (Review, 2002).

2.10 Cider manufacture

In the south and west of England, the traditional drink produced was cider from locally grown apples, as well as perry from pears. It was largely a farm-based craft although some small factories were established in areas close to urban markets by the late 19th century. The apples were first crushed or scratted to a pulp in a mill consisting of an edge runner in a circular stone trough, often driven by horse power. The pulp was then placed in hessian bags and the juice squeezed out in a hand-operated cider press before being fermented in open vats or closed

Figure 2.10 Cider mill, Hartlebury Museum, Worcestershire (© Amber Patrick)

casks. The industry is now almost entirely factory based but still located in the traditional cider-making regions.

Surveys of farms in these regions should always take into account the possibility of a cider mill, and evidence for the horse-powered mill as well as troughs and edge runners may remain.

Key sites

The most obvious evidence of cider-making are the circular stone troughs and edge runners, which are now commonly used for decorative purposes. A good example remains in the care of the National Trust at *Cotehele* in Cornwall. *The Cider Museum in Hereford* (http://www.cidermuseum.co.uk/index.htm) is set in a former cider factory and contains examples of cider mills and presses, as does *Worcestershire County Museum* (Fig 2.10), housed in part of *Hartlebury Castle* (http://www.worcestershire.gov.uk/cms/leisure-and-culture/museum.aspx).

Further reading

There are few books on cider manufacture, but M Quinion's Shire Album, *Cidermaking* (1982), is a good start, together with *Somerset Cider, The Complete Story* by P Legg & H Binding (Somerset Books, 1986). *Cider Making* by A Pollard & F W Beech (Rupert Hart-Davis, 1957) gives a list of equipment manufacturers. See also *Cider making on the Farm*, a Bulletin from the Devon County Agricultural Committee, 1934 (http://www.cider.org.uk/farm.htm).

2.11 The industrial archaeology of the food industry

Many industrial enterprises in the 18th century still served just regional, if not local, demand and their products were sold through markets and fairs. Many foodstuffs have regional origins, such as the oat bread of north Staffordshire and the Pennine region, Scottish oatcakes, laverbread in Wales and the West Country, and pasties in Cornwall. Some became associated with particular towns, such as Ashbourne gingerbread, Bakewell puddings or Banbury cakes. Bread was often prepared at home (from flour purchased from mealmen) and cooked at local bakeries since few homes possessed suitable ovens. However, the growth of London had created a demand for a more national distribution of goods, something commented on by Daniel Defoe during his *Tour through England and Wales* in the 1720s. Coastwise shipping had always been important, but the development of roads and canals, followed by railways in the 19th century, enabled regional foodstuffs to reach not just the capital but other major towns. The import of colonial foodstuffs also had a major impact on the British diet, with tea, coffee, sugar, and chocolate becoming available, together with tobacco. At first, such luxuries could be afforded only by the wealthy but the use of some of these products, especially tea and tobacco, percolated downwards in society, as can be seen from the numerous artefacts associated with their use found in archaeological digs. Further changes followed in the late 19th century, with increasing urbanisation. Dr Barrie Trinder, whose article on 'The Archaeology of the British Food Industry 1669–1900: a Preliminary Survey' is an essential starting point for studying this topic, argues that there were profound changes in some of the principal sectors of the British food industry in around 1870, which are paralleled by developments in other consumer goods industries, such as footwear, clothing, furniture, book production, etc. He also stresses the importance of marketing in persuading people that they needed products of which they were previously unaware.

Potential archaeological evidence from before 1870

Apart from the evidence of artefacts such as handles and spouts of tea pots and the ubiquitous sections of tobacco pipe stems found on so many post-medieval sites, building evidence can be found for bake ovens on village houses and farms, while urban redevelopment can aid the discovery of cellar bakeries or urban cow houses. Many manor houses and great houses constructed new bake ovens, and often pastry ovens as well. The rebuilding of farms on 'improved' models also led to the construction of purpose-built dairies, including some very ornamental ones on country house estates as at *Shugborough* in Staffordshire and *Wimpole Hall* in Cambridgeshire.

Bakeries after 1870

The introduction of the steam tube oven in the mid-19th century and mechanised kneading machines brought techniques of mass production to baking, and steam bakeries could be found in many towns. The Co-operative movement was responsible for the construction of many urban bakeries which can still be distinguished, as in Kettering, Northamptonshire, with associated housing for the workers.

Dairying after 1870

The development of the milk cooler in 1872 enabled farmers to dispatch milk by rail for long-distance transport, and so collection depots were set up. The buildings included a steam raising plant for cleaning and sterilisation, which may still be recognisable. Important areas for these collection depots were the pastoral districts west of London and north Staffordshire and Derbyshire, from where one-fifth of London's milk was supplied by 1900. Most towns had their own distribution dairies for transporting milk from the railhead to consumers, often elaborate in form.

Factories were constructed for making cheese or butter, sometimes also serving as milk collection depots. In Derbyshire, the local agricultural society founded the first experimental cheese factories in Derby and on the Longford Estate. Country creameries processed milk from remote farms into butter and, in the second half of the 19th century, into evaporated and condensed milk, a process developed in the USA. Some of the earliest of these can be found in the west of England, in Yeovil (St Ivel), Chippenham and Staverton (Nestlé), where redundant cloth mills were reused. Ice-cream also became more widely available from the mid-19th century, making use of ice imported from Norway and kept in huge wells.

Key sites

Semley milk collection depot, Wiltshire, opened alongside the Exeter to Waterloo Railway (now Dairy House Antiques); *Staverton* (former Nestlé factory, converted to apartments; *The Leek and Manifold Light Railway* and the *Churnet Valley Railway*, north Staffordshire and Derbyshire, both built to serve the dairying industry; *National Railway Museum*, York (milk carriages); *Regents Canal Museum*, London (built as an ice warehouse 1862–63 for Carlo Gatti, the ice-cream manufacturer).

Biscuits and breakfast cereals

The baking of biscuits for use at sea was a long-standing industry and mass production methods were used in the victualling yards of the Royal Dockyards from the early 19th century. Traditional biscuit manufacture was also mechanised, as in Reading where Huntley and Palmers was founded by two Quakers in 1841 and 20 years later employed nearly one-quarter of the working population of the town.

Evidence can be found in buildings and in artefacts, such as museum collections of tins and marketing posters.

Breakfast cereals were developed in the USA in connection with the vegetarian movement towards the end of the 19th century; Force wheat flakes were introduced into Britain early in the 20th century and advertised with the popular jingle, 'High o'er the fence leaps Sunny Jim, Force is the food that raises him'. Many other cereals followed, including corn flakes, developed by the two Kellogg brothers running a sanatorium in the USA based on Seventh Day Adventist principles. The first UK factory for Kelloggs was established in Manchester in 1978, followed by one in Wrexham, Clwyd. Shredded Wheat appeared in 1926, based in a purpose-built factory in Welwyn Garden City, Hertfordshire.

Key sites

Royal William Victualling Yard, Stonehouse, Plymouth; *Weston biscuit factory*, Llantarnam, South Wales; *Huntley and Palmers collection*, Museum of Reading; *Kellogg*, Trafford Park, Manchester; *Kellogg*, Wrexham; *Shredded Wheat factory*, Welwyn Garden City.

Industrial fishing ports

Many buildings for the storage and processing of wet fish can still be found in small fishing ports, such as Port Isaac and Port Gaverne in Cornwall. Tarred wooden lofts were also built for net and sail making, such as the 50 or so black wooden sheds in Hastings Old Town which date from the early 19th century. The market for fresh fish was confined to the hinterland of the ports before the extensive use of imported ice, and so the majority of the catch was preserved by salting, smoking or pickling. On the east coast, where herring were landed, curing houses were generally two-storey buildings with vents below the eaves and in the roof ridge, while larger ones had attached buildings for the manufacture of boxes and barrels in which the fish were exported. Ice plants were established in many ports in the second half of the 19th century, and distribution by railway enabled fresh fish to reach a much wider market. Covered fish markets were built in many inland towns with good rail access.

Figure 2.11 The ice factory, Grimsby, was built in 1901 to supply ice for the port's fishing industry. The Grade II* building is the largest and earliest purpose-built ice factory in England and houses, substantially intact, the ice-making equipment and compressors (© Great Grimsby Ice Factory Trust)

Key sites

Tower Curing Works, Yarmouth, dated 1880; smoke houses at *Craster*, Northumberland; *Fraserburgh*, Scotland; *Peel*, Isle of Man; *Mallaig*, Scotland; *Billingsgate Fish Market*, London (built 1849 onwards, closed 1982 and now a financial centre). Ice Factory, *Grimsby*. Fish markets in *Peterhead* and other ports such as *Grimsby* and *Newlyn*.

Meat processing

Droving reached its peak in the early 19th century with some 100,000 cattle being driven from Scotland alone into England. Their routes can often be traced by means of the network of drove roads which still survive as green tracks marked by stone walls in, for example, the Yorkshire Dales. Surviving toll-house tariff boards state the charges levied by the turnpike trusts for droves of cattle, sheep, and pigs. The latter were shipped from Ireland to Bristol and their road to London passed through Wiltshire, where a bacon-curing industry was established in Calne, Chippenham, and Trowbridge from the 1840s which survived after droving ceased. Droving had resulted in considerable weight loss on the part of the animals, and distribution by rail was consequently adopted quickly. Covered pens were built at both docks and railway yards. In towns, cattle markets and abattoirs were often designed to reflect Victorian municipal pride, and boasted elaborate gates and covered sales rooms, together with hide and skin markets.

Meat canning became important from the period of the Napoleonic Wars. Regional specialisation remained important for marketing, as with the Melton Mowbray pork pie, popular with fox hunters, and the Cornish pasty, the food of copper and tin miners. During World War II, buffer depots, strategic food stores directly operated by, or on behalf of, the government, were constructed adjacent to railways, some of which lasted until the 1990s.

Key sites

Smithfield Market, the largest wholesale meat market in the UK; *Cattle Market, East Croft*, Nottingham.

Colonial imports

British acquisition of colonies in the tropics greatly increased the range of foods available and helped create new types of buildings for processing them.

Sugar refineries were established in London and west coast ports such as Bristol and Liverpool. These processed cane sugar, but the huge refineries of Tate and Lyle and others have largely been demolished. Beet sugar was imported from Europe but shipping blockades during World War I caused the rapid expansion of home-produced beet and the construction of the large factories which still dominate the flat landscapes of eastern England. The sugar-refining process therefore moved from the west to the east as sources of the raw material changed.

Chocolate became popular as a drink in the second half of the 17th century, but its production was greatly boosted by the Temperance Movement in the 19th century. Three renowned Quaker manufacturers, Rowntree, Cadbury and Fry, in York, Birmingham and Bristol respectively, promoted its manufacture from the 1860s. Rowntree and Cadbury both created new industrial settlements with well-designed, spacious factories, surrounded by quality accommodation for workers. They also made chocolate and other confectionery, using sugar. Tea-drinking became popular in the 18th century and became the staple drink of the poor in the 19th century. Tea, like coffee and chocolate, was subject to import tax, and bonded warehouses, incorporating security measures such as small, barred windows, were constructed at ports including London, Liverpool, and Bristol.

Tobacco was first imported into Britain during the 16th century and achieved great popularity as pipe tobacco during the 17th century. Like other colonial imports, it was subject to excise duties and huge bonded warehouses were again constructed in ports such as Bristol, London, Liverpool, and Glasgow. Their size encouraged the early use of reinforced concrete in their construction. Cigarettes and pipe tobacco were manufactured in large factories such as those established by W D & H O Wills in Bristol and John Player in Nottingham.

Key sites

Chocolate: *Bournville*, Birmingham (Cadburys); *New Earswick*, York (Rowntree); *Terry's*, York. Tea: *Bush warehouse*, Bristol; *Port of London* (mostly converted). Tobacco: *Stanley Dock*, Liverpool; *Tobacco Dock*, London; *B bonded Warehouse*, Bristol, now partly used by Bristol Record Office.

Assessment of sites

- The architectural styles of food processing buildings were often intended to convey images of cleanliness and good living.
- Many of the large companies had their own styles of accommodation for workers, as at New Earswick and Bournville.
- Processed food required considerable packaging, and so additional buildings were needed for this purpose and should always be considered alongside the main structures.
- Many of the buildings of the food industry were easily adapted for new processes, and their location, especially in ports, has resulted in their frequent conversion to retail or living accommodation in the 20th century.

Further reading

A good starting point is B Trinder, 'The Archaeology of the British Food Industry 1669–1900: a Preliminary Survey' (*Industrial Archaeology Review* **15**:2, 1993, 119–39), which also has a comprehensive bibliography. See also his '18th- and 19th-century Market Town Industry: an analytical model' (*Industrial Archaeology Review* **24**:2, 2002, 75–89). Further historical background is provided by J Blackman, 'The Food Supply of an Industrial Town: A Study of Sheffield's Public Markets 1780–1900' (*Business History* **5**:2, 1963, 83–97), and K Hudson's *Food, Clothes and Shelter: Twentieth Century Industrial Archaeology* (John Baker, 1978), together with R Scola, *Feeding the Victorian City: the Food Supply of Manchester 1770–1870* (Manchester University Press, 1972).

Bakeries: J Burnett, 'The Baking Industry in the Nineteenth Century', *Business History* **5** (1963), 98–108, and his *Plenty and Want: A social history of Diet in England from 1815 to the Present Day* (Penguin, 1968).

Dairies: Economic histories include D Taylor, 'The English Dairy Industry 1860–1930' (*Economic History Review*, New Series **29**:4, 1976, 585–601), and V Cheke, *The Story of Cheesemaking in Britain* (Routledge & Kegan Paul, 1959). Regional studies include P J Atkins, 'The Retail Milk Trade in London, c 1845–1915' (*Economic History Review*, 2nd series, **33**:1, 1980, 522–37); R Sturgess, 'The Dairy Industry of Staffordshire and Derbyshire 1875–1900' (*Staffordshire Studies* **2,** 1989–90, 45–59), and P Sainsbury, *Tradition to Technology: A History of the Dairy Industry in Devon* (Tiverton: privately published, 1991).

Biscuits and breakfast cereals: T A B Corley, *Quaker Enterprise in Biscuits: Huntley & Palmers of Reading 1822–1972* (Hutchinson, 1972), while R J Butterfield,

'The Industrial Archaeology of the Twentieth Century: the Shredded Wheat Factory at Welwyn Garden City' (*Industrial Archaeology Review* **16**:2, 1994, 196–215), is a very good study of a 20th-century building.

Colonial imports: most sources on tea are about the artefacts of tea drinking rather than warehouses, such as R Emmerson, *British teapots and tea drinking 1799–1850* (London, HMSO, 1992), or histories of various companies. More interest has been taken in the industrial archaeology of primary sugar production in the West Indies rather than its refining in the UK, for which see N & A Wright, 'Hamilton's Sugar Mill, Nevis, Leeward Islands, Eastern Caribbean' (*Industrial Archaeology Review* **13**:2, 1991, 114–41), and D Hicks, *The Garden of the World; an historical archaeology of sugar landscapes in the Caribbean* (Oxford, Archaeopress, 2007). One study of a refinery is J A Watson, *The end of a Liverpool Landmark: the Last Days of Love Lane Refinery* (Liverpool: Tate and Lyle Refineries, 1985). For chocolate, an historical survey is R B Lees, *Sugar Confectionery and Chocolate Manufacture* (Aylesbury: L Hill, 1973), while M Harrison, *Bournville: Model Village to Garden Suburb* (Phillimore, 1999) looks at one of the Quaker model villages.

CHAPTER THREE

Power for industry

3.1   Introduction

The development of most industrial processes has run hand in hand with man's ability to find suitable sources of power beyond his own strength. The domestication of animals allowed a significant increase in the available power for a given task. Initially the strength of animals was principally harnessed for draught in such tasks as ploughing and wagon haulage. Once simple machinery began to be developed, its demands frequently ran ahead of available power resources, particularly for rotative power. The use of animals, mainly horses and oxen, to develop rotary power through suitable engines such as horse gins and tread mills for a multitude of purposes was a breakthrough. This was complemented by a growing understanding of mechanisms for developing mechanical advantage. Such understanding started with the use of the simple lever and developed through pulley systems and gear mechanisms. The treadmill was one of the earliest of inventions which allowed the power of several men or an animal to be harnessed, while the structure of both the treadmill and the horse gin also allowed a mechanical advantage to be developed through the use of varying diameters in the different elements of the mechanism.

As all forms of power source develop, there are effectively three factors in play after the initial invention has been proved as viable: the availability of appropriate skills, engineering machine tools, and suitable materials. This interplay of constraints can be most clearly seen in the development of the steam engine and the various forms of internal combustion engines. It has, however, applied historically to nearly all power sources. For example, the later generations of large suspension water wheels needed materials that were not available to an earlier generation. Newcomen's engines were limited by poor thermal efficiency and the ability to bore true cylinders, while the development of larger horizontal engines needed the invention of the planing machine. For the improvement of efficiency in the steam engine, better valve gear and more effective governors progressed as the understanding of thermodynamics increased. Just as the replacement of wooden components with iron allowed larger and more efficient power sources to be developed, so the introduction of modern steels in place of wrought and cast iron provided further advances. This evolutionary process can also be seen in steadily rising pressures used in steam boilers.

Wind and water power provided the ability to develop power outputs greater than that provided by horses and other draught animals; they also had the advantage of not suffering from the fatigue to which an animal source is prone. In the case of water power there was a heavy dependence on suitable sites adjacent to water courses with an appropriate volume and fall. Such sites were frequently expensive to develop and thus often required considerable capital. This limited large-scale industrial development to geographically suitable areas; the development of the mechanised spinning industry in the southern Pennines illustrates this dependence. Wind, as well as being a more intermittent power source, had considerable landscape constraints as hill-top sites were obviously desirable. As wind power was developed, less suitable locations were also made viable through building taller mills to catch the wind. All natural power sources suffered from the vagaries of weather. For water, droughts could cause no power to be available and floods could cause destruction. The range of wind speeds from a dead still day to gale force and higher affected wind engines in a similar way. However, all of these natural power sources had the advantage of minimal running costs once the initial capital cost had been recovered as the energy source was free. This often allowed them to compete with steam power for many years after they had become technically obsolete.

The spur to develop power sources that were independent of natural resources was driven by the mining industry. As shallow sources of ore and coal were exhausted, deeper mines became necessary and these encountered ever greater problems of water drainage. Newcomen's development of the first viable steam engine allowed power to be obtained for the first time in any location without recourse to the natural elements or animal power. The development of the steam engine in both its non-rotative form, when it was employed to pump water back for a water wheel, and in its fully rotative form, for the first time allowed industry requiring power to be developed away from suitable water courses. The viability of the steam engine on a given site was now governed by its running costs, and the challenge was to reduce these through a continuous quest for higher thermal efficiency and greater power. This encouraged industries to build bigger manufacturing sites which in turn required more power, a process which continued throughout the 19th century until the introduction of centrally generated electrical power. At the lower end of the power output scale, the relative cost of small steam engines continued to fall throughout the 19th century, making them economically viable in more and more locations. In the later 19th century the internal combustion engine was an alternative, providing a relatively cheap semi-portable source of power, and was particularly favoured where there was an intermittent demand for power such as in land drainage. Costs were significantly lower than for steam plant of equivalent power, since they did not require expensive boiler plant, used less labour and were thermally more efficient for small installations. It was frequently the use of the internal combustion engine rather than the steam engine that brought about the final demise of many old wind and water power sites.

At the same time as the potential output of available power sources was steadily increasing, the design of transmission systems to handle this power was also being developed. In early mills and factories large, slow-moving timber shafts were used to transmit power. These can be seen in many water mills and machinery driving tilt hammers. These heavy shafts evolved into the lighter, faster-moving iron-geared shafts used in early textile mills and later water corn mills. Later generation textile mills employed still lighter and faster systems in which cotton ropes drove line shafting with final power transmission to individual machines through flat belts. With the development of electrical power, the individual motor drive for each machine began to appear around the beginning of the 20th century. Many sites had hybrid power systems in the transition to electrical drive in which large electric motors would drive the line shafting previously driven by steam or water.

In the late 19th and early 20th centuries, the concept of centralised power generation was conceived. The first application of remotely generated centralised power was for hydraulic systems, although these were applied less often to manufacturing industry. At the same time the introduction of town gas, coupled with the development of the gas engine in the second half of the 19th century, allowed many industries to harness a centralised fuel supply to a local prime mover. Gas and electricity generation are considered further in Chapter 9. Throughout all of these developments there was a steady trend in the decrease in real terms of both the capital cost of the power source and the running costs per unit of power. It is only in the latter part of the 20th century with increasing fuel costs that this trend has been reversed.

3.2 Animal power

This section deals with animal-powered machines, not with the use of animals for traction which is referred to in the section on Early Railways in Chapter 6. Animals have been used since Roman times to drive machines for a large variety of purposes from agricultural activities, such as threshing, to turning spits for roasting meat and to water-raising for both water supply and mine drainage. Even after other methods of power were introduced, animal-powered machines were kept on standby in case these failed, particularly on mining sites. Donkeys and horses were the main animals used but elsewhere in the world camels, oxen and other animals and have provided motive power.

Types of machines

In most animal-powered machines, the effort of the animals is converted into rotary power by means of a wheel. In some cases, this wheel was vertical, the animal being placed inside it to provide motion, like the familiar wheel often placed in children's hamster cages. In others, the wheel was horizontal, and the horse moved above or below it in a circle around a central pivot, gearing providing the necessary transmission of power.

Vertical wheels have been used to power cranes and for raising water. In the

Roman period and beyond, these were often powered by men, usually slaves or prisoners, as was shown by the excavation of Roman water-lifting devices in London in 2003. They were also used in the construction of great buildings such as medieval cathedrals, where some remains still survive. Later, treadwheel cranes were used for lifting goods from water to land in docks or alongside canals. Small wheels were placed close to open fires in large kitchens and a small dog, the turnspit, was employed to turn them in order to keep the roast meat cooking evenly. The same principles could be used for raising water from wells or rivers, usually powered by donkeys or horses, and several horse engines survive on large country estates where connections to mains water was difficult because of their isolated positions and so older water-raising methods continued in use. Horses were also used to drive vertically placed stones or edge runners for crushing minerals, which were driven from a bearing in the centre of a circular stone base on which the vertical wheel ran. A similar system could also be used to drive a

Figure 3.1 Stone capstan base for a horse engine for lifting pumps from a lead and copper mine at Esgair Hir, Cardiganshire. The small roller carried the rope towards the shaft and the horse must have stepped across the trench, perhaps on a small bridge (© Marilyn Palmer)

Figure 3.2 Pumps for draining the Kilsby Tunnel, from J C Bourne's *Drawings of the London and Birmingham Railway*, London, 1839. The construction of this tunnel proved very difficult because of underground water problems and the two pumps shown in this drawing, together with a third worked by a steam engine, raised 1800 gallons per minute. The horse gins were used for raising and lowering material down the ventilation shafts, indicating that horse power continued to be used alongside steam even on large construction sites

capstan placed in the centre of the horse circle from which a rope ran over rollers and could, for example, be used to raise water from wells or lift pumping gear from mine shafts (Fig 3.1).

The overhead horizontal wheel driven by one or more horse is often referred to as a horse gin or horse whim, and was widely used to lift coal and metal ores from mines, most of which relied on them at least for standby purposes well into the 19th century. Horse gins were also used on construction sites especially where tunnelling was required: J C Bourne's famous lithograph of tunnelling work on the railway tunnel at Kilsby in Northamptonshire shows this very clearly (Fig 3.2). Many similar engines were also used on farms for grinding corn and crushing roots for animal feed etc.

There were other kinds of animal-powered engines, used mainly for agriculture, in which the animal walked on an oblique treadmill consisting of a moveable belt which powered threshing and other kinds of machinery. Experiments in the early days of powered cotton spinning also made use of horse power for driving textile machinery. Richard Arkwright's first cotton mill in Nottingham was powered by horses turning a capstan but it cannot have been entirely suitable for spinning where a steady movement is needed if the thread is not to break.

Landscape context

Horse-gin circles can be readily identified in the landscape, especially in mining districts, by gravelled circles which enabled horses to get a better grip on the ground. Often, too, these were surrounded by small earthen banks which enclosed the gin circle. Crushing sites can be identified by circles of flat stones. On farms, the remains of the bearings for horse engines can survive. Many of these were housed in small buildings, usually hexagonal or circular in shape, which indicate their origins as horse-gin houses. Buildings containing horse wheels for pumping water for large mansions were often disguised as classical landscape features.

Key sites

Animal-powered machines for agricultural purposes can still be seen in various folk museums, notably the *Museum of English Rural Life* in Reading, the *Museum of East Anglian Life* in Stowmarket, the *Weald and Downland Museum* in Sussex and the *Welsh Folk Museum* at St Fagans in South Wales. Horse gins originally used for mining can be seen at *Nottingham Industrial Museum* in Wollaton Park and the *North of England Open Air Museum* at Beamish, while the Peak District Mines Historical Society has re-erected one at *Magpie Mine*, Sheldon.

Horse engines for raising water can be seen at *Carisbrooke Castle* in the Isle of Wight, *Chilham Castle* in Kent, *Grey's Court*, Henley-on-Thames and *Burton Agnes Hall*, Driffield, Yorkshire, while some estates have elaborate water towers which housed horse engines in the base, as at *Houghton Hall* in Norfolk.

Treadwheel cranes for lifting building stone are preserved in *Peterborough* and *Salisbury Cathedrals*, and for goods transfer at *Harwich* and alongside the River Wey Navigation at *Guildford*.

A crushing circle for lead ore survives at the *Odin Mine* near Castleton in Derbyshire and the landscape around there, especially at *Eldon Hill*, contains the remains of several such circles. Many survive on *Dartmoor*, too. A horse-driven cider mill is displayed in the *Worcestershire County Museum* at Hartlebury Castle (Fig 2.10).

Further reading

J K Major made a special study of animal-powered engines; his *Animal-Powered Machines*, Shire Album **128** (1985) and his *Animal-Powered Engines* (Batsford, 1978) are very useful. For farm-based gin houses, see Further Reading in 2.3. The field remains of horse whims on mining sites has been covered recently in P Newman, *The Field Archaeology of Dartmoor* (English Heritage, 2011), chapter 11. The man-powered Roman water-lifting devices discovered in London are described in I Blair, 'Roman London's waterworks: the Gresham Street Discoveries', *Current Archaeology* **150** (2003), 509–16.

3.3 Water power

Before the advent of the steam engine, water was the only viable source of power other than wind or animal power. Water power was certainly introduced into Britain by the Romans as attested by numerous archaeological remains. Initially water power was used principally for the grinding of corn but subsequently became the power source for a very wide range of industries. At the time of the Domesday Book there were over 6000 mill sites recorded; by the early 19th century the total number of mills in the British Isles was estimated to be over 60,000.

Many of the advances in wheel and mill design in this period came from monastic sites. From the 12th century onwards, water power was employed in fulling mills for textile finishing, also known as walk mills. It also expanded to provide power for many other industries; in the iron industry uses included driving blowing engines, tilt hammers for forging, slitting, wire drawing, and boring machinery. In mining areas water power was used for pumping water, raising minerals, and crushing ore. Seed oil extraction, saw milling, paper making, bark crushing for tanning, pigment production, and gunpowder incorporating were just a few of the other water-powered medieval industries. As the early powered textile industry began to develop, water was used for driving spinning and scribbling mills. The successful development of powered silk throwing in Derby and cotton spinning by Richard Arkwright in the 18th century relied on water power. It was the textile mill, with its steadily growing demand for higher power, that really drove the development of more sophisticated water wheels. The availability of good mill sites was a key factor in the location of many early industries. This is particularly evident in the southern Pennines and in south-western England. Water power after a period of declining usage throughout much of the 19th and 20th centuries has seen a degree of resurgence in the later 20th century, with the development of hydro-electricity on both large- and small-scale sites.

Types of water power

The earliest mills, developed by the Greeks, were powered by a horizontal wheel mounted on a vertical shaft, acting in a similar way to an impulse turbine (Fig 3.3). This type of mill had the added advantage of simplicity of construction, generally having no gearing. The directly driven single pair of stones required only a small stream of water and the same stream could be used to power a series of wheels by making use of lades or leats. It only produced a relatively low power output, but was eminently suitable for single farms and small hamlets. These mills had characteristic oval or circular rubble walls containing the millstone, with the horizontal wheel beneath the building. Few survive intact but their former presence can be detected from abandoned millstones and rubble walls close to streams, as at Sandvaat on the Isle of Lewis (Fig 3.4).

The next generation of waterwheels are often known as Vitruvian wheels, after the Roman military inspector Marcus Vitruvius, although there is some evidence that these may also have been a Greek invention. They were built on horizontal shafts and were geared to allow faster rotational speeds. The simplest type was the undershot water wheel. This was best suited to fast-flowing streams or rivers with strong currents as it relied on the kinetic energy of the water to turn the wheel. The undershot wheel was somewhat inefficient but it utilised sites with comparatively small heads of water.

who were amongst the earliest water turbine builders. Modern hydro-electric installations use water turbines as the prime mover and these cover a huge power range, from a few kilowatts up to as much as 750MW. Pelton, Fourneyron, Boydon, Francis, and Kaplan all developed improved turbines through the 19th and early 20th centuries. In large 20th-century hydro-electric schemes the Francis turbine is the most common. Recently the reverse Archimedean screw in combination with a turbine has also started to be installed at some old mill sites for low to medium power electricity generation.

In addition to water wheels and turbines, certain types of engines driven directly by water pressure have been developed. These use the weight, pressure or kinetic energy of descending water to raise a smaller volume of water to a higher level. These engines range in size from small domestic hydraulic rams designed to raise water for single dwellings to very large mine drainage engines. The latter were usually mounted underground in mine workings or in sumps and so are rarely visible. Specialised types of water pressure engines are also used in hydraulic installations and these are covered in Section 3.6 on hydraulic power later in this chapter.

Landscape context and structures

Water-power sites are, self-evidently, usually located next to a water course. Some mills were built on naturally occurring sites but many water power sites have resulted in a significant impact on the surrounding landscape through the diversion and remodelling of ancient water courses. In seeking a suitable site for a mill the builder would have been attempting to balance obtaining the best available fall of water at the mill with the minimum capital cost of development. Most mills represented substantial investment when they were first constructed and for that reason many early sites would have been owned by the local lord of the manor or a monastic foundation, as at Fountains and Rievaulx in Yorkshire and Abbotsbury in Dorset. Many mills are built on sites that are far more ancient than the current buildings. Upstream of the site it is normal to find a substantial dam or weir to increase the head and impound or divert the water. This will be linked to the water-power site through a channel variously known as a leat, goit or head race or, if ground conditions require it, the water may be carried through a raised launder or through pipes to the wheel. At the entry to the leat there will normally be a control sluice and immediately adjacent to the wheel or turbine a further sluice or penstock. The leat frequently feeds into a mill pond situated immediately above the mill to allow for water storage. At this point there may also be a by-wash which allows surplus water to be returned to the main water course. Piped feeds are normally used for turbine installations as the water may be at considerable pressure.

The water wheels themselves are usually situated in a wheel pit which will generally have masonry sides. Some large overshot and pitchback wheels are built free standing, exemplified by the giant Lady Isabella wheel at Laxey in the Isle of Man and other wheels on the same site (Fig 3.5). Below the wheel or

turbine will be a tail race which returns the used water to the main water course. When wheels were used for mine drainage, the available water site could be some distance from the mine. In this case power was transmitted through flat rods from the wheel to the mine over distances which may extend to several miles. Even when the site is no longer in active use for water power, many or all of these landscape features can still be visible.

The type of wheel used in a given location was dictated by the available head of water, the gradient of the river, and the volume of flow. Overshot and pitch back wheels usually utilise a higher head and lower volume of water and are typically found in the head of valleys where gradients are steeper and volumes of flow smaller. Breast and undershot wheels, with their lower head of water, are usually found where river gradients are flatter, generally further downstream.

In certain locations where a large tidal range and a suitable coastal inlet coincided, tide mills making use of the rise and fall of the tide were built. These were situated alongside a dam constructed across the inlet in which a sluice allowed the incoming tide to be pounded. The stored water was then released through the wheel on the ebb tide when the head was adequate for milling. Some

of *in situ* survival with many examples having been restored to operational condition. Smock and post mills rarely survive in derelict condition but in the east of England many derelict and empty tower mills are still to be found, usually without their cap. Over 130 survive in Lincolnshire alone.

The buildings: development

The wind mill is frequently thought of only in the context of milling grain. However, as a prime mover, wind power was used for many varied processes wherever power was required, and usually where suitable water-based power was not available. In addition to grain milling, wind mills were used for pumping water, both for supply and drainage; the wind mill was attached to either a scoop

Figure 3.7 The seven-storey, five-sail Alford Tower Mill in Lincolnshire built in 1837 by Samuel Oxley (© Mark Sissons)

wheel for land drainage, or to displacement pumps for water supply and mine pumping (see Chapter 2.2). The use of the mill for crushing, where the sails usually drove a large set of edge runner stones, had many applications other than for corn milling. Amongst these were the crushing of seeds for oil extraction and the crushing of minerals, such as chalk, and clay. Mineral and seed crushing mills usually had vertically mounted edge runner stones rather than the horizontal stones used for cereals. Wind was also utilised to power saw mills where large reciprocating frame saws were used, and there were many other industrial processes where wind power could be harnessed.

The development of wind mill technology in the industrial period was initially driven by techniques imported from the Netherlands. In the 18th and 19th centuries, the technology perfected by British mill wrights, predominantly in East Yorkshire and Lincolnshire, surpassed that from abroad. The introduction of the fan tail in 1745/46 by Edmund Lee allowed the mill to be turned automatically into the wind. This freed the miller from having to be in constant attendance at the mill whether it was running or not. The common wind mill sail, on which a sail cloth is spread across the face of the sail frame, was universal until the introduction of the spring shutter sail by Andrew Meikle in 1772. In 1807 William Cubitt improved on this with the introduction of the patent sail. By the use of adjustable sail shutters actuated through a striking rod, carried through the centre of the main wind shaft, this allowed automatic control of the speed of the mill in response to variations in milling load and wind speed. Most mills had four sails but examples with two, five, six or eight do occur. Multi-sail mills with more than four sails are particularly common in Lincolnshire (Fig 3.7).

In addition to the mill itself, there may be several associated buildings, including a grain store and cart shed. Sometimes an engine house can be found adjacent to the mill when a steam or internal combustion engine has been used to drive the machinery in the mill instead of, or in addition to, the wind. Often, too, a portable engine was used outside the mill to supplement the power and small pulley wheels on the mill building indicate where the power take-off went into the mill. A miller's house is usually adjacent as constant attendance at the mill was necessary. A typical pair of mill stones consumed around 3.75Kw (5hp). A rough guide to the power output of a particular mill can therefore be judged by how many stones it could run concurrently.

Wind power was, until recently, viewed as a technology that became obsolete in the mid-19th century and effectively disappeared from commercial use in the mid-20th century. The advent of the modem wind turbine has ushered in a whole new phase in the development of wind power for electricity that is, unfortunately, outside the scope of this resumé.

Key sites

Post mills: Danzey Green at the *Avoncroft Museum of Buildings* in Worcestershire; *Wrawby* Lincolnshire; *Keston*, Kent; *Saxtead Green* in Suffolk; *Jack and Jill* in Sussex, a tower and post mill on adjacent sites; *Bourne*, Cambridgeshire;

Outwoods, Surrey; *Pitstone Green,* Buckinghamshire.

Smock mills: *Sarre Mill* and *Whitemill,* Kent; *Chaily, Rottingdean,* and *West Blatchington* in Sussex; *Cranbrook,* Kent.

Tower mills: *Skidby,* East Yorkshire; *Heckington, Alford; Maud Foster, Burgh le Marsh* and *Ellis Mill,* Lincolnshire; *North Leverton,* Tuxford, and *Greens Mill,* Nottinghamshire; *Wicken, Burwell* and *Swaffham Prior,* Cambridgeshire; *Lytham Mill,* Fylde.

Land drainage mills: *Berney Arms* and *Herringfleet,* Norfolk; *Wicken Fen,* Cambridgeshire.

Mine pumping: *Parys Mountain,* Amlwch, Anglesey.

Industrial mills: *Hessle Whiting Mill,* East Yorkshire.

Adaptive reuse

The most common adaptive reuse of mills is for domestic conversion. Such conversion normally involves many compromises, removal of machinery, alternative cap structures, the alteration of fenestration, and the building of extensions which can adversely affect the original context of the mill.

Further reading

A good general introduction to wind power can be found in M Watts, *Water and Wind Power* (Shire 2005). For fuller details of the use of wind mills as applied to corn milling and more technical detail see S Freese, *Windmills and Millwrighting* (David & Charles, 1971); R L Hills, *Windmills – a pictorial history of their technology* (Landmark Press, 2005); and C Moore, *Windmills: a new history* (History Press, 2010). For an understanding of the use of wind power for many other industrial processes, R Gregory, *The Industrial Windmill* (Phillimore, 2005), gives a detailed picture of many applications other than cereal milling.

There are several articles in *Industrial Archaeology Review* including K Major's article 'Wind Engines' (**14**:1, 1992, 55–63) and R Gregory on 'The Use of Power in the Early Industrial Development of Hull' (**15**:1, 1992, 7 –20).

For a gazetteer and lists of regional guides the following web sites are useful – http://www.windmillworld.com and http: //www.spab.org.uk/spab-mills (last accessed July 2011).

3.5 Steam power

Origins and development

While steam is frequently considered as a power source related to the 19th century, it is frequently forgotten that it is still the biggest provider of energy for the whole country. Most of our largest power stations, both nuclear and those

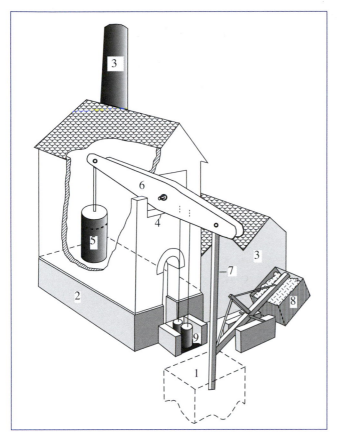

Figure 3.8 Simplified arrangements of a 'Cornish' beam pumping engine. 1, mine shaft; 2, engine house; 3, boiler house and chimney; 4, bob-wall supporting rocking beam trunnion; 5, steam cylinder; 6, rocking beam; 7, pump rod in shaft; 8, balance bob with weighted box to balance weight of pump rods; 9, condenser tank with air and water feed pumps linked to beam (© Marilyn Palmer)

burning fossil fuels, generate electricity using modern high-speed steam turbines.

The true origin of the steam engine is a much debated subject. While early inventors such as Hero and Dennis Papin realised the potential of steam, they failed to develop any commercially successful engines. In 1698 Thomas Savery patented 'an engine for raiseing water … by the impellant force of fire'. He named his invention 'The Miner's Friend' as the intended market for it was largely that of mine drainage, although the patent did include mention of water pumping and working mills. Savery's engine utilised a pressure vessel full of steam in which a partial vacuum was created by spraying in water to condense the steam, then allowing atmospheric pressure to suck up water from below, followed by the admission of live steam under pressure to eject the water up a pipe. It had major shortcomings, as the technology of that time had not developed sufficiently to permit the building of high-pressure boilers and the associated plumbing. The fuel consumption of his engine would have been prodigious.

His success in using these engines for raising water into private houses was limited, but there is some evidence that his engine was developed further in the late 18th century by a Manchester engineer, Joshua Wrigley, for pumping water to power overshot water wheels, particularly for early cotton mills in the area.

Thomas Newcomen, a Dartmouth ironmonger, is credited as being the first man to produce a commercially viable steam engine, but as Savery's patent covered all engines that raised water by fire, royalties had to be paid on subsequent developments until 1733. After years of experimentation, Newcomen erected his first successful engine on a coal mine at Dudley Castle in 1712. His atmospheric engine used the weight of atmospheric pressure to force down a piston in a cylinder in which a partial vacuum had been created by condensing the steam. The key difference from Savery's engine was that Newcomen's engines were beam engines in which the cylinder was attached to one end of a rocking beam and the pumps to the other end, which greatly increased its flexibility of use (Fig 3.8). The beam, or bob, was balanced at its mid-point on a wall of the engine house. His design was suited to the available engineering skills and boiler plant of the time which generated steam at very little more than atmospheric pressure. His major market was for mine pumping in both the deep metalliferous mines of south-west England and in collieries. Poor thermal efficiency was not much of an issue in coal mines where the engines burnt unsaleable coal slack. In other types of mine, though, frequently remote from a local source of coal, fuel consumption was a major cost.

Initially, when rotative motion was required, a Newcomen engine would be used for back-pumping water, in times of water shortage, to power a water wheel at an existing water-powered site or at isolated sites with no natural water supply. There were various experiments with rotative Newcomen engines in the mid- and late 18th century but most met with only limited success. Despite refinements by several engineers, notably John Smeaton, the Newcomen engine still had a thermal efficiency of less than 1%. It was James Watt, a Glasgow-born surveyor and instrument maker, who was the first to understand the cause of the fundamental inefficiency of the Newcomen engine. The practice of condensing steam in the working cylinder caused huge amounts of energy to be used in reheating the cylinder after it had been cooled by condensation of the steam in each power stroke. By condensing the steam in a separate vessel, Watt improved the thermal efficiency of the steam engine two- to threefold. The patenting of the separate condenser in 1769 therefore produced a major impetus in the development of more economical steam power. It needed the commercial drive of Matthew Boulton working in partnership with Watt from 1773 to develop and market engines built to Watt's patent, but they were limited at first to engines driving reciprocating pumps. Watt experimented with double-acting engines in which power was generated by supplying steam to both sides of the piston, and in 1783 developed his first satisfactory rotative engine which could, for example, be used to power textile mills. Rotary power generated by steam at last freed industry from using only locations where there was available wind or water power. It is questionable whether the restrictive use of Watt's extended period of patent protection encouraged the development of the steam engine through providing a protected market, or stifled innovation and allowed Watt's conservative designs to outlive their time. Even before the expiry of his patent in 1800, innovation in the development of the steam engine had started to move to Cornish engineers such as Woolf and Hornblower. Their work on using higher steam pressures culminated in the development of the Cornish engine by Richard Trevithick in 1812. This allowed higher-pressure steam to be used expansively and produced another huge improvement in thermal efficiency when compared with its predecessors, and thereby opened up the way for the development of the steam engine throughout the 19th century. Trevithick was also instrumental in the development of reliable higher-pressure boilers such as the Cornish boiler. The beam engine, with its comparatively simple engineering, reliability and the avoidance of a requirement for large machined flat surfaces, remained the commonest form of large steam engine until the mid-19th century. Indeed, in water and sewage pumping its popularity lasted, even for new installations, up to the beginning of the 20th century.

Although Trevithick developed a horizontal engine as early as 1802, the use of horizontal engines did not become widespread until the middle of the 19th century. After this date small single cylinder horizontal engines were produced in huge numbers to standard designs by a number of engineering companies. Many of these were sold complete with boilers to form a stand-alone power source. The cotton spinning industry provided the major demand for more powerful engines throughout the 19th century, with the construction of ever larger mills, containing faster machinery with higher power consumption. Initially many older beam engines were upgraded by installing new boilers and converting them to compound expansion by inserting an extra high-pressure cylinder, a process known as McNaughting. In a compound engine the steam is allowed to expand in stages in different cylinders to produce higher thermal efficiency. For higher power uses, large horizontal, multi-cylinder compound engines in a number of different configurations were built with power of up to c 4000hp. By the late 19th century this type was becoming the standard.

Developments in marine engines, where economy of fuel consumption was paramount, were fed back into land-based engines. In the late 19th century the inverted vertical engine, using marine practice, became more common in medium- to large-sized installations. At the same time the science of thermodynamics was developing through the work of men such as Carnot, Rankine and Kelvin, and a better understanding of the scientific principles of the steam engine allowed a more systematic development of new engines. This work led to more efficient valve gears and governors which allowed the output of engines to be more accurately matched with the power demanded from them.

Larger engines required more steam which in turn demanded bigger boilers. The Lancashire boiler developed by William Fairbairn in 1844 was effectively a twin-flue development of the Cornish boiler. It became the standard for medium-sized steam plant for most of the next 100 years. For larger plant the water tube boiler began to be used in the latter part of the 19th century. This was initially developed by George Babcock and Steven Wilcox in the USA and patented in 1867. It enabled still higher pressures and evaporative volumes to be achieved and derivatives of their original design are still used in most modern coal-fired stations today.

Other industries developed a market for their own specialist forms of steam engine. Foremost among these were the coal industry, with its demand for pit winding engines and the iron and steel industry that required huge high-powered rolling mill engines with outputs of up to 18,000hp.

Towards the end of the 19th century steam power began to be used in electricity generation, which required engines with a higher speed than those used in direct power applications. Much of the initial demand for electricity was driven by the mining industry and tramway companies. A number of special high-speed engines such as the Willans and the Bellis engines, usually directly coupled to dynamos, saw the final development of the stationary reciprocating steam engine. Many had short lives in large installations as the demand for electrical power soon outstripped the power output and economy of the reciprocating steam engine. Enter the steam turbine, patented in 1884 by Charles Parsons. His earliest turbine was used in electrical generation producing an output of 7.5Kw (10hp). As the demand for power for electricity generation rose, the improved thermal efficiency and reliability of the turbine over the reciprocating engine saw it become the standard for electrical power generation from the early 20th century onwards. In a modern power station steam turbines can now produce power outputs of as much as 1,500,000Kw (2,000,000hp).

The other area where steam power was used for central power generation was in connection with hydraulic schemes which are covered in the separate section on hydraulic power in 3.6 below.

Key elements and plan forms

The most characteristic buildings from the era of steam power are those housing the engines, which take many forms. The Newcomen engine house was the earliest. These can usually be distinguished from later beam engine houses by their almost domestic scale and the frequent lack of a separate boiler house. The most iconic is the Cornish engine house, normally built to house mine pumping engines. There are numerous semi-derelict survivors in the south-west of England and in other metalliferous mining areas. The houses for pumping engines are usually larger than those for winding as they contained engines with far larger cylinder sizes. Pumping engine houses for municipal utilities are frequently the most visually dramatic and can have the most architectural pretension. Many towns had both water and sewage pumping plant and the buildings associated with these frequently survive. (For fuller details see the sections on land drainage, water and sewage utilities in Chapters 2 and 9.)

Throughout the 19th century, steam plant was the most common source of power for larger industrial premises. Before 1850 most mill engines were low-pressure beam engines, usually installed in a tall, narrow, engine house that was

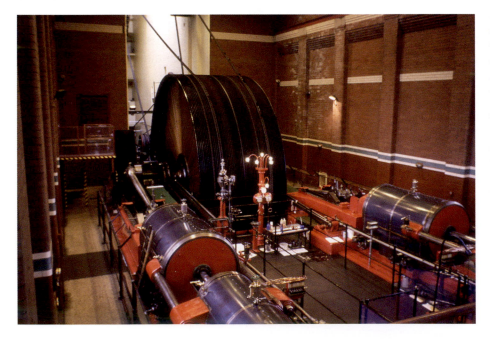

Figure 3.9
Trencherfield Mill, Wigan. Twin tandem triple expansion compound mill engine of 1907 by J & E Wood of Bolton. The engine developed 2500hp and drove the cotton spinning mill through rope drive. It was superseded by electric drive in 1968 (© Mark Sissons)

Figure 3.10 The beam engine and boiler at Shaddon Mill, Carlisle, a Grade II* building. These were part of the original steam-powered, fireproof, cotton spinning mill, designed by Richard Tattersall and built in 1835–36 for the leading Carlisle textile company Peter Dixon & Sons. This reconstruction shows the engine house with its two 80hp beam engines built by Rothwell & Co at their Union Foundry in Bolton. These shared a 25 ton flywheel 24ft (7.32m) in diameter from which the vertical and horizontal line-shafting was powered. A, boilers; B, water tank for boilers; C, steam engines; D, principal vertical drive shaft; E, horizontal secondary drive shaft; F, bevel gears for transmitting power from vertical to horizontal drive shafts. There were four Cornish boilers also built by Rothwell & Co. (© Michael Nevell)

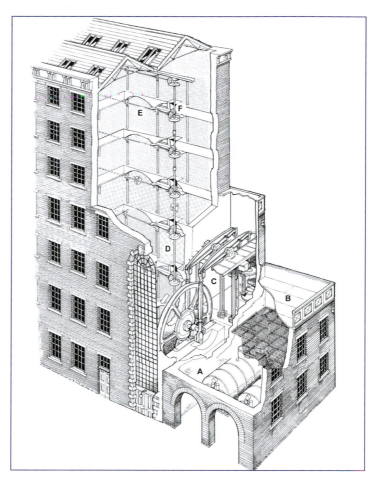

an integral part of the mill located either at a gable end or in the middle. These drove the mill by gearing and line shafting (Fig 3.10). After 1850 high-pressure beam engines, with their greater horse power, became much more common and mill engines were developed further from 1860 onwards with the introduction of horizontal engines, previously common in early steam ships. At the same time the rope drive was developed (Fig 3.9) and first used in Belfast by James Combe of the Falls Foundry in 1863 and by the late 1860s they were common amongst the new flax mills of Ireland. The transmission arrangement involved a series of heavy ropes which fitted grooves formed on the engine's flywheel. Individual ropes powered horizontal line shafting on each of the mill's floors, the ropes themselves being housed in a vertical chamber known as the rope-race. The adoption of rope-driving allowed for a more efficient power transmission over greater distances from the new larger steam engines, and rope-driven spinning mills were in use in Lancashire and Yorkshire by the mid-1870s. The rope-drive and the larger horizontal steam engines required the engine house to be moved outside the main mill, forming a prominent feature of later mills, although in smaller mills it is more normal for the engine house to be an integral part of the building (see also Chapter 5.7).

There are many other building and landscape elements connected with steam-power generation sites. The chimney, usually the biggest visual indicator of a steam-powered site is all too often the first element to disappear. Other elements include associated boiler houses, reservoirs for water supply and condenser cooling water (known as mill lodges in north-west England), condenser cooling towers, coal stores, and handling machinery.

Key sites

Newcomen engines can be seen at *Dartmouth*, where an engine originally from Hawkesbury on the Coventry Canal is displayed; at the *Elsecar Heritage Centre*, South Yorkshire, where there is a much rebuilt engine but still in its original house; and at the *Black Country Museum* where a modern replica gives a very accurate impression of what an original engine and its house would have looked like.

There are over 70 beam engines and numerous horizontal engines in preservation throughout the country. Some are in museums and some on their original sites. These engines cover a substantial number of types and end-power uses: the gazetteers in the Shire albums give a good selection of these. The UK engine database held by the Northern Mill Engine Society at http://www.nmes.org gives a listing of most preserved engines. The *Ellenroad Engine House*, Rochdale, has what is probably the world's largest fully working cotton mill engine, still possessing its original steam engine. In south-west England, the Cornish Engines Preservation Committee, now the Trevithick Society, campaigned for the preservation of Cornish engines as early as 1935 and now, with the help of the National Trust, maintain in steam an 1840 mine winding engine at *Levant*. In addition there are a large number of empty engine houses throughout most of the manufacturing and mining areas of the country. See also the web sites referenced for pumping engines in the section on water supply and sewage in Chapter 9.

Few early steam-driven electrical power stations survive from the dawn of the electrical age. None survives with its original machinery. *Lemington* near Newcastle of 1903 and *Lotts Road power station* of 1904 built by the Metropolitan District Electric Traction Company are two of the earliest of which the building survives. The timber cooling towers to be seen at many early power stations are now almost extinct. From the mid-20th century, examples include Giles Gilbert Scott's 1947 *Bank Side* (Tate Modern) and *Battersea* completed in 1933 and enlarged in 1953. There are few other survivors from the immediately post-war generation of power stations.

Adaptive reuse

As a building type, steam engine houses are generally not well suited to adaptive reuse. A few Cornish and Newcomen engine houses have been converted for domestic use, and their former use can often be detected by the presence of a

beam and arched window above it high up on the gable end. Some Lancashire mills retain engine houses, the shell of which is used commercially, but there has historically been a regrettable tendency to demolish the engine house and chimney and to leave the mill standing.

Further reading

A good introduction to the development of steam power can be found in G Hayes, *Stationary Steam Engines* (Shire, 2011) and *Beam Engines* (Shire, 2008) and, by the same author, *The Guide to Stationary Steam Engines* (Moorland Publishing, 1981). There is an interesting discussion of the early uses of steam power, including the later uses of the Savery engine, in A E Musson & E Robinson, 'The early growth of steam power' (*Economic History Review*, New Series, **11**:3, 1959, 418–39). For more detail on the development of early steam engines, L T C Rolt & J S Allen, *The Steam Engines of Thomas Newcomen* (Moorland 1977) is an excellent source. R A Buchanan & G Watkins, *The Industrial Archaeology of the Stationary Steam Engine* (Allen Lane, London, 1976) is a good guide to the development of the steam engine.

Figure 3.11 Former beam engine house converted for residential use at Pontesford, Shropshire. Note the infilled aperture where the rocking beam would have protruded and the surviving wooden beam for the trunnion (© Marilyn Palmer)

Stationary Steam Engines of Great Britain (Landmark Publishing, 2000), ten volumes covering the British Isles, is a series reproducing many of the images from the Steam Engine Record made by G Watkins between 1930 and 1980, which is now in the Watkins Collection at English Heritage's National Monuments Record at Swindon. His successor is C Bowden, whose *Stationary Steam Engines of Great Britain: a Checklist* (1979) and *The End of a Revolution: the last Days of Stationary Steam* (Landmark Collectors Library, 2008) are a record of his photographic achievements over many years.

R L Hills, *The Development of Power in the Textile Industry from 1700–1930* (Landmark Collector's Library, 2008) is very useful for the development of steam engines in textile mills. Cornwall Archaeology Unit's *Engine House Assessment: the Mineral Tramways Project* (1991) is a useful summary of standing remains in Cornwall.

Industrial Archaeology Review has many articles on detailed aspects of steam power of which C Bowden's 'The Stationary Steam Engine: A Critical Bibliography'

(**15**:2, 1993, 177–207) is a useful source for details of related publications providing information on stationary engines. There have been few excavations of engine houses, but see M Palmer & P A Neaverson, 'The Steam Engines at Glyn Pits Colliery: an Archaeological Investigation' (**13**:1, 1980, 7–34), and M Nevell, J Roberts & M Champness, 'Excavating the Iconic: The Rediscovery of the Fairbottom Bobs Colliery Pumping Engine (**26**:2, 2004, 83–93).

3.6 Hydraulic power

The word hydraulics refers to all aspects of the properties of water and other fluids. Hydraulic power itself can be defined as power that is created by releasing the potential energy held in a fluid under pressure. That fluid was historically water but in more modern installations is now usually oil. Hydraulic power is a means for transmitting power and not a primary power source in itself.

The earliest practical use of hydraulic engines was for mine pumping in the mid-18th century in the lead mines of the north Pennines. The hydraulic press was patented in 1795 by Joseph Bramah. His ideas were taken up by William Armstrong in Newcastle-upon-Tyne. Armstrong developed a hydraulically operated crane based on the hydraulic jigger, comprised of a ram in a closed cylinder arranged with multiple pulley sheaves at each end so as to multiply movement of the free end of a chain or rope wound around the sheaves when a pressurised fluid, normally water, was admitted into the cylinder. The hydraulic jigger operated in the reverse manner to the conventional block and tackle (Fig 3.12). The pulley system amplified the distance the lifting rope moved for a given movement of the piston, which meant that the load moved up or down a lot faster than the piston. The success of this crane encouraged Armstrong to set up a business to manufacture them and other hydraulic machinery. On docksides such as Newcastle, machines such as cranes and capstans were separated from each other over distances which made mechanical operation impossible, and Armstrong began to install some low-pressure hydraulic systems from the 1840s. A hydraulic network can be considered as analogous to a modern electrical system where power is transmitted to users from a central generating station, the pressurised water mains being the substitute for the cables of an electrical power transmission system. Armstrong then went on to develop the weight-loaded hydraulic accumulator in 1850, which allowed hydraulic fluid at pressure to be stored so making high pressure distribution systems viable.

The first public system was in Kingston-upon-Hull where the Hull Hydraulic Power Company began operations in 1877, authorised under an Act of Parliament with a pumping station situated on the corner of Machell and Catherine Street, now long since disappeared, and mains laid under most of the principal streets of the city. Edward Ellington was the company engineer; he was subsequently involved in most of the British public hydraulic systems and several overseas

Figure 3.12 Simplified
drawing of the
hydraulic jigger
(© C W White)

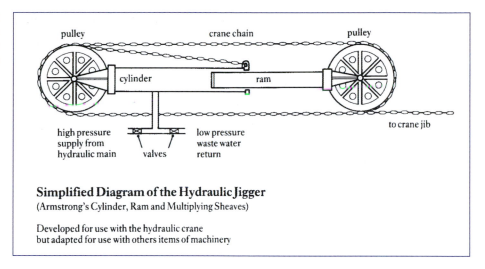

ones. Public hydraulic systems followed in London, Liverpool, Birmingham, Manchester, and Glasgow. The largest of these was the London Hydraulic Power Company which had, at its peak, 180 miles of mains with some 8000 machines connected. In the area of London between Tower Bridge and down the Thames to Blackwall Point there were 29 large hydraulic pumping stations of which two supplied the public system. Most of the others and many smaller local stations were for providing power on private dock or railway estates.

Each of these hydraulic systems had a centralised, steam-powered pumping station and a network of cast-iron mains. Pressure was regulated by weight-loaded accumulators, both at the pumping station and remote from it. Stop valves allowed sections of the main and machines to be isolated and relief valves prevented pressure from increasing too much. Localised private systems were installed within many factories but were most frequently to be found in dock estates and large railway yards. These would have been powered by a steam engine or occasionally a water turbine. Many of these private systems survived into the 20th century although the power source for the pumps had usually been converted from steam to either electrical or internal combustion. By the mid-1930s the cost of hydraulic power was over two and a half times that of electricity so its decline was inevitable. All of the public networks had ceased to operate by the mid-1970s.

Key elements and plan forms

Quayside cranes

Hydraulic pillar cranes had jiggers in pits or on the pillar of the crane, thereby multiplying the limited travel of a hydraulic cylinder so as to provide greater travel for a crane rope. Quay box cranes had jiggers within a wooden tower and the jib mounted on the box. Moveable hydraulic cranes, running on rails along the quayside, were built in response to increasing ship sizes in the 1870s. Portal cranes, both hydraulic and electric, allowed railway trucks to run beneath them. Semi-portal cranes and roof cranes were used where there was restricted space on the quay.

Warehouse cranes and external hoists

Goods were lifted into the upper floors of warehouses through loopholes (loading doors) by means of wall cranes or cathead hoists, sometimes protected by lucams. Hand-powered wheel-and-axle winches gave way, from 1850, to hydraulic jiggers usually mounted on the inside wall and protected by partitions to reduce the risk of fire spreading through the building. Control valves to move the load were operated using a rope which passed through all floors.

Internal hoists and lifts

From the 1850s, hydraulically powered hoists used jiggers, mounted either vertically in a shaft or inclined in the roof space. Hydraulic wagon hoists and goods lifts first appeared in the 1840s and became common at the larger railway depots from the 1860s. Lifts were increasingly used from the 1860s in large mansions and hotels, for both passengers and luggage. Two distinct types emerged, the direct-acting lift with a cylinder and ram in a well directly underneath the cage, and the suspended lift, with a jigger mounted within the lift shaft operating the lift through cables. Where a high-pressure supply was unavailable, low-pressure lifts could be worked from a town water main or by pumping water back up to a high-level tank.

Railway shunting capstans

Steam capstans were used for shunting railway wagons instead of horses from the 1840s. Hydraulic shunting capstans were first used at Paddington in the 1850s and were more generally introduced at large depots and dock estates after the development of a compact hydraulic motor in the 1870s. Besides moving wagons along by means of ropes, they could also be used to turn them on small wagon turntables. Associated with shunting capstans were snatch heads (unpowered dummy capstans) and rollers, the latter used to protect the corners of buildings. Electric capstans appeared in the early 20th century.

Dock gates and other nautical uses

As ships became larger, the lock gates admitting them to docks and navigation locks had to follow suit. The introduction of hydraulic power allowed large gates to be moved under the control of one man and the associated paddle gear to be operated remotely. Most large lock gates today remain hydraulically powered, but are now usually powered by local pumps worked by electric motors. The majority of large swing bridges and many lifting bridges are worked by hydraulic power.

The buildings

A hydraulic power station would normally have had as its key elements the boiler house with chimney, the pump house and associated water tanks for feeding the hydraulic pumps, and the accumulator tower. Below ground was a network of water pipes for transmitting the fluid under low or high pressure, and these may still be found during archaeological work on industrial sites.

Figure 3.13 Remains of the hydraulic accumulator at Somers Town goods yard near St Pancras Station, excavated by Museum of London Archaeology in 2011 (© MOLA)

Landscape context and adaptive reuse

Although many of the machines have disappeared, on both large manufacturing sites and waterside sites, care should be taken to ascertain if the remains of hydraulic systems remain below ground. For example, the excavation of the remains of the Somers Town goods yard next to St Pancras Station in London when the new British Library was being built revealed the remains of the hydraulic system which powered loading cranes and wagon hoists (Fig 3.13). On buildings, evidence for hoists, lifts and jiggers should always be sought. Care has been taken, for example, in the shopping centre conversion of the GWR's railway works in Swindon to conserve a number of the surviving wall-mounted cranes and hoists. Some accumulator houses in now popular waterside locations have been converted into restaurants and public houses.

Key sites

At the Underfall Yard in *Bristol Floating Harbour*, the hydraulic system is still operational. The main pump house, an accumulator tower, an outside accumulator and the main pump house are all visible. The dock tower in *Grimsby*, built in 1852 to provide power to Grimsby's dock gates and cranes, is perhaps the most iconic hydraulic accumulator tower in Britain. Over 300 feet (*c* 90m) high, it was modelled on the Torre del Mangia in Siena and is Grade I listed. The *Boat Museum* at Ellesmere Port has preserved a full hydraulic power station and accumulator house which still has steam-powered hydraulic pumps that can occasionally be seen in motion. In *Water Street* in Manchester, there is a former hydraulic power station in the grounds of City College, which was one of three built as part of a system for supplying hydraulic power to lifts and hoists of commercial warehouses in the city centre that continued in use until 1972. Railway examples survive in *Fitzwilliam Street, Huddersfield*, and *St Mary's goods yard* in Derby, as well as within the converted *Great Western Railway Works* in Swindon, now the Outlet Designer Shopping Centre.

Hydraulics in nautical use can be seen on many large lock gates, those on the *Thames* and *Weaver Navigations* being easily accessible at most locks. Some of the Weaver locks are still worked by Pelton wheel-powered winches rather than hydraulic cylinders and pistons. The *Anderton Boat Lift* on the Weaver shows a dramatic use of one very large hydraulic cylinder to raise each caisson of the lift.

The most famous hydraulically worked lifting bridge is *Tower Bridge* in which some of the original steam-powered hydraulic engines are still *in situ* although they no longer power the bridge. *Cross Keys Bridge* at Sutton Bridge in Lincolnshire has its own small hydraulic power station with adjacent accumulator tower alongside the River Nene. The bridges on the *Manchester Ship Canal* are all hydraulically operated although no longer using steam-powered pumping.

There are some remains of hydraulically powered domestic lifts in some large houses, notably Armstrong's own mansion of *Cragside* where lift mechanism is on display. The National Trust's recently acquired mansion of *Tyntesfield* near Bristol also had a hydraulic lift of which some remains can be seen.

Further reading

A good introduction to the subject is provided by A Jarvis's *Hydraulic Machines* (Shire Albums, 1985). More technical detail can be found in I McNeil's book *Hydraulic Power* (Longmans, London, 1972). For an understanding of a large system see T Smith's article 'Hydraulic Power in the Port of London' (*Industrial Archaeology Review* **14**, 1991, 64–88). The excavations by Museum of London Archaeology at the former Somers Town goods yard are reported in *Current Archaeology* **256**, 2011, 12–19.

CHAPTER FOUR

Extractive industries

4.1 Introduction

The complex geological structure of the British Isles and the consequent variety of rocks and minerals within comparatively small geographical areas has meant that few regions have escaped some form of extractive industry in the past. This section will deal with the buildings and structures that survive both from the extraction of minerals and also from the processing of them into manufactured objects. Many sites made use of forms of mechanical power for various processes and these are dealt with in Chapter 3 on power generation.

4.2 The clay industries

Clay is probably the most common mineral found in Britain and has been widely exploited since the prehistoric period. It is derived from the decomposition of feldspathic rocks, such as granite, but has generally been redistributed by water, for example by the melting of the ice sheets which covered much of Britain. This redistribution has increased the plasticity of clay, a property which enables it to be moulded into new shapes which can then be retained permanently by subjecting them to extreme heat in kilns. The firing process changes the chemical structure of the clay, driving off water and causing the clay particles to fuse. Mixture with other minerals, or fluxes, lowers the melting point at which these chemical changes occur, influencing the firing techniques and colours of the finished products.

Key sites are included for each type of clay processing with a further reading list at the end.

Extraction

Clay is more easily extracted from the ground than most minerals, but because of its bulky nature is usually dug as close as possible to the place where it is to be used. Consequently, the area surrounding surviving kiln structures should always be carefully searched for the source of the raw materials. There are some exceptions to localised exploitation, including that for the ball clays and china clays of south-west England which were sent to areas where fuel was available for their processing, such as Staffordshire. China clay and Cornish or china stone were essential in the production of English porcelain, and their use was patented by William Cookworthy, a native of Devon, in 1768. The extraction of china clay has created structures which have no parallel in other clay industries, since the clay, found near its parent granite rock, is mixed with unweathered minerals which have to be removed, such as mica and quartz. This is done by washing the extracted clay in a series of separate tanks or mica drags, earlier of wood but more recently of concrete, constructed with a slight gradient to enable the heavier minerals to be separated. The slurry flowed into tanks and settled slowly, the clear water being run off through a buttonhole launder, a plank with holes in it initially plugged with wooden pins which were removed sequentially as the clay settled. The clay then had to be dried in a pan kiln, a rectangular building with a furnace at one end and a chimney at the other, with flues running below a floor of porous tiles. The clay was allowed to flow from the settling tanks across the floor to dry out, and the dried clay was then stored in a linhay or lean-to structure attached to the building. The increasing mechanisation of the china clay industry in the 19th and 20th centuries led to use of either water or steam power for pumping the clay slurry and the construction of transport systems to take the dried clay to the coast for shipment. The 20th-century expansion of the industry has also destroyed much of its own past, but there are surviving examples of mica drags, pan kilns and linhays, as well as the remains of water wheels, steam engines, transport systems and the ports from which clay was shipped.

Key sites for china clay extraction (all Cornwall)

The landscape of the area to the north of *St Austell*, with its shining white mica sky tips and flooded workings is itself testimony to china clay extraction. *The China Clay Country Park Mining and Heritage Museum*, Carthew, near St Austell, deals with water-powered extraction, while *Parkandillick Beam Engine* at Treviscoe is the last surviving steam engine in the china clay area. The two ports of *Charleston* and *Par* were used for shipping the clay: the remains of mica drags can be found near the former, while the latter is still a working port for the industry.

Clay processing

The transformation of clay into ceramic artefacts including pottery, clay pipes, bricks, tiles, and drains, has created a range of structures whose basic form has varied through time only in terms of scale, fuel used, and increased mechanisation. Essentially, earlier kilns were generally used intermittently, and enabled labourers to work them when not needed for agricultural work. Increased demand from the later 18th century onwards led to the development of kilns for continuous working, manned by a full-time labour force. This does not mean that earlier intermittent kilns ceased to be used: for example, the demand for bricks as a result of canal and railway construction led to the construction of primitive clamps for bricks on the sites of bridges, tunnels and aqueducts. Many types of kilns have therefore survived into the archaeological record, and *in situ* fired features can often be dated by directional archaeomagnetism, a technique at its most precise for the post-medieval period.

The pottery industry

More has probably been written about pottery than any other archaeological artefact. This section deals only with the structures of the later post-medieval industry when mass production was needed to meet increasing demand both for quantity and quality of ceramic goods. Tin-glazed earthenware, salt-glazed stoneware, creamware and porcelain were produced in Britain from the later 17th century onwards. These new types of pottery made use of other raw materials added to the clay which helped to change its properties. Apart from the use of china clay and china stone for porcelain, ground flint was added to the clay body for the production of creamware and ground bone was essential for bone china. Both had to be calcined to break down the structure and then ground before addition to the clay body, processes carried out in water-powered or steam-powered mills close to Stoke-on-Trent.

Small, individual potteries continued in use into the 19th century, but new, purpose-built factories provided a series of workshops for all the processes of production in a systematic manner. When Josiah Wedgewood built his factory in Etruria in 1769, it was designed to divide the manufacturing process into various distinct stages such as turning, moulding, pressing, and decorating, and to use different workmen in each area as well as ensuring that the layout of the factory enabled ceramics in different stages of the process to be moved on in a logical manner. The Etruria factory succumbed to subsidence in the mid-20th century and was then demolished, but many other potbanks were designed using this principle, although other factors such as the size, shape, and location of the site resulted in modifications. As far as possible, though, the products would travel in a logical direction from the intake of raw materials to the sliphouse, clay making workshops, biscuit kilns and warehouse, dipping room, glost placing and firing, sorting and selection warehouse and then to the decorating departments and kiln. Generally, the aim was to have the lighter work on the first-floor levels and the heavier on the ground floor. Casting, dish pressing, plate making and decorating were mostly placed on the first floor, while throwing and turning were on the ground floor so that they could have access to a damp cellar. Saggar making with its heavy materials was usually located on the ground floor. Other potbanks tried to adopt a similar rationalisation of process within their existing layout by the addition of buildings or machinery. The potbank which is now the Gladstone Pottery Museum in Longton, Stoke-on-Trent, was created in the early 19th century from two houses fronting the main road, with a range of simple workshops and a kiln to the rear. Additional kilns and workshops were later erected, completing a form of courtyard development. Some degree of rationalisation of process-flow was introduced with the addition of a steam engine into the preparation area, which co-existed with the handcraft techniques

still practised elsewhere on the site. Purpose-built pottery factories and potbanks which had grown by degrees existed side by side. At the same time, many isolated potteries continued to operate in rural areas where there were good supplies of clay; these supplied ceramics to a local market, and occasionally a national one.

By the 18th century the standard pottery kiln was the bottle kiln, which had evolved from the multi-flued circular updraught kiln of earlier periods (Fig 4.1). Heat from a furnace below the floor passed through fireholes into the kiln itself, which was often reinforced by iron bands. The circular hovel around the kiln acted as a chimney as well as providing a working area for the operators, and could be up to 70ft (21m) tall. To protect decorated wares, a muffle kiln was devised which was an updraught kiln with an internal chamber to protect the glazing and had no outer hovel. Very similar kilns were used for firing clay pipes. However, there were many variations and glazed ware could also be protected from hot gases by being placed in saggars, rough clay containers which were stacked inside the kiln and sealed together with damp clay. Similar kilns were used to fire decorated ceramic tiles which were in great demand during the 19th century. The purpose of derelict or excavated kilns can often be deduced from the types of wasters or pottery fragments found in the vicinity.

Tunnel kilns, which allowed continuous rather than intermittent firing,

Figure 4.1 Excavated base of updraught pottery kiln from the Sunderland Pottery Company, later the Wearside Pottery Company, Millfield, Sunderland. The pottery was established in 1913, and produced a range of brown wares from local clay, together with yellow and white wares using clay imported from Wareham in Dorset. The kiln appeared to have been substantially rebuilt in the mid-1940s (courtesy of Oxford Archaeology Ltd)

were introduced into Britain in the early 20th century. A tunnel kiln is a long, rectangular structure lined with refractory bricks, through which the unfired pottery passed on cars through zones of first increasing, then decreasing temperature.

Warehouses for storage of finished pottery, together with packing houses, were generally built close to the means of transport, frequently a canal. Retail showrooms were an integral part of the pottery industry; these were usually built in a more elaborate architectural manner than other buildings and placed on the street frontage to attract buyers, but should be regarded as part of the production process.

Key sites

The *Gladstone Pottery Museum*, Longton, Stoke-on-Trent (Fig 4.2), is a good place to start, while nearby *Jesse Shirley's Bone Mill* and *Cheddleton Flint Mill* demonstrate the preparation of essential ingredients for white china. *Middleport Pottery*, Stoke-on-Trent, is one of the few remaining working potteries. The Ironbridge Gorge Museum Trust maintains *Broseley Clay Tobacco Pipeworks*, *Coalport China Museum* and *Jackfield Tile Museum*, which incorporates the *Craven Dunhill Works*. More isolated examples include *Sharpe's Pottery Museum*, Swadlincote, Derbyshire; *Bovey Tracey kilns*, Devon; *Fulham pottery kiln*, London; and *Corbridge kilns*, Northumberland.

Figure 4.2 The surviving bottle ovens at the Gladstone Pottery Museum, Longton, Stoke-on-Trent (© Marilyn Palmer)

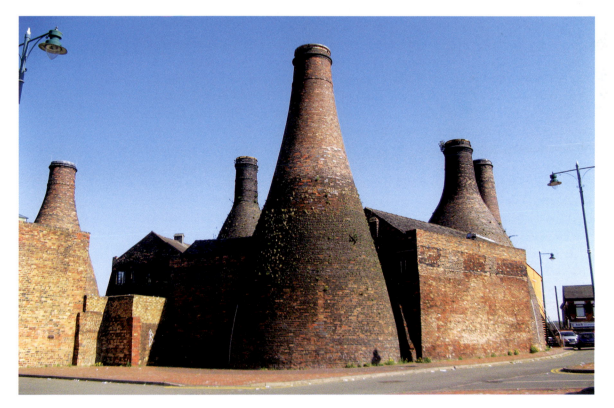

The brick and tile industry

Although the Romans had used brick in Britain, its use in the post-medieval period was confined to high-status houses, often using imported brick, and the chimney stacks and fireplaces which became such a feature of houses from the late 16th century onwards. Fireclay, which contains high proportions of aluminium and silicates, is resistant to high temperatures and was therefore used to produce bricks for lining furnaces as early as the 17th century, while in the same period the increasing shortage of timber for building opened up a new market for standard bricks in the building trades. The development of river navigations and canals also boosted the industry, since bricks were bulky and heavy to transport to building sites. Railways in the 19th century further aided distribution, and large brickworks had their own sidings onto main lines. In this period, too, the discovery that the Lower Oxford Clays of Bedfordshire and the area south of Peterborough contained sufficient carbonaceous matter to reduce the amount of fuel required for firing, and therefore reduced costs, led to the development of massive brickworks producing 'Flettons' (bricks named after one of the places they were first made). Their distribution slowly undermined the vernacular building tradition in many parts of Britain but undoubtedly boosted the growth of industrial towns. Blue bricks were originally made in Staffordshire from the local red clay, Etruria marl, which when fired at a high temperature in a low-oxygen reducing atmosphere became a deep blue colour and attained a very hard, impervious surface with high crushing strength and low water absorption, extensively used for bridges and tunnels in canal and railway construction.

Tiles had been used for flooring in medieval churches and abbeys as well as for roofing, and both types continued to be made in the post-medieval period, although roofing tiles were partly displaced by cheaper Welsh slate in the 19th century; this was lighter and so needed less substantial roof timbers. The decorative floor tile industry revived during the 19th century with increasing demand for use in Victorian villas and churches. Salt-glazed drainpipes of clay were needed both by agricultural improvers for draining land and by urban improvers for sewage disposal. Fireclay, because of its stability in kilns, was used for the production of sanitary ware which developed extensively in the second half of the 19th century. Different areas of the country developed their own specialisations, with decorative ceramic tiles being made in Shropshire and Staffordshire, while sanitary ware dominated the clay industries of east Staffordshire and west Derbyshire.

Brickworks were established in a number of different types of location. Large rural estates had their own brickworks, few importing bricks until the 19th century; examples survive on the National Trust estates of Blickling in Suffolk and Calke Abbey in Derbyshire. Farmers sometimes also produced their own bricks on an intermittent basis for repair of buildings. Some brickworks were developed as a subsidiary part of another industry, such as coal mining and iron working when clay was found in the Coal Measures, as was often the case in the Midlands. Temporary brickworks were set up for particular constructions, such as railways. Otherwise, independent commercial brickworks could range in size from small yards producing for a local market to large, integrated works supplying a national market, such as the huge late 19th-century brickworks at Stewartby in Bedfordshire.

Key elements and plan forms

As in the pottery industry, the preparation of clay for brick making demanded a whole range of processes housed in different buildings. Until modern times, clay was dug in the autumn and left to weather. It was then ground in a pug mill, once powered by horses but then by means of a steam engine, before being moulded either by hand, or by machine from the second half of the 19th century. The bricks were then dried and open-sided drying sheds were a feature of small brickworks; later, heated drying sheds were used. Kilns took numerous forms, different regions developing their own types (Fig 4.3). The simplest was the clamp kiln, a stack of unfired bricks which was then walled, capped, and left to burn. These are not easy to identify archaeologically, but evidence of burning or a surface of brick wasters may survive. It must not be forgotten that such clamps, although primitive, were still used on construction sites in the 19th century.

Most kilns were permanent structures but only used intermittently before the later 19th century, being cooled between each firing for loading and unloading. The most widespread intermittent kiln was the Scotch kiln, an open-topped rectangular structure with a wicket for loading at one end and a series of fireholes along the sides, often with a lean-to roof for shelter (Fig 4.3). The piled green bricks were usually temporarily capped during firing. Many such kilns went out

Figure 4.3 Some common types of brick kiln. A, Scotch kiln: W is the wicket through which the kiln was filled and F the fire grate; B, section of beehive downdraught kiln; C, plan of Hoffman kiln showing the firing sequence (© Marilyn Palmer)

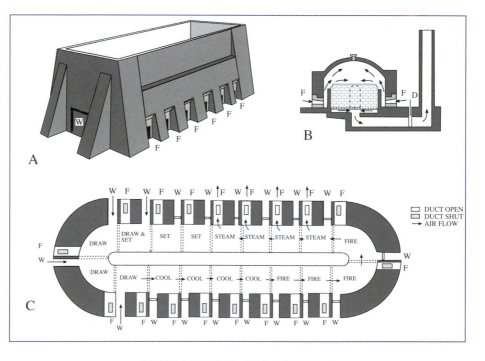

of use in World War II, as the smoke and flames from the open top contravened blackout regulations. The Suffolk kiln had parallel flues beneath the floor of the kiln and was also rectangular in form, usually with a vaulted roof. East Anglia had good clay resources and little building stone, and so many of these kilns were constructed. The Newcastle kiln was similar in form but lacked the parallel flues beneath the floor, having instead fireholes at one end and a flue or chimney at the other; this type of kiln had a permanent vaulted roof. Circular updraught and downdraught kilns, often known as beehive kilns, were also used for bricks. These had better control over air supply and so were used for the production of blue bricks and salt-glazed pipes. Rarely, bottle ovens were used for bricks as well as pottery.

Continuous kilns were introduced to meet increasing demand in the mid-19th century. In these, the waste heat from cooling bricks was used to dry green bricks before firing. This was achieved by means of a series of chambers around a central flue so that the firing process proceeded sequentially from chamber to chamber. The original Hoffman kiln, patented in Austria in 1858, was circular in form but most later ones were rectangular with rounded ends (Fig 4.3). Partitions between the chambers were blocked only temporarily and destroyed during firing, so Hoffman kilns that remain are huge, open spaces with no divisions and chimneys either in the centre or at one end. These were superseded, although not replaced, by transverse arch kilns or Staffordshire kilns which allowed greater control of temperature through elaborate systems of flues and dampers. Finally, as in the pottery industry, tunnel kilns came into use for bricks although not until the second half of the 20th century.

Key sites

These are scattered throughout the country. The *Chalk Pits Museum*, Amberley, Sussex, contains drying sheds and some machinery. The Hampshire Buildings Preservation Trust took on *Bursledon Brickworks* in Hampshire when it closed in 1974 and it is now run as an industrial museum by volunteers. Beehive kilns survive at *Great Linford*, near Milton Keynes, while an isolated bottle oven, later also used for lime, can be found at *Nettlebed* in Oxfordshire. A Scotch kiln survives in *Sutton-on-Sea*, Lincolnshire, while *Blists Hill Museum* in Ironbridge is preserving a large, 19th-century brickworks. An interesting coastal site is that of *Porthwen*, on the coast of Anglesey, which produced white silica bricks, and a Hoffman kiln is preserved at *Prestongrange* in Scotland.

Conclusion

The clay industries have left a wide range of structures; some remain as standing structures but many more have been discovered in urban excavations, as in the towns of the Potteries, which throw more light on different kinds of kilns. Attention should always be paid to the source of raw materials and fuel, the transport system for removing the product, and the range of ancillary structures for processing, storing and, in the case of the pottery, terracotta and decorative industries, the display of products for the retail trade. The transition from intermittent to continuous production is important, although it must be realised that many forms of intermittent production survived for specialist purposes.

Assessment of sites

- Sources of raw materials – local or imported? Local geology and topography.
- Preparation areas or buildings.
- Process-flow of site – planned area or organic growth over time.
- Type and purpose of kilns.
- Storage and/or retail sale of finished goods.
- Transport systems for raw materials or finished goods.

Further reading

More has been written on the history of the pottery industry and its artefacts than on its structures: see J Thomas, *The Rise of the Staffordshire Potteries* (Adams & Dart, 1971) and L Weatherill, *The Pottery Trade and North Staffordshire 1660–1700* (Manchester University Press, 1971). See also P Brears, *The English Country Pottery: its History and Techniques* (David & Charles, 1971).

For clay extraction, see R M Barton, *A History of the Cornish China-Clay Industry* (Bradford Barton, 1966), while its archaeology is covered in P Herring & J R Smith, *The Archaeology of the St Austell China-Clay Area* (Cornwall Archaeology Unit, 1991) and J R Smith, *Cornwall's China Clay Heritage* (Twelveheads Press, 1992). R Copeland, *A short history of pottery raw materials and the Cheddleton Flint Mill* (Cheddleton Flint Mill Industrial Heritage Trust, 1972) is a useful short introduction to the subject.

For pottery manufacture, a useful starting point is D Sekers, *The Potteries* (Shire Publications,1981) while D Baker, *Potworks: The History and Architecture of the Staffordshire Potteries* (RCHME, 1991), is an invaluable account of recording potbanks at a time when many were being demolished. A Peacey, 'The development of the Tobacco Pipe Kiln in the British Isles', *Internet Archaeology* 1,1997 (http://internetarch.ac.uk/issue1/peacey_index.html), surveys an important type of kiln and includes a detailed bibliography and many references to excavated structures. The excavation of a pottery kiln in Stoke-on-Trent is described in *Science for Historic Industries* (English Heritage, 2006, 8; see www.helm.org.uk/upload/pdf/Science-Historic-Industries). M Messenger, *North Devon Clay* (Twelveheads Press, 1982), deals with the relationship between a regional clay industry and its transport system.

For brick making, a good starting point is M Hammond, *Bricks and Brickmaking* (Shire Publications, 1981) and 'Brick Kilns: an illustrated survey' (*Industrial Archaeology Review* 1:2, 1997, 171–92). E Dobson, *A Rudimentary Treatise on the Manufacture of Bricks and Tiles: containing an outline of the principles of Brickmaking* (J Weale, 1850), is available electronically (http://galenet.galegroup.com/servlet/MOME?af=RN&ae=U106899972&srchtp=a&ste=14&locID=oxford).

A Cox, *Brickmaking: a History and Gazetteer* (Bedfordshire County Council, 1979), is a useful survey of an important brick-making area, while for Scotland see G Douglas, *Brick, tile and fireclay industries in Scotland* (Scottish Industrial Archaeology Survey, University of Strathclyde, 1993). The British Brick Society was founded in 1972 and carried out some important recording work on brick-making sites, and should be consulted about any sites found (http://www.britishbricksoc. free-online.co.uk/).

See also A Simco, *MPP: The Clay Industries* Steps 1 and 2 reports for English Heritage, 1998–2000.

4.3 Lime and lime burning

Limestone has always been valued as a building material (see 4.4 on quarrying) but, when burnt to change its chemical composition, was equally important both as an ingredient of mortar and cement and as a soil-improving agent. Both these uses increased in importance in the late 18th century when the wastes and commons were enclosed for agriculture and house building grew dramatically in towns. As in the clay industries, lime burning developed from an intermittent to a continuous process to meet demand, although many of the smaller intermittent kilns remained for the use of individuals. Limekilns are one of the most common types of industrial structure surviving in the landscape.

Limekilns

Limestone or chalk was burnt either where it was quarried or, because of the corrosive nature of burnt lime, transported to where it was needed and burnt there. Alternate layers of coal and stone were placed in an open-topped, bowl-shaped structure, occasionally lined with firebrick, and burnt over a period of days. At the base of the kiln were draw-holes or eyes, which enabled burnt lime, or quicklime, to be raked out, usually into an arch built in the side of the kiln to prevent it coming into contact with water. These were known as flare kilns or periodic kilns. Single kilns were often built into banks for ease of loading from the top (Fig 4.4), while in East Anglia kilns were generally below ground. Here, the pot was at ground level but chutes from it led into an underground chamber which was either annular or square in section and was accessed by a flight of steps. Another largely regional type was the sow kiln, a form of clamp used only for agricultural lime where impurities in the finished product did not matter. The lime was placed with layers of wood or coal in a bowl scooped out in the hillside, and covered with turves to ensure slow burning. The pye or pudding-pye kiln was a larger type of clamp used in some upland areas.

Greater demand during the late 18th century led to the development of draw kilns, generally larger structures lined with firebrick to withstand continuous firing over long periods. The pot of this type of kiln was generally an inverted

Figure 4.4. Limekiln, near Reeth in Swaledale; note the placing of the kiln against a slope to enable loading from above (© Peter Stanier)

cone, and had moveable fire-bars at the base to support the charge and enable the lime to be drawn out; as this was done, fresh layers of lime and fuel could be loaded into the top. The kiln pots were built unto sturdy stone structures for stability, generally in pairs or batteries comprising several kilns. For production of ash-free lime, kilns in which the fuel and charge were kept separate were developed in the second half of the 19th century. An example was the Dietzch kiln, in which powdered fuel was injected through a hinged door into a very tall kiln and did not mingle with the burning lime. Finally, the Hoffman kiln, first developed for bricks (see above), was adapted for lime production.

Loading the kilns was usually carried out by hand, but occasionally water power was used to haul the lime to the top of the kiln, as at Moorswater in Cornwall and Closeburn in Dumfriesshire.

Location

Single flare kilns are widely scatted across the UK, usually now ruinous, and their previous existence can also be deduced from field names. The small coastal kilns where limestone was brought in by sea for use on their hinterland were also usually only fired intermittently. Large numbers of kilns were also built on country estates, generally flare kilns where the lime was needed for estate purposes but also draw kilns where lime was sold off the estate, as at Calke Abbey in Derbyshire. Batteries of large draw kilns were often built adjacent to inland waterways, waggonways and railways during the 19th century for ease of transport both of raw materials and burnt lime. Most lime kilns were functional structures with no attempt at decoration; one notable exception is the kilns beside the Llanelly Railway at Llandybie near Ammanford, where the six ornate kilns were built in 1856 by the surveyor and church architect R K Penson who was heavily involved in the development of the quarries.

Assessment

- Location – in relation to source of raw material or to transport link for supply and distribution?
- Topography – set against a bank? Underground?
- Structure – type of kiln – intermittent or continuous? Single kiln or battery of kilns?
- Loading of kiln – any evidence of the use of power?
- Storage of burnt lime – adjacent to drawhole of kiln? Separate storage?

Key sites

Simple flare kilns can be seen in many places: good examples are at *Beadnell Harbour* and on *Lindisfarne* in Northumberland, and at *Solva* in Pembrokeshire and *Clovelly* in Devon. Larger draw kilns can be found along many canals and disused railways, for example at *Tenby* in Pembrokeshire, *Froghall Basin* in Staffordshire alongside the Caldon Canal, and at *Millersdale* in Derbyshire alongside the disused Midland Railway, together with *Charleston* and *Limekilns* on the coast of Fife. A Hoffman kiln for lime burning has been consolidated and interpreted at *Langcliffe* north of Settle, close to the Settle and Carlisle Railway. Other examples are preserved in a museum context, for example in the *Amberley Chalk Pits Museum* in West Sussex, the *Black Country Museum* in the West Midlands, the *National Stone Centre*, Wirksworth, in Derbyshire, and *Morwelham Quay* in Devon.

Figure 4.5 Excavated limekiln at Barrow-on-Soar, Leicestershire. This is a late type of kiln with flues to enable continuous working (courtesy of Danny McAree, Northamptonshire Archaeology)

Further reading

A useful starting point is R Williams, *Limekilns and Limeburning* (Shire Album, 1980). An old but useful book on the process of lime burning is A B Searle's *Limestone and its Products* (E Benn, 1935). There are many useful regional and local surveys of lime kilns, but see S Hughes, *The Industrial Archaeology of the Montgomeryshire Canal* (RCAHMW, 1983), for a useful survey of kilns in relation to canal transport. D Johnson, *Limestone Industries of the Yorkshire Dales* (Tempus, 2002), deals with an area where several different types of kilns survive. Many articles on lime kilns have been included in *Industrial Archaeology Review*: see R J Clarke, 'Closeburn Limeworks Scheme: a Dumfriesshire Waterpower Complex' (**10**:1, 1981, 5–22); M R G Trueman, 'The Langcliffe Quarry and Limeworks' (**14**:2, 1992, 126–44); G Marshall, M Palmer & P A Neaverson, 'The History and Archaeology of the Calke Abbey lime-yards' (**14**:2, 1992, 145–76); D Johnson, 'Freidrich Edouard Hoffman and the Invention of Continuous Kiln Technology: the archaeology of the Hoffman lime kiln and 19th century industrial development' (Part 1), **24**:2, 2002, 103–32; (Part 2), **25**:1, 2003, 15–29.

See also M Trueman, *MPP: The Lime, Cement and Plaster Industries Step 1 Report*, Report for English Heritage, 1996; M Trueman, *MPP: Lime Industry Revised Step 3 Report (with additionals)*, Report for English Heritage, 2000; G Chitty, *MPP: Lime, cement and plaster industries Step 4 Report*, Report for English Heritage, 2001.

4.4 Stone quarrying

The pre-19th-century buildings of Britain owe much of their distinctiveness to the immense variety of available building stone within such a compact area. Igneous, metamorphic, and sedimentary rock were all used for construction purposes and quarries, both large and small, were features of the stone regions of the country. Granite, the most intractable of igneous rocks, was used for buildings requiring strength, such as steam engine houses in Cornwall. It also played a major part in civil engineering structures, like bridges, as well as paving the streets of many industrial towns. Slate, the principal metamorphic rock, found more widespread use for roofing than as a building stone, as it could be cleaved very thinly and dressed to standard sizes, enabling economies to be made in roof timbers. Sedimentary rocks, which included gritstone, sandstone and limestone, have been used widely for both domestic and public buildings as, generally, they could be easily shaped in blocks (freestone) and carved to provide decorative features. Limestone was also quarried for use as a flux in iron furnaces. The Millstone Grit of the Pennines, as its name implies, was extensively used for stones for corn mills, edge runners for crushing minerals, and grindstones for the metalworking trades. Finally, both stone and gravel have been increasingly quarried for roadstone and other construction purposes since the early 19th century.

Extraction and processing

Methods of quarrying and processing vary according to the different rock types: quarrymen had to know their stone in order to make the best use of it. Most quarries were open, but in some cases, especially with the sedimentary rocks of southern England, the overburden was such that it was easier to extract the stone

Figure 4.6 Remains of
a smithy at Carbilly
Tor granite quarry,
Cornwall (© Peter
Stanier)

from below ground, using the pillar and stall method by which chambers were
mined, leaving pillars of stone between them to support the roof. Many of the
original stone mines were reused during the 20th-century World Wars for the
storage of ammunition and so took on a new role.

Until the mid-19th century, quarrying depended mainly on manual labour
although gunpowder was sometimes used for initial blasting and both powder
stores and quarrymen's blast shelters can still be found in abandoned quarries.
The stone was lifted by means of wooden shearlegs and cranes but dressing
remained largely a manual process until the introduction of mechanical
saw frames. In the small quarries located along the 'edges' of the gritstone
in Derbyshire and Yorkshire, unfinished millstones in various stages of
manufacture by hand can still be seen. The vast slate quarries of North Wales
still contain many open-sided sheds for manual splitting of slate, although later
water-powered saws were used for the initial shaping of the rock and large mills
were constructed in the valleys. Limestone has always been valued as a building
material, both for its colour and for the ease with which it can be dressed
and carved. It is a well-bedded rock, jointed into natural blocks, which could
be removed with crowbars and wedges. Away from the quarries themselves,

stone shaping was also carried out in masons' yards in towns, which may also contain the remnants of tools and machinery. By the late 19th century, quarries were increasingly dominated by heavy machinery for crushing and screening, the surviving concrete bases of which are difficult to interpret and the flimsy buildings containing them have usually vanished.

Quarries in the landscape

Quarries were usually formed of a series of galleries or 'benches', where one face had been worked out and another was started above or below it, resulting in some huge excavations such as that at Delabole in Cornwall or sculptured mountains like the Dinorwic Quarry at Llanberis in North Wales. The geological structure of Britain meant that many stone quarries were located in upland areas, with the attendant problems of obtaining the necessary labour and transporting the finished product.

Many quarry sites contain the remains of barracks where the men lived during the week, often recognisable by their hearths and ruined chimneys, as well as smithies for sharpening tools (Fig 4.6). The larger dressing mills may well contain the supports for powered machinery, with water courses if water wheels were used. Many deep quarries, especially those for gravel working, are now flooded and only too often used as rubbish dumps.

The problems of transporting dressed stone and slate to where it was needed was responsible for many early transport routes, none more spectacular than the inclines of the slate quarries in both North Wales and the Lake District, topped by small towers supporting brake drums for lowering wagons down the hillsides (Fig 4.8). Many narrow-gauge railways owed their origin to the carriage

Figure 4.7 Vivian Quarry, Llanberis, North Wales. Note the quarry benches at right and remains of the incline at left (© Marilyn Palmer)

of slate and stone, and harbours also had to be built for the coastwise shipping of materials to London or the industrial towns. A close study of the stone employed in public buildings, where prestige materials were used, is very instructive in giving some idea of the complex transport systems required to carry such a heavy material from its source to its destination.

Assessment of sites

+ Type of rock being quarried.
+ Evidence for extractive methods used, such as galleries, benches and spoil heaps as well as gunpowder stores, blast shelters etc.
+ Evidence for processing methods – splitting and shaping sheds.
+ Evidence for power sources – water wheels, machine bases.
+ Evidence for transport, such as cart tracks, self-acting inclines, railways, harbours, as well as standing buildings where the stone was eventually used.
+ The human landscape – barracks and other quarry-based settlements.

Figure 4.8 Remains of a winding drum for the incline at Honister Yew Crag Quarry, Cumbria (© Peter Stanier)

Key sites

The National Stone Centre, near Middleton in Derbyshire, is located in an area containing six disused limestone quarries, but also aims to tell the story of stone to the present day. The *National Slate Museum* at Llanberis in North Wales fulfils a similar function, and is situated in the former workshops of the Dinorwic Quarry with an enormous water wheel for powering the machinery. The site also includes four quarrymen's houses that recapture significant periods in the slate industry. The underground mining of slate has been recaptured at the *Llechwedd Slate Caverns*, near Blaenau Ffestiniog. Presentations and short tours are also available at the working slate quarries of *Delabole* in Cornwall and *Honister* in Cumbria. All these help to make sense of other abandoned sites. For transport, the *Haytor Tramway* was built in 1820 to move granite blocks from quarries on Dartmoor to the Stover Canal and thence the sea. Uniquely, it is constructed of L-shaped rails and points hewn from granite blocks and was used by horse-drawn wagons with flangeless iron wheels. The 'Great Little Trains of Wales', the narrow-gauge lines built to carry slate from the North Wales quarries to ports such as Dinorwig, Penrhyn, Portmadoc and Towyn, are all now run as tourist attractions (http://www.greatlittletrainsofwales.co.uk/index.html). By contrast, the disused limestone railways of the Brecon Beacons and the Clydach Gorge make exciting walking routes (see Van Laun below). In Derbyshire, *Bole Hill Quarry* near the National Trust's Longshaw Visitor Centre contains many unfinished grindstones alongside the railway track built to take them down to the main line. The quarry later provided stone for the dams of the Derwent and Howden reservoirs.

Further reading

Good general surveys are the books by P Stanier, including his *Quarries and Quarrying* (Shire Publications, 1985, reprinted 2009) and *Stone Quarry Landscapes; the archaeology of quarrying in England* (Tempus, 2000). For gravel quarrying, see T Cooper, *Laying the Foundations: a history and archaeology of the Trent Valley sand and gravel industry* (CBA Research Report **159**, 2008)

For many years, students from the Snowdonia National Park Study Centre at Plas-Tan-y-Bwlch in North Wales have been undertaking detailed surveys of the slate quarries, beginning with the exemplary study of *Rhosydd Slate Quarry* (M J T Lewis & J H Denton, The Cottage Press, 1974, reprinted by Adit Publications, 1994) and continued on an annual basis by D Gwyn, *Gwynedd: Inheriting a Revolution* (Phillimore, 2006).

More has probably been written on the transport systems from quarries than on any other aspect of their landscape. The Oakwood Press has published many of these: see especially J I C Boyd, *The Festiniog Railway 1800–1974* (2 vols, 1975), which includes descriptions of the quarry workings served by the railway. For the limestone quarries which fed the South Wales iron furnaces, see J Van Laun, *The Limestone Railways* (Newcomen Society, 2001).

See also S Gould, *MPP: The Alum Industry: Combined Steps 1–3 Report*, Cranstone Consultancy, 1993, and G Chitty, *MPP: The Alum Industry Step 4 report*, 1996.

Also J Ashbee, *MPP: The Quarrying Industry Step 1 Report*, Report for English Heritage, LUAU, 1996, and I Hedley, S Richardson & M Trueman, *MPP: The Quarrying Industry Step 3 Report (Revised)*, Report for English Heritage, LUAU, 1999.

4.5 The coal industry

Coal is one of the most common of Britain's natural resources, and has been mined since Roman times. It was of major national importance from the 17th century onwards when it began to be used extensively as a domestic as well as an industrial fuel, and reached its peak of output in 1913. However, large-scale exploitation in the 19th and 20th centuries, followed by the collapse of the industry in the second half of the 20th century and the subsequent rapid closure of mines and clearance of sites, has obliterated much of the field evidence for earlier periods of working.

Coal occurs in seams rather than the uncertain veins typical of non-ferrous metal mining, and consequently one area can be worked for a long period of time. The majority of coal seams occur in deposits of the Carboniferous period, and early coal mining took place where the Coal Measures outcropped. Later, mining had to follow the seams underground beneath the overburden into the 'concealed' coalfields and required considerably more capital expenditure to reach the coal and consequently a greater range of buildings and machinery.

Extraction

Early miners followed outcrops underground by means of adit or drift mines, a method still pursued by the Free Miners of the Forest of Dean. Where the terrain was not suitable for drifts, coal was extracted from shallow depths by bell pits, shafts being sunk into the seam through the overburden; the workings extended radially from the bottom, the coal being raised to the surface by a hand windlass. Where not obliterated by later workings, these survive in the landscape as circular mounds with a central depression and are scattered randomly over the area rather than being concentrated in a line following a vein, as in non-ferrous metal mining. They can be detected in ploughed ground by means of variation in soil colour and may also reappear in modern open-cast workings.

Seams at greater depth were extracted from shafts, and early timber-lined square-sectioned shafts 100ft (30m) deep and dating to *c* 1450 have been found at the Lounge opencast pit in west Leicestershire and more may remain to be discovered elsewhere. These gave access to pillar and stall workings, a method of operation designed to leave pillars of coal to support the roof, which may have been removed later (Fig 4.9). Where these were not far below the ground, their outline may often be detected on the ground by a grid pattern, especially in snowy conditions. In many coalfields, this method of working was replaced during the

Figure 4.9 Remains
of pillar and stall
workings, exposed
by opencast working,
Sharlston Colliery,
Wakefield, West
Yorkshire (courtesy
Oxford Archaeology
Ltd)

18th century by the long wall system, where the whole seam was removed, thus creating more surface subsidence. Large amounts of waste had to be brought up the shaft and dumped on the conical spoil tips which were once such a common feature of Britain's coalfields.

Drainage, haulage, and ventilation

Water was one of the major hazards in any underground mining. In suitable terrain, drainage soughs or underground tunnels could be used to drain the water into nearby rivers. Where this was impossible, hand-powered windlasses or *rag and chain* pumps, brought water to the surface by means of an endless chain of discs of leather in a wooden pipe. Horse power could be used for this purpose, but was more commonly used for winding coal to the surface. The most common version of the horse gin, the horse whim, developed in the 18th century, stood well away from the mine and the wooden frame supported a horizontal winding drum from which a double-ended rope ran over a pulley to the shaft head. The evidence for this in the landscape is usually a level, circular, often gravelled or paved, walkway, sometimes with a bearing block in the centre. Water power was less common on coal-mining than metal-mining sites, but water-balance engines were used, the weight of a bucket of water raising coal from a shallow shaft.

It was the invention of steam-powered pumping engines that really enabled the industry to expand from the 18th century onwards. Thomas Newcomen's atmospheric engine of 1712 (see Chapter 3.5) was rapidly adopted throughout the UK, and continued in use even after the improvements made by James Watt as its extravagant consumption of fuel mattered less on coalfields than it did for other types of mines. Consequently, some survive and converted examples of

Figure 4.10 A mid-19th-century pithead scene on the Staffordshire coalfield, from Tomlinson's *Cyclopaedia of the Useful Arts*, Vol.II, 1852. On the right can be seen the then old-fashioned haystack boiler for a rotative beam winding engine which is raising coal from the shafts. In the background, two other steam engines can be seen, each of them winding from shafts some distance from the pithead

engine houses can be recognised by their shape, which was taller and narrower than later types of engine houses since the boiler was beneath the cylinder rather than separately housed. The infilled aperture for the rocking beam or bob at top-floor level is often retained as a feature. Watt's development of rotary engines was invaluable to the coal industry in enabling steam-powered winding. Later engines usually had the winding drum mounted above the cylinder, resulting in a tall engine house and headstocks. By the 20th century, huge steel and concrete structures housing Koepe winders, driven by electric motors, were introduced, a hoisting system in which the winding drum is replaced by large wheels or sheaves over which passes an endless rope. In other collieries, beam engines were replaced in the 19th century by faster horizontal engines, often with twin cylinders, housed in single-storey buildings of considerable height to accommodate the winding drum. These in turn gave way to electric winders in the 20th century, with associated generating stations.

Ventilation

Ventilation was of particular importance in coal mines, since many coal seams gave off methane gas or fire damp, which forms an explosive mixture with air, together with carbon monoxide, whose popular name of choke damp indicates its lethal properties. As shaft depth increased, the problems of mine ventilation became more acute. At first fire baskets were suspended in shafts to draw up foul air; furnaces at the base of shafts served the same purpose, their presence sometimes marked above ground by small chimneys. Both of these methods often led to explosions, which were common until mechanical means of ventilation could be provided. Both the Waddle fan and the Guibal fan were introduced in the second half of the 19th century, the latter enclosed in an easily recognisable building with a funnel-shaped outlet or evasée from which the foul air was expelled.

Coal preparation

By the late 19th century, pits tended to extract whole seams rather than just good coal, and so coal preparation became a necessity. The processing plant included picking belts, screens for separating different sizes of coal, and washeries to extract dirt. These were often collected together in a heapstead, a structure usually built above a railway line so that the coal and waste materials could be removed easily. Thomas Hair's *A Series of Views of the Collieries in the Counties of Northumberland and Durham*, first published in 1844, gives some idea of the extent of above-ground structures at large colliery sites.

The major secondary product produced from coal at the colliery was coke, the result of heating coal in the absence of air to drive off volatile material to produce something close to pure carbon, used for iron smelting and many other industrial purposes. At first performed in open heaps, long ranges of brick-built beehive-shaped structures or coke ovens were being constructed from the late 18th century onwards, the bases of which show up in excavations, for example by North Pennines Archaeology at Framwellgate, County Durham (Fig 4.11). At first, the gas and tar driven off went to waste, but they were later recovered once larger and more complex coke works were constructed with tanks for gas, tar and other by-products. Most of these were on or near colliery sites, but others were attached to ironworks.

Figure 4.11 The remains of coke ovens, once part of an extensive coking works, at Framwellgate, County Durham, excavated in 2009 (© North Pennines Archaeology)

Transport

The bulky nature of coal meant that transport systems were vital to enable it to reach the points of sale. Although previously carried in panniers by pack-horses, canals, rivers and coastwise shipping were obvious means for the carriage of coal by the 18th century. However, on colliery sites themselves, wheeled transport was vital and it is not surprising that the earliest forms of waggonways or railways were developed in association with collieries and the evidence for these should always be sought (see Chapter 6). Wooden rails for waggonways have been found on many cleared colliery sites, for example a waggonway of 1815 found in 1995 during reclamation works on the site of the former Lambton D pit in County Durham.

The human landscape

Coal mines employed a large workforce, whose welfare was commonly ignored by mining companies in the UK well into the 20th century. Pit-head baths were introduced in Europe long before they were in Britain, but the establishment of the British Miners' Welfare Fund in the 1920s led to their construction at many pits. Lamp-rooms were another important ancillary building, together with locker rooms for clothing. Since shiftwork was common in most mines, miners needed to find accommodation close to the pits and many companies provided whole settlements of houses for rent, occasionally with railways providing coal to the houses, as at Ashington in County Durham. These mining settlements have survived beyond the closure and clearance of the collieries themselves, and should always be regarded as part of the mining landscape in any recording process (see Chapter 6).

Conclusion

Despite the former importance of coal mining in the UK economy, wholesale clearance of collieries has removed much of the physical evidence. Valuable recording work was carried out at the time of many pit closures by the Royal Commissions on Historical Monuments in England, Wales, and Scotland, and a considerable archive of drawings and photographs built up. However, opencast working and land clearance schemes often reveal evidence from past mining activity, and should always be monitored. Evidence from pre-20th-century collieries can still be found in the forms of horse-gin platforms, ventilation chimneys, coke ovens, fan houses, ancillary buildings etc, together with transport systems such as pack-horse routes and waggonways.

Assessment of sites

- Topography – mining by adit, bell pit or shaft. Spoil tips.
- Evidence for haulage or pumping, such as horse-gin platforms.
- Evidence for ventilation, such as chimneys or fan houses.
- Evidence for coal preparation – heapsteads, coke ovens.
- Evidence for transport, such as waggonways, loading staithes on rivers and canals.
- The human landscape – pithead baths, miners' barracks, settlements, monuments to pit disasters.

Key sites

The collapse of the coal industry in the 1980s and 1990s and its previous importance in the economy led to the retention of some collieries as mining museums, conserving many of their surface buildings and sometimes running underground tours. Among these are *The National Coal Mining Museum*, Caphouse Colliery, West Yorkshire, where wooden headstocks survive; *Woodhorn Colliery Museum*, Northumberland, with two sets of headstocks and a fan house, together with a collection of paintings by the Ashington Group of pithead scenes; *Snibston Discovery Park*, Coalville, Leicestershire, which preserves surface buildings from the mid-20th century, together with exhibits including the unique late medieval timber-framing from a shaft. The *Scottish Mining Museum*, Lady Victoria Colliery, Newtongrange, preserves most of the buildings and machinery from a late Victorian colliery. In South Wales, *Big Pit National Coal Museum* at Blaenavon and the former Lewis Merthyr Pit, now the *Rhondda Heritage Park*, also with two sets of headstocks and a large fan house. The open-air museums at *Beamish* in County Durham and the *Black Country* also have important examples of colliery buildings.

Outside the museum environment, the remains of collieries on the Cumbrian coast are worth seeing: *Jane Pit*, Workington, retains a gin circle and a later steam engine house, and is a rare example of a coal mine that demonstrates the evolution of a horse-powered winding to steam power, while at Whitehaven, the scanty remains of *Duke's Pit* include a large Guibal fan house. *Haig Colliery Mining Museum* preserves the winding engine house and headgear of a pit closed in 1986. The engine house and other buildings at *Saltom Pit* have recently been conserved. *Clipstone Colliery* in Nottinghamshire retains its impressive steel headstocks for a Koepe winder, while the earlier *Pleasley Colliery* on the boundary between Nottinghamshire and Derbyshire has won several awards for its sympathetic restoration by volunteers.

Further reading

More has been written about the history of the coal industry than about its archaeology, and there are many regional accounts as well. J U Nef, *The Rise of the British Coal Industry* (Routledge, 1932), was the first to stress the importance of coal mining in the late 16th and 17th centuries. A good general account of the types of structures discussed above is A R Griffin, *Coalmining* (Longman, 1971). T H Hair's important *A Series of Views of the Collieries of the Counties of Northumberland and Durham* (1844) was reprinted by Davies Books in 1966 and is available as an electronic resource, http://galenet.galegroup.com/servlet/MOME?af=RN&ae=U105677785&srchtp=a&ste=14&locID=oxford (accessed 02/09/2011).

The closure of coal mines in the 1980s gave rise to national recording exercises, published for England by R Thornes, *Images of Coal* (RCHME, 1994), and S Gould & I Ayris, *Colliery Landscapes: an aerial survey of the deep-mined coal industry in England* (English Heritage, 1998). Similar work for Wales resulted in S Hughes, B Malaws, M Parry & P Wakelin, *Collieries in Wales: Engineering and Architecture* (RCAHMW, 1997), together with an article by B Malaws, 'Process recording at industrial sites' (*Industrial Archaeology Review* **19**:1, 1997, 75–98), based around a working colliery site. For Scotland, see M K Oglethorpe, *Scottish Collieries: an inventory of the Scottish coal industry in the nationalised era* (RCAHMS, 2006).

See also MPP reports on the coal industry from English Heritage: S Gould & D Cranstone, *MPP: The Coal Industry: Step 1 Report*, The Cranstone Consultancy, 1993; E Instone & D Cranstone, *MPP: The Coal Industry: Step 3 Report – Pre-20th Century Collieries*, The Cranstone Consultancy, 1994; S Gould, *MPP: The Coal Industry Step 3 Report – 20th-Century Collieries*, The Cranstone Consultancy, 1994; G Chitty, *MPP: The Coal Industry Step 4 Report*, 1995.

For the Cumbrian coast, what may be the first reference to industrial archaeology can be found in I Fletcher, 'The Archaeology of the West Cumberland Coal Trade' in *Transactions of the Cumberland and Westmorland Antiquarian and Archaeological Society*, **3**, 1878, 266–313, while D Cranstone, 'The Whitehaven Coast, 1500–2000: post-medieval, industrial and historical archaeology?' in A Horning & M Palmer (eds), *Crossing Paths or Sharing Tracks: future directions in the archaeological study of post-1550 Britain and Ireland* (Boydell & Brewer, 2009, 205–19), presents an original viewpoint on the 'long Industrial Revolution', based around the extractive industries of this coast.

For coke ovens, see K Reedman & M Sissons, 'Unstone Coke Ovens' (*Industrial Archaeology Review* **8**:1, 1985, 78–85), and S Gould, 'Coke Ovens at Vobster Breach Colliery (*Industrial Archaeology Review* **17**:1, 1994, 79–85). The excavation of a large coking plant in County Durham is described in M Railton, 'The Excavation of the Remains of a 19th century Coking Works at Framwellgate Moor, Durham', *North Pennines Archaeology Online Magazine* **3**, 2007, www.nparchaeology.co.uk/npa-om/NPA_OM_Vol03_download.pdf (accessed 19/10/2011).

References to waggonways are included in Chapter 6 but see particularly I M Ayris *et al*, 'The Archaeological Excavation of Wooden Waggonway Remains at Lambton D Pit, Sunderland' (*Industrial Archaeology Review* **20**:1, 1998, 2–22).

4.6 Non-ferrous metal mining and processing

The chief non-ferrous minerals that have been mined in the British Isles from very early times are tin, copper, and lead. These are found mainly in the north-west of the Exe-Tees line with some copper and lead in the Peak District as well. Unlike coal seams, mineral veins run erratically through their parent rock and hence those who exploited them were often known as 'Adventurers' in the 16th and 17th centuries. The veins, also known as rakes or lodes, which had outcropped at surface were soon worked out and so shaft mines had to be dug, as in the coal industry, with all the consequent problems of draining the mines and getting both miners and materials up and down the shafts. Many metal mines were located in remote hilly areas; this means that structures have often survived since mines were frequently only worked for short periods of time and so, unlike coal mines, did not destroy their own past. Although some metal mines belonged to large companies which introduced the latest technology, other small mines retained old forms of technology long after new machines had been introduced, which can be useful to the industrial archaeologist.

Lead mining and processing is dealt with first, but the techniques used were similar for other minerals, and so Section 4.7 could also be of use to those seeking information about the processing of other types of metal ore, particularly copper.

Further reading

J Day & R F Tylecote (eds), *The Industrial Revolution in Metals* (The Institute of Metals, 1991), is a useful introduction to the development of the most important metal industries, including ferrous and non-ferrous minerals, in the early modern period. *R R Angerstein's Illustrated Travel Diary, 1753–1755: Industry in England and Wales from a Swedish perspective*, trans T & P Berg (Science Museum, 2001), is a fascinating account of the state of British industry in the mid-18th century, particularly metal mining and smelting as Angerstein was representing the Swedish ironmasters who were increasingly afraid of British competition.

N Jones, M Walters & P Frost, *Mountains and Orefields: metal mining landscapes of mid- and north-east Wales* (CBA Research Report **142**, 2004), is a well-illustrated report on a series of detailed archaeological surveys which covered mining for lead, copper and coal, making extensive use of aerial photography as well as field survey.

4.7 Lead mining and processing

Mining

The most frequently exploited ore of lead is galena. From the Roman period onwards lead veins were often detected by hushing, a process whereby water was collected in a small reservoir high up in the hills and then released all at once to wash away the overburden. Such hushes are obvious scars on the hillsides of the Yorkshire Dales and the North Pennines. Once veins had been located, they were exploited by shallow shafts or horizontal adits. A shallow horizontal vein or rake may be marked by a number of filled-in shafts in a formation resembling a string of beads across the landscape. Once these shallow veins were worked out, shafts were dug to deeper levels.

Drainage was a problem in metalliferous mines as well as coal mines, and again drainage soughs were used where the terrain was suitable, as in the Peak District of Derbyshire. Hand-powered pumping methods were very common in small mines, but as mines became deeper, the hilly terrain in which lead was

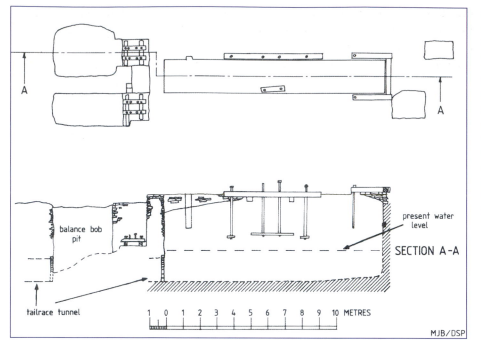

Figure 4.12 Plan and section of pumping wheelpit, Esgair Hir, drawn by M Bannister and D Palmer, from M Palmer, *The Richest in All Wales*, 1983. Note the timbers bolted along the edges of wheelpit and the balance bob pits for the weighted balance box at one end of the wheelpit (© Marilyn Palmer)

usually found enabled the use of water wheels with flat rods to drive pumps at the shaft, since the shafts were often at some distance from the water source. The water wheels could be very large, over 70ft (22m) at Great Laxey Mine in the Isle of Man, constructed in 1854, but frequently over 40ft (12m), and must have been spectacular features in the landscape. Heavy timbers held down by substantial bolts were placed along the edges of wheel pits to strengthen them against the thrust of the crank on the wheel. This drove the flat rods, which were kept in tension by a box weighted with rocks or balance box on each end; these sank into pits on each stroke. Wheelpits for pumping can be recognised by these pits and traces of supports for flat rod systems can often still be found.

In some areas where coal was available, such as North Wales, steam pumping engines were used. However, these were often too expensive to run away from the coalfield and cheaper methods like drainage soughs were preferred if at all possible. For example, a new drainage sough was dug in 1873 at Magpie Mine in Derbyshire, despite the earlier installation of steam pumping engines.

Processing

The mining of ore was usually carried out by small teams of miners who stored their ore separately from other teams in large storage bins, often known as bouse teams, prior to dressing the ore. These were substantial stone structures, generally built against a bank so that they could be filled from above, with a sill at the base to retain the ore until it was removed for processing.

Dressing, or separating the ore from the unwanted minerals (gangue) in which it was still embedded, involved crushing and washing. Before the late 18th century, crushing was sometimes done by means of hand-held hammers on a bucking floor (a buck was a hammer); these can be identified from a spread of gravel-sized fragments near spoil tips. Horse-driven edge runners in a gin circle were also used; this differed from the horse whim used for winding from shafts in having a circular paved area with a central bearing which supported the shaft on which the edge runner was mounted, and can still be found on former lead-mining sites, particularly in Derbyshire. Where water power was available, use was made of Cornish rollers, a technique developed in the late 18th century by the Cornish mining engineer, John Taylor. The ore was crushed between two sets of iron rollers suspended from a beam in a crushing house; this reduced the ore to the size of gravel but did not pulverise it, which would result in considerable loss as slimes. The remains of these can be recognised by the water-wheel pit alongside and the slots for the heavy beams which supported the iron rollers; the weights which regulated the gap between the rollers can occasionally also be found.

Once crushed, the ore was classified to sort it into sizes for further concentration. This remained fairly primitive until the late 19th century and was generally done by making use of the principle that the specific gravity of most metals is higher than that of the gangue minerals. The ore was washed through a series of gently inclined pits or sunken wooden boxes, from which the different grades of ore could be dug out separately and much of the waste washed away. The coarser ore was then treated in jiggers, wooden boxes full of water containing moveable sieves which further graded the ore. The form of these developed considerably in the 19th century; most were worked by hand but water-powered jiggers were known on larger mines. Few survive intact, but the remains of sieves can often be found during excavation. The finer material was processed in a series of sloping tanks or buddles, whose form again underwent many changes in the

Figure 4.13 Reconstructed rectangular buddle at the North of England Mining Museum, Killhope, County Durham, based on excavations by David Cranstone at the site (© Marilyn Palmer)

Further reading

A good starting point is L Willies, *Lead and Lead Mining* (Shire, 1982), written largely from a Derbyshire viewpoint. Of use too is T D Ford & J H Rieuwerts, *Lead Mining in the Peak District* (4th edn) (Landmark Publishing and Peak District Mines Historical Society, 2000). More about the heritage of lead mining in Derbyshire can be found in an excellent archaeological account by J Barnatt & R Penny, *The lead legacy: the prospects for the Peak District's Lead Mining Heritage* (Peak District National Park Authority, 2004). The Peak District Mines Historical Society has produced many useful publications, among them P Claughton (ed), *Water Power in Mining* (The Peak District Mines Historical Society, 2004).

For the north of England, A Raistrick's two volumes on *The Lead Industry of Wensleydale and Swaledale* (Moorland, 1975) are invaluable, while R T Clough, *The Lead Smelting Mills of the Yorkshire Dales* (privately published, 1961), contains his architectural drawings of many of the smelt mills before they were damaged by vandalism. D Bick produced many books on the remains of Welsh mines, notably the series *The Old Metal Mines of mid-Wales* (The Pound House, 1974–78). M Palmer's '*The Richest in all Wales!': The Welsh Potosi or Esgair Hir and Esgair Fraith Lead and Copper Mines of Cardiganshire* (Northern Mines Research Society, 1983) has an account of the survey and partial excavation of an important lead mine. M Atkinson (ed), *Exmoor's Industrial Archaeology* (Exmoor Books, 1997), covers the mining of various minerals, particularly lead and silver.

For the archaeological remains of ore-dressing plant, see M Palmer & P A Neaverson, 'Nineteenth Century Tin and Lead dressing: a comparative study of the evidence' (*Industrial Archaeology Review* **12:1**, 1989, 20–39), and D Cranstone, 'The Archaeology of Washing Floors: Problems Potentials and Priorities' (*Industrial Archaeology Review*, **12:1**, 1989, 40–9).

See also L Willies, *MPP: Underground Metal Mines (excluding iron) Step 1 Report*, Report for English Heritage, Cranstone Consultancy, 1993, and G Chitty, *MPP: The Lead Industry Step 4 Report*, Appendix II: 'Protection of underground metal mines', Report for English Heritage, 1995.

4.8 Copper and brass production

Copper has been valued for thousands of years as an alloy: with tin as bronze and with zinc as brass. The copper ores mined were usually sulphides such as chalcopyrite which needed careful processing to be of use. Zinc was extracted from calamine and later from blende.

In the 16th century, copper was in considerable demand for armaments in the European wars of that period, since cannon were generally made from copper alloys before cast-iron barrels came into widespread use. The UK imported copper from Europe, notably Germany and Sweden, and Elizabeth I's government attempted to improve home copper production by encouraging the immigration of German miners, as well as the creation of monopoly companies, the Company of Mineral and Battery Works and the Society of Mines Royal. Many mines, particularly in Cumbria and Wales, date from that period but the monopolies were disliked by landowners and were disbanded in the late 17th century, following Parliamentary intervention.

Extraction and processing

Copper has been mined in the UK and Ireland since prehistoric times, hammer stones occasionally being found on later mining sites which demonstrate their antiquity, as on the Great Orme above Llandudno in North Wales, Ecton Hill in Staffordshire, Alderley Edge in Cheshire, and Ross Island, County Kerry, in Ireland.

The methods of winning and dressing copper ore were very similar to those for lead and so the reader is referred to the section on lead mining and dressing. The major differences were in the methods of smelting. Many mines produced both minerals, Esgair Fraith in Cardiganshire being an example, while in Devon and Cornwall, copper was found in association with tin.

Copper output in the UK was revolutionised in the mid-18th century by the discovery of vast deposits of copper in Parys Mountain on Anglesey, where in the 1780s production was greater than that of any other mine in Europe, amounting to over 3000 tons a year. The ore was first worked by means of shafts and levels, but eventually the whole mountain became a vast pit worked by open-cast methods. This was initially pumped out by means of a windmill (Fig 4.14), but a steam engine was eventually installed. The water thus extracted was rich in copper sulphate, and the copper was recovered by pumping the water into pits. Scrap iron was deposited

Figure 4.14 The devastated landscape of former copper working at Parys Mountain, Anglesey, showing the derelict windmill which was once used to pump out the workings (© Mark Sissons)

in these, to be dissolved by the copper sulphate, leaving a copper-bearing sludge in the pits which could then be processed. Similar precipitation pits can be found on other copper-dressing sites in the UK.

Cornwall is usually thought of as primarily a tin-mining area, but in fact it reached the height of its industrial development during the copper boom of the mid-19th century; many of the engine houses that can still be seen were originally built for copper mining. However, the subsequent redevelopment of both mines and dressing floors for tin ores in the later part of that century has obliterated much of the other evidence for the copper-mining period.

Copper smelting and brass production

The association of copper with sulphide ores made the smelting process more complex than that for lead smelting, and its melting point was also far higher. Generally, the ores had first to be roasted repeatedly before smelting, and fuel consumption was therefore far greater. The process was speeded up in the late 17th century by the use of the coal-fired reverberatory furnace, in which the ore was roasted for a long period before the resulting mass, or matte, was removed and broken up in advance of further roasting and smelting. This development took place first around Bristol, where copper ore was used for its extensive brass industry, but the copper smelting process was eventually centred in South Wales where coal was plentiful.

Reverberatory furnaces were long, low buildings in which the fuel and metal being smelted were kept in separate compartments, thus preventing contamination of the ore by the fuel. Heat was forced over the ore by the up-draught created by the tall chimney at one end of the building. The landscape around Swansea was dominated by these structures and the fumes they produced, but the collapse of the industry in the 20th century when richer copper deposits were being worked elsewhere in the world resulted in one of the largest areas of industrial dereliction in Europe. Much was cleared away during the Swansea Valley Project from the 1960s, but growth in interest has recently led to the excavation of the remains of some foundations of these furnaces along the banks of the River Tawe. Few remains of copper smelters survive elsewhere, but their former existence can sometimes be detected by the use of black copper slag blocks for walling, for example at Whiston in Staffordshire, where the Ecton ores were smelted, and around Hayle harbour in Cornwall, where several copper smelters were situated before the industry moved across the Bristol Channel into South Wales.

An important subsidiary of the copper industry was the manufacture of brass, particularly around Bristol. This involved the shaping of brass sheet into hollow-ware vessels, such as pans, bowls, and vats. Large water-powered hammers were used to beat the brass ingots into sheet, but these were replaced in the 18th century by water-powered rolling mills which produced brass sheets more evenly. Faster hammers shaped the sheet into hollow-ware, a process known as battery; the mills in which it was carried out were known as battery mills. The brass was malleable enough to be worked cold, but rolling and hammering could continue only for a limited period before work-hardening took place, which caused cracking, and so the partially worked brass was periodically softened by heating, or annealing it. By the late 18th century, this was being done in large furnaces heated with local coal. The brass goods were protected from damaging coal fumes by an inner sealed arch, introducing a new type of large-scale 'muffle' furnace. These were tall, tapering furnaces with arches in the front and rear through which the furnace was loaded. A long, vertical slot in the front wall accommodated a pivoted wooden beam upon which the loading door was hung. Brass production spread to Cheshire and to Flintshire, the furnaces supplying brass to the workshops of Birmingham for manufacture into the small items or 'toys', such as horse brasses, buckles, and candelabra, for which the town was famous.

Key sites

The copper mines on *Great Orme* near Llandudno enable the visitor to experience the adit mining carried out in the Bronze Age. *Sygun Mine*, in the Snowdonia National Park, has displays on processing as well as an underground tour. By contrast, *Parys Mountain* in Anglesey is a spectacularly coloured landscape where the amount of copper extracted can still be appreciated and the remains of the copper precipitation pits found. Mining trails have been developed to demonstrate the extent of mining and dressing the ores in the *Coppermines Valley*, near Coniston in Cumbria. Many of the mines in Cornwall and west Devon were begun for copper and subsequently reworked for tin, but the landscape indicates the extent of the copper boom of the mid-19th century. Cornish engineers took their technology round the world, including the important *Allihies* mines in County Cork in Ireland where a striking Cornish engine house still dominates the site.

The clearance of the Swansea Valley has meant that few remains of the reverberatory furnaces survive, but excavation has revealed some of the foundations and many of the walls in nearby *Morriston* were built of copper slag blocks. The structures for annealing and rolling brass are best seen at *Saltford Brass Mill* on the River Avon near Bath.

Further reading

There are more historical than archaeological accounts of the copper industry, but see

M B Donald, *Elizabethan Copper: the history of the Company of Mines Royal, 1568–1605* (Michael Moon, 1989); D B Barton, *A History of Copper Mining in Cornwall and Devon* (Truro, 1961); D E Bick, *The Old Copper Mines of Snowdonia* (The Pound House, 1968), and E Holland, *Coniston Copper* (Cicerone Press, 1987). J R Harris, *The Copper King: a biography of Thomas Williams of Llanidan* (Liverpool University Press, 1964), is a masterly study of the 17th- and 18th-century copper industry and the importance of Parys Mountain.

Fundamental to an understanding of the effects of copper smelting on the landscape is S Hughes' splendid *Copperopolis: landscapes of the early industrial period in Swansea* (RCAHMW, 2000). A good account of the brass industry is J Day's *Bristol Brass* (London, 1976).

See also D Cranstone, *MPP: Copper Industry Step 1 Report*, Cranstone Consultancy, 1993; J Day, *MPP: The Brass Industry: Step 1 Report*, Cranstone Consultancy, 1992; D Cranstone, *MPP: The Brass Industry: Step 3 Report*, Cranstone Consultancy, 1993; G Chitty, *MPP: The Brass Industry Step 4 Report*, Report for English Heritage, 1996.

4.9 Tin mining and processing

The ore of tin is cassiterite (tin oxide), which in the UK is found only in veins or lodes of quartz and other minerals associated with the granite mass of south-west England. Many of these lodes were washed out by water and so early miners were able to extract tin from alluvial workings which have left traces across the moorlands of Devon and Cornwall, a process known as tin-streaming. Tin was certainly exploited here in the prehistoric period and may well have had a continuous history until the closure of the last deep tin mines in the late 1990s (they may renew activity when the price of tin makes it worthwhile). By the medieval period, the importance of tin to the economy of south-west England was recognised by the imposition of Stannary Law, giving the miners certain rights and privileges but also ensuring payment of royalties to the Crown and to landowners. Later mining went deep into the hard granite rock, and so Cornish miners gained a worldwide reputation for their engineering. They were thus able to take their skills to other mining areas in, for example, Spain, Australia, and California when Cornwall's mines went into recession in the mid-19th century and later, resulting in other 'Cornish' mining landscapes elsewhere in the world. The mining area of Cornwall and West Devon was designated as a World Heritage Site in 2006 because of the excellent survival of its industrial monuments.

Cassiterite is finely disseminated through the parent rock, which therefore has to be crushed very finely to concentrate the ore. The high price of tin has meant that even small quantities have been worth extracting, with the waste material from the dressing processes being reworked time and again. This has resulted in rather different industrial archaeology on tin sites from those of lead or copper.

Extraction, dressing and smelting: key elements and plan forms

Medieval and post-medieval

The tin ore washed from the parent lodes by streams was deposited as pure tin gravel, along with other minerals reduced to the same size. The much higher

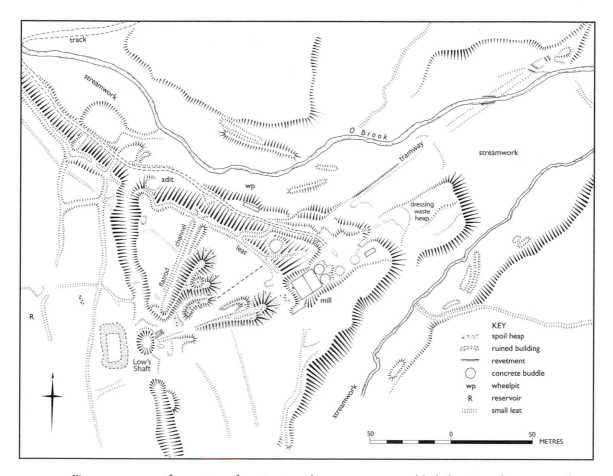

KEY

⟍⟍⟍	spoil heap
⟍⟍⟍	ruined building
⟍⟍⟍	revetment
◯	concrete buddle
wp	wheelpit
R	reservoir
⋯⋯⋯	small leat

50   0   50
METRES

Figure 4.15
Hexworthy Mine
upper dressing floor
at Hooten Wheels.
The underground
pumps were powered
by flat rods from a
remote water wheel
further down the
valley. This mill
and dressing floor,
with round concrete
buddles, was one of
the last to be built
on Dartmoor c 1905
and used electricity
to power some of the
machinery (RCHME
1:500 earthwork
survey, courtesy of
Philip Newman
© English Heritage)

specific gravity of cassiterite, about 6.8 to 7.1, enabled the tin to be separated out by the use of moving water, as in lead dressing. The terrain of south-west England enabled early miners to lead water off the streams into a network of water channels, known as streamworks, in which the tin could be concentrated and waste material washed away. The process was repeated downstream to extract as much tin as possible, and so a streamworking valley is a network of braided channels, often dotted with the ruins of stone-built huts where the miners lived while working the tin.

By the late medieval period, lode tin was being exploited as well as stream tin, and this needed crushing and refining before smelting. Tin mills were small, stone-built, rectangular structures with a wheel pit alongside. The water wheel-powered heads of stamps, from which the crushed ore, suspended in water, flowed into various buddles for refining. The worn mortar stones on which the ore was crushed beneath the stamps can provide a clue to the existence of a former tin mill.

Other small stone buildings may well be the remains of early blowing mills in which the tin was smelted. These used water-powered bellows to create the necessary heat in a small furnace to smelt the tin, which ran off into mouldstones, pieces of flat-topped granite with a rectangular hollow cut out for the molten tin, which cooled to become an ingot. These, like mortar stones, are good clues to the former existence of tin blowing mills.

Tin streaming continued long after deep mines were sunk, the streamers reworking the waste from dressing plants at the mines, so valuable was tin. By the 19th century, more sophisticated dressing machinery was available but water power continued in use because of its lower costs.

19th and 20th centuries

The intensive exploitation of Cornish minerals during the 19th and 20th centuries has left few traces of earlier workings. The tin-mining landscape designated as a World Heritage Site is mainly a 19th-century one, its most characteristic feature being the engine houses which were built for pumping and winding the mines and crushing the ore. These are dealt with in more detail in Chapter 3.5 on power sources, but many mines had pairs of engines in separate houses which pumped and wound from the same shaft. Those for pumping were usually much larger than those for winding as more powerful engines were needed, the cylinders being up to 90in (2.3m) in diameter. Winding engine houses had massive structures known as loadings in front of them which supported the winding drum and cranks, and were often situated well away from the shaft, whereas pumping engines were usually adjacent to the shaft.

Stamping engine houses, for crushing the ore, also had large stone or concrete loadings ranged in front of them to support the heads of stamps, often much longer than those near winding engine houses. Wheal Peevor, near Redruth, is a good place to compare the different types of engine houses. Most mining companies remained faithful to the Cornish engine but some adopted more elaborate engines, such as the inverted beam engine installed at Marriott's Shaft near Camborne in 1900. Compressor houses of very solid construction were built on some of the larger mines to provide the compressed air needed for driving rock drills in the mines.

Dressing floors can still be found on some sites as they were built of concrete by the second half of the 19th century. Rectangular buddles, described above for lead processing, gave way to the more sophisticated round buddles and Cornish frames which were designed to extract the much more finely disseminated black tin. What is missing from all such sites is the superstructure of wood and iron, together with the numerous wooden channels which conveyed the ore suspended in water from one end of the site to another; it is essential to study the numerous archive photographs which exist for Cornish mining to gain an idea of the complexity of tin dressing floors. In the late 19th and 20th centuries, technological transfer from the USA led to the adoption of more elaborate machinery for tin extraction, such as shaking tables and Frue Vanners, but generally only the concrete bases of these remain, apart from those in the last surviving dressing mills such as that at Geevor (see below). Only by looking at these survivals is it possible to identify many of the concrete structures which can still be found in many Cornish stream valleys.

A building found on many Cornish tin-mining sites is the calciner, designed to heat the partly dressed ore to drive off impurities such as sulphur and arsenic. The ore was heated on a slowly rotating iron plate, and the circular interior of the squat, square building helps to identify its function. The vapour passed through a flue to a chimney, but once arsenic was found to have saleable value as an insecticide, the vapour was directed though a labyrinth of flues to the chimney. Arsenic condensed on the interior of the flues and, as in the lead industry, had to be manually scraped off when the labyrinth cooled (see Fig 1.4).

The Stannary Laws which regulated the tin industry in Devon and Cornwall forced smelting to take place within the two counties, since all tin ingots had to be coined or sampled for assay before sale. Coal-fired reverberatory furnaces replaced the old blowing mills by the 19th century, but the cost of importing coal into Cornwall led eventually to the transfer of the smelting process to South Wales, particularly after the abolition of tin coinage in 1838. Smelted tin was extensively used for coating iron sheet by the second half of the 19th century, and tinplate works were often added to iron and steel strip rolling mills. These were foundry-like buildings with large numbers of chimneys, each above a hearth for the tin baths inside the building where the coating took place. Few have survived the extensive clearance around Swansea, as discussed above.

The landscape

Landowners in south-west England attracted miners to the mines from which they received royalties by allowing them to build cottages on land cleared from the moorland, resulting in the scattered settlement pattern which is characteristic of much of Cornwall. At least one Nonconformist chapel was to be found in most of the hamlets and villages, since John Wesley and other preachers had a very strong influence here. The landowners themselves, profiting from their royalties, built large houses on their estates, such as Godolphin near Helston. The terrain of Cornwall made canal building impossible, and networks of horse-drawn tramways and later small railways were developed for the import of coal and the export of metal to be smelted. The coast was generally inhospitable, and great difficulty was experienced in building and maintaining small harbours for the tin trade. The results of the long exploitation of metals can be read in much of the Cornish landscape.

Assessment of sites

- Evidence for tin streaming – braided stream channels, earthworks, stone huts, blowing mills, mouldstones and mortar stones?
- Crushing ore – evidence for water-powered stamps?
- Types of engine houses – pumping, winding or stamping?
- Classification and dressing – remains of tanks, buddles, concrete bases for shaking tables etc.
- Evidence for the extraction of arsenic – calciners, labyrinths.

- Later reworking of site and rebuilding of structures for discarded minerals?
- The human landscape – tin-workers' huts, scattered settlements, chapels, mine-owners' houses?
- Reverberatory furnaces for smelting and tinplate works?
- Transport networks and access to harbours?

Key sites

Tin-streaming sites are scattered across Dartmoor and the Dartmoor Tinworking Research Group http://www.dtrg.org.uk/ (accessed 1/03/2011) organises numerous walks and carries out archaeological work with volunteers.

East Pool pumping and winding engines, in the care of the National Trust, provide an entry point for the exploration of the Cornish Mining World Heritage Site http://www.cornish-mining.org.uk/ (accessed 1/03/2011).

Basset Mines, south-east of Camborne, is a good example of a large mine where the remains of the dressing floors and arsenic calciner survive, while nearby *Marriott's Shaft* preserves its miners' 'dry' for changing to go below ground, a compressor house, and an engine house for an unusual inverted beam engine.

The machinery used for tin dressing can be understood by visits to *King Edward Mine* near Troon http://www.kingedwardmine.co.uk/contact.html and *Geevor Tin Mine* http://www.geevor.com/ (both accessed 1/03/2011). These visits will help to interpret remains of dressing floors at, for example, *Botallack Mine* near St Just where a splendid arsenic labyrinth has been conserved. Nearby *Levant Mine* contains the only working Cornish beam engine on its original site and demonstrates the tenacity of Cornish miners in tracing lodes under the seabed http://www.nationaltrust.org.uk/main/w-levantmineandbeamengine.

Little remains of the smelting or tinplate processes in South Wales, but a small museum at *Kidwelly*, near Llanelli, preserves one of the first tinplate works and explains the processes http://www.kidwellyindustrialmuseum.co.uk/.

Further reading

Early tin working has been studied more fully in the Dartmoor area than elsewhere: see P Newman, *The Dartmoor Tin Industry: a Field Guide* (Chercombe Press, 1988), for a detailed and accessible account of the archaeology of early tin streamworks, together with his *The Field Archaeology of Dartmoor* (English Heritage, 2011). Newman also edited *Mining and Metallurgy in South-West Britain* (Peak District Mines Historical Society, 1996), a valuable collection of papers on aspects of mining from Somerset to Cornwall. See also S Gerrard, 'The medieval and early modern stamping mill' (*Industrial Archaeology Review* 12:1, 1989, 9–19). P Herring, A Sharpe, J R Smith & C Giles, *Bodmin Moor: an Archaeological Survey Vol. 2. Industrial and Post-medieval Landscapes* (English Heritage, 2008), is a detailed report on an archaeological survey covering mining, quarrying, china clay, industrial settlement and public amenities, transport and communications.

Later mining landscapes in the south-west are best approached through the various documents drawn up in connection with World Heritage status, notably *Nomination of the Cornwall and West Devon Mining Landscape for inclusion on the World Heritage List* (Cornwall County Council, 2004), which contains detailed maps and a comprehensive bibliography as well as discussion of the whole mining landscape. Cornwall was also one of the first counties to adopt Historic Landscape Characterisation, see P Herring, *Cornwall's Historic Landscape: presenting a method of historic landscape character assessment* (Cornwall County Council, 1998); this was useful in identifying whole mining landscapes rather than individual mines. S Rippon, P Claughton & C Smart, *Mining in a Medieval Landscape: the Royal Silver Mines of the Tamar Valley* (Exeter University Press, 2009), is a more recent and very detailed example of the use of Historic Landscape Characterisation for a mining landscape in south-west England.

Many books have been published on the history of both Cornish mining in general and on specific mines, such as D B Barton, *A History of Mining and Smelting in Cornwall* (Cornwall Books, revised edn 1989) and P Joseph, *Hard Graft: Botallack Mine in the Twentieth Century* (The Trevithick Society, 2010). For an early archaeological study by volunteers, see M Palmer & P A Neaverson, *The Basset Mines: their History and Archaeology* (Northern Mines Research Society, 1987), which led to their 'Nineteenth Century Tin and Lead Dressing: a comparative study of the evidence' (*Industrial Archaeology Review* **12:1**, 1989, 20–39). Since then, archaeological work has been mainly undertaken by Cornwall Archaeological Unit, which has devoted considerable attention to mining, both in field survey and building assessment: see particularly *Engine House Assessment: the Mineral Tramways Project* (1991) for a detailed study of surviving engine houses and arsenic calciners.

See also D Cranstone, *MPP: Tin Industry, Step 1 Report*, Cranstone Consultancy, 1992; A Brown, *MPP: Non-Ferrous Metals (Tin, Copper, Arsenic and Minor Metals) Industries. Part 1 The South-West Peninsula, Step 4 Report*, Report for English Heritage, 1998; A Brown, *MPP: Non-Ferrous Metals (Tin, Copper, Arsenic and Minor Metals) Industries. Part 2 England outside the South-West Peninsula, Step 4 Report*, Report for English Heritage, 1999.

4.10 The iron and steel industries

Iron and steel are the most widely used metals in the world, and the physical remains of their manufacture are common in the archaeological record from prehistoric times onwards. Iron ores occur widely in the UK, but the extraction of metal from them is complex, depending on what other minerals are present. Consequently, early iron manufacture used the purer oxide ores such as magnetite and haematite, as well as bog ore or goethite. The iron ores of the Jurassic ridge in eastern England, including limonite, could not be utilised to any great extent until ways were found of eliminating impurities such as phosphorus from the smelted metal.

Extraction and preparation

Before the 19th century, most iron ores were mined, either from bell pits or adits, although there were some deep mines, as in the Cumbrian ore field. Surface buildings such as engine houses were therefore less common than in other kinds of mining, and foundations have been obliterated. When it became possible to utilise the Jurassic ores in the second half of the 19th century, these were removed by open-cast methods. Several feet of ironstone were taken out, first by hand and later by powered excavators and draglines, and the soil then replaced, with the result that many roads and isolated farmsteads in the East Midlands now stand above the level of the surrounding countryside, an interesting example of the way in which past industrial activity can transform a landscape yet leave little trace of itself behind. The 19th-century industry was based upon an extensive network of narrow- and standard-gauge railway lines, and abandoned tracks, inclines and bridges enable former lines to be traced.

Many iron ores, particularly the carbonates and Jurassic ores, need calcining before smelting. The latter were often calcined *in situ*, large heaps being set alight beneath the quarry faces, with resultant pollution of the atmosphere. Other ores were calcined in kilns similar to lime kilns, but where large amounts of ore were extracted, as in the North York Moors, huge calcining kilns of brick were used, the remains of which stand alongside abandoned railway tracks in Rosedale.

Smelting

Both surviving and excavated structures illustrate the chronological development of furnaces for smelting iron, which was influenced by changes in sources of fuel and types of power as well as by consumer demand. Early iron smelting was carried out in bloomeries, but hand-operated bellows or natural draught did not enable molten iron to be achieved, only lumps of iron which could be forged into wrought iron, removing slag and other impurities; the former presence of these can thus sometimes be identified by slag scatters. Some bloomeries were adapted to make use of water-powered bellows, but these had largely disappeared by 1700, when charcoal-fired blast furnaces became more common. These were located near good water-power sources for driving the bellows and also near charcoal supplies, which limited their distribution mainly to hilly, forested areas such as the Lake District and the Weald of Kent and Sussex. The furnaces were solidly constructed, usually of stone, over 20ft (6m) high with arches in two or three sides for the tuyeres which took the blast into the furnace and for tapping the molten iron into a sand-filled pig bed (Fig 4.16). The fourth side was either built into a bank or had a bridge to the top to enable the furnace to be charged, or loaded. Adjacent was a wheel pit and space for bellows, a pig-bed of sand which was often covered to form a casting house, together with extensive stores for both charcoal and ore.

The introduction, firstly, of coke as a fuel and, secondly, of steam power to drive the bellows, freed the iron industry from the constraints of proximity to wood and water. Coke was also a more solid fuel than charcoal, which enabled

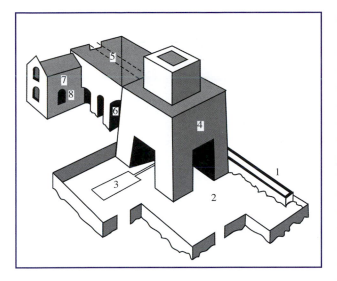

the furnaces to sustain larger charges of ore and so increase in size. Although Abraham Darby had used coke fuel in Coalbrookdale in 1709, it took the remainder of the century for coke to replace charcoal and even then some furnaces continued with charcoal as it was thought to produce purer iron; this was the case even longer in heavily forested parts of Europe such as Sweden. Iron-cased furnaces replaced stone-built ones by the mid-19th century, but the superstructures of these have largely gone although their stone- and brick-built bases do sometimes survive. Large blowing engines became part of the ironworks complex, supplying banks of furnaces rather than single ones.

The product of the blast furnace was pig iron, which could either be remelted for castings or converted into wrought iron. The former took place in foundries, the latter in forges which remained dependent on water power and charcoal, often using the same water source as the blast furnace. Wrought iron was also rolled into sheets and then passed though slitting mills to produce iron rods which could, for example, be used for making nails. In the late 18th century, the invention of the puddling furnace greatly speeded up the production of wrought iron and, since it was a coal-fired reverberatory furnace, all the components of the iron industry could now be brought together near to the coalfields.

Steel

Steel, an alloy of iron and carbon, was in demand for edge tools, weapons, and springs. By the 18th century, wrought iron was converted into blister steel in a cementation furnace, resembling a pottery kiln in shape (Fig 4.17). Wrought-iron bars were packed into fireclay chests with charcoal and heated by a coal fire, the wrought iron absorbing sufficient carbon to become steel. For better-quality steel, this product was remelted in a crucible furnace to distribute the carbon throughout the steel (Fig 4.17). Tall, rectangular chimney stacks to create the necessary draught characterise the exterior of crucible furnaces. Few of these survive, as the Bessemer process for the mass production of steel rendered them redundant, but excavations in, for example, Sheffield, centre of the steel industry, have revealed just how densely packed they were in an urban environment (see Further Reading). Water power was also often used to drive the grindstones for sharpening edge tools and cutlery, but hand- or steam-powered workshops for this purpose can be found in the densely packed tenements of Sheffield, recognisable by the distinctive remains of the grinding wheels.

Assessment of sites

- Evidence for extraction – bell pits, adits, open-casting.
- Topography – water courses, banks against which to set furnaces.
- Fuel supply – charcoal pitsteads, sledways for carriage, storage.
- Power sources – water wheel pits, bases of steam engines.
- Type of blast furnace – charcoal, coke, iron-cased.
- Ancillary buildings – fuel and ore stores, forges, rolling and slitting mills, grinding mills, puddling furnaces.
- Cementation furnaces and/or crucible furnaces denote manufacture of steel.
- Settlement – furnaces require continuous supervision.
- Transport – for fuel and ore, often from a distance; for molten metal on site.

Key sites

Cleveland Ironstone Museum at Skinningrove in north-east England maintains an ironstone mine, while the *Rutland Railway Museum* near Oakham deals with the relationship between transport and ironstone quarrying. The only deep mine remaining in the UK for ironstone is the *Florence Mine* at Egremont in Cumbria, which is open to the public. Massive calcining kilns can still be seen in *Rosedale* in the North York Moors.

There are more survivals of stone-built charcoal blast furnaces than the much later iron-cased ones, partly because of their rural setting. Good examples are at *Duddon* in the southern Lake District, *Whitecliff* in the Forest of Dean and *Bonawe* in southern Scotland, to which iron ore was sent from Cumbria in order to tap local charcoal supplies (Fig 4.16). Abraham Darby's first coke-fired furnace is a remarkable survival in *Coalbrookdale*, although now caged behind glass. Other early coke-fired furnaces are at *Morley Park* and *Moira* in Derbyshire, the latter brick-built and remarkable for its size. Later banks of furnaces can be seen at *Blaenavon* in South Wales, now a World Heritage Site, and some remains at *Blists Hill* in Ironbridge. Water-powered forges for the manufacture of edge tools survive at *Sticklepath* in Devon, *Patterson's Spade Mill* in Northern Ireland and *Wortley Top Forge* near Sheffield.

For steel manufacture, a good place to start is at the *Kelham Island Museum* in Sheffield which preserves not just machinery but also the story of the 'little mesters' who maintained Sheffield's steel industry on an almost domestic basis. Few cementation furnaces survive, the most complete being that at *Derwentcote* south-east of Newcastle, where recent excavations have uncovered a crucible steel furnace and forges. *Abbeydale Industrial Hamlet* near Sheffield preserves the only intact example of a crucible steel furnace which worked until the 1940s, together with a water-powered scythe works. Hand forges in the Black Country made nails and chains rather than edge tools: a nailer's forge and chain shop were moved to the *Avoncroft Museum* near Redditch, while at *Mushroom Green* near Dudley a chain shop still operates occasionally. Redditch itself became the centre for needle making and a water-powered needle mill forms the basis of the *Forge Mill Museum*.

Further reading

A good starting point is W K V Gale's *Ironworking* (Shire Album, 1981). More detail of both iron and steel is given in J Day & R Tylecote (eds), *The Industrial Revolution in Metals* (Institute of Metals, 1991). The landscape of iron mining and its railways in the Midlands is detailed by E Tonks in nine regional volumes, *The Ironstone Quarries of the Midlands*, all with detailed drawings, published by Runpast Publishing between 1988 and 1992. Steel making is covered in two books by K Barraclough, *Steelmaking before Bessemer*, published by The Metals Society: Vol. 1 *Blister Steel: the birth of an industry*, 1984; Vol. 2, *Crucible Steel: the growth of an industry*, 1984.

From an archaeological viewpoint, *The Iron Industry of the Weald*, by H Cleere & D W Crossley, details the introduction of the blast furnace to England, while Crossley's excavations of early blast furnaces can be found in *Post-Medieval Archaeology*: 'A 16th-century Wealden blast furnace: excavation at Panningridge' (**6**, 1972, 42–68), and, with D Ashurst, 'Excavations at Rockley Smithies, a water-powered bloomery of the 16th and 17th centuries' (**2**, 1968, 19–54). Crossley's *The Bewl Valley Ironworks, Kent, c 1330–1730* (Royal Archaeological Institute, 1975) is an account of an exemplary excavation of a forge and furnace, while M Bowden, *Furness Iron: the physical remains of the iron industry in southern Lakeland* (English Heritage, 2000), deals with the furnaces and the landscape charcoal production in Cumbria. P Riden, *A Gazetteer of Charcoal-fired Blast Furnaces in Great Britain in use since 1660* (Merton Priory Press, 1993), is very useful. *R R Angerstein's Illustrated Travel Diary, 1753–1755*, trans T Berg & P Berg (Science Museum, 2001), contains drawings and details of ironworking and furnaces since these were the particular interest of a Swedish ironmaster.

The coke-fired furnaces have been less well served, but D Cranstone's excavations at *Moira Furnace* were published as a monograph by North-West Leicestershire District Council in 1985, while C Barber's *Exploring Blaenavon Industrial Landscape World Heritage Site* (Blorenge Books, 2002) deals with an important industrial landscape. For a crucible steel furnace, see D Cranstone's *Derwentcote Steel Furnace; an industrial monument in County Durham* (Lancaster Imprints, 1997). The results of urban excavations in Sheffield are well explained and illustrated in J Symonds, *Steel City: an Archaeology of Sheffield's Industrial Past* (http://www.hrionline.ac.uk/matshef/symonds/MSsym.htm, accessed 26/07/2011), while J Symonds (ed), *The Historical Archaeology of the Sheffield Cutlery and Tableware Industry 1750–1900* (ARCUS Studies in Historical Archaeology 1, 2002), covers both the artefacts and buildings of the cutlery industry, as does a volume in the Informed Conservation series, *One Great workshop: the Buildings of the Sheffield Metal Trades* (English Heritage, 2001). Further archaeological studies of the early iron industry are included in *Science for Historic Industries* (English Heritage, 2006), while J Bayley, D Crossley & M Ponting, *Metals and Metalworking: A research framework for archaeometallurgy* (Historical Metallurgy Society Occasional Publication 6, 2008), is particularly useful on iron and steel. There are some useful articles in *Industrial Archaeology Review*, such as M D A Coulter, 'Patterson's Spade Mill, Northern Ireland' (18:1, 1995, 96–105) and I Richardson & M Watts, 'Finch's Foundry, Devon' (18:1, 1995, 83–95).

See also D Crossley, *MPP: The Iron and Steel Industries Step 1 Report*, Report for English Heritage, 1992; D Crossley & I Hedley, *MPP: Iron and Steel Industries Step 3: Introduction to Site Assessments*, Report by Lancaster University Archaeological Unit for English Heritage, 1998.

4.11 Charcoal and gunpowder production

These two industries are considered in this chapter as they both were connected with extractive industries, charcoal providing much of the fuel for the iron industry until the late 18th century and gunpowder used extensively in underground mining as well as for military purposes. Both also generally took place in woodland, although there were exceptions in the case of gunpowder production.

Charcoal production

Manufacture

Charcoal is made by the controlled slow burning of wood with a restricted air supply, driving off water and other volatile substances to leave a high-carbon fuel with about twice the heat potential of the original wood. Unlike coal, it is free from possible contaminants such as sulphur and phosphorus which could affect

Figure 4.18 Building
a charcoal clamp
(courtesy Weald and
Downland Museum,
Singleton, Sussex)

the quality of the smelted iron. Coppiced wood was stacked around a central flue on a prepared base, often beaten clay, and covered with turves to exclude the air (Fig 4.18). This clamp was then fired by dropping lighted charcoal down the flue and left to burn for several days. The clamps or pitsteads had to be carefully watched to avoid, for example, changes of wind direction which could incinerate the wood very quickly, so charcoal burners usually lived in huts nearby. By the end of the 19th century, portable metal kilns were introduced and attempts were made to conserve the volatile products of the process such as wood oils, tar, and acetic acid. Some large-scale wood distillation plants were established, such as those in the Forest of Dean, near Crinan in Scotland, and at Blackpill near Swansea but there is now little evidence of their existence. In other areas of the world stone-built kilns were used for charcoal burning, as in Death Valley in California, for example, but no evidence of such structures has been found in the UK.

Landscape context

Charcoal burning was essentially a woodland industry along with others such as bark stripping for the tanning industry, hurdle making, bobbin turning and burning bracken for potash. Woodland management had been practised since the medieval period to make the best use of the resource, with numbers of trees left to grow as standards and others felled to leave boles around which coppice poles would regenerate. It took an average of fourteen years for coppiced woodland to become sufficiently mature for industrial use, although the period was longer in Scotland. The iron industry was one of the largest consumers of charcoal, and it has been calculated that in the Forest of Dean, for example, a large iron furnace and its forge required about 13,000 acres of coppice for continuous operation. Charcoal was very friable as well as bulky and so iron furnaces and forges were often located close to this source of fuel so long as good water-power sites could be found, even if the iron ore itself had to be transported some way: the Bonawe furnace was built near Oban in Scotland to smelt Cumbrian ore using local wood resources. Consequently, the area around iron-working sites should always be scrutinised for evidence of woodland coppicing, the flat bases for the charcoal clamps and the routeways, designed for use by sleds, which transported the product to the furnaces.

Key sites

Woodlands in areas such as *Sussex*, the *Forest of Dean* and the *Lake District* show clear evidence of previous coppicing and charcoal clamps. Some museums in these areas demonstrate charcoal burning, particularly the *Dean Heritage Centre* in the Forest of Dean and the *Weald and Downland Museum* at Singleton in Sussex which uses both clamps and iron kilns. The popularity of barbecues has prompted several environmentally friendly projects making charcoal from locally sourced wood, such as one in Sussex: see http://www.charcoalburners. co.uk/charcoal.php. Other wood colliers operate in the Wey River area in south-east England: see http://www.weyriver.co.uk/theriver/industry_6_charcoal.htm (accessed 25 November 2011).

Further reading

An excellent discussion, if available, is D W Kelley, *Charcoal and Charcoal Burning* (Shire, 1986), while L Armstrong, *Wood Colliers and Charcoal Burning* (Coach House Publishing, Weald and Downland Open Air Museum, 1978), also deals with the structures of the industry. D Crossley drew attention to the landscape of charcoal preparation in his *Post-Medieval Archaeology in Britain* (Leicester University Press, 1990), as did J Marshall & M Davies-Shiel in *Industrial Archaeology of the Lake Counties* (2nd edn, Beckermet: Michael Moon, 1977). M Bowden (ed), *Furness Iron: the Physical Remains of the Iron Industry and related Woodland Industries of Furness and Southern Lakeland* (English Heritage, 2000), describes one of the few surveys undertaken of the landscape of charcoal burning and the archaeological evidence for pitsteads and charcoal-burners' huts.

Gunpowder production

Historical development

Gunpowder is a mixture of saltpetre (potassium nitrate), charcoal and sulphur, generally in the proportions of 75:15:10. Often referred to as black powder, it was developed for military purposes but began to be used for blasting in mines and then quarries from the 17th century in Britain, possibly first at the Ecton copper mines in Staffordshire, followed by mines in Somerset and Cornwall.

The early industry supplied gunpowder for military and naval use and for merchant shipping, both for trading and for ships' own defence. It was concentrated in south-east England, mainly within easy distance of London and the Thames. A water-powered industry to begin with, the earliest recorded mills were on the Thames at Rotherhithe in the 1540s and were probably tide mills. Government policy required the building of more mills from the 1560s onwards, particularly after the Armada in 1588. In the second half of the 16th century the Evelyn family established mills in Surrey at Tolworth, Wotton, and Godstone, and there were mills on the lower Lea in Essex. A powder maker is recorded at Faversham in Kent in 1573. The number of mills increased rapidly after an early monopoly was abolished by the Long Parliament in 1641.

In the 1720s, the first of a group of mills was established in north Somerset in the hinterland of the port of Bristol. These were followed by mills near Liverpool in the 1750s and, with increasing demand for gunpowder in mines and civil engineering, by developments in Westmorland and Furness from the 1760s onwards, in Scotland from the late 18th century, and in Derbyshire, Yorkshire, Devon, and Cornwall in the 19th century.

The government obtained supplies from private manufacturers until it acquired the mills at Faversham in 1759, followed by Waltham Abbey (1787) and Ballincollig in County Cork (1804). In this period it promoted a scientific approach to manufacture at the Royal Laboratory under Sir William Congreve and his son, William the younger.

Steam power was adopted by many mills in the 19th century. Some mills closed because of the requirements of new safety legislation, in particular the Explosives Act of 1875. A new class of chemical explosives and propellants, based on the nitration of glycerine, cellulose, and other organic compounds, began to replace black gunpowder for many applications; factories for their manufacture were added to some existing black powder works. Several company mergers took place in the 19th century and a major rationalisation of the industry was organised after World War I. Many factories closed but the industry continued in Kent and in the Lake District until the 1930s and in Scotland until the 1970s. Black powder manufacture ceased in Britain at ICI Ardeer in Ayrshire in 1977.

Gunpowder mills

Manufacturing sites owe their distinctive character to the large number of processes involved in combining these ingredients and finishing the product; the need, historically, for water power to drive machinery at successive stages; and improvements in safety standards from the late 18th century onwards. Sites tended to be located away from centres of population, well-wooded, linear and spacious, with process buildings at intervals along a mill stream and a system of secondary leats.

The preferred wood for charcoal to make gunpowder was alder, willow, and

Further reading

A good start can be made with G Crocker's *The Gunpowder Industry* (Shire, 1986, 2nd edn 1999, reprinted 2002). Her research notes on many gunpowder sites for the Gunpowder Mills Study Group were published in 1988 as *Gunpowder Mills Gazetteer: Black Powder Manufacturing Sites in the British Isles* (SPAB Mills Section, 1988). An electronic edition with addenda was placed with The Mills Archive 2007, www.millsarchive.com, and is invaluable. Her article with K R Fairclough on 'The introduction of edge runner incorporating mills in the British gunpowder industry' (*Industrial Archaeology Review* **20,** 1998, 23–36), looks at the technology of black powder manufacture. The important site at Chilworth in Surrey is covered by W D Cocroft & C Tuck with J Clarke & J Smith, 'The Development of the Chilworth Gunpowder Works, Surrey, from the mid-19th Century' (*Industrial Archaeology Review* **27**:2, 2005, 217–34).

For Waltham Abbey, see W Cocroft, *Dangerous Energy: the Archaeology of Gunpowder and Military Explosives Manufacture* (English Heritage, 2000) and S Foreman, 'Nitro-glycerine washing house, South Site, Waltham Abbey Royal Gunpowder Factory, Essex' (*Industrial Archaeology Review* **23**:2, 2001, 125–42), for an archaeological survey of a building which was part of the production of chemical-based explosives developed in the late 19th century.

See also I Tyler, *The Gunpowder Mills of Cumbria* (Blue Rock Publications, reprinted 2010). Useful articles include A Pye, 'An example of a non-metalliferous Dartmoor industry: the gunpowder factory at Powdermills (*Devon Archaeological Society Proceedings* **52**, 1994, 221–39, and B Buchanan & M Tucker, 'The manufacture of gunpowder; a study of the documentary and physical evidence relating to the Woolley Powder Works near Bath' (*Industrial Archaeology Review* **5**:3, 1981, 185–202). B Buchanan has also edited *Gunpowder: the history of an international technology* (Bath University Press, 1986), which includes chapters on 'The Royal Gunpowder Factory at Waltham Abbey: the field archaeology of gunpowder manufacture', by P Everson & W Cocroft (pp 377–94) and 'The Royal Gunpowder Mills, Ballincollig, County Cork', by B Kelleher (pp 359–75). For the latter, see also C Rynne, *The Industrial Archaeology of Cork City and its Environs* (Stationery Office, Dublin, 1999). For Scotland, J E Dolan & M K Oglethorpe produced *Explosives in the Service of Man: Ardeer and the Nobel Heritage* (RCAHMS, 1996).

See also S Gould, *MPP: The Gunpowder Industry: Combined Steps 1–3 Report*, Cranstone Consultancy, 1993; G Chitty, *MPP: The Gunpowder Industry: Recommendations for Protection*, Hawkshead Conservation, 1996.

CHAPTER FIVE

Manufacturing industries

5.1 Introduction

The factory as a concept, a dedicated place of mass manufacture, can be traced to the stone axe quarries or flint mines of the Neolithic. The term, however, is of more recent origin, coming from the Latin *factorium* meaning 'a place of making' and being first recorded in Britain in 1582. Used to describe the trading stations along the Indian coast during the 17th and early 18th centuries, it became increasingly applied to the new textile mills of 18th-century Britain. The phrase proto-factory, which describes the workshop dwellings (see Chapter 6.2) that were very common in the metal and textile trades during the 18th and 19th centuries, is a 20th-century term for these small-scale, multi-storey, semi-industrial structures. The developed industrial factory, however, was usually not a single building, but a group of linked structures set around a courtyard within a piece of land defined by a wall or a fence. Paul Belford, in two stimulating articles ('Monasteries of Manufacture: Questioning the origins of English Industrial Architecture', *Industrial Archaeology Review* **26**:1, 2004, 45–62; 'The World of the Workshop: Archaeologies of Urban Industrialisation', in A Green & R Leech (eds), *Cities in the World, 1500–2000*, Society for Post-Medieval Archaeology, 2006, 133–50), has recently traced the development of the industrial urban courtyard as a means of organisation and control which was central to the layout of many of these developed urban factories.

The earliest industrial factory, the textile mill, with its labour-intensive machinery, integrated process-flow, and need for distributing energy around the site, was a compact multi-storey structure. Later factories, such as the integrated engineering works, and those used for motor vehicle and aircraft manufacture, benefited from newer forms of power and building materials, which allowed a more sprawling complex, or at least much bigger sites. Many were purpose-built for the processes they contained and increasingly used architects who specialised in industrial structures.

During the 20th century the adoption of new building materials, such as steel, concrete, and plate glass, and the increasing use of electricity as a source of power, allowed more flexible designs for manufacturing buildings, many on greenfield sites associated with the by-pass, motorway, and trunk road network. The decline in the traditional 18th- and 19th-century manufacturing centres of central and northern England, southern Wales and the Greater Glasgow area led to the demolition of many factory sites. Some manufacturing buildings, particularly those associated with the textile industry, have been converted for other uses, although other industries such as engineering have few examples of successful conversion, and some industries such as glass making have little chance of finding an alternative use outside the museum.

5.2 Integrated engineering works

In the 19th century Britain could justifiably claim to be the 'workshop of the world'. Thousands of engineering works and factories across the country supplied the tools, locomotives, plant, and machinery that enabled global industrialisation. Today the classic engineering works is a thing of the past. The rise of the industry was spectacular in its speed and extent, and its contraction was equally rapid and traumatic. Its heritage is both unrepresentative and fragmentary and what does survive is problematic and vulnerable.

The Industrial Buildings Selection Guide produced in 2007 by English Heritage's Heritage Protection Department makes a convenient, if perhaps over-simplified, distinction between 'works' and 'factories' based on the emphasis within the site on manufacturing as opposed to assembly. Locomotive and agricultural engineering works might be seen to fall into the former category, motor car and aircraft factories into the latter. The difference is not a technical one but was adopted to distinguish between sites that essentially revolved around the erecting shop and those that did not. This section focuses upon integrated engineering works built around an erection shop. A discussion of car and aircraft factories can be found in 5.3 and 5.4 below.

Historical development

The engineering works in its most recognisable expression was effectively a creation of the last two decades of the 18th century and the first half of the 19th century. Prior to that, machinery was the province of the millwright, mechanic, blacksmith, and carpenter, who would come together to erect the machinery on site whether it be a water-powered installation, a steam engine or a textile mill. The rising demand for pumping engines led to a proliferation of ironworks teaming up with foundries, such as Harveys of Hayle which manufactured many of the great Cornish engines, while from 1722 the Darbys at Coalbrookdale pioneered the use of cast iron as opposed to expensive brass cylinders and became one of the major supplier of engine parts for the succeeding 50 years. Construction on site remained the norm, while the cylinders themselves were often bored by specialist firms such as John Wilkinson of Bersham.

The Boulton and Watt rotative engine was much more demanding in terms of engineering precision and by the end of the century was being wholly constructed within an engineering works environment. Indeed the firm of Boulton and Watt, whose famed Soho Manufactory on the outskirts of Birmingham initially produced steam engine parts alongside its many other products, developed, in the 1790s, an entirely new site – the Soho Foundry in Smethwick – for the manufacture of steam engines. At the same time Matthew Murray's Round Foundry in Leeds was to emerge as the foremost engine manufacturer in terms of technical quality. It was from this factory's manufacture of steam engines and its demand for precision machine tools that the integrated engineering works with its many specialist branches was to evolve.

The industry developed rapidly in the first decades of the 19th century with notable concentrations in London, Manchester, Leeds, Tyneside, the Black Country, and Cornwall. Already there were indications of specialist emphasis building on the universal manufacture of steam engines – machine tools in London and Manchester, textile machinery in Lancashire, Manchester, and Leeds. Before long, locomotive manufacture in Tyneside and Leeds and agricultural machinery in an arc in the east of England from Leeds to Bedfordshire were to produce the next leap forward in scale and mass production. By the second half of the century the main railway companies were manufacturing their own locomotives and carriages in huge integrated works at sites such as Crewe, Derby, and Swindon, while even greater numbers of locomotives were being constructed by private companies in Leeds, Glasgow, Manchester, and Tyneside. Meanwhile, agricultural engineering firms making traction and stationary engines and all sort of implements for the domestic and world market had developed in towns such as Bedford, Gainsborough, Grantham, Ipswich, Leeds, Leiston, Lincoln, and Thetford. There were of course outliers of all these industries in other locations and further specialisms such as crane building in Bath, Carlisle, and Leeds, and oil engines in Keighley.

Key elements and plan forms

All these works, however, shared a need for a common stock of specialist building components which might include: a foundry, multi-storey pattern makers and carpenters' shop, smithy, forge, boiler shop, machine shop (with its lathes, drilling and planing machines), fitting and erecting shops, and an office and drawing office.

The erecting shop dominated the integrated engineering works, with foundries and forges clustered around it. It was a high building divided into bays, producing a tall, long, brick and iron structure where new machines were assembled. A key feature of such buildings was the overhead crane; Sir John Rennie in 1816 had designed cranes of this type for the West India Docks. Although Robert Stephenson & Co in Newcastle were still using shear legs to lift large locomotive parts, the use of overhead cranes was popularised by the Great Western railway, which used them extensively at their Swindon works. The use of such steam-powered, later electric-powered, overhead cranes was the norm from the 1850s.

The general office was often combined with a drawing office in a multi-storey structure, the drawing office usually being at the top of the building where roof lights provided natural lighting. Furthermore, a glazed inspection bay could often be found overlooking the machine or erecting shop floor. The office-cum-drawing building, as the commercial and public interface of the works, usually attracted the most architectural treatment although, during the industry's golden age in the later 19th century, considerable attention was paid to the external appearance of the works. The surviving office and drawing room at Budenburg Gauge Co Ltd in Altrincham, dating from 1913–14, was a three-storey brick structure with a taller stair tower-cum-clock tower decorated with stained-glass windows. Occasionally railway companies employed architects such as Francis Thompson for the Derby Works while Stothert & Pitt in Bath provided their riverside premises with an architect-designed gracious frontage.

With the notable exceptions of some railway and agricultural engineering works and car factories, the buildings of the industry have not attracted much scholarly attention and the rapid contraction of the industry in the second half of the 20th century largely wrong-footed the preservation movement. Consequently most of the first-generation sites have gone without adequate assessment or recording as they typically occupied urban locations which were redeveloped in the 1960s and 1970s. More recently the huge second-generation sites, again without adequate assessment, were often designated brownfield sites and hence were ripe for regeneration; only a handful are adequately preserved or protected.

Key sites

There have been some notable achievements in the preservation and/or reuse of a few historic engineering sites: *Garrett's Long Shop* at Leiston; the *Charles Burrell Museum* in Thetford; *Enginuity* at Coalbrookdale, formerly the engine assembly shop for the Coalbrookdale Company; and the buildings in the care of the *Robert Stephenson Trust* in Newcastle upon Tyne. The *GWR Railway Works* at Swindon is perhaps the supreme example, with *STEAM Museum* occupying an 1846 Brunel building, English Heritage based in the General Office and the workshops of 1846 and the 1870s converted sympathetically into a vast Outlet centre. Elsewhere, however, *Marshall's* of Gainsborough has not fared so well, while under the current redevelopment scheme only the façade will survive of *Stothert & Pitt* in Bath.

Further reading

A good overview of the development of the 19th- and early 20th-century engineering works and its various products (from textile machinery and steam engines to cars and aeroplanes) is provided by Chapter 6 of M Stratton & B Trinder's *Industrial England* (Batsford & English Heritage, 1997). C Rynne's monumental *Industrial Ireland 1750–1930. An Archaeology* (The Collins Press, Cork, 2006) has a chapter on the Irish engineering and shipbuilding industries. K Falconer's article on the Swindon railway works is a classic study: 'The Rolt Memorial Lecture, 1998. Swindon – Brunel's Ugly Duckling' (*Industrial Archaeology Review* **22**:1, 2000, 3–20), together with his book with J Cattell,

Swindon: the Legacy of a Railway Town (RCHME, 1995). E Course reviewed rural and agricultural machinery engineering works in 'The Rolt Memorial Lecture, 1994. Engineering Works in Rural Areas' (*Industrial Archaeology Review* 18:2, 1996, 151–64). R Hayman's article 'The Archaeologist as Witness: Matthew Harvey's Glebeland Works, Walsall' (*Industrial Archaeology Review* 19, 1997, 61–74), is an excellent study in terms of process-flow and use of space in a working small ironworks-cum-engineering works in the early 1990s. W K V Gale's article, although more personal reminiscence, is another good study of how a small-scale iron and engineering works functioned: 'The Rolt Memorial Lecture, 1991. Researching Iron and Steel: A Personal View' (*Industrial Archaeology Review* 15:1, 1992, 21–35). There is, however, a significant gap in published material on the archaeological development of engineering works, although there are a number of grey literature survey reports on engineering works. Work along the M74 in Glasgow involved the excavation of several engineering erecting sheds and offices and this material is in press.

Several articles on the products of engineering works can be found in the pages of *Industrial Archaeology Review*, such as R Fitzgerald 'The Development of the cast iron frame in textile Mills to 1850' (**10**:2, 1988, 127–45); R Fitzgerald 'Historic Building Record and the Halifax Borough Market Doors' (**29**:1, 2007, 51–70); D R Harper & T M Day, 'The 19th-century Suspension Footbridges of Harpers of Aberdeen' (**32**:1, 2010, 21–34); R W Rennison 'The influence of William Fairbairn on Robert Stephenson's bridge designs: four bridges in north-east England' (**20**, 1998, 37–48); and the building of the iron bridge at Ironbridge in D de Haan's 'The Rolt Memorial Lecture, 2003. The Iron Bridge – New research in the Ironbridge Gorge' (**26**:1, 2004, 3–20). M Bailey and J Glithero's study of the history and conservation of the steam locomotive Rocket, *The Engineering and History of Rocket* (National Railway Museum, 2000), is, literally, an object lesson in how to read an engineering artefact archaeologically.

5.3 Motor vehicle manufacturing sites

Most British car factories in the early phase of the industry were adaptations of textile mills, engineering shops, tram car works, and other light engineering buildings. Those manufacturing sites of the prestigious marques, such as Aston Martin and Lotus, originated in second-hand buildings, and evolved by adaptation and the accretion of sheds. Their location was determined not by any drawn-out evaluation of options but simply by what was on the market. Herbert Austin hit upon Longbridge as the site for what was to become Britain's largest and longest-lasting car-making complex following an exploratory visit to a closed-down tin printing works over a weekend in November 1905, and the site survived in production until 2005. Other car makers gained workspace through taking over workshops built for the assembly of bicycles or sewing machines, and, after the two World Wars, for aircraft or armament manufacture. The evolution of the British car factory shows an overwhelming preference for adaptation.

Shadow factories

During the spring of 1936 some of the leading firms in the British motor industry were approached by the Air Ministry to see whether they were interested in participating in a scheme under which they would be acting virtually as manufacturing agents, producing components for the Bristol air-cooled aero-engine. Negotiations continued throughout 1936, with an announcement in November that Austin, Daimler, Rover, and Standard were to join the scheme to produce the aero-engine components, while Austin and Bristol would assemble the engines, and Austin and Rootes Securities Ltd, in their Humber factory at Coventry, would also manufacture airframes. The output of components and completed engines would be carefully coordinated by these firms, or, in other words, they would 'shadow' each other's production – hence the scheme's name.

Work on constructing the factory buildings commenced early in 1937, and they were ready for official inspection by that October. They were in production by the end of the year. The Midlands shadow factories administered by car firms were: Rootes, Daimler, and Standard in Coventry; Rover at Acocks Green, Birmingham; and Austin at Longbridge.

One common feature of all the shadow factories was that the complete plant and services were all housed under one roof. Their construction employed fairly conventional steel sheds, with either saw tooth or A-framed trusses, one variation being the umbrella roof whereby the main beams might be set into the apex as opposed to supporting the bottom of the truss to maximise the clear working height.

The post-World War II factory

The advent of monocoque construction, with the body and chassis integrated into a single unit, resulted in major producers making additional investment in body plants and introducing new conveyor systems, often with bridges to carry bodies from one works to another. The major reorganisation at Longbridge following the War included a 1000ft (305m) long tunnel to feed bodies to the new assembly building, CAB 1, with electronic controls overseeing the selection and feeding of bodies and parts to the assembly tracks. Completed in 1951, this was of steel-framed, top-lit construction, and with sufficient height for overhead feed lines and walkways.

In the years around 1960, several British firms had the opportunity to rethink from scratch how a car factory should best be laid out and built, as the Board of Trade forced them to implement their expansion plans in areas of high unemployment rather than by extending their works in Dagenham or Coventry. Layouts were determined through drawings arranged within precise datum lines that coincided with the location of the steel stanchions. Ford's plant at Halewood and Standard-Triumph's at Speke, both on Merseyside, Vauxhall at Ellesmere Port on the Wirral, and Rootes at Linwood near Glasgow were all laid out as discrete blocks, for the most part of one storey, that could be accumulated across the spacious sites, evolving logically to emerge as an integrated factory.

The first new building to juxtapose modern building forms and robotics was the Metro plant erected at Longbridge during 1976–77 to designs by the Harry

Weedon Partnership. An area module of 118 x 59ft (36 x 18m) was combined with a clear unobstructed height of 29ft (9m) to allow overhead conveyors and body slings to move panels to and from sub-assembly zones and from final assembly tracks to dispatch areas. A major section of the building was allocated to an automated panel store with a clear roof height of 50ft (15m). The shallow-pitched lattice roof trusses had to be made strong enough to carry 2000 tons of services and over 5000 tons of conveyors. With so much equipment being suspended from the roof, illumination had to be primarily artificial.

Key elements and plan forms

Early factories

Having produced a successful prototype, an engineer could establish production by erecting no more than an extra range of north-lit sheds, if the engines and bodies were supplied by outside firms. Greater confidence might justify a small machine shop, a sawmill, and a fronting office and showroom block to impress potential customers.

Car manufacturers, large and small, juggled with a range of options concerning their factories: whether they should adapt and extend their existing plants, or move and re-establish as demand expanded. One option that every manufacturer rejected was to rebuild from scratch on the same site, due to expense and the dislocation to manufacturing and delivery.

The workshop

Most of Britain's pioneering car manufacturers occupied modest workshops in or close to the centre of industrial towns and cities. Cars were made in Birmingham's New Street and just off Oxford Street in London. The remains of Rover's Meteor works can be found behind Coventry's main shopping precinct, while one of Triumph's early factories lies under that city's post-war cathedral. The majority of the first-generation manufacturers built their first dozen cars in a Victorian workshop. The street frontage would be little more than an archway leading through to top-lit sheds or multi-storey workshops, arranged round a cobbled courtyard.

A firm could gain extensive accommodation without the delay and expense of engaging architects and builders by moving into a redundant works. The end of the Victorian period was marked by a series of economic and technological changes: slumps in the bicycle industry or the textile trade of the Midlands, and the development of electric traction, left a number of cycle works, mills and horse tram depôts redundant. Almost any building could accommodate a modest level of car production, while a larger block or complex might be shared with other firms. Cheap accommodation allowed pioneers to experiment without being constrained by heavy bank loans.

The most notable conversion of a textile mill was to form Britain's first car factory, the Motor Mill in Coventry, occupied by Daimler from 1896. Triumph took over a seven-storey silk spinning mill. Most mills forced manufacturers to assign machining, and chassis and body manufacture to different floors. However, there were many other types of single-storey building that might be purchased cheaply, such as a tin printing works at Longbridge by Austin, a skating rink in Lowestoft by Davidson, a tramcar building works in Trafford Park by Ford, and, also in Manchester, a tram depôt in Hulme by Bell.

Once a firm progressed to a significant scale of car production, say over twelve units a week, its requirements, both in terms of space and machinery, could increase dramatically. Growth might be facilitated by the erection of further sheds as exemplified by Austin at Longbridge or Morris at Cowley, or the purchase of additional sites.

Before the advent of powered track production, the major manufacturers were likely to visualise their factories as a type of engineering works, arranged according to the workshop system. Each shop was housed in a separate building or a sectioned-off part of a larger building, and contained the machinery and equipment necessary to produce a specific component or larger assembly of components.

Steel or concrete?

Advances in American factory design became closely associated with the take up of a relatively new building material: concrete. It offered an alternative to traditional 'mill' construction, which, with its combination of timber columns and brick walls, became increasingly discredited due to the small spans that wooden beams allowed, the mediocre levels of internal natural lighting, and a susceptibility to fire. Concrete permitted spans of around 30ft (9m), dimensions that managers considered necessary to accommodate car production efficiently. Being fireproof, it brought lower insurance costs. If incorporated as a full framed system, concrete allowed deep window openings, and ceilings free of dark obstructions.

Henry P Joy of Packard in the USA believed that a factory should be handsome as well as practical. His architect Albert Kahn agreed. Stone facings, tile inserts and even gothic or Renaissance decorative elements, were also seen as a means of persuading city authorities to permit the erection of major factories in residential areas. Kahn never pursued the multi-storey form as an absolute dogma, including a single-storey machine shop with saw-tooth roof in Ford's Highland Park complex before adding a six-storey building of concrete construction with mushroom columns in 1918. He adopted single-storey, steel-framed construction for sites where it seemed more appropriate.

The Packard and Ford plants became idealised as archetypes of industrial efficiency. A number of European architects and car makers adopted the form of a multi-storey block without considering its rationale and efficiency in their own context. The closest British derivative of Highland Park was to be Arrol Johnston's model factory, built 1912–13 on farmland outside Dumfries. Based on the American designs, it was a multi-storey plant in which each floor was designed to have a distinct purpose, the overall system being that materials should proceed, if not flow, from the top floor to ground level.

Key sites

Since the 1980s many of the larger British car factories of the mid-20th century have been either extensively rebuilt (*Cowley* in Oxford) or almost completely demolished (*Longbridge* in Birmingham). However, a significant number of earlier car factories built before 1939 survive across Britain, from Glasgow to London. Amongst the earliest are the administrative buildings for the *Clement-Talbot Automobile Works* on Barlby Road in London which were built in 1902–03 and where the single-storey assembly shops were fronted by a massive classical wing; the near complete *Vulcan Motor Works* at Crossens in Southport, opened in 1909, which retains its single-storey assembly shops and classical-style administrative buildings; and Henry Ford's first European car factory in *Cork*, Ireland, designed by the architect Albert Kahn using his concrete system and completed in 1919 in a modernist style.

Further reading

A starting point for any study of motor car manufacture is P Collins & M Stratton, *British Car Factories from 1896* (Veloce, 1993). There is a brief section in M Stratton & B Trinder, *Twentieth Century Industrial Archaeology* (E & F N Spon, 2000). Good examples of regional archaeological and historical studies of the car industry are provided by A D George, 'The rise and fall of the Manchester motor industry', in D Brumhead & T Wyke, *Moving Manchester. Aspects of the History of Transport in the City and Region since 1700* (Lancashire and Cheshire Antiquarian Society, 2004, 194–209), and D Thomas & T Donnelly, *The Coventry Motor Industry: birth to renaissance* (Ashgate, 2000). The development of the car factory, particularly production methods and flow systems, is covered by P Collins & M Stratton, 'From Trestles to Tracks: the influence of the motor car manufacturing process on the design of British car factories' (*Journal of Transport History* **9**:2, 1988, 198–208).

Most other studies of the car industry concentrate on particular marques or are preoccupied with economic matters. K E Richardson, *The British Motor Industry 1896–1939* (Macmillan, 1976), provides an overview, while R Church, *Herbert Austin: The British Motor Car Industry* (Europa, 1979), is a detailed study of the role of Herbert Austin in the development of the British car industry. A large number of well-captioned illustrations of factories and machinery can be found in M E Ware, *Making of the Motor Car 1895–1930* (Hartington, 1976).

5.4 Aircraft manufacturing sites

The aircraft manufacturing sector, like car making, is often seen as one of the new hi-tech industries of the 20th century but both developed from small-scale, hand-craft production sites run by a few individuals in reused buildings across Britain. Indeed, there were strong links between early aircraft manufacture and boat building, created by the use of similar construction materials such as wooden frames, canvas, and dope, and the coastal location of some early makers. The industry was largely split between companies building engines and those assembling aircraft. Like the car industry, aircraft manufacturers developed flexible factories that had offices in a multi-storey range behind which were single-storey workshops. Unlike car manufacture, however, the use of an automated mass-production line was not possible with aircraft production and until the arrival of computer-aided design and robotic production techniques in the later 20th century most aircraft production involved hand-crafted parts applied to a static frame and the use of sub-assembly on external sites. The latter technique, of course, is still used at, for instance, the BAE site at Broughton, north-east Wales, which manufactures all the wings for Airbus planes, and has become a feature of the British aircraft industry in the early 21st century.

Historical development

The first manufacturers

The first generation of aircraft firms from *c* 1907 to 1914 were located close to major industrial centres with a skilled workforce, and also along the southern and eastern coasts of England where there was suitable access to launching sites for seaplanes. The earliest buildings used for aircraft manufacturing were adapted buildings: cotton mills, garages, skating rinks, railway arches, even airship hangars, were used for the first small-scale production of British aeroplanes. Early factories converted from previous uses include: Brownsfield Mill in Ancoats, Manchester, the basement of which was used by A V Roe from 1910 for building his triplanes; the Dick Kerr (later English Electric) electric railway and tramcar works in Preston, which was used to build seaplanes and flying boats from 1914; and the Royal Aircraft Factory at Farnborough was established in 1911 in sheds used for making airships.

Early purpose-built factories

The vast increase in production during World War I required the construction of the first purpose-built factories by the leading manufacturers, and also by the Ministry of Munitions which sponsored a series of national aircraft factories. With the growth of civil airliners and larger bombers and the introduction of the monoplane fighter a major relocation took place in the late 1920s and early 1930s to large new aerodrome sites outside city centres where new production, assembly, and flight test facilities were created. However, the need to rearm in the mid- to late 1930s encouraged the survival of older city-centre manufacturing sites.

In the mid-1930s the introduction of new materials such as steel alloys for the stressed skin and aluminium spars for the new monoplane designs, coupled with an upsurge in Air Ministry specifications and procurement after 1934, initiated a programme of new factory building and the relocation of test-flight facilities by the leading firms. Shadow factories (see above), so-styled because they duplicated existing facilities at aircraft or motor works and were intended to be brought into use in times of national emergency, were built from 1937 beyond what was thought to be the range of enemy bombers in the north Midlands, north-west England and Scotland. These new factories were divided into engine and aircraft sites and some were managed by car makers such as Austin at Longbridge, Ford at Trafford Park in Manchester, and Standard at Coventry. The layout of these factories set the design standard for the rest of the century.

Consolidation and closure

With the concentration and rationalisation in the industry from 1960 many sites were closed or substantially rebuilt, although aircraft factories could still be found in most parts of Britain: at Prestwick in Ayrshire, Belfast in Northern Ireland, Warton in Lancashire, and Woodford in Cheshire. Very few new factories were built in the later 20th century, the industry continuing its tradition of investing in a skilled workforce, new materials such as carbon-fibre, and up-to-date assembly equipment rather than investing in new purpose-built structures that might rapidly become redundant. This is indeed what happened to the new BAE assembly hall erected at Hatfield in 1987 for civil aircraft production and which became redundant in 1992 when that was moved north to Woodford near Manchester.

Key elements and plan forms

The first aircraft factories

The earliest purpose-built factories were split between an administrative-cum-design range, usually a multi-storey building with some architectural flourish, and a series of manufacturing workshops for wood working, wing assembly, and engine building. A third element was a runway for flight testing the aircraft although many factories during the 1920s and early 1930s did not have this facility, the aircraft being assembled at a nearby airfield. The production of flying boats required the addition of a concrete slipway into the sea leading from the assembly hall.

Shadow factories and later structures

By the 1930s aircraft engineers needed high and wide production spaces for assembling bigger aircraft in larger batches, and particularly civilian aircraft after 1945. The shadow factories were built from 1937 and exemplified this with the complete plant and services all under one roof. The steel-framed, top-lit, main hall was typically around a quarter of a mile long (c 400m) with a roof clearance of 40ft (12m). The roof structure was formed from lattice girders and the walls clad with asbestos sheets, and there were long sliding gable doors. The interior could be subdivided by movable screens to create offices, part stores, and an erecting shop with parallel production lines from fuselage assembly to the fitting of engines, propellers, and instruments. A plain two-storey office range fronted such complexes and there was an adjacent concrete apron and runway. The new Brabazon hangar at Bristol, erected in 1947, followed these design principles.

Key sites

Examples of surviving buildings that were converted to manufacturing use by early plane makers include *Dick Kerr's engineering works* in Preston and *Brownsfield Mill* in Manchester. The original 1916 portions of the current British Aerospace factory built by Blackburn Aviation at *Brough* in East Yorkshire are typical of purpose-built north-light factories of this period. Many had waterside locations to facilitate the launching of flying boats. Shadow factories survive across the Midlands and north of England although not normally in use for aircraft or aero-engine production: *Broughton* near Chester and *Woodford* in Cheshire are exceptions. Parts of the pre-war assembly hall at *Shorts* in Belfast, along with the original three-storey offices, survive and the assembly hall at *Prestwick* also still stands. The *museum at Brooklands* in Surrey, although usually identified for its association with motor sport, is on a site which has many buildings dating back to the earliest days of British aviation. Buildings from the *Grahame-White factory at Hendon* built in 1911 can be seen in the grounds of the RAF museum. Amongst the post-1945 buildings, the large 1947 *Brabazon hangar* at Filton near Bristol survives and is now best known as the birthplace of Concorde. There are very few sites which retain remains relating to early 20th-century airship manufacture but of these the best known are the huge hangars at *Cardington* in Bedfordshire, dating from 1917, where the airship R101 was built in 1929.

Further reading

The development of the British aircraft factory from the 1900s to the 1960s is covered in M Stratton's article 'Skating Rinks to Shadow Factories: the Evolution of British Aircraft Manufacturing Complexes' (*Industrial Archaeology Review* **18**:2, 1996, 223–44), and in D George's booklet *Aircraft Factories. Origins, Development and Archaeology* (Manchester Polytechnic Occasional paper, 1986). M Stratton & B Trinder have a chapter on cars, ships and aircraft in their *Twentieth Century Industrial Archaeology* (E & F N Spon, 2000), and they provide a general overview of the development of the 20th-century factory in chapter 3 of their *Industrial England* (Batsford & English Heritage, 1997). Individual company histories which discuss aircraft production and assembly hall layout include H Holmes, *The Story of Manchester's Aircraft Company* (Salford, 1993); J W R Taylor, *Fairey Aviation* (Tempus, 1997); and *The De Havilland Legacy* (University of Hertfordshire, Hatfield, 2010).

The Airfield Research Group has recorded a number of manufacturing sites associated with airfields (http:/www.airfieldresearchgroup.org.uk/). There are also a few developer-funded factory studies although these remain as grey literature.

5.5   The glass industry

Standing structures are comparatively rare survivals in the glass industry because, like other furnaces subject to intense heat, glass works were frequently rebuilt and many have disappeared as the huge glass cones of the late 18th and 19th centuries were fundamentally unstable. On the other hand, the glass industry, like the pottery industry, has attracted more archaeological work in the past couple of decades than most areas of industry, which has contributed extensively to our understanding of it. Not only have both rural and urban sites of production been excavated, but considerable attention has also been paid to the analysis of both artefacts and residues.

Historical development

The medieval industry was based in woodland areas such as the Weald of Surrey and Sussex, using wood as a fuel as well as obtaining some raw materials locally, notably sand and potash, derived from the ash of woodland plants such as beech, oak or even bracken. Since glass making in Britain lagged behind that of many European countries, the government encouraged the immigration of European glass makers into England in the 16th century; they greatly improved the quality of the glass produced, including window glass. The transformation of the glass industry in the 17th century to make use of coal as a fuel, with far more substantial and permanent furnaces, was, however, well in advance of what was happening in Europe where wood continued to be used – a change which also, of course, affected other industries such as iron making. The industry was relocated to areas where coal was easily obtainable such as the West Midlands, north-east England, Bristol, London and south-east Scotland, but distance from markets was also a locational factor.

Glass production in England was hampered by the Excise Act of 1745 which taxed glass according to the weight of materials used. The tax was increased twice in the late 18th century and remained in force until 1845. Ireland was free of the tax until 1825 and took advantage of this to develop glass factories in Cork, Dublin, Belfast, and Waterford, which produced some of the finest cut lead crystal glass of the period. In the 19th century, innovations in the production of flat glass made possible some of the architectural splendours of the age such as the Crystal Palace, railway station roofs, and the greenhouses of country estates. Crown and cylinder glass (see below) was replaced by cast and sheet glass, but it was not until the 1920s that continuous glass casting became possible, and then in the 1950s Pilkingtons of St Helens invented the process of floating glass onto a bath of molten tin to ensure perfect surfaces on both sides. This in its turn had a dramatic effect on the architecture of the late 20th and 21st century.

Structures

Much of what we know about glass furnaces has been derived from archaeological excavation, since the most striking features of these structures were the underground flue systems which carried heat to the crucibles or pots in which

the raw materials for glass were melted and fused together. Traditional woodland glass furnaces consisted of two low walls known as sieges, on which the crucibles were placed, with a fire trench in between. Fires were set at either end, and the heat drawn through arches at each end of the trench into the centre. The furnace was covered with a dome-shaped clay or stone roof with openings in it which both helped to provide draught and enabled the glass blower to 'gather' glass from the crucibles. The partial remains of only one arched roof survive, that of Shinrone in County Offaly, Ireland, where the interior is heavily slagged. The reader is referred to the further reading section below for information about the excavated examples, since more may well be discovered.

Coal has a shorter flame than wood, and so for the heat to reach the crucibles, a drastic redesign of the furnace was necessary. The fire was placed on an iron grate in the centre of the furnace, with the draught provided by deep, stone-lined flues. Again, excavations have demonstrated this development. Most furnaces were rectangular in shape with one or two which were circular, but it has been less easy to discover the nature of the furnace covers. Better known visually are the conical structures placed over the furnaces which date from the 18th century onwards, which, like the hovels of pottery kilns, were designed to induce greater draught for the process. These were often huge, as contemporary illustrations show that glass working took place around the furnace within them. However, they were fundamentally unstable and only four have survived intact to the present day. Other buildings would have been placed around the cone to provide space for the storage of raw materials, making the crucibles, and decorating the glass.

From the middle of the 19th century, flat glass and bottle glass was made in tanks using a process invented by Siemens which did away with the need for crucibles. The regenerative process pre-heated the gases coming into the furnaces and so saved fuel and increased heat. These furnaces were surrounded by fire-brick flues filled with bricks set on edge and arranged in such a way as to have a great number of small passages between them. The bricks absorbed most of the heat from the outgoing waste gases and returned it later to the incoming cold gases for combustion. An excavation on the Hotties site in St Helens demonstrated how these worked and parts of the site has been conserved as a component of the *World of Glass* exhibition. Parts of the site, including the Siemens, were housed in large, rectangular buildings as can still be seen at St Helens.

Artefacts

The manufacture of glass involves the fusing together of a source of silica, such as sand, crushed flint or quartz, with fluxes, for example lead oxide or alkali fluxes derived from plant ash. A great deal has been written about glass products and this section just gives a brief outline. Tablewares were blown but early vessels had a characteristic brown or greenish colour due to traces of iron oxide in the sand used. The breakthrough came in the 17th century when George Ravenscroft experimented first with crushed flint as a source of silica and then with the addition of lead oxide, giving rise to what is known as lead crystal and much more brilliant than previous forms of English glass. By the 18th century some of the best cut crystal glass was produced in Waterford in Ireland. Windows were made from crown glass, in which a bubble of glass was blown, then rotated on the end of the pontil rod near the furnace mouth. This caused the glass to open out into a circular disc which was then cut up into panes, with the characteristic 'bull's eye' at the centre where the rod had been attached; this is often now put in to simulate 'bottle glass' in windows. Another method was to swing a bubble of glass to elongate it into a cylinder, which could be cut, opened out and flattened. Later, glass could be blown into moulds for bottles and tableware. Good-quality glass was decorated by engraving, cutting or etching to create a wide variety of forms which are on display in many museums.

Glass fragments and waste found on archaeological sites can provide a great deal of information about the process, and the residues from several sites have been analysed by the English Heritage Archaeological Science team (see further reading section).

The human landscape

Glass working was a skilled process. Following the making of crucibles and melting the raw ingredients for glass, the glass makers worked in teams. The gaffer sat in the glass maker's chair, which had elongated arms suitable for

Both of these methods were ubiquitous throughout the medieval and post-medieval periods. Although apparently not subject to guild regulation (unusually, for a trade of this value), tanning in the medieval period was both subject to heavy government regulation and heavily taxed. Most communities had at least one tannery, and concentrations could be particularly dense in market towns, where tanneries were associated with their traditional source of raw hides, the cattle markets and butchers' quarters. In broad terms, tanners were tied to their sources of oak bark and hides, although some regions, such as the West Riding, are known to have actively imported hides from other areas from at least the late medieval period. The trade was essentially craft-based, with little mechanisation and an emphasis on trade secrecy and small- to medium-scale production.

This situation continued until the early 1800s. The end of the Napoleonic Wars and the reopening of trade with Europe brought about a reactive economic slump which badly affected the leather trade. To aid recovery, tanning regulations were rescinded. Increases in population and advancements in other technologies (such as the development of machinery driven by leather belts) increased the market for leather. At the same time, the growth of the British Empire both opened new markets and exponentially increased the available sources of raw materials such as hides and exotic tannages. Over the course of the 19th century, major changes in the tanning industry included an increase in the varieties of leather as different uses were devised for the material, the concentration of tanneries within cities with good transport links and an increase in the size and uniformity of workspaces, small workshops being replaced by large factories. At the same time, increased understanding of the chemistry of the process led to standardisation of both procedure and product. This was accompanied by the advent of formal technical training in the field and the introduction of professional associations and technical publications. Chrome tannage, the third most common tanning method, was perfected during the third quarter of the 19th century. This consisted of treating hides with either chromium sulphate or chromic oxide, in automated drums rather than in pits. Leather was tanned in a matter of hours rather than months, revolutionising the process and the market. Uptake of the technology in the British Isles was regrettably slow, and as a result, the British market was flooded with cheaper German, American and latterly Indian leather, and the industry had all but collapsed by the 1920s.

Key elements and plan forms

The key elements of tanneries remained common throughout the historical life of the industry, until the introduction of chrome tannage. Before the 1890s, the characteristic requirements of a tannery were: an abundance of soft water; good drainage; sufficient level space for a number of pits, which were normally set into the ground surface; close communication between the pits and the areas for leather processing before and after immersion, to minimise the handling of heavy leather 'packs'; sufficient space for hanging and drying the finished hides, in areas where ventilation and lighting could be carefully controlled; and an element of fireproofing or fire retarding within the storage and leather-oiling areas.

Although the exact form of individual tanneries varied widely depending on location, available capital, and length of active life, the above requirements resulted in a number of physical characteristics common to tanneries in general. The most pronounced of these are the consistent pairing of multi-storey buildings with adjacent open yards or (after the mid-1850s) large single-storey sheds. Although superficially resembling the buildings of a textile mill, tannery structures are distinguished by a lack of powered working in the yard or shed, open communication between the yard/shed and the ground floor of the multi-storey (often by means of an arcade), and ranks of interconnected brick-, stone- or timber-lined pits in the single-storey element. The pit yards, shed or sheds may be arranged across sloping ground to facilitate drainage. The height of the multi-storey buildings varied, but the upper floor was usually arranged as a drying loft, with characteristically broad and tall window openings often either wholly louvered or part-glazed to permit temperature and ventilation control. The chosen site usually contained a borehole or other source of free or cheap soft water (since the amounts used were too large to make the use of town water economic). Power requirements on most tanneries were low, and engine houses, where found, are usually small. Other buildings on site may include offices, laboratories, hand- or machine-workshops and storage buildings, the majority of which lack distinctive elements. The few purpose-built chrome tanneries were constructed without pit yards on compact sites, and can be difficult to identify on the basis of building morphology.

Boot and shoe manufacture

Shoe-making was carried out by cordwainers and others in most towns and many villages of Britain. It really became an industry once large amounts of footwear were needed for military purposes: Oliver Cromwell's order for 4000 pairs of shoes and 600 pairs of boots for Lord Essex's army serving in Ireland was placed with a Northamptonshire shoemaker in 1642, and the county continued to supply huge quantities of army boots for military purposes thereafter.

The boot and shoe industry remained as a home-based industry (Fig 5.3) for even longer that the hosiery industry, and the workshops in which this was carried out are discussed in Chapter 6. Production was split into separate processes, which were carried out by different operatives, usually in separate premises. Consequently, part-finished goods were transferred from one place to another by what became known as the basket-work system. Cutting the leather to avoid waste was a highly skilled process, known as 'clicking', and by the 19th century was carried out in small workshops in which the leather was also stored. These workshops can often be recognised by the small wall-mounted cranes for lifting the bales of leather into the building. Closing, or stitching the uppers together, was usually done in backyard workshops rather than factories. The

the standing buildings is H Gomersall's article, 'Departed Glory: the archaeology of the Leeds tanning industry 1780 to 1914' (*Industrial Archaeology Review* **22**:2, 2000, 133–44). Useful comparative material can be found in two articles by R S Thomson: 'The Industrial Archaeology of Leather' (*Leather* **180,** 1978, 189–93) and 'Leather manufacture in the Post-Medieval Period with special reference to Northamptonshire' (*Post-Medieval Archaeology* **15**, 1981, 161–75).

Contemporary text books can be very useful in understanding the processes encountered in standing buildings and on excavated sites and H R Procter, *A Textbook of Tanning* (New York, E & F N Spon, 1885), is a good place to start.

A very useful publication on the footwear industry is K Morrison & A Bond, *Built to Last: the Buildings of the Northamptonshire Boot and Shoe Industry* (English Heritage, 2004). See also several publications by P Mounfield on the history and buildings of the footwear industry (http://mounfieldpublications. com/northamptonshire/footwear_industry.html), accessed October 2011.

5.7   Textile manufacture

Domestic textile production appears in the archaeological record in the late prehistoric period in the British Isles, whilst the export of woollen cloth was an important part of the economy of Roman Britain. During the medieval era the woollen industry of the Cotswolds and East Anglia helped to fund a wave of parish church building in these areas, whilst the economy of the monasteries of northern Yorkshire was built on sheep rearing and wool production. Thus, for many thousands of years wool was the staple textile product of Britain. This changed rapidly with the introduction of first mechanised silk production and then mechanised cotton production during the 18th century. By the mid-19th century all four major branches of the textile industry (cotton, flax and jute, silk, and wool) had been mechanised and the textile districts, with over 10,000 mill sites, became notorious for their mill landscapes dominated by tall buildings and chimneys. The textile industry contracted enormously in the mid-20th century so that today woollen production, on a much reduced scale, is once more the dominant part of the sector. The number of working textile mills in Britain is now very small, although the production of artificial fibres in reused cotton and woollen mills became very common in the mid-20th century. A large part of the reason for the collapse of the textile industry was overseas competition; textile production, in particular cotton, was and remains a swift and cheap way of introducing industrialisation into a country and in the early 21st century the centres of global cotton manufacturing and clothes production are the rapidly industrialising economies of China and India.

The textile factory, often referred to as a mill, is one of the iconic images of industrialisation. Such sites comprised a number of buildings that might include spinning blocks, weaving sheds, finishing works, leats, and reservoirs. Textile works were primarily functional buildings, constructed and run with profit as the over-riding motive. Their form and appearance were related to the processes which they housed, and any attempt at architectural pretension was very much a secondary consideration. As a result of their commercial importance, the design of these buildings underwent a continual process of development centred on improvements in both their construction and operation.

Geographically, the industrial remains of at least one of the four branches of the textile industry can be found in most parts of the British Isles. Silk manufacture was the first of the textile industries to be mechanised, at the beginning of the 18th century, in Derby. However, the complexity of the 'throwing machines', the cost of building the mills to house this machinery, and the difficulty of securing a reliable supply of raw silk meant that mechanised silk production was never very extensive. In the 18th century the industry was largely confined to London and the north Midlands (Derbyshire, northern-eastern Staffordshire and eastern Cheshire), with outliers in south-west England at Sherborne and Tiverton, and at Paisley in Scotland. In the 19th century the industry became focused upon eastern Cheshire and West Yorkshire, although there were exceptions such as Nottingham and Sudbury in Essex.

Mechanised, water-powered cotton production was pioneered in the valleys of the north Midlands, particularly along the River Derwent, during the 1770s and 1780s, and quickly spread to most of central and northern England, London and to the Scottish Lowlands and Borders. However, the rise of the urban, steam-powered cotton factory in Manchester in the 1790s helped to concentrate the industry in north-west England. After 1800 the cotton industry came to be dominated by the steam-powered mills of Lancashire and its associated areas in north-western Derbyshire around Glossop and eastern Cheshire around Congleton and Macclesfield. There was cotton production elsewhere in Britain, most notably in the Clyde Valley around Glasgow, in West Yorkshire (in the Calder Valley, Craven District and Saddleworth areas) and in northern Cumbria around Carlisle. The Lancashire industry, however, remained dominant until its demise in the mid-20th century.

The production of woollen cloth was an important industry in Britain from the medieval period onwards, and the manufacturing processes involved changed slowly over a long period in contrast to the sudden development characteristic of the cotton industry. Many processes still took place in domestic dwellings well into the 19th century. The evidence for the factory-based woollen industry, which developed in the late 18th century, is mainly concentrated in five areas: the south-west of England from Devon to Oxfordshire, West Yorkshire, the landscape around Cork in southern Ireland, the Scottish Lowlands and Borders, and north-west and south-west Wales. Many of the mills of the woollen industry reflected local, vernacular, building traditions and were often stone-built. Their design did not on the whole reflect technological innovation, although there are some exceptions such as Stanley Mill at King's Stanley, Gloucestershire.

Linen production, from the flax plant, had been a common feature of late medieval and post-medieval Britain. Its mechanisation began with the patenting of a flax spinning machine in 1790 and mechanised weaving followed in the mid-

patented only in the 1820s. It was not widely used in other parts of the woollen industry until the 1850s.

The emergence of the integrated mill coincided with the gradual adoption of the steam-powered loom from the 1820s to the 1850s. Many mill complexes achieved integration through the addition of extra processes to an earlier specialised mill. In the cotton and flax industries this was usually through the addition of a weaving shed adjoining an existing spinning mill. In the woollen branch powered spinning and later weaving might be added to existing scribbling and fulling mills. The worsted spinning industry usually continued to separate the preparatory processes of scouring and combing from spinning and weaving.

Early integrated mills shared a common power system but increasingly a separate power system for the weaving shed was thought appropriate. Integration achieved by piecemeal addition often resulted in sprawling, irregular complexes or split sites. Purpose-built integrated mills were less common, being most frequently found in the Lancashire cotton industry of the 1830s to 1850s. On these sites the weaving sheds usually abutted one side of the spinning and warehouse range, as at Gilnow Mill in Bolton, or more rarely flanked a central spinning block and often shared a single engine house and boiler house.

The mid-19th century saw a revival in dedicated mills specialising in one production process. Thus, in Lancashire the cotton weaving mill as a separate company and site developed in the 1840s and 1850s, although the focus of the weaving industry became the mills of the Ribble valley around Blackburn, Colne, and Nelson. In other parts of Lancashire and in Yorkshire new large block spinning mills dominated the landscape. The mechanisation of the finishing processes (bleaching, dyeing, and printing) during the 1840s and 1850s also ensured that this side of the industry remained distinctive.

Architectural details

Throughout most of its functional life the textile mill subordinated style to function and form, and until the arrival of the railway such structures usually reflected the vernacular style of the locality in their use of building materials. Arkwright's first mills at Cromford showed little concession to decoration or flamboyance, although 18th-century silk mills showed some limited classical influences with the use of shallow projecting central bays topped by a clock pediment, as at the now lost Old Mill in Congleton built in 1753 or Frosts Mill from 1785 in Macclesfield. Arkwright's Masson Mill from 1783 shows a similar classical influence allied to the use of Palladian features such as Venetian and semi-circular windows arranged in a regular pattern beneath a bell cupola. This appears to have set the pattern of mill design for a generation, and mills as far apart as New Lanark on the Clyde, Brownsfield Mill in Manchester, and Stanley Mills near Stroud all used these features.

The early 19th century saw the spread of steam-powered mills and a growing emphasis by mill builders and engineers on the embellishment of mill offices and stair towers of the spinning block, usually in a classical style. In the mid-

Figure 5.7 Coppull Ring Mill, Chorley, Lancashire, a Grade II building, is an outstanding example of an early 20th-century steam-powered spinning mill. Built in 1906 for the Coppull Spinning Co Ltd, it was designed by the mill architects Stott & Sons. The terracotta decoration is typical of mill building design from the early 20th century. It is steel-framed with concrete floors and has projecting engine and boiler houses (© Michael Nevell)

19th century specialist mill architects and builders, such as David Bellhouse of Manchester, began to emerge in the manufacturing towns. Many of these architects promoted classical or Renaissance, Italianate, styles, such as those which adorned the mill colony of Saltaire, West Yorkshire, designed by the architectural practice of Lockwood and Mawson and built between 1853 and 1876. These designs included tower staircases topped by cupolas and loggias, pilaster corner columns, and detached chimneys such as the 310ft (94m) campanile chimney at India Mill in Darwen (1859–77) and the 249ft (76m) campanile chimney at Manningham Mills in West Yorkshire (1871–73). In Dundee, the vast jute mill of Camperdown boasted an ornate polychrome brick campanile chimney 282ft (86m) high, designed by local architect James McLaren. By the end of the 19th century many northern architectural practices were specialising in mill design, such as Bradshaw & Gas in Lancashire, Horsfall & Williams in Yorkshire, and Stott & Sons in Oldham.

The introduction of new building materials in the late 19th century, such as concrete, steel, and terracotta (see below), freed architects to concentrate on even more elaborate exteriors (Fig 5.7). The first use of concrete on brick arches in a British factory was at No. 3 Mill for George Knowles & Son Ltd of Bolton. Designed by George Woodhouse, the exterior used so much glass it was known locally as the 'The Glass Factory' as two sides consisted entirely of glass held in place by light iron pillars. This external design was, however, exceptional, and in most cases the exterior treatment of textile mills remained conservative. The use of Renaissance and classical traditions remained strong in both the cotton and woollen branches of the industries down to the end of large-scale mill building in the late 1920s, with little sign of any shift towards the late Victorian gothic style or the modernist styles of the 1920s. The period from the 1880s to the 1920s saw

wholly iron-framed building. Each floor had three ranks of cruciform cast-iron columns supporting iron cross-beams, whilst the spaces between were spanned by brick arches. This mill set the pattern for many of the fireproof mills of the early 19th century. Thus, William Strutt's correspondence with Charles Bage led to a similar construction being adopted for his North Mill in Belper in 1803–04, replacing the original mills on the site which had burnt down; further examples could be found in other textile regions. The Salford twist mill (now demolished) was probably the earliest such cotton mill in the North-West, whilst one of the earliest in the South-West was the woollen spinning block at Stanley Mills of 1812–13 which used cast iron extensively in its fireproof construction (Fig 5.10). The development of mill fireproofing covered much of the first half of the 19th century and was led by, amongst others, the mill engineer William Fairbairn who worked with the scientist Eaton Hodgkinson to perfect a distinctive brick-arched system supported by parabolic cast-iron beams on circular-section cast-iron columns. Even so, fireproofing was slow to spread amongst textile mills before 1850 and as late as 1853 when the first mills at Saltaire were opened their cast-iron structure was described by contemporaries as best practice, rather than the usual form.

The use of steam power in mills led to the addition of distinctive engine houses, while the development of rope driving from the 1860s allowed for more efficient transmission over longer distances from larger steam engines and so even bigger mills (see Chapter 3.5). Since these engines required three or four boilers, the mills featured chimneys typically around 220ft (c 67m) high. In Lancashire, these usually carried the name of the mill or in some cases an appropriate symbol, such as Anchor Mill in Oldham, and Swan Lane Mills in Bolton. The introduction in the late 19th century of steel girders and concrete, while retaining the cast-iron columns, allowed wider spinning mills to be built. Mills built during the Edwardian period were very large, housing in excess of 100,000 spindles, and typically 140ft (c 42m) in width and 300ft (c 91m) in length. Sprinkler systems for firefighting were now

Figure 5.10 The elegant cast-iron frame of Stanley Mill, King's Stanley, Gloucestershire, dating from 1813. Note the circular apertures for the power transmission from the water wheel (© Marilyn Palmer)

provided, the header tank being installed in a water tower over the staircase, which was used to form an architectural feature, often carrying the name of the mill.

There was experimentation in the late 19th and early 20th century with single-storey spinning sheds, inspired by the development of the weaving mill (see below), but the multi-storey spinning block remained the usual form down to the end of the cotton, flax, and silk industries. The last traditional cotton spinning mill to be built in Lancashire is considered to have been Elk Mill, Oldham, built 1925–28, and demolished 1999. This was a multi-storey mill powered by a horizontal steam engine with a rope-race. Mills for spinning woollen and worsted yarn were never quite as large as cotton mills and remained more conservative in construction. There were numerous specialised branches in the woollen trades, which may have been one reason why mills remained somewhat smaller than in the cotton branch. However, the building of traditionally designed flax, silk, and wool spinning mills all finished in the mid-20th century.

Weaving mills

Although many early power looms were installed in multi-storey mills, the weight and reciprocating action of the cast-iron and wooden looms made it normal practice to install power looms in single-storey sheds. These had north-light roofs, saw-tooth roofs with glazing facing as close as possible to north (Fig 5.11). This gave a good light but excluded direct sunlight. Such sheds were built from the late 1820s in the cotton, flax and jute industries and in the woollen industry from the 1830s. By the mid-19th century separate weaving mill firms were being founded across the cotton and woollen sectors, although the biggest concentration was to be found in the cotton weaving firms of north-east Lancashire in the

Figure 5.11 Weaving sheds along the Leeds and Liverpool Canal at Burnley, Lancashire. Note the downpipes from the drainage gutters which indicate the presence of a north-light roof behind the plain façade (© Marilyn Palmer)

Figure 5.12 Interior of weaving shed, Queen Street Mill, Harle Syke, Burnley. Built in 1894, it closed in 1982 and is now maintained by Lancashire Museums as the world's only surviving steam-driven weaving shed (© Marilyn Palmer)

Ribble Valley. Up to about 1880, north-light roofs were built with timber frames supported by cast-iron columns; thereafter, iron-framed roofs were developed. Fireproofing seems never to have been a problem in weaving sheds themselves but warehouse and preparation blocks were susceptible to fires, and consequently a few fireproof examples are known and sprinkler systems were sometimes fitted.

Weaving mill engines underwent similar technical developments to those seen in the spinning sector, moving from beam engines to horizontal engines, and from gear driving to rope driving. Weaving mill engines were smaller than spinning mill engines, the largest being of the order of 1000hp, which required two boilers, whilst only a single boiler was needed at smaller mills. Chimneys were typically 120ft (c 36m) to 150ft (45m) high and were often ornamented in a similar fashion to those of the spinning mills.

Over time, weaving mills increased in size to accommodate more looms (Fig 5.12). During the Edwardian era weaving mills of up to 2000 looms were being built in the Pendle area of Lancashire. Elsewhere in Britain weaving mills tended to be smaller, with very few exceeding 1000 looms. The last weaving mills were built after World War I and only a handful are still weaving. Other survivors have been put to a variety of commercial and industrial uses, but weaving sheds have not generally been seen as suitable for conversion to residential use.

Finishing sites

The finishing of yarn and cloth through bleaching, dyeing, and printing was common throughout the medieval and post-medieval periods but the growing output of mechanised textile production led to a bottleneck at the finishing stage of production until two technological changes emerged to speed up the process. The first was the introduction of chemical bleaching and the second the application of steam power to the bleaching, dyeing, and printing processes.

Previously linen and sometimes cotton cloth had been spread out in the sunlight for bleaching, and huge bleachfields which can be identified from map evidence were routinely located close to textile mills, often guarded by watchmen to prevent theft. Chlorine bleaching was first perfected in 1785 by the French chemist Berthollet, who demonstrated that a solution made by passing chlorine through potash had a very strong bleaching action. This process reduced the time taken to bleach cloth from four or five months to days and allowed the process to be moved under cover. In 1788 a Manchester chemist, Thomas Henry, exhibited a yard of cloth bleached in the 'new way' to a meeting of textile finishers and merchants in Manchester, already the regional centre of the textile finishing trade. This helped to popularise the process in the area, and further encouragement for its use was given in 1799 when Charles Tennant introduced chlorine-based bleaching powder. Traditionally the cloth was treated in bundles by hand, but in 1828 David Bentley invented a washing machine that used lengths of cloth pieced or sewn together to form a near continuous process. However, it was not until 1845 that John Brooks, of the Sunnyside Print Works in Crawshawbooth, first used steam power to carry the ropes of cloth through all the stages of the bleaching process. This continuous process used a pulley system, and the cloth ropes were pulled through the walls separating the various bleaching and dyeing rooms via glazed bricks with large holes in them, known as pot eyes. As the 19th century progressed the separate processes of bleaching and dyeing were usually combined on a single site. In the late 19th century this continuous process was supplemented by the use of high-pressure kiers (large vats) for batch processing and, in the 20th century, were replaced by long multi-process linear continuous process machines that could be used for bleaching and dyeing.

The mechanised bleach and dye works were characterised by a central core of buildings (including bleaching and dyeing crofts, multi-storey warehouses and offices, and stables), flanked by artificial reservoirs and a complex leat system which exploited a local river. It was the latter two elements which had the greatest impact on their surrounds. Some of the largest bleach and dye works in Lancashire and Yorkshire (where most of this industry was based in the 19th and 20th centuries) covered tens of hectares with their reservoirs and leat systems and led to a fundamental reworking of their immediate landscape.

Linen usually underwent a further process called 'beetling', in which the cloth was pounded by heavy wooden hammers mounted on a cylinder, often driven by water power in Northern Ireland, and later by steam power. This gave the linen cloth its hard, shiny appearance, which was then finished off by 'calendering', or passing the cloth between cylinders. The latter process was frequently undertaken by the bleachworks although specialist calendering mills were built. Linoleum and floorcloth factories are characterised by the great height of the drying stoves in which loops of linoleum are cured, after linseed oil and cork is pressed into jute cloth.

The use of fast colour dyes in hand block printing was first introduced into Europe in imitation of Indian fabrics around 1670 and the first English print works to use this method was founded on the River Lea at West Ham in East London in 1676. This early process initially used engraved wooden blocks up to 12in (305mm) square, but from the mid-18th century copper plates from 1ft to 1yd (305–914mm) square became very popular because of the ability to create more finely detailed designs. Both printing processes involved stretching the fabric across a table, the blocks being applied by hand using pins as guides. A print works would normally have a number of tables in one or more rooms, and there was usually a print carriage, or small trolley on rails, that ran parallel to the blocking tables, which carried the dyes for refreshing the blocks or plates. This early printing industry remained centred on London until the 1780s, with a notable concentration in the Wandle Valley.

The introduction of cylinder printing coincided with the shift of the calico printing industry from London to southern Lancashire and Manchester. The earliest experiments in the use of wooden hand block printing in the county took place during the 1760s at the Mosney Works in Walton-le-Dale, at Bamber Bridge, and at Brookside in Oswaldtwistle by Robert Peel. The industry did not take off, however, until the later 1780s, when many Lancashire printers led by the Manchester merchants started to adopt cylinder printing. By the early 19th century cylinder printing of linen, silk and wool had also been developed, allowing the mechanised printing industry to spread into those areas of Britain with these industries.

Although initially water power was used to run the cylinder rollers, steam engines rapidly took over this role early in the 19th century. Steam engines were also used to power the new steam fixing kiers, washing machines, heated drying rooms, and calenders which were needed to finish the printing process and to cope with the increased through-put of printed cloth. Cylinder printing remained the normal means of production in the cotton and woollen industries down to the mid-20th century, and as with bleaching and dyeing, the woollen printing industry became concentrated in Yorkshire and the cotton printing industry in the Lancashire area.

Textile print works from the 19th and early 20th centuries were usually sprawling single-storey complexes, associated with a series of leats and reservoirs, in valley or upland locations. Multiple chimneys and boiler houses tended to dominate these sites and the only architectural embellishments were to be found on the main offices.

Key sites

Despite the decline of the industry in the mid- to late 20th century, and the demolition of hundreds of mill sites, standing textile buildings remain common in south-west England, north-west England, West Yorkshire and the Scottish Borders, and scattered examples, sometimes grouped in towns, sometimes in rural river valleys or standing in splendid isolation, can be found across the rest of the British Isles. In Northern Ireland, small scutching mills do survive in rural areas, and a beetling mill at *Wellbrook*, Cookstown, County Tyrone, is preserved by the National Trust. In England more than 200 mill buildings are listed although many other fine examples are not. A few are now preserved as museums with working machinery: these include the *Cambrian Mills* at Drefach Felindre in Carmarthenshire in Wales, now designated the *National Woollen Museum*; *Helmshore Mills* in Lancashire, with intact fulling stocks; *Coldharbour Mill*, Uffculme, Devon, which demonstrates worsted combing and spinning by both water and steam power; *Quarry Bank Mill*, Styal, Cheshire, a cotton mill owned by the National Trust; *Queen Street Mill*, Burnley, Lancashire, one of the few places where the scale of powered weaving can be appreciated; *Stanley Mills* on the River Tay near Perth, run by Historic Scotland (see also Chapter 1.4); and *Stott Park Bobbin Mill* in Cumbria, owned by English Heritage. In Dundee in Scotland, the Verdant Works, run by the Dundee Heritage Trust, tells the story of jute manufacture in the locality. Others have been given World Heritage Site status (*The Derwent Valley Mills*, *New Lanark*, and *Saltaire*).

During the 20th century most archaeological research on the textile mill was concentrated on the upstanding remains. Since 2000, however, there has been an upsurge of interest in the excavation of such sites. The redevelopment of brownfield

Figure 5.13 Dunkirk Mill, Nailsworth, Gloucestershire. The earliest building in this complex was water powered and dates from 1798. The elegant chimney was built for a steam engine added about 1820 while the sections on the right were unpowered loomshops built in the 1820s. The complex has now been converted to residential use but includes a small museum run by the Stroudwater Textile Trust (© Marilyn Palmer)

sites has led to the targeted excavation of dozens of mill sites, mostly in north-west England, but excavated examples are known from Glasgow and London. Most of this work has been done ahead of redevelopment and consequently much remains to be published. The existing published material covers work in the Greater Manchester area, including the cotton spinning mill complex of *A & G Murray* in Ancoats, Manchester, which was surveyed and the boiler and engine houses excavated as part of the restoration of the site; the excavation of the wheel and engine houses of the 19th- and early 20th-century *Portwood Mills* site in Stockport; and the excavation of a large part of one of the bleachcrofts at *Wallsuches Bleach Works* in Horwich near Bolton. This work demonstrates the kind of structures likely to be encountered on such sites (building foundations, drains, pits and vat bases, engine beds, boiler foundations, machine bases, restraining rods, flues, chimney bases, pipe works, and even remains of the steam engines and water wheels). Understanding the development of different types of process machinery and power features such as engine houses, boiler houses, and wheel pits, is a way of revealing the technological history of a textile site where there are no standing remains.

The rural location of many mills, especially in the East Midlands and south-west England has made them prime locations for housing conversion, such as *Maythorne Silk Mill* near Southwell, *Bliss' Tweed Mills* near Chipping Norton in Oxfordshire, *Dunkirk Mill* and *Stanley Mills* in Gloucestershire, all now converted into flats (Fig 5.13). Mills in the urban textile towns of northern England and central Scotland have presented more of a challenge: a continuing industrial use is difficult because of the changes in methods of transport and the lack of car-parking space. However, Netherdale Mill in Galashiels has found an appropriate reuse as the School of Textiles and Design of Heriot-Watt University, and the massive former jute mill in Dundee, Tay Mills, houses students from Dundee University. The growing demand for urban apartments has saved some of them, notably *Murray's Mills* in Manchester where the canalside location is marketed as an asset. Ironically, the very importance of the Derwent Valley Mills and their inclusion in a World Heritage Site has made reuse more difficult. This has been achieved successfully at *Belper North Mill*, where some commercial use is combined with a Visitor Centre and small museum. *Cromford Mill* has proved more difficult, despite the extensive excavations that have taken place in the interior courtyard to ascertain the original water courses, but the interpretation of that major site is moving forward. In contrast, the World Heritage Status of the cotton mill colonies at *New Lanark* in the upper Clyde Valley and *Saltaire* in Yorkshire came after most of the conservation and restoration work had been completed at these sites, and has been an aid to the marketing of the complexes.

Further reading

Any study of the archaeology of the textile mill in Britain should begin with the three pioneering studies of the 1990s: C Giles & I Goodall, *Yorkshire Textile Mills: Buildings of the West Yorkshire Textile Industry 1770–1930* (HMSO, 1992); M Williams with D A Farnie, *Cotton Mills in Greater Manchester* (Carnegie, 1992); and A Calladine & J Fricker, *East Cheshire Textile Mills* (HMSO, 1993). These three volumes provide the foundation for the understanding of the development of the processes in the standing buildings of the cotton, linen, silk, and woollen branches of the textile industry. E Jones' *Industrial Architecture in Britain 1750–1939* (Batsford, 1985) remains the best introduction to the influence of the architect on industrial building design and has several chapters that deal with textile mill design, although P Belford's article 'Monasteries of Manufacture: Questioning the origins of English Industrial Architecture' (*Industrial Archaeology Review* **26**:1, 2004, 45–62), provides more of a social archaeology perspective on mill design. Since 1990 an increasing amount of developer-funded planning archaeology has been focused on the excavation of the remains of the textile industry. M Fletcher, 'Old Mill, Congleton, Cheshire – Brindley's Grand Design' (*Industrial Archaeology Review* **30**:1, 2008, 49–70), and J Milln, 'Power Development at the Northern End of Quarry Bank Mill, Styal, Cheshire' (*Industrial Archaeology Review* **18**:1, 1995, 8–28), show the potential of targeted excavations on the power systems of a textile mill. However, most of this material lacks any synthetic overview and remains unpublished as grey literature, such as the important study of Manchester's first cotton mill, the 1780s' Arkwright's Mill, undertaken by TV's *Time Team* in 2005, although this is available as a pdf from the Wessex Archaeology website, http://www.wessexarch.co.uk/reports/59471/arkwrights-mill.

Many more developer-funded evaluations can be downloaded from the ADS website archive. A useful introduction to the importance of textile mill excavation is provided by M Nevell, 'Excavating the Cotton Mill. Towards a Research Framework for the Below-Ground Remains of the Textile Industry', in P Belford, M Palmer & R White, *Footprints of Industry. Papers from the 300th anniversary* conference at Coalbrookdale, 3–7 June 2009 (BAR British Series **523**, 2010, 153–68). A summary of the kind of archaeological deposits that can be encountered on textile sites is given in D Dungworth & S Paynter, *Science for Historic Industries; guidelines for the investigation of 17th- to 19th-century industries* http://www.helm. org.uk/upload/pdf/Science-Historic-Industries.pdf (English Heritage, 2006).

Industrial Archaeology Review is a good source of individual and methodological case studies, containing over 30 articles on the textile industry, including two special textile mill editions: *Industrial Archaeology Review* **10**:2 (1988) and **16**:1 (1993). Amongst the highlights in these two volumes are A Calladine, 'Lombe's Mill: an exercise in reconstruction' (**16**:1, 82 –99); R S Fitzgerald, 'The Development of the Cast Iron Frame in Textile Mills to 1850' (**10**:2, 127–45); and C Giles, 'Housing the Loom, 1790–1850: a study of industrial building and mechanisation in a transitional period' (**16**:1, 27–37). Recent work at Stanley Mills in Scotland is presented in an exemplary volume by M Cressey & R Fitzgerald, *Force and Fabric: Archaeological Investigations at Stanley Mills* (Archaeology Report No. 5, Historic Scotland, 2011).

Since the three classic volumes published in the early 1990s there have been further significant regional archaeological studies that include the archaeology of textile industry such as the Derwent Valley Mills World Heritage Site Partnership, *The Derwent Valley Mills and their Communities* (2001); M Palmer & P A Neaverson, *The Textile Industry of South-west England: a Social Archaeology* (Tempus, 2005); D Gwyn, *Gwynedd: Inheriting a Revolution. The Archaeology of Industrialisation in North West Wales* (Phillimore, 2006), chapter 4; C Rynne, *Industrial Ireland 1750–1930. An Archaeology* (The Collins Press, Cork, 2006), chapter 8; and S Nisbet, *The Rise of the Cotton Factory in Eighteenth-century Renfrewshire* (BAR British Series **464**, Archaeopress, 2008).

Noteworthy case studies of groups of mills or individual sites include: A Calladine & J Fricker, 'Pickford Street: A Study of Macclesfield Textile Mills' (*Industrial Archaeology Review* **10**:2, 1988, 146–61); R N Holden, 'The End of an Era: Elk Mill 1926–1999' (*Industrial Archaeology Review* **26**:2, 2004, 113–27); A Menuge, 'The Cotton Mills of the Derbyshire Derwent and its tributaries' (*Industrial Archaeology Review* **26**:1, 1993, 38–61): I Miller & C Wild, *A & G Murray and the Cotton Mills of Ancoats* (Oxford Archaeology North, 2007), which combines excavation, historic building survey and documentary analysis to form a textbook holistic study of this nationally important urban cotton mill complex; and M Williams, *Bridport and West Bay. The buildings of the flax and hemp industry* (English Heritage, 2006). A useful study of adaptive reuse is *Northern Lights, Finding a Future for the Weaving Sheds of Pennine Lancashire* (Lancashire County Council in conjunction with English Heritage and the Heritage Trust for the North West, 2011). The lesser textile industries of felt hat making and jute production have been less well studied but two useful archaeological introductions are: M Nevell with B Grimsditch & I Hradil, *Denton and the Archaeology of the Felt Hatting industry* (The Archaeology of Tameside 7, Tameside MBC and the University of Manchester Archaeological Unit, 2007), and M Watson, 'Jute Manufacturing: A Study of Camperdown Works, Dundee' (*Industrial Archaeology Review* **10**:2, 1988, 175–92) and his *Jute and Flax Mills in*

Dundee (Hutton Press, 1990). Historic Scotland has carried out a re-survey of listed buildings in the Scottish Borders mill towns, published as part of the *The Scottish Burgh Survey* in partnership with the CBA between 2006 and 2010: see especially M Rorke, D Gallagher, C McKean, E P Dennison, G Ewart, *Historic Galashiels* (2011). *Historic Dunfermline* was published separately by Dunfermline Burgh Survey Community Project (2007) while *Hawick and its place among the Borders Mill Towns* is available as a free download from Historic Scotland – see http://www.historic-scotland.gov.uk/hawick-burgh-publication.pdf

The development and identification of textile machinery, and its context within the various branches and buildings, is covered in a fine series of booklets written by experts on the subject and published by Shire Publications Ltd. A Benson provides a very good overview in *Textile Machines* (1983). Machinery for the cotton industry is covered by Chris Aspin in *The Cotton Industry* (1981); flax is covered by P Baines in *Flax and Linen* (1985); S Bush writes about *The Silk Industry* (2nd edn 2000); and C Aspin covers *The Woollen Industry* (1982). Finally, two volumes deal with specific parts of the textile process: A Benson & N Warburton, *Looms and Weaving* (1995) and H Clark, *Textile Printing* (1985).

Studies placing the textile mill in its landscape, social and technological context include: B Cooper, The Transformation of a Valley: the Derbyshire Derwent (Heinemann, 1983); S D Chapman, 'The Arkwright Mills – Colquhoun's Census of 1788 and the Archaeological Evidence' (*Industrial Archaeology Review* 6:1, 1981–82, 5–27); R N Holden, *Stott & Sons: Architects of the Lancashire Cotton Mill* (Carnegie, 1998); R N Holden 'Water Supplies for Steam-powered Textile Mills' (*Industrial Archaeology Review* 21:1, 1999, 41–52); R N Holden, 'Lancashire Cotton Mills and Power', in A Horning & M Palmer (eds), *Crossing Paths or Sharing Tracks? Future Directions in the archaeological study of post-1550 Britain and Ireland* (Boydell & Brewer, 2009, 261–72); I Mellor, 'Space, Society and the Textile Mill', in D Gwyn & M Palmer (eds), *Understanding the Workplace. A Research Framework for Industrial Archaeology* (*Industrial Archaeology Review* 27:1, 2005, 49–56); M Nevell, 'The Archaeology of Industrialisation and the Textile Industry: the Example of Manchester and the South-western Pennine Uplands During the 18th Century, Part 1' (*Industrial Archaeology Review* 30:1, 2008, 33–48) and Part 2 (*Industrial Archaeology Review* 30:2, 2008, 97–100); and M E Rose with K Falconer & J Holder, *Ancoats: Cradle of Industrialisation* (English Heritage, 2011).

5.8 The hosiery and lace industries

The East Midlands, particularly Leicestershire, were known for the quality of the wool produced by local sheep but the area never developed a large weaving industry like East Anglia or the south-west of England. The origins of its hosiery industry lie in domestic hand knitting which dominated the trade until the end of the 17th century, well after the invention of the stocking frame. Most hand knitting took place in the 'open' parishes not subject to manorial control, where the supply of labour outstripped the level of agricultural work, and the poor supplemented their wages by knitting hose.

In addition to the invention of the stocking frame, what prompted this growth in hand knitting was the transition in men's fashion during the 16th century from long robes to doublet and hose, putting the legs on display. Aristocratic stockings were knitted of silk, but knitted worsted and later cotton stockings also became popular. It is generally accepted that William Lee of Calverton near Nottingham patented the stocking frame in 1589. The machine was undoubtedly one of the major textile inventions,

Figure 5.14 A German postcard showing a family at work on a glove frame *c* 1890. The man on the right is working the glove frame, while the women are engaged in finishing the gloves

nearly two centuries before equivalent developments in mechanised spinning or weaving. The early frames were used in London and then in France, centres of the fashion trade, and there is little evidence for the existence of stocking frames in the East Midlands before the second half of the 17th century. The adoption of the frame was faster in Nottingham than Leicester, probably because both Nottingham and Derby concentrated on the production of silk stockings, whereas Leicester continued with the hand knitting of worsted stockings before the frame was adapted to cope with worsted yarn. By the time of the Framework Knitters' Report, a government enquiry into the poverty of the stocking knitters in 1844, 90% of the hosiery industry was located in the East Midlands. Nottinghamshire specialised in cotton stockings, Leicestershire in worsted (the largest sector) and Derbyshire in silk, with Nottingham following on behind. At that time there were nearly 4000 silk hosiery frames within reach of Derby, Nottingham, and Belper, the main putting-out centres. In 1847, nearly 6000 people were employed in the silk factories of Derbyshire and Nottinghamshire, 13.7% of the total in England.

Hose were knitted flat on the stocking frame, being shaped to fit the leg, and then seamed up the back by hand. Consequently, the early hosiery industry was very much a family concern, the men using the frame, the women seaming the stockings, and the children winding bobbins for the frame. By the end of the 18th century, the frame had been adapted to knit gloves (Fig 5.14), produce ribbed fabric, turn off three or four stocking pieces at once – in fact, it is said that by 1800 it could produce 40 distinct types of fabric. One of the most important developments was the invention of the thread carrier which saved the knitter laying the thread across the needles by hand, and so enabled wider pieces of fabric to be made. This wide frame was the genesis of the East Midlands knitwear industry, enabling knitted fabric to be made which could be turned into combinations, shirts and so on, thereby greatly increasing the versatility of the frame. Although resisted at first as the fabric could also be cut into stockings, which were cheaper, although poorer quality than those produced on the narrow frame, wide frames were to prove the salvation of the Leicester industry once men's fashion changed in the early 19th century and long hose were no longer required, merely socks to go with long trousers.

Historical development

By the late 18th century, the yarn for hosiery was usually being spun in factories, whether silk, cotton or worsted, which are themselves an important aspect of the industrial landscape. The yarn was distributed by master hosiers, who usually owned warehouses from which the knitters had to collect their yarn on a weekly basis and where the finished products were kept; these were often more elaborate in design than the spinning factories. Some hosiers as well as knitters made use of middlemen to distribute yarn and collect the finished products. The system created a series of nodal points throughout the East Midlands, with knitters in scattered villages working for hosiers in the towns.

Stocking knitters' houses

The hosiery industry was one of the last branches of textile manufacture to survive in a domestic environment as hosiery factories did not really develop until the second half of the 19th century. The surviving buildings are therefore important

Figure 5.15 Elevation of a master hosier's house, Albert Street, Nottingham, showing the attached workshop for stocking frames (© Gary Campion)

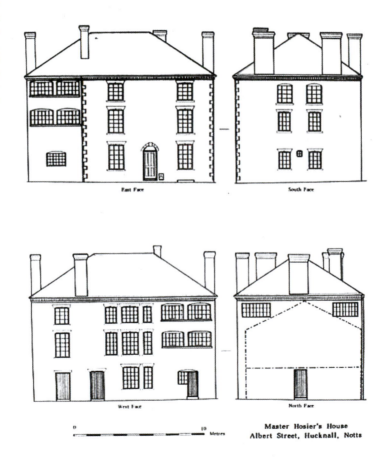

East Face

South Face

West Face

North Face

Master Hosier's House
Albert Street, Hucknall, Notts

as one of the rare opportunities to see how the domestic system functioned and are more fully discussed in Chapter 6.2. It is important to remember, however, that homes adapted to house knitting frames were probably in the minority and, as with handloom weaving, many operatives just worked where they could find a space.

Although purpose-built stockingers' houses continued to be built into the second half of the 19th century, an increasing number of unpowered workshops were constructed, where frames could be grouped together and worked under supervision. Some of these were added to master hosiers' houses, as in Albert Street in Hucknall, where the style of the hosier's living quarters differs sharply from that of the attached workshops (Fig 5.15). Separate workshops were often built to house wide frames which were unsuitable for domestic use, but this was not always the case. The two museums of framework knitting are both housed in former workshops at Ruddington in Nottinghamshire and Wigston in Leicestershire. Some hosiery workshops survive as they were taken over by the boot and shoe industry later in the 19th century when hosiery factories began to be built, especially in south Leicestershire.

The growth of the mechanised factory

By the middle of the 19th century, house and workplace had generally become disassociated and the truly domestic aspect of the industry lost, although women still seamed the stockings and children wound the bobbins. The principal drivers of the move to powered factory production were, firstly, the development of commercially viable powered knitting machines from the 1840s onwards; secondly, the development of the sewing machine; and finally, the emergence of a mass market for hosiery and associated clothing for the British middle classes. Pressure from cheaper European imports, particularly from Germany and America, further accelerated the trend. There were, however, many entrenched practices that led to the domestic hosiery industry proving surprisingly resilient when compared with the impact of mechanisation in other areas of textile production. The merchant hosiers, on the whole, preferred to tie up their capital in stocks of yarn and finished goods rather than in buildings and plant. Equally, many people made money out of rents to framework knitters and acting as middlemen or the distributors of their products. The Education Acts of the 1870s, by insisting on a period of compulsory primary schooling, broke up the family unit of production and deprived the knitters of the services of their children, although the oral evidence from people living in the 20th century shows that the effect was not immediate and that many children were obliged to wind and seam out of school hours. Finally, renting frames out to workers in their own homes was becoming increasingly anomalous and was finally abolished in 1874. This all paved the way for the growth of the powered hosiery factory.

Viable power-operated knitting machines were late in development when compared with mechanisation in most other segments of the textile industry. Various inventors, including Sir Marc Brunel in 1816, developed circular knitting machines; none were taken up by the industry to any significant extent. It was the work of the Pagets and others from 1844 onwards, and of Matthew Townsend in developing the latch needle in 1847, which led to the development of a practical circular fabric knitting machine. Developments in stocking machines were even slower as automating Lee's hand frame, with its complex reciprocating motion, and the need to narrow or widen the knitted piece, proved very difficult. It was not until 1864 that William Cotton succeeded. Cotton's early machines were sold to a restricted group of manufacturers, thereby further limiting take up. The concurrent development of the sewing machine in the 1850s produced a further incentive to move seaming operations from domestic workshops into factories. The production of true hosiery (stockings and socks) long remained the biggest single part of the industry by volume and value, still representing 41% of the total output value of all knitted products in 1937 but dropping to 23% of the total by 1969 as fabric production and fully fashioned outer garment production played a more significant part.

The 19th-century industry was concentrated in the area covered by south Derbyshire, south Nottinghamshire, and Leicestershire, with a significant outlier in the Scottish Borders, especially Hawick and Galashiels, where luxury knitwear predominated by the 20th century.

Lace factories

Although lace made by hand using a lace pillow was a feature of many areas of Britain from the 18th century onwards, the extensive lace industry of Nottinghamshire owes its origins to the knitting frame. This was adapted to produce a regular mesh or 'point net' which could then be hand embroidered. Hand-operated lace frames were worked in buildings similar to those for framework knitting, often in upper storeys of houses as the industry tended to

Figure 5.16 Bridge Mills, Long Eaton: a late 19th-century lace factory alongside the Erewash Canal (© Marilyn Palmer)

Midlands. For example, the large factory of *Atkins* in Hinckley, Leicestershire, has been converted for mixed use, including creative studios and office space. *Brettles* in Belper in Derbyshire had a huge number of home-based knitters working for them, and their 1834 warehouse survives. The results of an important project to document the East Midlands hosiery industry can be found at http://www.knittingtogether.org.uk/home.asp?cat=594 (accessed September 2011). Hosiery was also a major employer in Baldock, Hertfordshire, in the mid- 20th century and *Kayser Bondor's Art Deco factory* has been converted into a superstore.

The larger lace mills have had a mixed fate. Some have been converted to flats, notably *Victoria Mill*, Draycott, built in successive blocks by Terah Hooley and completed by Jardine from 1888 until 1907, which eventually reached over 600ft (183m) in length; *Springfield Mill* in Sandiacre in its canalside location; and the unusually elegant *Anglo-Scotian Mills* at Beeston (Fig 5.17). *Long Eaton* in Derbyshire remains the best place to see a landscape of large and small lace mills, while *Lace Market* in Nottingham, especially the *Adams Building*, dating from the 1850s onwards, is a prime example of the urban landscape of lace warehouses (see Fig 8.4).

Further reading

There is a substantial literature on the East Midlands hosiery industry. Overview works on the development of the industry include S D Chapman, *Hosiery and Knitwear: Four Centuries of Small-Scale Industry in Britain c. 1589–2000* (Pasold Studies in Textile History, Oxford University Press, 2002); S Mason, *A History of the Worshipful Company of Framework Knitters* (The Worshipful Company of Framework Knitters, 2000); S Mason, *Nottingham Lace, 1760s–1950s* (Alan Sutton, 1994); M Palmer, *Framework Knitting* (Shire Publications, 1984, reprinted 2010); and F A Wells, *The British Hosiery Industry* (Barnes & Noble, 1972). A more archaeological approach to the industry can be found in D M Smith, *The Industrial Archaeology of the East Midlands* (David & Charles, 1965) and M Palmer & P A Neaverson, *Industrial Landscapes of the East Midlands* (Phillimore, 1992). A contemporary 19th-century study is provided by W Felkin, *A History of the Machine-Wrought Hosiery and Lace Manufactures*, originally published 1867 but the centenary edition included an introduction by S D Chapman (David & Charles, 1967). Historic Scotland's re-survey of listed buildings in the Scottish Borders mill towns included some hosiery workshops and factories, especially for Galashiels and Hawick (see Further Reading 5.7).

The buildings of the hosiery industry are dealt with in several articles including G Campion, 'People, process and the poverty pew: a functional analysis of mundane buildings in the Nottinghamshire framework-knitting industry' (*Antiquity* **70**, 1996, 847–80); G Campion, 'Familiarity Breeding Contempt? Understanding and Conserving Outworking Buildings and Landscapes' (*Industrial Archaeology Review* **27**:2, 2005, 195–216); and M Palmer, 'Housing the Leicester Framework Knitters: History and Archaeology' (*Transactions of the Leicestershire Archaeological and Historical Society* **74**, 2000, 59–78).

CHAPTER SIX

Housing the workforce

6.1 Introduction

Industrial-period housing took a variety of forms from the country houses of the elite to the cellar dwellings of the poorest. This section looks at the archaeological and standing buildings evidence for housing directly associated with industry during the 18th, 19th, and early 20th centuries: structures commonly known as workers' housing. Although many such structures were superseded or replaced from the mid- to late 19th century by social housing and large-scale speculative housing projects, considerable quantities of industrial housing still survive, long after their associated factories have closed and been demolished.

The major difference in the type of workers' housing was between those dwellings that combined work and domestic functions (the workshop dwelling) and those that were purely domestic in function (industrial dwellings associated with factories). Both types have been studied since the beginning of industrial archaeology as a discipline, but workshop dwellings, with their strong association with proto-industrialisation and their survival into the early 20th century in some industries, have attracted more systematic study, from the woollen workshops of the textile industries of south-west England, lowland Scotland, and Yorkshire, to the boot and shoe workshops of the East Midlands. They could, however, be found across much of Britain, particularly where raw materials and poor agricultural land encouraged the search by poorer tenant farmers for a second income.

Industrial dwellings, from the terraced house to the tenement, have been less intensively studied, with research focused upon groups of standing buildings that were erected adjacent to manufacturing sites either with money from the factory owner (as factory colonies) or as early speculative developments that were rented to the factory workforce. However, factory colonies associated with textile production have attracted more attention, particularly those in World Heritage Sites such as the Derwent Valley of Derbyshire (Strutt and Arkwright mills), New Lanark (Dale and Arkwright mills), and Saltaire (Titus Salt mill). Since 1990, and especially during the economic boom decade of 1997 to 2007, developer-funded archaeological work has enabled the targeted excavation of many areas of workers' housing in some of the most important industrial urban centres of Britain such as Glasgow, London, and Manchester.

Although much of this material has yet to be published as either technical monographs or synthetic studies, it is already clear that the excavation of large areas of workers' housing allows the archaeologist to look at the way in which industrialisation changed people's domestic lives, as well as their work lives. Furthermore, the analysis of material culture from such sites provides a way of charting increasing consumption and the globalisation of trade networks during the industrial period.

6.2 Workshop dwellings

The workshop dwelling, also known as a vernacular workshop, was a composite building used for a variety of hand-production processes from textiles and hat making to metal working and boot and shoe manufacture. The domestic rooms could be on either ground or upper floors. The workshop was a room in which a skilled workman or woman had a degree of control over the rhythm and intensity of the processes undertaken to produce something which could be a finished article or only one component of that article, regardless of whether any mechanical power was used within the workshop. Such structures are found all over Britain, including the two-room, single-storey, woollen weavers' cottage of lowland Scotland; the two-storey, ground floor and cellar, cotton weavers' workshop of north-eastern Lancashire; the two- and three-storey woollen weavers' workshops of West Yorkshire and south-west England; the three-storey silk workers' workshops of east Cheshire; and the integral as well as garden workshops of the East Midlands boot, shoe, and hosiery industries.

Workshop dwellings were one of the most successful building types of the industrial period, their history running from the beginning of the 18th century to the end of the 19th. Their construction reflected the vernacular traditions and buildings materials of the regions of Britain, and thousands of examples survive into the early 21st century, many of them listed.

Historical development

The handloom weaver's cottage was probably the earliest workshop dwelling to emerge as a distinctive building type. Its origins lie in the investment of some of the capital generated by the growing woollen domestic-based textile industry of the late 17th and early 18th century, particularly in south-west England and West Yorkshire. The Spitalfields area of London emerged in the late 17th century as an area of silk weavers' workshop dwellings, with a distinctive hybrid workshop-tenement building type (see below). The wills and inventories of parishes in Gloucestershire, Lancashire, and Yorkshire often refer to 'shops', meaning workshops, being used for metal, shoe, textile, or some other form of domestic industry by tenant farmers from the late 17th century. By the beginning of the 18th century many farmhouses had either a dedicated room for domestic textile manufacture or an additional one- or two-storey workshop range (Fig 6.1). Separate and dedicated three-storey textile

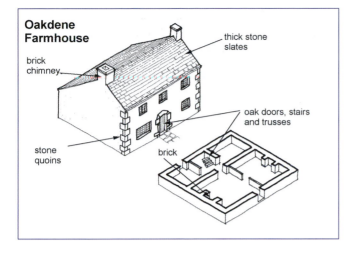

Oakdene Farmhouse

brick chimney

thick stone slates

stone quoins

oak doors, stairs and trusses

brick

workshops began to be built in the valleys of the Cotswolds in the late 18th and 19th centuries, and attracted hostile responses from the weavers who preferred to work in their domestic environments. Such workshops were also built in the Pennine valleys around Leeds and Manchester, and came to be used for cotton spinning and weaving in Lancashire. By the early 19th century, however, a two-storey variant which might have the workshop on the ground floor or on the first floor had emerged in north-eastern Lancashire and in the Bethnal Green area of London.

Such workshops, along with the one- and two-storey farmhouse workshop additions found in upland areas such as the Pennines, were a physical expression of the growth of the textile industry during the 18th century. They reflect two different ways of organising production. The first of these was artisan production which was the domestic manufacture of textiles by independent, skilled, craftsmen. In these households a significant proportion of the total family income was derived from the manufacture or processing of such goods for sale. Such artisan production was very common in the woollen-producing areas of West Yorkshire and in the uplands of south-east Lancashire around Rochdale, Littleborough, and Oldham. The second was merchant capital production whereby the preparation, manufacture, and finishing, as well as the marketing, of textiles was organised by a few clothiers but carried out by many workers on a commission or order basis. Within the woollen industry of Wiltshire and Gloucestershire and the Lancashire fustian and cotton industry, this was usually done on the 'putting-out' system, where the entrepreneur clothier raised the capital to buy the raw material and then organised production by putting-out parts of it to spinners, weavers, and finishers working at home. In other words this was dispersed production under a central capitalist control. The boom in the fustian industry of Lancashire encouraged speculative house builders, and during the mid-18th century hundreds of weavers' cottage were built and rented to fustian weavers in the area now known as the Northern Quarter of Manchester. Clusters of wool weavers' houses were also built in villages and in many of the towns in Wiltshire and Gloucestershire, particularly Trowbridge and Bradford-on-Avon (Fig 6.2).

Although mechanisation in the cotton and woollen industries during the early 19th century slowly brought an end to domestic textile production in these manufacturing areas, the building type survived for a surprisingly long time in silk, cotton, and woollen weaving and even more so in other less mechanised industries such as hosiery where outworking remained popular down to the end of the 19th century. Spinning was successfully mechanised well before weaving, and the increased output from spinning mills from the late

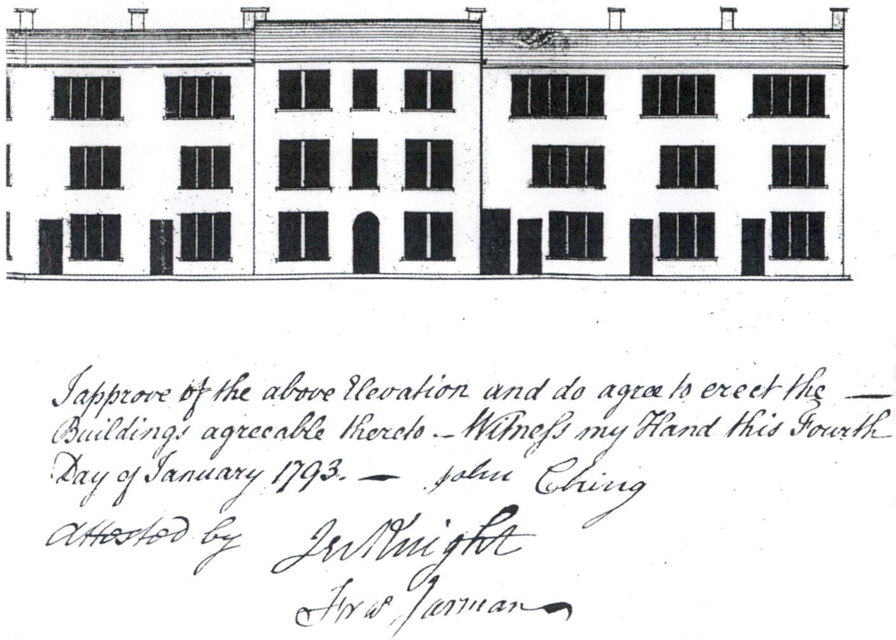

*I approve of the above Elevation and do agree to erect the ___
Building: agreeable thereto ___ Witness my Hand this Fourth
Day of January 1793. ___ John Ching
attested by Jno Knight
Thos Jarman*

Figure 6.2 A weavers'
terrace in Trowbridge,
Wiltshire: part of
the original drawing
showing 'the new
intended street there
to be called Yerbury
Street', signed by
the developer John
Ching, a local
plumber and glazier,
in 1793 (reproduced
by permission of
Wiltshire and
Swindon Archives)

18th century onwards encouraged the construction of workshop dwellings for
handloom weavers well into the 1830s and for even longer in the silk industry. It
is important to remember that mechanisation in one branch of an industry did
not mean that other branches immediately followed suit: it was a long drawn-
out process.

Key elements and plan forms

The earliest type of purpose-built workshop dwelling appears to have been a
two- or three-storey structure with a single workshop space occupying the whole
of the upper floor and lit by long rows of mullion windows in at least one wall at
this level. These could be found in the late 17th and early 18th century in London,
the South-West, the Midlands, northern England and southern Scotland. A large
window frontage is one of the hallmarks of a weaver's dwelling, its function being
to allow as much natural light as possible into the working area (Fig 6.3). Access
to the workshop was through the house itself, via an internal stair, but often the
upper floor included an external taking-in door to facilitate the movement of
materials. They can occur attached to a farmhouse, in individual pairs or in long
rows. Some cottages, particularly in Lancashire, also had a half-cellar workshop
which was used for spinning and was lit by similar windows.

Since handloom weaving persisted for so long in the woollen and silk industries,
many examples of houses built or converted for weaving survive. Most have larger
windows than normal, and the workshops could be placed on one or more
floors of the house. A schematic diagram of possible positions of workshops is
illustrated in Figure 6.4.

Figure 6.3 A set of three, three-storey, handloom cotton weavers cottages built by John and Ann Morehouse, landlords of the adjoining Gunn Inn, Hollingworth, Tameside, in 1781. These appear to have been built as speculative housing as part of the boom in handloom weaving in the Pennines during the period 1770 to 1810 (© Michael Nevell)

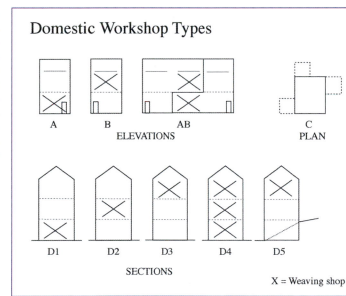

Figure 6.4 A suggested classification of types of weaving workshops in Gloucestershire and Wiltshire. Most urban workshops were of types D4 and D5, while rural ones, with less obstruction of light, tended to be D1 or D2 (© Marilyn Palmer)

It is difficult from the physical evidence alone to identify archaeologically which form of production was taking place in any particular workshop, not just whether these workshops contained cotton, fustian, knitting, lace, linen or wool production, but also whether they were associated with artisan or merchant capital production. However, by comparing the documentary evidence for the vernacular workshop with the physical evidence for these buildings in areas such

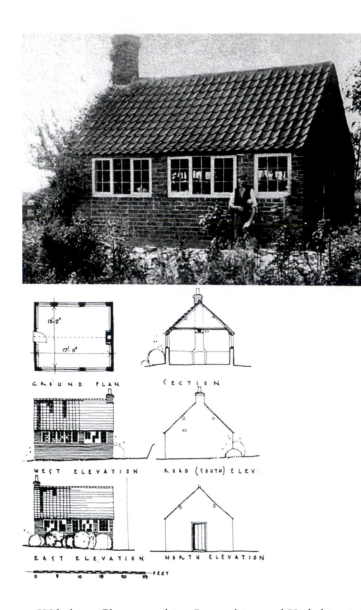

GROUND PLAN

SECTION

WEST ELEVATION

ROAD (SOUTH) ELEV

EAST ELEVATION

NORTH ELEVATION

as Wiltshire, Gloucestershire, Lancashire, and Yorkshire, it is possible to suggest a very broad correlation between rows of workshop dwellings which appear to have been sponsored by merchant capital production, and those workshops (including the one-, two-, and three-storey varieties) associated with farmsteads which appear to reflect artisan production.

The hosiery industry was one of the last branches of textile manufacture to survive in a domestic environment as hosiery factories did not really develop until the second half of the 19th century. The surviving buildings of the East Midlands (particularly in Leicestershire and Nottinghamshire) are therefore important as one of the rare opportunities to see how the domestic system functioned. The main characteristic of stockingers' houses is the existence of long or large windows to enable as much daylight as possible to reach the frame; many rooms which housed frames are through rooms with windows on both sides. It is important to remember, however, that houses adapted to house knitting frames were probably in the minority and, as with handloom weaving, many operatives just worked where they could find a space. There are three phases of stockingers' houses in the East Midlands:

- The insertion of workshops into existing timber-framed houses, which can be recognised by additional windows. Good examples survive in Sutton Bonington (Nottingham) and Shepshed (Leicestershire);
- The construction by speculative builders of purpose-built houses with workshops incorporated, generally financed by people outside the trade as a means of investment. Most of these date from the very end of the 18th century and continued to be built until late on in the 19th century; an example at Calverton in Nottinghamshire has the date of 1857 in brick headers in the gable end of the row of houses. Those in urban areas usually had the workshop on the top floor to maximise light penetration; as late as the 1880s the industrial town of Hucknall in Nottinghamshire still had rows of two- and three-storey terraces with functioning attic workshops for outworkers of the hosiery industry. In villages, where interruption to light was less of a problem, stockingers' houses often had the workshops on the ground floor as this did not have to be strengthened to support the frame; good examples survive at Calverton, particularly Windles Square which dates from 1834;
- In the third phase, purpose-built stockingers' houses continued to be lived in and even newly built. Their occupants may well have carried out tasks such as winding bobbins and seaming stockings in them, but increasing numbers of unpowered workshops were constructed, where wider frames could be grouped together and worked under supervision. These are further discussed in Chapter 5.8.

Within the textile industries, silk weaving in three-storey domestic workshops continued to be a significant part of the industry in eastern Cheshire and northern Staffordshire during the late 19th century. The boot and shoe industries of Northamptonshire used domestic workshops until the late 19th century, built at the back of the terrace house or even against the back garden wall, often with a separate alleyway providing access to the rear. These were generally heated and rows of small chimneys above a back garden wall can still be seen in, for example, Earls Barton and Kettering. The lace industry frequently made use of similar houses to those occupied by the framework knitters of the East Midlands and it is difficult to tell except from documentary evidence to which industry they belonged from the late 18th century onwards, particularly in Nottingham, where good examples survive at Bramcote and Stapleford. Many others have been demolished during urban renewal.

The domestic workshops of the metal industry sometimes took the form of the three-storey workshop familiar from the textile industry and common in the West Midlands. Some of these can be seen in the Birmingham Jewellery Quarter (Fig 6.6), the buildings of the Sheffield steel cutlery industry, and the watch-

making industry in, for example, Prescot in Lancashire. One- and two-storey workshops attached to the rear of terrace houses continued to be used until the end of the 19th century. A decreasing number of workshops for the outworkers of the boot, shoe, and hosiery industries of the East Midlands, and those of the felt and straw hat industry around Denton and Stockport in the North-West and Luton in Bedfordshire, continued to be used into the 20th century.

Key sites

Standing workshop dwellings can be found in many parts of the country in both rural and urban locations. However, they are most common in the five great industrial textile districts of England: the silk zone of eastern Cheshire (in *Congleton and Macclesfield*) and northern Staffordshire; the woollen zone of Gloucestershire and Wiltshire, notably *Trowbridge, Bradford-on-Avon* and villages in the Gloucestershire valleys such as *Chalford*; the Lancashire cotton region (especially in and around *Blackburn* and *Manchester*); the woollen zone of West Yorkshire, including the important *Saddleworth* district now in Greater Manchester; and the lace making and hosiery making areas of Leicestershire and Nottinghamshire. Elsewhere, silk weavers' domestic workshops can still be

Figure 6.6 The interior of J W Evans' Silver Factory in the Jewellery Quarter in Birmingham. Opened in 1881, its contents remained intact after its closure and it was taken over by English Heritage in 2008. Behind the frontage of four terraced houses, the workshops retain their original drop stamps and fly presses, and are packed with thousands of dies for the manufacture of silverware, as well as the whole of the working equipment, stock and records of the business (© Marilyn Palmer)

found, heavily altered, in *Spitalfields* in London; boot and shoe workshops survive in parts of Northamptonshire, while metal workers' domestic workshops can still be seen in the centre of Birmingham, notably in the *Jewellery Quarter*. Single-storey weavers' cottages remain common in lowland Scotland, where there is a well-preserved planned weavers' village at *Newcastleton*, dating from the decades either side of 1800.

Further reading

The best starting point is P S Barnwell, M Palmer & M Airs (eds), *The vernacular workshop: from craft to industry, 1400–1900* (CBA Research Report **140**, 2005). This contains many articles on the regional variation of this building type in England, and is introduced by a more theoretical article on their role and function by M Palmer, 'The workshop: type of building or method of work?'. Her Rolt Memorial Lecture, 'Industrial Archaeology: Continuity and Change' (*Industrial Archaeology Review* **16**:2, 1994) was one of the first to draw attention to the importance of the variety of surviving domestic workshops.

Other useful regional studies include several more from England for the East Midlands, the North-West and the South-West: G Campion, 'People, Process and the Poverty Pew: a Functional Analysis of Mundane Buildings in the Nottinghamshire Framework Knitting Industry' (*Antiquity* **70**, 2001, 847–60); M Nevell, 'From Linen Weaver to Cotton Manufacturer: Manchester During the 17th and 18th Centuries and the Social Archaeology of Industrialisation', in M Nevell (ed), *From Farmer to Factory Owner. Models, Methodology and Industrialisation. The Archaeology of the Industrial Revolution in North West England.* (Archaeology North West **16**, CBA North West, 2003, 27–44); M Palmer & P A Neaverson, 'Handloom weaving in Wiltshire and Gloucestershire in the 19th century: the building evidence' (*Post-Medieval Archaeology* **37**:1, 2003, 126–58) and 'Home as Workplace in nineteenth-century Wiltshire and Gloucestershire' (*Textile History* **35**:1, 2004, 27–57); D Shrimpton, 'Buildings for Framework Knitters in Ruddington, Nottinghamshire' (*Industrial Archaeology Review* **8**:1, 1985, 70–7); G Timmins, 'Handloom Weavers' Cottages in central Lancashire: Some problems of Recognition' (*Post-Medieval Archaeology* **13**, 1979, 251–72) and his 'Domestic Industry in Britain during the 18th and 19th centuries: field evidence and the research agenda', in D Gwyn & M Palmer (eds), 'Understanding the Workplace: a Research Framework for Industrial Archaeology in Britain' (*Industrial Archaeology Review* **27**:1, 2005, 67–76). The workshops of the boot and shoe industry in Northampton are covered in K A Morrison with A Bond, *Built to Last? The Buildings of the Northamptonshire Boot and Shoe Industry* (English Heritage, 2004). The domestic metal workshops of the Midlands are discussed in J Cattell & B Hawkins, *The Birmingham Jewellery Quarter. An Introduction and Guide* (English Heritage, 2000), and J Cattell, S Ely & B Jones, *The Birmingham Jewellery Quarter: an architectural survey of manufactories* (English Heritage, 2002). For hosiery and framework knitters' housing, see Chapter 5.8.

The surviving physical remains of the domestic woollen weaving industry in

and brick in the lowlands was largely adhered to, although the cheaper and more mass-produced brick became the increasingly dominant material as the railway network spread during the mid-19th century. Nevertheless, the houses of individual factory communities often took on a particular identity in the form of small architectural details that reflected the company that built them. At Bestwood in Nottinghamshire all the houses built by the Bestwood Coal and Iron Company in the 1870s bore their crest in rubbed brick (Fig 6.8). The railway town of Swindon, built by Brunel in the 1840s and early 1850s, included rows of two-storey, brick-built, two-up-two-down terraces and pairs of two-roomed cottages with Elizabethan details such as diamond-set chimneys and projecting gabled bays. Larger end-terrace properties with five or even eight rooms appear to have been set aside for the foremen and their families. However, multiple occupancy of many of the cottages and terrace houses became common due to the high rents charged by the Great Western Railway.

A common development from the mid-19th century onwards was the addition of an extension at the rear of the building. This was typically of two storeys but narrower than the width of the full building plot. The result was known as a 'tunnel back' (Fig 6.9) and the increased room space which was created allowed a change in room function. The ground-floor room in the extension became the scullery, while the back room in the main part of the house became the kitchen and living room area. Most of the main activities of the day took place within this rear room, which was now also heated. The front room of the house became the 'parlour', a showpiece room set aside for 'best'. The parlour was rarely used but contained the most expensive furnishings within the household; it functioned as a room for guests and may have been used by the family on special occasions and perhaps for Sunday dinner. In tunnel backs, which still exist in large numbers in many industrial towns, access into the parlour could be directly by the front

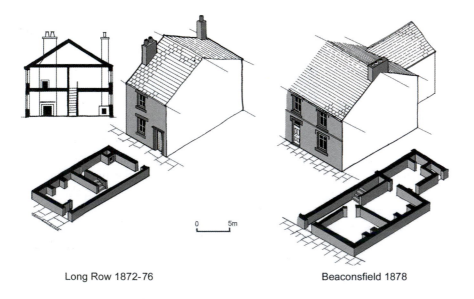

Long Row 1872-76   Beaconsfield 1878

Figure 6.9 Some examples of late 19th-century Local Board housing from the Carrbrook textile community, Stalybridge, Tameside, showing the room arrangements. Left: a through-house from Long Row, a stone-built terrace of 21 properties built in the period 1872–76. Right: an example of one of seven tunnel-back properties from Beaconsfield Terrace built in 1878 (© Michael Nevell)

door, but increasingly a hall, in the form of a narrow corridor, separated the two. Although of lowly status in this situation, the function of the hall as the first point of entry for guests harks back to the rooms of a more grandiose past. The hall introduced into the terraced house a choice of room circulation by containing separate doorways into the rear room and parlour, which also gained in privacy. Another addition to the late 19th-century terraced house was the front garden. This very often took the form of a shallow paved area enclosed by a wall, but had the significant function of distancing the front door from the street. Usually the rear of the house took the form of a cramped yard still with an external privy and a coalshed. Excavation can reveal this progress, as with examples investigated at Ancoats in Manchester, where progressive backyard development, particularly the introduction of one privy per household, was noted.

The external treatment of the later 19th-century terraced house was in some respects even more monotonous than that of the earlier terraces, largely as a consequence of the standardisation brought in with bye-law housing. Doors and windows became of regulation size and the houses themselves took on a more uniform height. Despite this general regularity, the facades of some terraces did display a development not only in architectural styles and building materials but also in terms of aesthetics and the changing attitudes of the occupier. The use of pressed, machine-made brick, with its polished red or yellow appearance, became commonplace, with houses often incorporating different coloured brickwork. Ornamental brickwork or terracotta was also frequently found on the terraced house. The use of stone as the sole constructional fabric became less common, but its use as a facing material only was popular in the late 19th and early 20th centuries. A further significant development of the terrace was the adoption of the bay window, popularised in factory colonies such as Swindon, which with the abolition of the window tax in the 1850s became a popular form among all types of buildings. The external embellishments of the terraced house, whether in the form of a garden, a bay window or a terracotta panel, all indicated the relative wealth and status of the occupants, as can be seen at Saltaire and Akroydon. The backs of houses, which were unseen from the street, were not affected by such developments.

Back-to-back housing and its variants

Several other industrial housing types, notorious at the time and which were the product of the rapid urbanisation brought about by industrialisation, rarely survive as standing structures: back-to-back houses, cellar dwellings, and court housing. Cellar houses and back-to-back housing were outlawed in the mid- to late 19th century by a succession of housing acts giving local authorities the power to improve sanitary and health conditions in their areas. As a result such types of housing were either demolished or so radically improved that few examples now survive. Leeds has a significant grouping of converted back-to-backs, whilst converted cellar dwellings can still be seen in Chorley, Lancashire, and in Manchester's Northern Quarter. In most regions excavation is the best

Figure 6.10 The excavation of back-to-back houses with yards on Loom Street, Ancoats, Manchester, by the University of Manchester Archaeology Unit in 2007. These were built during the years 1831–48 as part of the many rear courtyard developments in the city during this period and are an example of the way in which such houses were crammed onto every available plot of urban land (© Michael Nevell)

way of recovering archaeological information about their evolution and use (Fig 6.10).

Back-to-back houses were found in most of the industrial towns of midland and northern England and in the larger industrial cities of Scotland (Glasgow) and Wales (Cardiff and Swansea). Each back-to-back house shared a pair of brick chimney stacks whilst on the ground floor was a door and a single window. The staircases were located against the central spine wall, except for those in the side-to-backs. The upper rooms were lit by a single window, heated, and were open to the roof space. Such properties only had one wall facing outwards and were thus badly lit and poorly ventilated. Unlike ordinary terraced houses they lacked space for an outside privy. Instead, these were set up on spare ground nearby. Excavations in a number of cities (Glasgow, London, Manchester, and York) have all shown that these structures were poorly built with one-brick thick outer walls, no running water and sometimes only clay floors. Even the chimneys could be rudimentary, whilst some examples only had ladders giving access to the upper floors.

Cellar dwellings were found, as the name implies, in the basements of buildings and were notorious for their poor living conditions. These were almost always converted cellars from earlier housing, although some examples of excavated back-to-back houses in Manchester were built with cellar dwellings. These were built during the peak period of that city's population expansion, the decades from 1800 to 1840, and this seems to be a common theme across Britain. Documentary accounts indicate that they were common in many of the industrial towns of the Midlands and northern England as well as London, and occur as early as the 1790s in both London and Manchester.

The courtyard house was also a product of rapid population expansion and rising land values. These were small-scale structures, usually two rooms but sometimes just a single room, built on the rear yards of earlier housing. In historic city centres, such as those of Glasgow, London, and York, this might be on the rear plots of the medieval burgages, and such structures could only be accessed via narrow alleys between the property boundaries. Excavations off Angel Street in Manchester showed that the foundations of some of these structures had been built directly on top of the earlier paving of the yard. Like cellar dwellings and back-to-back terraces, this form of housing was noted for its insanitary conditions owing to poor construction, lack of lighting and the lack of adequate privies.

Courts can occasionally be identified by surviving plaques on walls, either with a number or the name of the court; those in Nottingham, for example, were unrealistically given names such as 'Pleasant Place' or 'Vine Court'.

Tenement housing

Tenements were a common form of shared housing in Scotland and Europe from the 17th century onwards, but were rarer in England. According to Adam Smith, writing in 1776 as industrialisation took hold in Britain, 'A dwelling-house in England means everything that is contained under the same roof. In France, Scotland, and many other parts of Europe, it frequently means no more than a single storey'. Early tenements usually had three or four storeys, were two rooms deep, might contain four two-storey apartments, and were often built in ashlar stone. Early examples often occurred in pairs but more commonly in the 19th century as terraces. Many surviving tenement blocks from the early 19th century have a circular or turnpike stair at the rear, accessed from a passageway that ran from the front to the back of the property, whilst the ground-floor flats on the street frontage had separate entrances.

Tenements could be found in 18th-century London and the Spitalfields district contained a large grouping used by silk weavers. These structures were a cross between the artisan workshop dwelling and the Scottish tenement: one-room workshop homes with a front communal staircase. Tenemented flats above commercial premises first appeared in Glasgow in large numbers during the mid-18th century and contained multiple apartments used by the merchants and middle classes. The preference of Glasgow's inhabitants, or at least its house builders and architects, for multi-storey tenement dwellings ensured that this kind of structure emerged as the dominant working- and lower-middle-class building type during the period 1770–1846 in the city's new industrial suburbs. Beyond the industrial city, some of the earliest surviving tenements are those built by Robert Owen at his New Lanark Mills in the early 19th century. These terrace tenements were stone-built, three- and four-storey structures, with shared staircases and washrooms. Whilst tenements remained a popular housing form throughout the 19th century, their construction came to be dominated by commercial building companies, many examples of which were excavated in Glasgow along the line of the M74. The tenements themselves showed little in the way of development from earlier 19th-century examples.

community life in (post) industrial England (Manchester University Press, 2010). N Jeffries & A Owen's work on backyard clearance groups combines historical and artefactual evidence to suggest new insights about urban living: A Owens, N Jeffries, D Hicks, R Featherby & K Wehner, 'Rematerialising metropolitan histories? People, places and things in modern London', in A Horning & M Palmer (eds), *Crossing Paths, Sharing Tracks: Future Directions for Archaeological Study of post-1550 Britain and Ireland* (Boydell & Brewer, 2008, 323–49). K Matthew's study of 19th-century housing at Hamilton Place in Chester provides a type-site for the way in which archaeology can show how the introduction of bye-laws and regulations could take decades to affect existing housing; see K Matthews, 'Familiarity and contempt: the archaeology of the modern', in S Tarlow & S West (eds), *The Familiar Past? Archaeologies of later Historical Britain* (Routledge, 1999, 155–79).

Extensive published overviews of the developer-funded excavations of workers' housing during the 2000s are, as yet, still rare. M Nevell, *Manchester: The Hidden History* (History Press, 2008), provides a summary of the work on 18th- and 19th-century workers' housing in the centre of that city, much of it in areas written about by the social commentator Frederick Engels during the 1840s. A further article, entitled 'Living in the Industrial City: Housing Quality, Land Ownership and the Archaeological Evidence from Industrial Manchester, 1740–1850', is in press for the *Journal of Historical Archaeology*. Summaries of the important excavations of 19th- and early 20th-century workers' housing at Hungate, York, the living conditions of which were recorded and published by the philanthropist Seebohm Rowntree in 1901, can be found in *Current Archaeology* **215** (2008, 26–33) and two articles are in press for the *Journal of Historical Archaeology*: P Connelly, 'Flush With The Past: An insight into late 19th century Hungate and its role in providing a better understanding of urban development', and J Rimmer, 'People and their Buildings in the Working-Class Neighborhood of Hungate, York, UK'. A detailed overview of the recent work along the M74 corridor in Glasgow which involved the excavation of more than 60 tenement blocks, back-to-backs and factory houses, is currently in press. However, an overview of the project is provided by D Morton, 'Involving the public in Glasgow's Industrial Archaeology: the M74 Dig' (*The Archaeologist* **74**, 2009, 36–7).

CHAPTER SEVEN

Moving around

7.1 Introduction

Adam Smith stated in the first book of his *The Wealth of Nations* (1776) that

> Good roads, canals and navigable rivers, by diminishing the
> expense of carriage, put the remote parts of the country nearly
> on a level with those in the neighbourhood of the town; they are,
> upon that account, the greatest of all improvements.

Transport is often treated as a discrete area of study in contemporary
economic history and industrial archaeology; it is, however, a key primary enabler
to most other industries. The cost of transport related to total product cost has
always been critical in establishing broader markets for products. Raw materials
and goods have little value if they cannot be moved to their point of conversion
or consumption at a competitive rate. Most developments of transport routes by
both water and rail in the mid-17th century were driven by the need to access
raw materials. The coal and limestone industries were frequently the earliest
to try to improve routes suited to carrying these commodities in bulk. Other
than between large towns, most early inland routes covered comparatively short
distances, usually conveying minerals from their point of extraction to a point
of shipment by waterborne transport. An exception to this was the number of
droving roads that allowed livestock to be moved over large distances on the hoof.
Turnpikes allowed more rapid movement of people and mail but were never a
solution for moving large volumes of raw materials or finished merchandise over
large distances. Early transport developments on core routes were, in turn, often
followed by more speculative developments which normally aimed to benefit
developing the economy of an area through enhanced transport links.

New techniques of manufacture usually produce improved efficiency, and hence
reduced costs, in the manufacturing process. These improvements are, however,
of little value to anything other than a local market if the costs of transport cancel
out the saving brought about through new processes. As industries became more
capital-intensive in the early modern period, they required a growing market to
drive larger sales volumes in order to show an acceptable return on capital. Such
markets only became economically accessible through reduced transport costs and
the ability to ship higher volumes and obtain sufficient raw materials. Similarly
the regional concentration of certain industries that developed during this period

reversed and Western markets which had successfully resisted the cost advantages of the East could no longer do so. Again and again, once the combination of the removal of tariff barriers and huge reductions in transport costs and transit times occurred, the advantage of many home-based industries was effectively destroyed. This could not have taken place without the development of air transport as well as sea-borne containerisation on which so much of our global economy now depends.

7.2   Roads and turnpikes

Between the departure of the Romans and the turnpike acts (see below), the road system of most areas of the British Isles saw little, if any, development. Nevertheless, people and goods did move around the country and John Ogilby's road atlas, the *Britannia* of 1675, portrays a web of eleven major routes centring on London. Most roads were unsuitable for wheeled traffic throughout the winter and frequently for much of the rest of the year. The carriage of most goods over any distance was by pack animal, which could carry loads of up to 250lb (113kg) on special wooden frames and could cover up to 25 miles (40km) per day. In the north of England the Galloway pony was a much-favoured pack animal. A typical pack horse train would have 30 or 40 animals, sometimes under the control of only one man. All sorts of materials were carried, from heavy minerals and salt through to finished products like woollen cloth. The pack horse era produced a group of distinctive routes, often on radically different alignments to our modern roads. The constant wear of hooves produced sunken tracks or hollow-ways, which could easily degenerate into water courses. Where stone was available, many of these were built up and paved with a single or double row of flagstones and were known as causeys. One of the best known Derbyshire causeys crosses Stanage Edge from near Hathersage and then forms the Long Causeway towards Sheffield.

Associated with these routes were pack horse bridges, mainly built from the 16th century onwards; these were usually narrow with low parapet walls to clear the pack. Many distinctive single-arched, hump-backed examples survive. Alongside established pack horse routes, inns developed to provide overnight accommodation and stabling. Many of these survive, often with names that refer to pack horses, although the stable blocks have usually been demolished or adapted for other purposes. As road improvements during the 18th century permitted the use of wheeled vehicles all year round, the use of pack horses declined, although in remote and hilly areas, such as the north Pennines, where the rate of road improvement was slower, their use persisted well into the 19th century.

Drove roads for cattle and sheep were wider than pack horse tracks and unpaved, usually running between walls and hedges to contain the stock. Many of these survive as green ways, for example in the Pennines. The vestiges of these old road systems are still recognisable in the present upland landscape, but while many lowland routes have disappeared beneath modern road construction, old names such as 'Salter's Way' still survive.

The coming of the turnpikes

Prior to the passing of turnpike acts, the care and maintenance of roads was the responsibility of the parish through which the road ran. This system was formalised by a statute of 1555 'for the mending of highways'. Under this statute each parishioner was required to spend four days a year on road maintenance. Despite later statutes that increased the number of days required, this system was frequently inefficient and failed to provide any form of consistent maintenance of the highways. It worked moderately well where the principal users of the roads were local, but where a nationally important road, such as the Great North Road, ran through a parish it became increasingly difficult to supply adequate labour for maintenance from the parish.

These circumstances led to the passing of the very first turnpike act in 1663. Under this act local justices were empowered to erect gates and levy tolls on a section of the Great North Road in Hertfordshire, Huntingdonshire, and Cambridge. Although seven more trusts had been authorised by 1700, it was not until 1706 that the first act was passed to allow the appointment of independent trustees empowered to raise tolls. The act enabled a trust to be set up with powers to collect road tolls and use the revenue to maintain the road and to raise loans against the security of the toll income. Most turnpike acts were passed between 1751 and 1772. At the peak of the turnpike system in the 1830s there were over 1000 trusts covering 18,000 miles of road. This represented about one sixth of the national road mileage total. Acts were generally valid for a specified number of years, after which a renewal had to be applied for. Investment in turnpike trusts was appealing as they gave higher rates of interest and security of capital than many other forms of contemporary investment. Most acts covered relatively modest distances of road, typically between 20 and 40 miles. The new roads, with superior standards of surfacing and more even gradients, led to a major improvement in the speed of long-distance land transport and delivered significant benefit to both the local and national economy. The turnpikes were only one part of the complex story of the development of road transport in this country. In some cases they took over existing routes, normally trunk routes, and improved them, but in other areas they built completely new routes. Major through routes were usually controlled by several trusts, not all of which were formed at the same time. It took nearly 50 years to turnpike all of the London to Bath Road westwards towards Newbury, which was managed by six separate trusts.

Although most roads were built with commercially raised capital, in the Scottish Highlands a different pattern of road building was employed. Here, following the Jacobite uprising of 1715, General George Wade was commissioned by the British government to build military roads to control the Highlands.

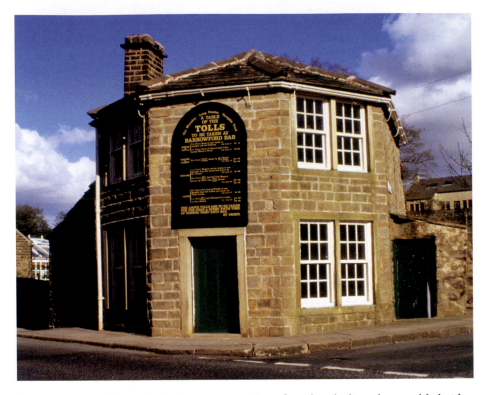

Figure 7.1 Barrowford Tollhouse in Lancashire, dating from 1804–05 and now owned by the Trust which operates the nearby Pendle Heritage Centre. The board lists charges levied by the Marsden to Long Preston Turnpike Trust (© Marilyn Palmer)

Between 1725 and 1737 he built over 300 miles of road including the notable bridge over the Tay at Aberfeldy. However, the gradients of many of his roads were too great for them to be used by commercial wagons and coaches. His successor William Caulfield built a further 800 miles of military roads up to his death in 1767 when the programme ceased. Several of these roads still form the principal routes through the Highlands, although many sections were improved in the second half of the 20th century. In the lowlands, the first turnpike act was passed for Midlothian in 1714, but other counties did not follow suit until the second half of the century. In south Wales, some turnpike acts were passed from the mid-18th century onwards, but abuse of the system by some of the trustees, including the multiplication of toll gates, led to the Rebecca riots of 1842–43, during which many gates and toll houses were destroyed. As a result, south Wales became the first region where roads became the responsibility of county boards.

Turnpike roads developed consistent methods of road surfacing. The major developers of road building and surfacing techniques in the 1820s, which largely followed French practice, were Thomas Telford, John Metcalfe, and J L McAdam. All of these engineers dictated processes for building proper foundations for roads with carefully graded top dressings. These surfaces, when compared with unimproved roads, allowed up to three times the load and greater speeds to be achieved, with 10mph averages being common for stage coaches in the 1830s. Original surfaces have invariably disappeared under years of later resurfacing and reconstruction. Modern concrete, asphalt and tarred road surfaces were developed in the middle of the 19th century but their adoption in Great Britain was slow. The suction effect of the rubber-tyred wheels of faster-moving motor vehicles caused stone and macadamised surfaces to break up into fine clouds of dust. It was not until the early 20th century that there was a major drive to upgrade stone surfaces by bonding them with tar.

Following a long period of decline in the face of railway competition, many turnpike trusts were wound up under general acts of parliament passed between 1873 and 1878. The winding up would see the extinction of any arrears and the disposal of the assets of the Trust to repay loans and was supervised by the Local Government Board. The Local Government Act of 1888 passed the entire responsibility for the maintenance of main roads to the county councils, and the last turnpike act expired in 1895. With the expiry of the acts the toll gates were removed.

With the passing of the era of the turnpike trusts and the supremacy of rail transport until the 1920s, there was little new road building other than in some major urban areas. As numbers of motor vehicles increased rapidly in the 1920s and 1930s, new road construction accelerated but was still was mainly focused on the construction of by-passes and arterial roads in and around major conurbations. The progress of building major roads in many areas was hampered by the inability of adjacent local authorities to agree on route and priorities. Towns such as Colchester, Winchester, Coventry, Oxford, and Shrewsbury were by-passed by the early 1930s. Major routes out of London were modernised and rebuilt. Alongside these new roads, such as Western Avenue, new housing and industrial estates were built, often leading to sprawling ribbon development along their routes. At the same time the main roads were classified using the A and B road numbering prefixes still in use today. This road structure, with few major modifications, carried on until the start of the motorway age.

Nevertheless, many of today's major roads follow routes originally created, or improved, under a turnpike act. Bridges, cuttings, retaining walls and embankments on these routes will frequently have remnants or entire structures dating from the original turnpike road, particularly on sections where the main road has subsequently been diverted.

Buildings and roadside structures

When toll roads were built, toll houses were normally constructed at each gate or turnpike point to provide living accommodation for the collectors. The toll house was typically, but not exclusively, single storey, and frequently of three bays with a projecting centre bay and situated very close to the roadway. There is often a large blank space on the wall above the main door where a board detailing the tolls would have been displayed. The very situation of these buildings, close to major roads, has led to a high rate of loss from both road widening and, occasionally, vehicle impact. Most surviving houses are in domestic use and have usually been extended due to the small size of the original structure (Fig 7.1).

Roadside milestones are another prominent remnant from turnpiked roads (Fig 7.2), although many have disappeared through road widening and theft.

Legislation in the mid-18th century made it compulsory for trusts to erect them along their routes, and many developed their own distinctive styles of road markers from stone blocks to cast-iron pillars; a good selection of the latter, painted white with black lettering and carrying the foundry name, survives on the Derbyshire turnpikes.

Bridges

Before the advent of the main railway system, the turnpike trustees were responsible for commissioning many of the major bridges built in this country. These were designed by some of the most eminent engineers of the time. The forefather of modern bridges was Abraham Darby's Iron Bridge of 1779. The iron bridge then evolved through such developments as Burdon's Wearmouth Bridge in Sunderland, built in 1796. However, it was Thomas Telford who became the major exponent of its development with such bridges as Craigellachie on the River Spey of 1814 (Fig 7.3), Waterloo Bridge of 1815 over the Conwy at Betws-y-Coed, and Holt Fleet and Mythe of 1828, both over the Severn. At the same time turnpike trusts were building larger stone bridges; Telford's 1828 Severn Bridge at Over is an excellent example.

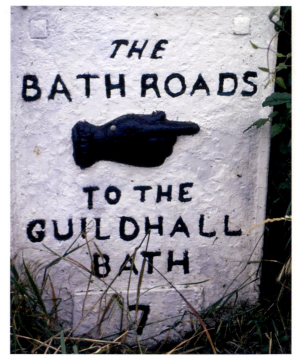

Figure 7.2 One of the 'Terminus Stones' on the Kingsdown Road, Bath, erected by the Bath Turnpike Trust to mark the end of their roads leading out of the town (© Marilyn Palmer)

In the early 19th century the suspension bridge was being adopted for larger clear spans. The early work of Captain Samuel Brown is still to be seen, albeit in a somewhat modified form, in the Union Bridge of 1820 over the River Tweed, some 6 miles upstream from Berwick-upon-Tweed. Other notable early examples are Telford's Menai Bridge of 1826 and I K Brunel's Clifton Suspension Bridge of 1864. A minor but significant suspension bridge of this period survives virtually as built at Horkstow on the River Ancholme in North Lincolnshire; it was constructed in 1836 to a design by Sir John Rennie. An interesting variation on the suspension bridge was designed by James Dredge; surviving examples are Victoria Bridge in Bath of 1836 and the Bridge of Oich of 1854 in the Highlands.

In the 20th century steel replaced iron in large road bridges; the Tyne Bridge of 1928 and the new Wearmouth Bridge of 1929 are outstanding examples. The use of concrete reinforced with iron and steel in bridge construction became more common in the early 20th century, particularly under the influence of L G Mouchel; bridges built this way include the Horseshoe Bridge in Spalding, Lincolnshire, and the Royal Tweed Bridge of 1928 in Berwick-on-Tweed.

Where navigable rivers requiring large head room were crossed, some form of opening bridge was usually required. Various types of draw bridges, swing bridges and bascule bridges were the most common solutions. William Jessop's swing bridge at Selby of 1791 over the Yorkshire Ouse was an early timber-built example that was not replaced until 1970. Newcastle Swing Bridge over the Tyne of 1876, the 1890s' swing bridges over the Manchester Ship canal and Boothferry Bridge over the Yorkshire Ouse of 1929 illustrate the evolution of this type of structure. The Scherzer rolling bascule bridge gained popularity for large opening bridges in the early 20th century; King George V Bridge at Keadby, Lincolnshire, of 1916 and Duke Street Bridge in Birkenhead of 1931 are good examples. The alternative of tunnelling was used in some locations such as the Blackwall Tunnel of 1897 and in the early 20th century in the Rotherhithe Tunnel of 1908 and the Mersey Tunnel of 1934.

The late 20th century saw new road bridges built across many of the largest estuaries of the British Isles; major examples are the Firth of Forth Road Bridge of 1964, the Severn Bridge of 1966, and the Humber Bridge of 1981. Each of these modern suspension bridges incorporated major design modifications learnt as a result of the USA's Tacoma Narrows Bridge collapse of 1940.

The transporter bridge in which a travelling gondola deck was suspended from a high-level gantry was briefly popular in the early 20th century in flat locations where long approaches to a traditional high-level bridge would have been impractical. Examples of this rare type survive at Newport in Wales (1906), Middlesbrough (1911), and Warrington (1915).

Figure 7.3 Telford's cast-iron bridge of 46m span over the River Spey at Craigellachie. Cast at Plas Kynaston Foundry, the bridge was completed in 1815 (© Mark Sissons)

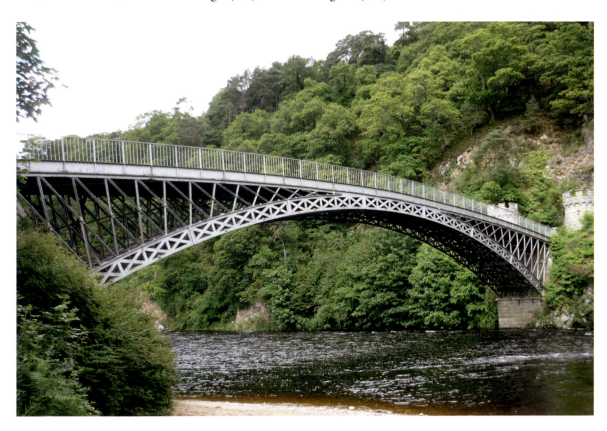

Key sites

Good examples of toll houses can be seen in *Avoncroft Museum* which is home to the reconstructed Little Malvern Toll House, *Blists Hill Museum* houses a Telford-designed toll house from Shelton on the Holyhead Road. Aberystwyth South Gate Toll House of 1771 is now at *St Fagans Museum* near Cardiff. Houses in their original locations can be seen at *Steanor Bottom Toll House*, Calderbrook Road in Todmorden, Calderdale, *Barrowford*, Lancashire (see Fig 7.1), and *Butterow Toll House*, Rodborough, Gloucestershire. There are several good Telford toll houses on the original alignment of the A5 in Shropshire and in Anglesey, where *Llanfair Pwllgwyngyll* still retains its toll board. Abraham Darby's *Iron Bridge* of 1779 is in the care of English Heritage; a board on its toll house lists tolls payable, showing that not even the royal family was exempt from payment.

Further reading

D Hey, *Packmen, Carriers and Packhorse Roads* (Leicester University Press, 1980), is an excellent account of the landscape of trade and communications in North Derbyshire and South Yorkshire, while T Prevett's *Roads and Trackways of North Wales* (Landmark Collector's Library, 2008) deals with an area where many structures from the pre-turnpike era survive. R K Morriss, *Roads: Archaeology and Architecture* (Tempus, 2005), is the best introduction to the subject. G N Wright's *Turnpike Roads* (Shire, 1992) provides a good introduction to turnpike roads; for more detail on the legislation and their history, W Albert *The turnpike road system in England 1663–1840* (Cambridge University Press, 1972) and J Copeland, *Roads and their Traffic, 1750–1850* (David & Charles 1968) are both useful. For a recent study of an entire road, see J Quartermaine, B Trinder & R Turner, *Thomas Telford's Holyhead Road* (CBA Research Report **135**, 2003).

There are a number of regional and local histories such as those by T Jenkinson and P Taylor on Toll Houses in North and South Devon and Essex (Polystar Press, 2009–10). *The Iron Bridge* by N Cossons & B Trinder (Phillimore, 2002), as well as giving a history of the original iron bridge, discusses the evolution of iron road bridges. For bridges, see McFetrich, *An Encyclopaedia of Britain's Bridges* (Priory Ash, 2010). For the development of roads in the 20th century see M Stratton & B Trinder, *Twentieth Century Industrial Archaeology* (Spon, 2000).

For a list of turnpike trusts see http://www.turnpikes.org.uk/The%20 Turnpike%20Roads.htm (site last accessed July 2011).

7.3   Early railways

It is often assumed that the history of railways starts in 1825 with the opening of the Stockton and Darlington Railway, but this is very far from the truth and this section looks at the early railways which pre-dated the coming of the locomotive railway, and for which considerable archaeological evidence remains.

Historical development

There is clear evidence from Germany of the use of track-guided vehicles running on rails in use in mines as early as the 15th century. Much of this technology came to the British Isles from Germany in the middle of the 16th century, when the government imported German mining experts to improve British copper production. They may well have developed horse-drawn railways here as well as in their native land, but we have no actual evidence of this. It is difficult to judge whether these developments had any effect on what we think may be the earliest English horse-drawn railway (also referred to as waggonway, tramway or gangway) for which there is documentary evidence, built from pits at Strelley and Billborough to Wollaton, near Nottingham, by Huntingdon Beaumont in 1603. Like many of the later locomotive railways, it was built because of the demand for cheaper coal in major markets. Beaumont subsequently moved to north-east England where he continued to be involved in the development of early railways, building three railways down to the River Blyth *c* 1605. There is evidence of railways being built at Broseley in Shropshire at around the same date. The more extensive development of early wooden railways in Britain took place from the second half of the 17th century onwards in the North-East and also in Shropshire during the 18th century, the lines being built to convey coal to the Rivers Tyne, Blyth, and Wear for coastwise shipment in the first case, and coal and ironstone to ironworks and to the River Severn in the second. Between 1700 and 1800 the mileage of waggonways in the North-East grew from 37 to 146.

Figure 7.4 Plan of part of the waggonway at Lambton Pit Colliery, Sunderland, excavated in 1996. Constructed *c* 1812–17, these wooden rails were mainly of oak and ran through a series of points, as can be seen here at the junction of two of the tracks (© Northern Counties Archaeological Services for the City of Sunderland)

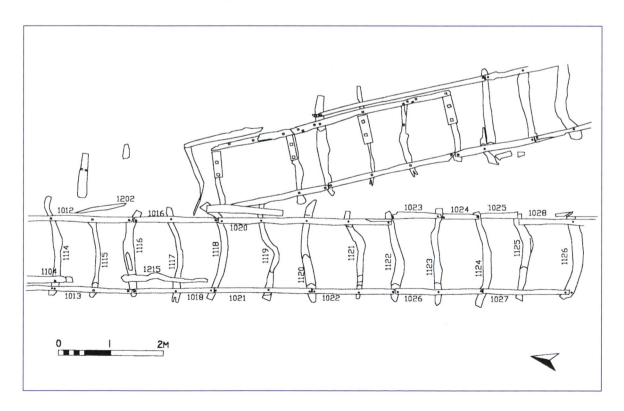

Early railways consisted of two parallel wooden rails carrying four-wheeled horse-drawn wagons (Fig 7.4). The wooden rails wore very quickly despite the often-used addition of an extra strip of wood and later iron strips on the bearing surface of the rail. Cast-iron rails pegged to heavy stone blocks set in a foundation of broken stone were introduced in Shropshire from the mid-18th century. Within the last decade, archaeological evidence has been found for at least three such systems, at Bedlam in the Ironbridge Gorge, Bersham in north Wales, and Lambton Colliery on Wearside (Fig 7.4). Other structures such as the Bowes Railway, Causey Arch at Tanfield, the dry stone embankments and inclines of the Cromford and High Peak, and Dunston Staithes, survive to illustrate this phase of railway development. Two distinctly different types of rail were used, each favoured by different engineers: the plateway, in which a plain wheel ran on track with an L-shaped flanged plate to constrain its direction; and the railway in which the wheel carried a flange and ran on edge rails. The flanged wheel eventually came to be seen as superior, and composite iron and wood rails were eventually replaced by wholly metal rails.

The canal mania of the later 18th century boosted the construction of new pre-locomotive railways. Where canals sought to penetrate hilly ground and building large numbers of locks proved to be too expensive, railways were used as an alternative. These railways also provided feeders to canals from quarries and mines in place of building a branch canal. It became common for acts of parliament licensing canals to include provision for the construction of railways to the more remote mines and quarries. Many of these were also constructed using wayleaves with the land owner in place of an act of parliament. This solution, although seemingly economical in terms of initial capital investment, often proved to be ruinously expensive as the annual payment made to land owners for wayleave costs rose rapidly. Extensive systems of canal-related railways were constructed in many areas, for example, in conjunction with the canals of south Wales, Shropshire and in the East Midlands.

In a later phase, a transitional type of railway was built; the Surrey Iron Railway, Kilmarnock and Troon, and the Hay Railway are all examples of this genre. These were true cross-country railways but still normally connected with waterborne transport rather than any other railway system. They continued predominantly to employ horse power on the level and stationary engines or gravity on inclines. The promotion and development of some of these lines overlaps with the arrival of locomotive-worked railways. Examples of this last generation include the Cromford and High Peak, Whitby and Pickering, and Stanhope and Tyne railways.

The engineering of these early railways resembled that of contemporary canal engineering. Long level sections, tight curves, and a route that frequently clung to a contour, produced a relatively level trackway which gave easy passage for horses at minimum cost. Where a change in level was required, the usual solution was an inclined plane. These planes were gravity-worked where the normal flow of traffic was downhill or employed a winding engine or water balance when the principal traffic was either travelling in both directions or against the gradient. The second generation of horse-worked railways used cast-iron track, employing either edge or plate rails, usually of fish-bellied profile, with a length of *c* 3ft (1m). Rail weight was typically 30 to 50lb (13.6–22.7kg) per yard. The rails were usually laid on large dressed stone blocks which had a wooden plug inserted in a hole in the block to which the rail was then spiked. Conventional transverse timber sleepers were also used. None of these types of rail was suited to locomotive working. The track was too light and, in the case of cast-iron rail, too brittle. With stone block sleepers, the gauge was prone to spread under the weight of the locomotive. From the mid-1820s, wrought-iron rails in 15ft (4.6m) lengths began to be laid; these were far better suited to locomotive working.

Buildings and landscape context

Early railway companies constructed very few purpose-built buildings and virtually none in the form of stations as currently understood. The main building types were horse stables and weighbridge houses, along with haulage drums and winding engine houses at the heads of inclines. Small warehouses and transhipment buildings were also constructed, normally where the railways met a canal. This phase of railway construction has left few extant buildings other than a handful of examples of the types detailed above, but there is much more in the way of landscape remains. The courses of many early railways, although often abandoned over 100 years ago, are still clearly visible. Landscape features in the form of cuttings, embankments, inclines, and bridges still remain on many early routes. Stone sleeper blocks are occasionally found *in situ* and can frequently be seen reused in adjacent buildings and retaining walls. Some early railway routes have been converted into footpaths and cycleways.

Power sources

Early railways relied on the horse and the power of gravity. In their later phase water balance systems and steam-driven stationary winding engines were introduced on some inclined planes. The preserved beam winding engine at Middleton Top on the Cromford and High Peak and the electric winder on the Bowes Railway at Blackham's Hill both illustrate how rope haulage was applied to early railways. Many routes were subsequently modified and rebuilt into conventional railways but the use of steam locomotives on lines as originally built was rare, mainly due to the problems with the strength of the track and sharply curved alignment outlined above.

Key sites

The *Haytor Tramway* on Dartmoor, built to convey granite to the Stover canal and thence to the sea, illustrates an early stone-built guided trackway and is a scheduled monument (Fig 7.5). The *Bowes Railway* in Tyne and Wear is a rare survivor of the early railways built to carry coal from the Great Northern

Figure 7.5 Points on the Haytor granite railway of *c* 1820, Dartmoor; iron flanges would have moved the wagons from one rail to another (© Marilyn Palmer)

Coalfield down to the Tyne. *Causey Arch* near Stanley in County Durham is possibly the earliest surviving railway bridge in the country, and well interpreted. The route of the Monmouth and Brecon canal, particularly around *Clydach*, contains the remains of numerous tramways serving the canal. The course of the *Cromford and High Peak Railway* in Derbyshire is a long-distance footpath at the southern end, and a very good example of how early horse-drawn railways were engineered; the *Middleton Top engine house* is open to the public. The *Leicester and Swannington Railway* was built as a composite railway with locomotives on sections, but at its northern end the railway descended the *Swannington Incline*, where a steam winding engine was used to draw trucks uphill. The area is maintained by the Swannington Heritage Trust and the engine itself is housed in *York Railway Museum*, which also has a display of the track used on early railways, as does *Amberley Museum* in Sussex.

Further reading

A recent good general guide is A Guy & J Rees, *Early Railways* (Shire, 2011). The classic introduction to this early phase of railways is B Baxter's *Stone Blocks and Iron Rails* (David & Charles, 1966). M J T Lewis's definitive work, *Early Wooden Railways* (Routledge & Kegan Paul, 1970), gives a full and detailed context for early railways. J Simmons, *The Railways of Britain: an historical introduction* (2nd edn, Macmillan, 1968) puts early railways into context with later railway developments.

Among specific histories of individual lines, which are helpful in understanding the detail of these railways, are S Hughes, *The Brecon Forest Tramroads: the archaeology of an early railway system* (RCAHMW, 1990); J Marshall, *The Cromford and High Peak Railway*, (Martin Bairstow, 1996), and J van Laun, *Early Limestone*

Railways (The Newcomen Society, 2001), which covers parts of south Wales and Monmouthshire. The collected papers from the Early Railway Conferences are also a very useful source; see http://www.steamindex.com/library/earlyrly.htm.

There are several articles in *Industrial Archaeology Review*: particularly relevant are Stephen Grenter, 'A Wooden Waggonway Complex at Bersham Ironworks, Wrexham' (**15**:2, 1993, 195–205) and 'The archaeological excavation of wooden waggonway remains at Lambton D Pit, Sunderland', by I Ayris, J Nolan & A Durkin (**20**:1, 1998, 5–22). The *Journal of the Railway and Canal Historical Society* should also be consulted; see http://www.rchs.org.uk/trial/gwpf.php?wpage=publications (accessed August 2011).

7.4 Rivers and canals

Historical development

River navigations and early canals

Until the beginning of the canal age river navigations, complemented by coast-wise shipping, had formed the main communication arteries for trade in the British Isles. Road development had been limited to pack horse routes and some early turnpikes, neither of which were ideally suited to the transport of raw materials in bulk. With the exception of the Roman Foss Dyke, linking the River Witham to the Trent, no canals were built in Britain before the 16th century.

The early technology of river navigation came originally from China and developed in Europe from the 11th century onwards. In the 16th century, acts for improving river navigations in Britain began to be passed. The Exeter canal of 1566, which by-passed a part of the River Exe, was the first canal in the country to use conventional mitre-gated pound locks but was still essentially a river navigation. Many of the major river navigations in the British Isles were improved in the 17th century through dredging, straightening of the water course, and the building of pound locks to replace flash locks. However, river navigations, in addition to suffering from flood damage, were always an uneasy balance between the conflicting interests of mill owners, land drainage and navigation.

Britain was behind the rest of Europe in developing non-river navigation canals but after a slow start expansion was rapid. The Newry canal in Ireland, opened in 1742, was the first non-river navigation in the British Isles. On the mainland, the opening of the Sankey canal in 1757 was followed by the Bridgewater canal in 1761. The latter halved the price of coal in Manchester and triggered a period of 'canal mania' in Britain. Between 1760 and 1820 over 100 canals were built, and the total mileage of navigable rivers and canals rose from around 1000 miles (c 1610km) in 1750 to 4250 miles (c 6840km) by 1850.

Early canals, with their constant depth when compared with river navigations, were usually built with the objective of permitting better movement of mineral resources to their end market; 50 tons could be hauled in a canal barge by one horse compared with 30 tons by river boat or 2 tons by wagons on a surfaced road. Coal and limestone were two of the major cargoes carried on early canals. A second generation of canals, often referred to as the Grand Cross, joined up the major river navigations of the Humber, Thames, Mersey, and Severn, and helped to solve the transport problems of the landlocked Midlands. James Brindley was the foremost engineer in this early phase of canal building. Early canals tend to follow contours and have few heavy engineering works, which is illustrated very well along the unimproved stretches of the Oxford canal. The success of these early canals is demonstrated by the huge concentrations of industry that built up around many of them. Prior to the canal age all the major cities of the country lay on the coast or on a major river, but canals facilitated the development of large inland cities. In the late 18th and early 19th centuries the network was expanded by canals providing shorter routes between major population centres and also by speculative canals accessing areas with a mainly agrarian economy. The latter were often financial failures although their impact on the surrounding area was frequently positive in terms of access to heavy goods such as bricks and coal. The successful canals from this later building phase are frequently characterised by heavier engineering works with large cuttings and embankments and flights of locks grouped together. New routes to serve towns and industry are typified by the Grand Junction Canal completed in 1805 and the Birmingham and Liverpool Junction Canal opened in 1835. The major engineers of this great phase of canal building were William Jessop, Thomas Telford, and John Rennie. The canal engineers had the task of organising engineering works and managing contractors on a scale not seen before in this country. They developed surveying and estimating techniques that would be essential for the subsequent development of railways.

Nearly all English and Welsh canals were financed by private capital which was frequently raised locally. In contrast, many of the canals in Scotland and Ireland were funded by exchequer loans and other government financing instruments. The lack of any central control resulted in two distinct types of canals emerging in Britain. Those connected to the great rivers of Scotland, northern England and southern England are usually broad, that is with locks over 12ft (3.6m) wide, whilst the canals of Wales and the English Midlands were predominantly narrow with locks only 7ft (2.1m) wide. The length of vessel varied but was usually between 58 and 70ft (17.7–21.3m) on these canals, whereas the broad canals could take wider vessels. These variations inhibited the establishment of a national canal network and often prevented the use of larger boats even on broad canals if they had to traverse narrow canals en route.

The 19th century

Competition from the railway network from the 1850s onwards saw freight volumes and traffic receipts fall. Throughout much of the 19th century and after the coming of the main line railways, most of the British canal system was in a state of atrophy. Years of petty squabbles, paying high dividends and not investing in developing the system, coupled with toll systems that did not encourage through traffic, made much of their business an easy target for the railways. As canal share prices fell, the canal companies were frequently purchased by the competing railway company. Most of these starved the canals that they owned of capital investment which led to a long period of decay and also ironically to many of their original features surviving. The exceptions to this were where the canal system provided a useful feeder to the railway, as in much of Birmingham and the Black Country, and where a canal provided access to an area covered by a rival railway company.

In the 20th century, road competition made many of the narrow canals obsolete for most commercial transportation, and many British canals fell further into decay. Only the Manchester Ship Canal, the Weaver Navigation, and the Aire and Calder Navigation continued to be developed in the late 19th and early 20th centuries. The canals were nationalised under the 1948 transport act and many were formally abandoned at this time while others were categorised as 'remainder waterways'; with no requirement to maintain them in a navigable condition, minimal money was spent on them. Commercial carrying saw another drastic decline in the face of cheap road transport. The Inland Waterways Association was founded in 1946 as a charitable organisation dedicated to the maintenance and restoration of the British canal system, and fought hard political battles in the 1950s and 1960s to prevent the closure of the smaller canals; without their efforts, much of what does survive today would have been lost. In 1962 management of the canals was transferred to British Waterways and although commercial traffic continued to dwindle to almost nothing, there has been a dramatic expansion in leisure use since then. This increased activity has seen extensive refurbishment of much of the network and also the reopening of many miles of derelict canal, often with considerable assistance from volunteers. Currently (2011), the Environment Agency has responsibility for rivers used for navigation like the Thames and those in the fens and the Broads, as well as some other waterways as part of its flood control management remit, while proposals have been put forward to hive off the responsibilities of British Waterways to a charitable trust.

Landscape context

Canals in the lower reaches of river valleys normally follow the course of the river quite closely, or even use the river as a part of the navigation. In the higher reaches of a river valley the canal will frequently climb away from the river into a valley-side location as it gains height towards the watershed of the area. Many of the early canals were built along a natural contour line to minimise engineering works at the expense of greater length and a winding course; in consequence their landscape impact is comparatively low. Canals from the second generation and later often have much more visible landscape impact in the construction of substantial cuttings and embankments, along with large feeder reservoirs.

The final generation of ship canals have a huge landscape impact and their construction frequently involved rerouting large rivers and produced massive associated earthworks.

Buildings

Each canal tended to develop its own architectural style. The most common surviving buildings are the houses for lock keeper and lengthsman, usually small functional structures built from local materials and frequently on narrow strips of land adjacent to locks. Some canal companies produced architectural embellishment on their houses and others had characteristic forms. The two most notable of these are the barrel-shaped roofs of the Stratford Canal cottages and the round houses of the Thames and Severn Canal. At most canal junctions, where canals owned by different companies met, toll houses can be found, often with a characteristic bay window. Superior properties may be found at certain locations for engineers and district managers. Many canal companies built offices, normally in urban locations and frequently with some degree of architectural style. They also built their own maintenance workshops and many of these survive, frequently with enclosed dry docks and associated facilities for building lock gates and general blacksmiths' work. Typical examples are Icknield Port on the Birmingham Canal Navigations, Bulbourne on the Grand Union, and Clachnaharry on the Caledonian Canal. Canalside warehouses are frequently found both along the course of the canal and particularly near to junctions with other waterways; these are covered in Chapter 8. Whilst not built by the canal company itself, the public house became a typical canalside building as a refreshment stop for boatmen (and now leisure boat passengers) but there is no clear typology of these. Canal companies also frequently built stables but surviving structures are rare. It is fortunate that under the management of British Waterways the conservation of canal buildings and structures has generally been carried out in a sympathetic manner.

Structures

Many characteristic canal structures survive on both active and abandoned canals. Bridges are one of the most visible landscape features and were built wherever a road crossed the canal or to allow access to fields separated by the building of the canal. These are usually to a standard design for any particular canal and of local building materials. The hump-back bridge is the most characteristic but for the sake of economy many canal companies used draw bridges and swing bridges. These were usually built of timber but have often been replaced by later steel structures. The southern Oxford Canal and the Leeds and Liverpool both have a large number of such structures. Bridges built to transfer the towing path from one side of the canal to the other can have a particularly satisfying aesthetic form, those of the Macclesfield Canal being especially good. In areas where there are industrial branches from the

Figure 7.6 Roving
bridges cast in the
Horseley Ironworks,
at Smethwick
Junction on the
Birmingham
Canal Navigation
(© Marilyn Palmer)

canal, as found in the Birmingham Canal Navigation system, or the route has
been straightened, as on the northern Oxford Canal, many elegant arched iron
tow path bridges are to be found. Those built by the Horseley Iron Works are
particularly common in the West Midlands (Fig 7.6).

The locks and the lock equipment vary greatly from one canal to another,
both in size and in construction detail. Other details such as overflow weirs and
by-washes tend to have a characteristic form on different canals. Where gradients
had to be surmounted, flights of locks were built; these differ from staircase locks
in that the locks are separate from one another and there is a navigable pound
or stretch of water between the locks. The Tardebigge Flight on the Worcester
and Birmingham Canal is the longest flight of locks in the UK, comprising 30
narrow locks over 2¼ miles (3.6km) and raising the canal some 200ft (61m), while
the Caen Flight on the Kennet and Avon Canal has 29 locks over 2 miles and
raises the level by 277ft (84m); this includes a particularly steep flight of sixteen
locks with extensive side ponds to conserve water. Where there was a sudden
change of level, it was cheaper to build staircase locks with shared gates, as on
the Grand Union Leicester Line at Watford and Foxton; these too made use of
side ponds. The most dramatic of these staircase locks are the great set of eight
locks at Banavie on the Caledonian Canal, the longest staircase in the UK and
now hydraulically operated, and the Five Rise locks at Bingley on the Leeds and
Liverpool Canal in West Yorkshire which are the steepest. There are many other
examples of two- and three-rise staircase lock sets on other canals.

There have been several attempts to develop alternative methods of managing
changes in height in canals whilst avoiding the use of locks, since passage through
these was time-consuming as well as wasting water. Most of these involved canal

lifts or inclined planes. The sole surviving functioning example of a vertical canal lift in the UK can be found at Anderton in Cheshire, built in 1875 and recently restored, which moves boats between the Trent and Mersey Canal and the River Weaver. The use of inclined planes involved moving the boats on trolleys or water-filled caissons between the levels, partly by gravity but making use of a steam engine for ancillary power. The remains of such planes can be found at Foxton on the Leicester section of the Grand Union Canal and also at the Blists Hill site of the Ironbridge Gorge Museum, where the Hay Incline took the Shropshire tub boat canal down to the River Severn. There are far more impressive inclined planes in Europe, but a modern method of moving boats between two levels of waterway is the Falkirk Wheel in Scotland, which links the Forth and Clyde Canal with the Union Canal.

Visually, the most impressive of canal features are the great aqueducts (Fig 7.7). Once again both form and constructional detail vary on different canals. Early aqueducts are usually squat with low short-span arches. The Dove aqueduct by James Brindley, where the Trent and Mersey Canal crosses the River Dove just east of Burton-on-Trent, is a typical example. As the engineers' confidence grew, larger span masonry aqueducts were built. Good exemplars are Rennie's Lune aqueduct on the Lancaster Canal and his Dundas aqueduct over the River Avon on the Kennet and Avon Canal. Jessop and Telford further enhanced the masonry aqueduct by inserting an iron trough to contain the water inside a masonry structure, as at Chirk on the Welsh borders. Finally the iron trough aqueduct was developed by Jessop and Telford and from modest beginnings in

Figure 7.7 The Bridgewater Canal between Worsley and Manchester originally crossed the River Irwell on an aqueduct of 1761, one of the first of its kind in the world. The construction of the Manchester Ship Canal in 1893 led to its replacement by another unique structure, the present swing aqueduct which forms a sealed tank to contain the canal, pivoting on an island and operated by hydraulic power (© Michael Nevell)

Derby and at Longdon-on-Tern, they went on to build the great aqueduct at Pontcysyllte on the Ellesmere Canal which was opened in 1805. Many smaller iron and masonry aqueducts can be found on other canals.

Water supply was a continual problem for many canals. Adjacent to the summit levels, large reservoirs can often be found with substantial earth embankment gravity dams. The other solution to water supply was to pump the water from adjacent rivers or streams, by means of either water or steam power (Fig 7.8); some survive in working order, but there are many other locations where the buildings of old canal pumping engine houses can still be found.

When a canal had to pass through hilly terrain, there was sometimes no alternative but to construct a tunnel, and techniques that had been developed by mining engineers were used. This was very much an action of last resort as costs for both the construction and maintenance of canal tunnels were very high, and their construction frequently led to lengthy delays in the completion of a canal. The characteristic landscape features in addition to the tunnel portals are ventilation shafts along the route of the tunnel, which are frequently surrounded by spoil heaps from the construction of the tunnel. As most early tunnels had no tow path, there is usually a horse path passing over the top of the tunnel route. The longest canal tunnel was the Standedge Tunnel on the Huddersfield Narrow Canal through the Pennines, over 3 miles (4.8km) long and recently reopened.

Canalside furniture is a further feature on most canals; once again its design varies with each canal. This includes such items as milestones, bridge name or number plates, bollards, rope rubbing strips, rope rollers, and cranes to name but a few. Many structures associated with other industries are to be found in canalside locations; typical of these are lime kilns and brick works. Small dry

Figure 7.8 The restored pumping wheel at Melingriffith near Cardiff, which lifted water from the tailrace of the Melingriffith Ironworks into the Glamorganshire Canal (© Marilyn Palmer)

docks used by canalside boat builders and repairers can also be found which often drained into an adjacent water course or were situated at the head of a lock flight.

Key sites

Thanks to a massive restoration programme, many canal features have survived in a modified form; many original features remain to be seen along derelict stretches of abandoned canals. The canal museums at *Gloucester*, *Stoke Bruerne* and *Ellesmere Port* provide an excellent overview of many canal features and are also situated at sites which encompass many features of the canal system, notably its warehouses.

Examples of water-powered pumping engines still exist on the Kennet and Avon at *Claverton* and the *Melingriffith Water Pump* on the Glamorganshire Canal (see Fig 7.7), while steam-powered canal pumping stations still containing their machinery can be seen at *Leawood* on the Cromford Canal and *Crofton* on the Kennet and Avon Canal. The *Anderton Boat Lift* in Cheshire has recently been restored and opened to canal traffic. The tunnel portals of the *Sapperton Tunnel* on a disused stretch of the Thames and Severn Canal are impressive, while the *Braunston Tunnel* on the Grand Union in Northamptonshire has a good example of the horse path and spoil heaps from the original tunnel construction.

There are many notable canalside settlements which survive, often with their original canal furniture and buildings: *Shardlow* on the Trent and Mersey, and *Stourport* at the junction of the Staffordshire and Worcestershire Canal and the River Severn, are good examples.

Adaptive reuse

Many lock-keepers cottages survive in private ownership, and converted canal warehouses are covered in Chapter 9. Occasional conversions of other buildings can be found, such as the former beam engine house near *Hillmorton Locks* on the Oxford canal.

Further reading

There is a huge collection of publications on canals and inland waterways. The best book to begin with is N Crowe's *English Heritage Book of Canals* (1994), written by someone who was British Waterways' first Heritage Manager. The many books by L T C Rolt deal not just with the history of inland navigation but also with the fight to save the canal system in the 1960s; see especially *Landscape with Canals* (2nd edn, Alan Sutton, 1984) and *Navigable Waterways* (2nd edn, Penguin Books, 1985). The best history of early waterways is still T S Willan, *River Navigation in England* (1936), while R Russell, *Lost Canals and Waterways of Britain* (David & Charles, 1982), is a useful guide to abandoned waterways.

The series of regional histories in the books by C Hadfield (ed) in the *Canals of the British Isles* series (David & Charles, 1967–77) are still very useful. Detailed maps of all bridges, locks, and other structures can be found in the series edited by D Perret,

Regional Canal Guides (Collins/Nicholson). Probably the best archaeological study of any canal is S Hughes, *The Archaeology of the Montgomeryshire Canal* (2nd edn, RCAHMW, 1988). D Tew's *Canal Inclines and Lifts* (Alan Sutton, 1984) is a useful short discussion, while the development of early canal pumping and water supply is studied in J H Andrew, 'Canal Pumping Engines' (*Industrial Archaeology Review* **15**:2, 1993, 140–59). S Hughes, 'The Swansea Canal: Navigation and Power Supplier' (*Industrial Archaeology Review* **4**:1, 1979–80, 51–69), is an excellent discussion of a canal used partly as a source of water-power supply to various industries, something that could well be studied on other industrial canals. For more detail on specific canals there are numerous local histories, many published by David & Charles and also a substantial number published by local canal societies. A website that gives a full list of opening and closure dates for nearly all British waterways is to be found at http://www.jim-shead.com/waterways/mwp.php?wpage=Introducing-Canal-History.htm (last accessed July 2011). See also M Nevell & T Wyke (eds), *Bridgewater 250: the archaeology of the Bridgewater Canal* (Centre for Applied Archaeology, University of Salford, 2011).

7.5   Locomotive railways

There is an enormous body of literature on the history of locomotive railways, so this book does not attempt to duplicate that. Rather, it deals with the buildings and structures which are most likely to be encountered by those working on sites of the industrial period. Archaeologically, most excavated railway remains have been from the period of horse-drawn railways which was covered earlier in this chapter. Locomotive railways, however, had a massive impact on the landscape. By the time of the Great Exhibition in 1851, there were already more than 6000 miles of railway in England and Wales. Construction involved engineering works on a scale not previously seen because of the need to minimise gradients. Railways also influenced the pattern of settlement to a much greater extent than canals had done, not just with planned settlements for railway workers as in Derby and Swindon, for example, but also by enabling the transformation of what had been villages on the outskirts of towns into commuter suburbs. Leisure patterns, too, were affected, enabling those who had never gone far from home to visit the capital and to take seaside holidays. Railways even changed the character of sport in the second half of the 19th century, turning local matches and meetings into national events. The social influence of the railways was therefore far greater than that of any earlier forms of transport.

Buildings

Much of the architecture and infrastructure of the 19th-century railway system survives today, with a significant part of it still in daily use. The archetypical railway building is the station. However, it should be remembered that many early passenger railways, whether steam or horse powered, used systems for selling tickets and handling passengers that owed far more to stage-coach practice than to the modern railway. Local hostelries were often used by early railways to provide these services, and most railways built before 1840 had little dedicated architecture; where buildings were required they were usually of modest size and often reflected the local vernacular. On most railways the station does not emerge as a discrete architectural form until the 1840s when railway companies saw the benefit of impressing the public by employing leading architects to design their principal stations (Fig 7.9). They were frequently pioneers in the use of building materials and many of the earliest examples of the use of materials such as cast iron, wrought iron and concrete are to be found in railway structures. The subsequent range of buildings is vast, ranging from iconic London termini such as *St Pancras* and *Paddington*; great city centre stations like *Bristol Temple Meads* and *Newcastle*; and through to the smallest wayside station. Some railway companies used standard designs, most notably the Midland; others gave architects a free hand. Architectural styles run the full gamut through Tudor, Elizabethan, neoclassical, Italianate and gothic. Some railways retained 'in house' architects, notably the North-Eastern, while others drew their design work from a pool of external architects. It was usual to have the major buildings on the platform that handled the most outbound passenger traffic, with frequently little more than a timber shelter on the other platform. The station master's house was usually built as an integral part of the station offices.

The train shed has long been recognised as an outstanding achievement in both architectural and engineering terms, stations with such sheds sometimes being viewed as the cathedrals of the industrial age. Their history in the 19th century seems to be one of ever-increasing spans. Large train sheds have survived comparatively well with the great London termini illustrating a range of styles. Outside London, Brunel's *Temple Meads* and the fine train sheds at *York*, *Newcastle*, and *Hull* are outstanding examples. The former *Manchester Central* train shed, now an exhibition centre, is an excellent example of adaptive re use. The train shed has been particularly at risk in many smaller stations, frequently demolished as passenger numbers fell and maintenance costs rose; early examples of this form are really quite rare, but in the north of England there are several survivors. At *Selby* the original shed of the Leeds and Selby Railway opened in 1834 has survived showing a composite construction of timber trusses supported on cast-iron columns. Some early stations had an overall train shed roof and foremost among the architects for employing smaller train shed roofs were I K Brunel and G T Andrews. Brunel usually used timber for the various companies for which he was engineer. An excellent example of this type built in 1850 by J R Hannaford survives at *Frome*. For the York and North Midland Railway, the York architect George Townsend Andrews built many station train sheds using an adapted form of the original Euston wrought-iron truss. A few of these survive such as *Richmond* and *Filey* of 1846 and a modern replica of 2011 at *Pickering*.

While many station buildings survive, both in active railway use and converted for domestic and other purposes, it is often the other buildings associated with

Figure 7.9 The
former Low Level
railway station in
Nottingham, designed
by T C Hine for
the Great Northern
Railway in 1857
(© Marilyn Palmer)

the railway that have disappeared. At present, it is not perhaps the stations and
their associated buildings, such as hotels, which are most at risk, but the broader
aspects of railway structures and engineering. The plethora of minor buildings
once to be found around both large and small stations has in many cases suffered
far more than the core station buildings. These minor buildings are frequently
omitted from sites which otherwise carry statutory protection. The list of such
structures is long and includes signal boxes, goods offices, goods sheds, coal sale
offices, water tanks, engine sheds, coal staithes, lime cells, and lengthsmen's
cabins to name but a few.

Among the most endangered of railway buildings is the goods warehouse (see
also Chapter 8). As miles of sidings have been lifted and the transport of goods
moved to the road, the railway warehouse has become superfluous. Many are
small in size and in rural or semi-rural locations, and it is perhaps these that have
survived better, being more easily adapted to light industrial or office uses and
sometimes for residential purposes. The archetypical rural goods warehouse was
single storey with arched access for railway vehicles offset to one side, an internal
platform, usually with a small crane, and a side loading bay for road vehicles. The
large and complex goods warehouses in many big cities and centres of industry
have largely been demolished, although excellent examples survive in *Manchester*
and at *Huddersfield* together with a nearby associated hydraulic pumping station
that once operated its cranes, lifts and capstans. These large warehouses were
often multi-storey buildings and many had internal wagon lifts allowing railway
vehicles to access several floors.

Many of the early railway companies built hotels adjacent to their principal
stations. These generally have a good rate of survival, with the former *Midland
Hotel* in Derby being one of the earliest. Many examples survive in London
with George Gilbert Scott's exuberant, recently reopened, *Midland Grand at St*

Figure 7.11 Cast-iron columns supporting the railway viaduct to Central Station in Manchester. Opened in 1880, this particular short stretch of urban railway demonstrated the problems of traversing the cityscape of the 19th century. The viaduct passed over the 18th-century Castlefield Canal basin and ran alongside the viaduct for the 1849 Manchester South Junction and Altrincham Railway. Further on, the building of the viaduct and station involved the demolition of hundreds of houses
(© Michael Nevell)

Figure 7.12 Bennerley Viaduct, Ilkeston, Derbyshire, is 1452ft (0.44km) long and crosses the River Erewash between Derbyshire and Nottinghamshire. Its foundations were liable to mining subsidence, so the lighter wrought iron was chosen in preference to brick. Constructed 1876–77, it formed part of the Great Northern Railway Derbyshire Extension which was built partly to exploit the local coalfields. The cost of demolition helped ensure its survival although it is on the Buildings at Risk Register
(© Marilyn Palmer)

such as Granger and Bourne's *Tees Viaduct* at Yarm on the Leeds and Thirsk Railway, the spectacular *Ribblehead Viaduct* by J S Crossley on the Settle and Carlisle line, J U Rastrick and David Moccata's *Ouse Valley Viaduct* at Balcombe, William Cubitt's *Digswell Viaduct* at Welwyn, and Brunel's *Maidenhead Bridge*. Taking railways into and above towns was a particular challenge; the great brick viaduct towering over *Stockport* was designed by George Watson Buck, and when completed in 1840 was the largest in the world. With textile mills nestling below its arches, it was and, to some extent still is, a magnificent tribute to Victorian engineering. London presented an even greater challenge, as demonstrated by the many viaducts and bridges throughout the city; some of these have recently been studied by the Museum of London as a result of the reconstruction of the East London Line.

In the second half of the 19th century some large wrought-iron viaducts were built, particularly on secondary main lines. Of the many that were constructed the only substantial survivors are W R Galbraith's *Meldon Viaduct* and Johnson's *Bennerley Viaduct* (Fig 7.12) on the border of Derbyshire and Nottinghamshire. Crossing the great estuaries of the country produced some truly monumental bridges of which the *Forth, Tay, Tamar*, and *Menai Straits* particularly stand out.

The engineering problems associated with the construction of tunnels were well understood by the beginning of the 19th century. Canal builders and mining engineers had already addressed many of the problems of building lengthy tunnels. While the function of the tunnel is to provide a safe passage through high ground, the entrance or portal of the tunnel provided an opportunity for architectural display – or not, for the tunnel portal is something one rarely sees as the train rushes inside. This did not prevent engineers giving architectural embellishment to some as at *Summit*, high in the Pennines, on the Manchester and Leeds line, or architectural elaboration as at *Bramhope* on the Leeds and Thirsk Railway with contrasting portals at either end, one gothic, one classical. Brunel's *Box Tunnel* and Stephenson's great tunnel at *Kilsby* in Northamptonshire also have considerable architectural style in their porticoes and, in the case of Kilsby, there are also monumental ventilation shafts. The building of many of these was recorded by the great artist J C Bourne, whose drawings of the building of the London and Birmingham Railway and the Great Western Railway give us an idea of the scale of engineering work required which is difficult to obtain from any other source. He also recorded some of the railway construction work in London, but the tunnels and stations for the Underground are a study in themselves and beyond the scope of this book.

Adaptive reuse

The closure of minor stations and complete branch lines from the 1930s through to the Beeching era resulted in the loss of many station buildings and other railway structures. Additionally, poor maintenance allowed buildings to fall into decay, or be disfigured by inappropriate additions. The demolition of some fine monuments, largely in the second half of the 20th century, particularly those of

Euston Station in London and St Enoch's in Glasgow, led to a public outcry. In the latter part of the 20th century the British Rail board and its successors began to take a more enlightened view of railway architecture and recognised the historic engineering of many other structures. In 1985 British Rail set up the Railway Heritage Trust as an independent company, to assist the operational railway in its preservation and upkeep of listed buildings and structures, and to facilitate the transfer of non-operational premises and structures to outside bodies willing to undertake their preservation (see http://www.railwayheritagetrust. co.uk/, last accessed August 2011). Additionally, the 681 railway buildings and structures listed in 1985 in England, Scotland, and Wales had increased to some 1650 by 2009; Ancient Monuments increased from 45 to over 100 in the same period, while numerous parts of the railway estate fall within Conservation Areas. Refurbishment of stations and structures began to celebrate many of the earlier features as opposed to the 1960s' trend for unsatisfactory embellishment or demolition. The National Railway Heritage Awards, given to public as well as private railways, provide some motivation for such restoration (see http://www. nrha.org.uk/, accessed September 2011).

Of all the categories of railway building it is the rural station that has fared best, being readily suitable for conversion for domestic use. Many examples, particularly on closed lines, have been successfully converted but retain the key elements of the former station buildings. Small goods warehouses survive in both light industrial use and have also seen successful conversion for housing. On preserved and heritage railways there are many examples of conserved railway architecture although some have suffered from inappropriate additions. For a full list of locations see http:// heritagerailways.com/ (site last checked July 2011). Several old railways have now been turned into cycle tracks; the first route created in 1977 by Sustrans, the sustainable transport network charity, was a cycleway along the disused track bed of the former Midland Railway from Bristol to Bath which had been closed for passenger traffic in the late 1960s. As well as leading to the conservation of the route this often results in the better preservation of bridges, stations, and other structures along the line.

Further reading

A good basic introduction can be gained from R Morriss, *The Archaeology of Railways* (Tempus, 1999), and F G Cockman's *Railway Architecture* (Shire, 1976). For more detail see M Binney & D Pearce's *Railway Architecture* (Orbis Publishing, 1979), together with G Biddle's books, *Victorian Stations* (David & Charles, 1973), *Great Railway Stations of Britain* (David & Charles, 1986), and *Britain's Historic Railway Buildings* (Oxford University Press, 2003). For more local detail, the series edited by D St John Thomas, *A Regional History of the Railways of Great Britain* (David & Charles), is a collection of regional volumes which provides good background information. There are also many other regional railway history books of which, unfortunately, many concentrate on everything but the architecture. There are however some excellent histories of the architecture of the pre-grouping

railway companies which were grouped to form the 'Big Four' railway companies in 1923. Amongst the best are A Vaughan, *A Pictorial Record of Great Western Architecture* (Oxford Publishing Company, 1977), and W Fawcett, *North Eastern Railway Architecture* (North Eastern Railway Association, 3 vols, 2001–05). R S Fitzgerald's *Liverpool Road Station, Manchester: an historical and architectural survey* (Manchester University Press, 1980) is a comprehensive survey of the oldest surviving purpose-built railway station in Britain, while J Cattell & K Falconer, *Swindon: the Legacy of a Railway Town* (RCHME, 1995), is an historical and architectural study of both the town and the railway works. For signal boxes, the Signalling Study Group's *The Signal Box: a Pictorial history and guide to design* (Oxford Publishing Company, 1986) is very useful and for engine sheds, R Griffiths & P Smith, *The Directory of British Engine Sheds* (Oxford Publishing Company, 2 vols, 1999). For small goods warehouses see M Nevell, 'The Archaeology of the Rural Railway Warehouse in North-West England' (*Industrial Archaeology Review* **32**:2, 2010, 103–15). A good recent archaeological study, undertaken by Museum of London Archaeology during the upgrade of the overground railways in east London, is E Dwyer,

Figure 7.13 Archaeological recording of the smoke-blackened flues which carried the waste gases from the boilers for the hydraulic pumping station at Somers Town goods yard near St Pancras Station (© MOLA)

The Impact of the Railways in the East End 1835–2010: historical archaeology from the London Overground east London Line (Museum of London Archaeology, 2011).

7.6 Air transport

The air transport industry has three key elements: aircraft construction, civil and military airfields. Civilian airfields have not generally been a subject of study by industrial archaeologists until the start of the 21st century. By then, the greater interest being taken by English Heritage in 20th-century landscapes, together with proposals for the redevelopment of both civil and military airfields, prompted several reports. On the whole, interest has been centred on military sites as part of English Heritage's Monuments Protection Programme, looking at 20th-century military defence rather than civilian airfields. Buildings for aircraft manufacture, particularly the shadow factories of World War II, have also received some attention. In the 1990s, an international Raphael programme (with Germany and France) was set up to increase public awareness (*L'Europe de l'Air*) and England's contribution to this project focused on Speke (Liverpool). The listing of the Speke complex has resulted in exemplary reuse but the parallel hoped-for thematic listing programme on civil aviation by English Heritage has not been systematically followed through.

The earliest flying fields were no more than a suitable field without buildings or associated structures. Timber buildings were constructed on early flying fields for aircraft storage and repair but were not of any particularly distinctive form.

First-generation civil airports all initially used grass runways and most were adapted from former RAF stations. Concrete runways and many of the facilities that we associate with an airport today were not developed until the late 1930s. World War II hugely accelerated the rate of development of all types of aviation and also produced large numbers of cheap surplus aircraft at the end of hostilities.

The principal UK airports are in the London area and their development is typical of many other aviation sites. The earliest London site for civil aviation was Croydon, which evolved from two adjacent World War I aerodromes and opened for commercial flying in March 1920. The airport was extended in the mid-1920s and a new purpose-designed terminal and other buildings were constructed on the eastern side of the site. After being requisitioned by the RAF it reverted to civilian usage at the end of World War II; it was too small a site for modern aeroplanes and the last scheduled flight departed in September 1959. Hendon in north London was always principally a military site and is now home to the excellent RAF museum.

Heathrow started life as the privately owned Great Western Aerodrome in the 1930s. At this time it was mainly used for the assembly and testing of aircraft, with Croydon remaining as the dominant commercial aerodrome for the capital. In World War II the RAF developed Heathrow as a transfer base rather than an operational frontline station. Civilian use commenced in May 1946 and its principal runway pattern was developed by 1947. Initially the airport was serviced from a rambling group of temporary buildings. The first permanent terminal called the Europa Building, which is now part of terminal 2, was opened in 1955.

Gatwick evolved from the Surrey Aero Club's site at Hunt's Green Farm in 1930. Early on it was used for a flying school and as a base for people flying in to watch races at the adjacent race course. Commercial flights started in 1936. After being requisitioned by the RAF, Gatwick was returned to civilian use after the war when a number of charter companies started to operate from there using war surplus aircraft. In 1952 Gatwick's status as London's second airport was confirmed. Stansted in Essex was opened in 1943 as a US air force base and developed for civilian charter business in the 1960s.

Between the wars there was an extensive programme of building municipal airports, many of which no longer exist. These airports mainly handled low passenger volumes on internal flights aimed at competing with road and rail transport.

Buildings

The aviation industry had requirements for specific building types quite unlike those built by any other industry. The major types were large hangars, for both construction and maintenance of aircraft, airport terminal buildings and control towers.

Some of the first-generation aircraft hangars used the principle of the Belfast Truss to obtain a satisfactory clear roof span. This design of roof had already been used in dock warehouses. Examples of this technique, which employed wooden trusses made out of a lattice work of short timbers, can be seen at the *Imperial War Museum* at Duxford in Cambridgeshire and at *Bracebridge Heath* in Lincolnshire. Many World War II hangars survive at locations all over the country. Later large examples of hangars are the *Brabazon hangar* of 1947 at Filton and *the Owen Williams-designed hangar at Heathrow*. Many specialist research buildings can be found at the *Royal Aircraft Establishment at Farnborough*. Early control towers survive at several civil airports and at many military fields, both active and disused. Most are distinguished by the glazed observation area on the top storey of the building. The greatest concentration of surviving military aviation buildings is in the county of *Lincolnshire* and there is excellent information at http://www.raf-lincolnshire.info/index.htm and for the whole of the country see http://www.controltowers.co.uk/Site%20Map.htm which has a useful directory of sites (both sites last visited August 2011). The Lincolnshire site includes a listing of hangar types used on military airfields. Many former hangars have found reuse for warehousing but the number of 1940s' and earlier buildings is now declining as redevelopment, rust, and age all take their toll.

Several examples of first-generation civil airport terminal facilities survive. At *Croydon* the current Airport House complex is an adaptive reuse of the world's first purpose-built airline terminal which was opened in 1928. The adjacent Airport Hotel survives as an independent hotel and restaurant. At Gatwick, the *Beehive terminal building* of 1936 can still be seen and the 1939 *Birmingham Airport terminal at Elmdon* survives although it is no longer a part of the current passenger terminal. Other examples of early terminal buildings can be found in *Brighton* in the joint control tower, the 1936 terminal at *Shoreham Airport*, and *Liverpool Airport's 1939 terminal at Speke*.

In the 1930s the focus for long-distance air travel moved towards flying boats in place of conventional ground-landing aircraft and facilities were constructed in Southampton Docks. Successive generations of long-haul flying boats operated by Imperial Airways provided services to most parts of the Empire until they ceased in November 1950. The pre-war terminal building at Southampton survives, now adapted to offices as *Imperial House*. Early development proposals for both Heathrow and Glasgow Prestwick included facilities for handling flying boats.

Further reading

An overview of aviation developments can be found in M Stratton & B Trinder, *Twentieth Century Industrial Archaeology* (Spon, 2000, 169–74). For a guide to airfield buildings see G B Innes, *British Airfield Buildings: Expansion and Inter War Periods (Aviation Pocket Guide)* (Midland Publishing, 2000), also *British Airfield Buildings of the Second World War* by the same author. *L'Europe de l'Air* stimulated considerable public interest and resulted in two books: a popular and lavishly produced book edited by P Smith & B Toulier, *Berlin Tempelhof, Liverpool Speke, Paris Le Bourget* (Editions du Patrimoine, 2000) and the proceedings of three conferences, B Hawkins, G Lechner & P Smith (eds), *Historic Airports: proceedings of the International L'Europe de l'Air conferences on aviation architecture* (English Heritage, 2005). A profile of the development of aircraft factories is given in M Stratton's 'Skating Rinks to Shadow Factories: the Evolution of British Aircraft Manufacturing Complexes' (*Industrial Archaeology Review* **18**:2, 1996, 223–44).

The English Heritage MPP on 20th-century military defence has produced some on-line publications, such as *Military Aviation Sites* (Conservation Management Guidance, 2003), see http://www.english-heritage.org.uk/ professional/research/landscapes-and-areas/characterisation/military-heritage/ free-and-online-publications/. See also J Lake, 'Historic airfields: evaluation and conservation', in J Schofield, W G Johnson & C M Beck (eds), *Matériel Culture: the archaeology of twentieth century conflict* (Routledge, One World Archaeology **44**, 2003, 172–88).

Commercial buildings

8.1 Introduction

This section covers those commercial building types involved with the distribution and sale of raw and manufactured industrial goods: the warehouses and retail premises of the industrial period. The distribution of raw and finished goods was, arguably, as important as the manufacturing of new products during this period. Whilst the trading and transporting of goods by land and water has long played an important part in Britain's economic activity, the 18th and 19th centuries saw the establishment of new types of building associated with this activity. Specialist warehouses emerged for carriers on the canals and railways, commercial warehouses were built in the new manufacturing towns of the 19th century, purpose-built offices in the great cities of Britain became the seats of many firms controlling the complex industrial distribution network, and food outlets such as co-operative shops and public houses emerged as processing and retail centres in these new towns. Traditionally, distribution and consumption have been studied by archaeologists through the artefactual remains from excavations, but the role of buildings archaeology is crucial to understanding these new commercial building types. They are often clustered in groups, around transport termini or in dedicated warehouse or business areas, and their style was influenced not just by the needs of the particular manufacturing sector they served but also by the role of planning legislation from 1870 onwards which increasingly influenced building design. Such structures are not only the physical expressions of the new economic system of the industrial period but also reflect the widespread influence of industrialised distribution and consumption on the social structure and work life of Britain.

8.2 Canal warehouses

Industrial canals were developed from the mid-18th century onwards and became the heavy goods routes of the nation. They linked manufacturing to markets and became a distinctive industry in their own right, with ports, docks, wharves and, importantly, warehouses, built to store and facilitate the handling of a wide range of agricultural and industrial cargoes. Canal warehouses are a building type specific to the canal network, and although there are many similarities with dockside and urban warehouses, this type of carriers' warehouse had a number of unique features. The first canal warehouses were built during the 1770s and the last at the beginning of the 20th century. Recent work on this building type, which is almost exclusively confined to standing buildings, has been able to categorise four main types, as discussed below.

Historical development

Canal warehouses were built by canal companies, canal carriers, and private waterside businesses. They were typically located at rural wharves (such as Rednal Wharf on the Montgomery Canal), town wharves (such as Devizes, Louth, and Market Harborough), inland ports (such as Gloucester and Stourport) and industrial centres like Birmingham, Brentford, and Nottingham. Representative numbers survive and the best preserved are likely to be designated as listed buildings and protected from inappropriate development or demolition. The earliest canal warehouses (1770s to c 1830) were usually small in scale, with the notable exceptions of those in Liverpool and Manchester. In plan-form these early examples were not dissimilar to agricultural storage buildings and barns; they were built in local materials and often in the local vernacular style. The development of the railway network allowed the building of larger, multi-storey, brick-built structures (1830s–1890s). Later still in the 20th century (principally during the 1950s and 1960s), there were concrete or steel-framed warehouses (eg in Birmingham and Sheffield) clad in steel, concrete or other modern man-made materials and often given large overhanging canopies.

Architectural details and interior forms

Few canal warehouses had any architectural pretensions, but their very plainness could occasionally make them appear sublime, as J M Richards pointed out in his classic book *The Functional Tradition* (1958). Typical examples, from both the early and late 19th century, like those in Gloucester Docks or the Castlefield area of Manchester, consisted of unadorned brick walls punched though at regular intervals by small windows. Occasionally a warehouse was given a large classical pediment to break up its elevations and give it a sense of grandeur and dignity. The Grain Warehouse (Duke's Dock, Liverpool, now demolished) was a good example, as is the Terminal Warehouse in the Sheffield Basin and the Palladian terminus warehouse on the remote Westport Canal (opened 1840, closed 1875). Few warehouses were as consciously designed as the Flyboat Warehouse on the Aire and Calder Dock in Leeds. This palazzo-styled warehouse dating from c 1830 has a Renaissance-inspired arcade to the water, with a strong rhythm of windows and loading doors above, and was clearly intended to impress. It has now been converted, as have many other warehouses, to living accommodation. It was not uncommon for warehouses to be extended; the Navigation Warehouse in Wakefield (recently restored by British Waterways) was originally two separate 18th-century warehouses which were joined together and enlarged in the early 19th century.

Internally, the canal warehouse was divided into a number of long open bays, with loading bays to both canal and road sides and at least one roadside cart entrance. The earliest canal warehouses had a single open space on each floor and were quite narrow. These floors were wooden and were sometimes supported by a row of wooden or cast-iron columns. Nineteenth-century multi-storey canal warehouses had cross-walls or occasionally longitudinal dividing walls (such as the Grocers' Warehouse at Castlefield in Manchester), with the wooden floors being supported by a forest of cast-iron columns. Sometimes these columns had slots for vertical boards which allowed individual bays within a floor to be partitioned and even rented separately (as in Tariff Street, Manchester). In early period canal warehouses hoists were usually gravity powered, with the mechanism found in the loft space – often in the form of large fly wheels (eg Tariff Street, Manchester). Occasionally, the hoist system was driven by a water wheel supplied from the canal (Portland Basin Warehouse, Ashton-under-Lyne) or by a steam engine. From the 1870s onwards hydraulic power, with distinctive hydraulic rams in the roof and accumulator towers attached or adjacent to the building, were used as a power source. During the 20th century most of these earlier power sources were replaced by mains electricity, and sometimes small motors can still be found attached to hoists.

Key elements and plan forms

Type 1

Internal canal arm(s) for internal split-level loading. Multi-storey structure built flush to the canal and sometimes terraced into a hillside. Earliest examples date from the 1770s (Shardlow, Leeds, Manchester, and Wigan). Usually brick with timber floors supported by posts or columns.

Type 2

Detached from the canalside. Multi-storey structure with external internal hoists. Brick or stone with timber floors often supported by posts or columns. A few spanned narrow canals, enabling hoisting direct from the boat, as at the former Pickford's warehouse on the Chesterfield Canal in Worksop (Fig 8.1). Late 18th century to late 19th century.

Type 3

Flush with the canalside. Multi-storey structure with external internal hoists. Brick or stone with timber floors often supported by posts or columns. Very similar to, and contemporary with, the Type 2 canal warehouse and has the same date range.

Figure 8.1 The former Pickford's warehouse, on the Chesterfield Canal at Worksop, now a public house. This type was often called a 'straddle' warehouse and enabled boats to load either upwards into the building directly from the canal, or to make use of the adjacent yard (© Marilyn Palmer)

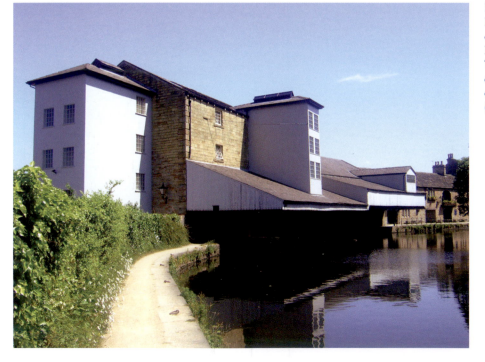

Figure 8.2 Manchester Road Wharf, Burnley, on the Leeds and Liverpool Canal. The wooden loading canopies are carried on cast-iron pillars (© Michael Nevell)

Type 4

Open-sided, single-storey shed built flush to the canalside. The open side is by the canal and internally there are hoists but often with a separate but adjacent jib crane. Appears to be a design copied directly from dockside buildings. Introduced on the canal system in the mid-19th century and examples were still being built during the 20th century.

Key sites

Despite the collapse of the canal system as a commercial enterprise during the mid-20th century, several hundred canal warehouses survive along the waterways of Britain. Most of these are small single structures associated with rural wharves and have been reused either to service the new pleasure traffic along the canals or as waterside apartments or pubs. The 1779 three-storey warehouse at *Stourbridge* is a good example of an early canal warehouse. The most impressive examples are those multi-storey structures that survive as striking urban groups, such as the late 18th- and early 19th-century canal warehouses at *Stourport-on-Severn* on the Staffordshire and Worcestershire Canal; the early to mid-19th-century carrier warehouses of the *Castlefield Canal Basin* in Manchester on the Bridgewater Canal; and the carrier warehouses at *Gloucester Docks* on the Gloucester and Sharpness Canal. Several canal warehouses are now used as museums, including the *Gloucester Waterways Museum* in the Llanthony Warehouse, the *London Canal Museum* on the Regent's Canal, the *National Waterways Museum* at Ellesmere Port, and the *Portland Basin Canal and Industrial Museum* in Ashton-under-Lyne on the Ashton Canal.

Further reading

There are many books on the industrial archaeology of the canal, from publishers David & Charles' classic series of regional studies, *Canals of...*, written in the 1960s to N Crowe, *English Heritage Book of Canals* (Batsford & English Heritage, 1994), the latter having a chapter that includes canal warehouses. Regional studies of canal warehouse structures and plan forms include M Nevell, 'The Archaeology of the Canal Warehouses of North-West England and the Social Archaeology of Industrialisation' (*Industrial Archaeology Review* 25:1, 2003, 43–58), and A D George, 'Housing the Bulk Cargoes: an introduction to canal warehouses', in R McNeil & A D George (eds), *The Heritage Atlas 3: Warehouse Album* (Field Archaeology Centre, University of Manchester, 1997, 24–5). For the warehouses of Gloucester Docks, see H Conway-Jones, *Gloucester Docks: an Illustrated History* (Alan Sutton and Gloucestershire County Library, 1984).

8.3 Industrial warehouses

Most manufacturing towns had a warehouse district by the mid-19th century, usually focused upon the canal, port or railway system, although these areas were not the exclusive preserve of the carriers. Aside from the carriers' warehouses three forms of industrial warehousing developed: the general-purpose private warehouse which could be found in large numbers in many port areas from Liverpool to London; the textile warehouse which was typified by the Lace Market in Nottingham and the Manchester warehouse district of the mid- to late 19th century; and the commercial showroom warehouse of the later 19th and early 20th centuries, which could be found attached to an industrial process building or on its own. All these warehouses were multi-storey structures with a broadly rectilinear plan, often with a clear separation between secured storage and transhipment handling. Each usually contained an office that controlled the flow of goods into and out of the warehouse, a series of roadside loading bays and, in larger structures, a cart entrance.

Historical development

Beyond the dockside, British urban warehousing during the 17th and early 18th centuries was usually small in scale, and focused upon the townhouses of specific merchants and the courtyards of inns and taverns as important hubs in the transport system. Private mercantile and purpose-built carriers' warehouses began to be constructed during the 18th century in the major manufacturing towns and ports of Britain and by the end of that century formed a significant feature of not just the great industrial cities such as Birmingham, Glasgow, and London but also the emerging smaller industrial towns such as Leicester and Northampton. During this period large, purpose-built warehouses were also starting to be built as part of the industrial complexes for several industries.

Private mercantile warehouses could be found in the hinterland of the docks of the major ports from Bristol, Glasgow, and Liverpool to London and Newcastle. From the early 18th century multi-storey brick structures for secure storage with roadside loading bays could be found adjacent to the houses of the more important merchants in these ports. By the mid-19th century the warehouse agent, or keeper, had emerged, offering secure storage space for hire in their own buildings. By the late 19th century these agents had developed into large companies owning dozens, and in the largest cases (eg The Liverpool Warehouse Co Ltd) hundreds, of warehouses in the ports and manufacturing centres of Britain.

The textile warehouse emerged as a distinctive building type in several midland and northern textile towns, most notably the cotton warehouses of Manchester, the woollen warehouses of Bradford and Dewsbury, the hosiery warehouses of Leicester and Nottingham, and the lace warehouses of the latter, in the late 18th and 19th centuries. They were needed for the supply of raw materials to outworkers and the temporary storage of materials and products at factories. The commercial textile warehouse was a showplace, wholesale shop, and office, as well as serving as secure storage. It provided the commercial link between the local textile industry and the international market for British textiles. Most of these warehouses, though, were run by companies separate from the mill owners, thus developing a large dedicated wholesale sector within the textile towns.

The showroom warehouse, which emerged in the mid-19th century, may have been inspired by the classic textile warehouse and performed a similar function but was smaller in scale, plainer, and often found in association with production buildings. Furthermore, unlike most textile warehouses, they were built and run by the company which manufactured the products on display. Many were based in London, particularly the warehouses of manufacturers of luxury goods such as the porcelain and china works of the Midlands since they could expect to meet prestigious customers there.

The peak in the construction of both types of warehouse was the Edwardian period and, like many traditional warehouse forms, 20th-century changes in the way goods were packaged affected how they were handled, stored, and secured. Containerisation of bulk cargoes, the rise of the combustion engine at the expense of the horse, and the introduction of the fork-lift truck with its high vertical reach made such buildings redundant by the mid-20th century.

Architectural details and interior forms

Private mercantile warehouses had a numbers of forms, the earliest types being similar to other types of contemporary warehousing: long, narrow, multi-storeyed buildings (three to six storeys high) with central roadside loading bays for a manual hoist. Pedestrian access and the stairs were also at the roadside end and the internal structure usually comprised wooden floors supported by wooden or cast-iron columns. These buildings can often be found adjacent to a private residence where the merchant resided, or at the end of a terrace. By the mid-19th century new structural forms had emerged: mixed secure storage with transhipment handling by combining open ground floors with secured storage above; bonded warehouses providing secure, regulated storage associated with the administration of excise duties on imported goods; the loss of the adjacent private dwelling, allowing dedicated warehouse zones to emerge; and new structural materials. Structurally, the main innovations were fireproof designs involving cast-iron columns and brick vaulting allowing multi-bay warehouses with rows of loading bays, sometimes with an open ground floor for ease of transhipment handling. Albert Dock in Liverpool combined the security features of the bonded warehouse (bars on the windows, iron doors) with fireproof construction to form a courtyard of pillared warehouses set around the dock. In the late 19th century hydraulically powered hoist systems replaced the manual systems or the occasional steam-powered systems of earlier structures and these were often associated with the use of cast- and wrought-iron roof structures. The limited warehouse companies of the late 19th century often advertised their presence with bold signs, like the railway companies, sometimes in white brick. At the end of the century one- and two-storey warehouses also began to emerge and these made

Figure 8.3 Canada Warehouse, a packing warehouse for cotton textiles in Chepstow Street, Manchester, 1905–09, designed by W & G Higginbottom for H S Booth Ltd (© Michael Nevell)

use of the new structural materials of steel beams and concrete. Road and rail access were separated by the use of internal partitions in order to provide secure storage and transhipment handling. These were typified by the new warehouses of Trafford Park in Manchester built in the years either side of 1900.

The textile warehouse, which could be as large as a cotton-spinning mill complex, can be divided into three main types: home-trade warehouses, multiple-occupancy warehouses, and overseas warehouses. Within the home-trade warehouses each floor was divided into departments that specialised in particular types of goods, in the charge of a foreman who oversaw assistants and salesmen. The lightest goods were stored on the upper floors and the heavier goods on the lowest floors. These sales floors were used as sample and pattern rooms, with benches for cloth examination; this required plenty of light, so there were many windows. In the basement of the warehouse was the packing floor with boilers, presses, later on hydraulic gear, and other services such as inspection and making-up; orders were lowered to the packing floor via hoists. Opposite the main entrance was a grand staircase that penetrated the full height of the building to impress prospective buyers, and led to the ground floor, where the company's offices were located, along with entertainment. Many home-trade warehouses were at the same time multiple-occupancy warehouses where the structures were owned by a company that provided secure storage, display, office, and packing space which was rented to a number of smaller companies, rather on the lines of the room-and-power textile mills of the early 19th century.

Architecturally these multiple-occupancy warehouses tended to be plainer than those belonging to single companies, though there was still a clear division between the elaborate main face and the functional rear with its multiple loading bays, often to be found backing onto a canal. The later steel-framed structures built between 1890 and 1914 marked the pinnacle of this type of warehouse and, in Manchester, included the hydraulic hoist systems run from the city's newly installed hydraulic supply (Fig 8.3). The use of steel-framing allowed for larger structures and freer use of more architectural styles from classical and Italianate, Elizabethan and Scottish, to Renaissance and French Baroque.

The showroom warehouse combined showrooms with wholesale storage and office space; early examples in Shoreditch in London and the Birmingham Jewellery Quarter looked superficially like a workshop dwelling – a three-storey structure dominated by a plain facade with wide windows and a loading bay. However, internally the arrangement was very similar to the textile warehouse with offices on the ground floor and showrooms above that were well-lit undivided floor spaces, often with an internal lift. Later examples were three to five storeys high and usually had a basement. The facade was often more elaborate, as can be seen in several examples in Birmingham, Northampton, and Shoreditch, although the loading bays usually remained at the front of the building, like the carriers' or general-purpose warehouse.

Figure 8.4 The five-storey lace warehouse in the Lace Market, Nottingham, built for Adams and Page in 1855, and designed by local architect T C Hine. There were rooms for mending lace on the top floor, together with a library, chapel and tearoom for the workforce (© Marilyn Palmer)

Key sites

Although London had the largest collection of mercantile and bonded warehouses in Britain most of these have been lost, the Museum of London's dockland site at *West India Quay* preserving a small flavour of this landscape. *Liverpool* probably retains the best grouping of mercantile and agent warehousing in Britain, although smaller groups of such structures can still be found in the zone behind the docks in *Bristol, Glasgow, Lancaster,* and *Newcastle.* The most notable groups of textile warehouses can be found in *Bradford* (wool), *Manchester* (cotton) and *Nottingham* (lace). The *Lace Market* in the latter dates from the 1850s, the most impressive warehouse being the *Adams Building*, now in part a college (Fig 8.4). The Manchester grouping runs along the Rochdale Canal and Princess Street, the finest surviving examples being *Asia House, Central House, India House,* and *Lancaster House.* The variety of tall elaborate facades provides a visual feast that stops the line of warehouses from being monotonous, whilst groups of showroom warehouses in *Birmingham* and *Shoreditch* in London are clustered along narrow streets, giving these urban landscapes a canyon-like feel.

Further reading

The most accessible overview of the subject is provided by M Stratton & B Trinder in the *English Heritage Book of Industrial England* (Batsford & English Heritage, 1997) which has a chapter devoted to warehouses. A collection of papers edited by A Jarvis & K Smith discusses the functional and structural development of warehouses and transit sheds in general: *Albert Dock: Trade and Technology* (National Museums and Galleries on Merseyside, 1999). There are also several very good city-based studies that discuss commercial urban warehouses in the context of a variety of trades: C Giles & B Hawkins, *Storehouses of Empire. Liverpool's Historic Warehouses* (English Heritage, 2004), and J Smith & R Rogers, *Behind the Veneer. The Shoreditch Furniture Trade and its Buildings* (English Heritage, 2006). A study of textile warehousing can be found in S Taylor, M Cooper & P S Barnwell, *Manchester. The Warehouse Legacy. An introduction and guide* (English Heritage, 2002), and there are sections on textile warehousing in C Giles & I Goodall, *Yorkshire Textile Mills. The Buildings of the Yorkshire Textile Industry 1770–1930* (HMSO, 1992), and M Williams, *Bridport and West Bay. The Buildings of the Flax and Hemp Industry* (English Heritage, 2006). M Palmer & P A Neaverson, *Industrial Landscapes of the East Midlands* (Phillimore, 1992), details lace, hosiery, and footwear warehouses, while S Mason, *Nottingham Lace 1760s–1950s* (Sutton, 1994) has an extensive section on lace merchanting. Buildings associated with dockside distribution and storage are discussed in chapter 7 of M Stammers, *The Industrial Archaeology of Docks and Harbours* (Tempus, 2007).

8.4 Railway warehouses

The railway warehouse has its origins in the carrier warehouses of the canal network, in quayside storage, and in the storage sheds associated with the early colliery tramways. They were an integral part of the railway network during the 19th and early 20th centuries. Usually built by the railway companies themselves, although there were private examples serviced by sidings, the railway warehouse demonstrates the Victorian approach to industrialised transhipment and redistribution brought about by the railways. The earliest example dates from 1830 whilst the latest ones are early 20th century. These buildings include single-storey and multi-storey structures in a variety of materials and styles, but all have the common feature of internal loading directly from the railway.

Historical development

The first purpose-built urban railway warehouse was the 1830 warehouse at Liverpool Road Station in Manchester, whilst amongst the last were the two Liverpool Shipping warehouses on Trafford Road in Trafford Park, Manchester, which were built between 1927 and 1932. As a building type its development lasted just 100 years, although railway warehouses continued to be used on the main line railway network down to the mid-20th century.

The peak period for construction was the decade after the establishment of the main line network in the 1840s, and during the 1870s when the branch line network was rapidly developing, although railway warehouses were built throughout the development life of the network. Rising urban land values and rising urban populations encouraged the building of multi-storey warehouses as a way of speeding transfer times and goods volumes into and out of the industrial towns and cities of Britain. One of the largest examples is the building of the five-storey, hydraulic-powered, 26,730m² Great Northern Railway Company's Warehouse in Manchester in 1896–98 (Fig 8.5). However, sometimes the competition between Victorian railway companies for railway freight traffic could lead to a large concentration of warehousing, as at Carlisle which had six goods depots built around a city a quarter of the size of Birmingham.

The 20th century witnessed a change in the way goods were handled for redistribution which affected the role of the railway warehouse. This change was driven by the introduction of the motor vehicle in the 1900s, containerisation in the 1950s, and later by computer technology. At the same time the concept of long-term storage fell out of use, and the transhipment centre became the dominant form of store. These trends led to the abandonment of multi-storey city-centre warehouses in favour of single-storey transit sheds located close to, or at, road junctions. The fate of the railway warehouse was sealed by the sharp contraction in Britain's railway system in the mid-20th century. Those that were not demolished or converted to other uses became redundant, cut off from the main railway network or abandoned in sidings no longer used by rail freight. Few examples are protected as listed buildings.

Architectural details and interior forms

Structurally the warehouse developed rapidly, from the non-fireproof, timber-framed and brick-walled 1830 warehouse to the 1860s' barrel-vaulted, multi-storey, fireproof structures of the railway termini and sidings of the industrial midland and northern towns, as in Birmingham and Leeds. In the 1880s warehouse design evolved again with the introduction of hydraulic power and the building of accumulator towers. This reached a zenith with the construction of the Somers Town goods yard at St Pancras in London, built 1883–87, with its internal, hydraulic-powered hoists and high-level sidings (see Fig 3.13), together with those of the Great Central Railway in Nottingham, Leicester, and Marylebone, dating from the same period. In the early 20th century railway warehouse building slowed dramatically, as did branch-line construction, but the Liverpool Shipping warehouses in Trafford Park, which lie at the end of the classical railway warehouse tradition, show the continued innovation in building materials with their extensive use of steel-framing and concrete.

External elevations were often used to advertise the railway company running the building, through large signs and elaborate facades. Architecturally, there was a distinction between single-storey transfer sheds and multi-storey, longer-term warehouses, with the latter having more architectural embellishments, external company names and large hydraulic towers.

Internally, railway warehouses were dominated by hoist mechanisms and railway tracks. The track usually ran through the building with the platform to one side. Road access was sometimes through a separate cart entrance in the gables, sometimes along the exterior of the elevation opposite the railway line, or sometimes both. The area underneath the platform could be used for storage and there was usually a small office attached to the building. Gravity hoists could be found in the roof spaces of early single-storey warehouses, although larger

Figure 8.5 Great Northern Railway Warehouse, Manchester (1896–98). Built on Deansgate, this was intended to provide an interchange between the railway, the canal system, and road transport (© Marilyn Palmer)

warehouses had steam-powered, and by the end of the 19th century hydraulically powered, hoist systems. The layout of the multi-storey urban railway warehouse emerged almost complete with the building of the multi-storey, curved, 1830 railway warehouse at Liverpool Road Station in Manchester. This had split-level internal loading and unloading, with railway wagons being taken into the warehouse directly, via turntables in front of access bays. Ironically, the design was probably adapted from a rejected plan for a canal warehouse for the Gloucester docks.

Key elements and plan forms

By the late 19th century three types of warehouse had emerged, including multi-storey urban warehouses, although most structures were still single-storey buildings.

Type 1: Transhipment shed

The most common type in smaller towns and associated with rural-based industries was the single-storey, linear transhipment shed, with a railway track running right through the building. Here goods were loaded directly onto other forms of transport without being stored on site. This form is common to quayside and dockside locations and one of the best examples is the Great Western transhipment shed at Albert Dock on the Liverpool Quay, built around 1890.

Type 2: Combined internal and external loading single-storey goods shed

Also common in smaller towns and on the rural branch lines was the combined internal and external loading single-storey goods sheds. These had similarities with the transhipment shed, being of a single storey and usually having a railway track running through the building, but they also had a limited amount of storage space, an internal raised platform, and generally some form of architectural embellishment externally.

Type 3: Multi-storey urban railway warehouse

A significant element of the railway network in the industrial towns of Britain, from Glasgow to London, was the multi-storey warehouse. This was distinct from both the Type 1 transfer shed and the Type 2 single-storey goods shed, since it specialised in the longer-term storage of bulk goods. The multi-storey warehouse was built by the railway companies, often as part of a dedicated goods station, and played a pivotal role in the movement of goods into and out of the Victorian town and city.

Key sites

Railway warehouses, unlike the warehouses along the canals, tend not to cluster in large groups but like the canal warehouses several examples are now incorporated into museum complexes. These include the multi-storey 1830 Liverpool Road Warehouse which is now part of the *Museum of Science and Industry* in Manchester, and the transhipment shed which is now the main exhibition hall at the *National Railway Museum* in York.

Further reading

Despite the traditional interest of industrial archaeologists in the archaeology of the railway, specific literature on the archaeology of railway warehouses is comparatively sparse. A general overview of railway buildings, which includes a chapter on such structures, is provided by R Morriss, *The Archaeology of Railways* (Tempus, 1999). There are several regional- and city-based overviews which provide the background on the development and plan forms of the various types: T Allison, 'Industrial Building Design and Economic Context: The Railway Freighthouse in Chicago, 1850–1925' (*Industrial Archaeology Review* **29**:2, 2007, 91–104); and A D George, 'Manchester Railway Warehouses – A Short Note' (*Industrial Archaeology Review* **4**:2, 1980, 177–83); and M Nevell, 'The Archaeology of the Rural Railway Warehouse in North-West England' (*Industrial Archaeology Review* **32**:2, 2010, 103–15). P Greene, 'An Archaeological study of the 1830 Warehouse at Liverpool Road Station, Manchester, (*Industrial Archaeology Review* **17**, 1995, 117–28), remains the best published site-specific archaeological survey of a railway warehouse, while P A Neaverson, M Palmer & S Warburton produced a detailed survey of the Leicester Great Central Railway Warehouse and its adjoining hydraulic and electric power station in *Bulletin of the Leicestershire Industrial Archaeology Society*, **15**, 1994, 27–76. E Dwyer, *The Impact of the Railways in the East End 1835–2010* (Museum of London Archaeology, 2011), includes drawings and photographs of the Bishopsgate Goods Station and warehouses and their hydraulic accumulators, while their excavation at The Somers Town Goods Yard at St Pancras was featured in *Current Archaeology* **256** (2011), 12–19.

8.5 Co-operative buildings

The emergence of the co-operative movement was a key feature of the 19th-century retailing revolution, although its roots can be traced to the late 18th and early 19th centuries in the newly emerging industrial towns of central and northern England and Scotland. The majority of Co-operative premises were more than just shops and assembly rooms. They were self-sufficient units involved in the production, storage, retailing and distribution of goods. Consequently, a variety of buildings can be found on these sites, from stables and warehouses to dairies and bakeries.

Historical development

In the early 19th century many factory owners controlled the supply of housing and food for their workforce, with the result that both were usually of poor quality. As a response to these poor conditions groups of workers banded together in order to guarantee quality goods at a reasonable price. It was not until the Rochdale Society of Equitable Pioneers was set up in 1844 that a successful model was established that was copied by hundreds of groups over the next 30 years. Membership was a few pence per week and the profits of the society were invested by the committee for the social and economic benefit of the members and the needy of the district. Two and a half per cent of all profits were set aside for educational purposes. The main period of expansion for new societies was during the 1850s, 1860s and 1870s when societies were established in many of the new urban industrial centres. In 1863, 300 of these new societies in Lancashire and Yorkshire came together to form the North of England Co-operative Society as a way of improving their buying power and production facilities. This became the Co-operative Wholesale Society in 1872 and was owned by its member co-operatives. The CWS rapidly expanded into the mass production of goods, such as boots, shoes, and textiles in the East Midlands, where Kettering in Northamptonshire was an important centre from 1866 and the Wheatsheaf boot and shoe works in Leicester, built 1891 and enlarged 1900, was one of its flagship factories and at that time the largest boot and shoe factory in the world. The CWS also expanded into agricultural production through the purchase of farmland, and into grain milling and warehousing; there is a large complex in Glasgow on the Clyde, for instance. In 1933 the CWS formed a retail division to take over failing local co-operatives.

Architectural details

The stores operated by early co-operative societies were usually established in existing buildings, and were often unassuming and plain in appearance by comparison with the emerging shop fronts (*Market Street, Hollingworth, Tameside*). They could form part of a row of terraces or be housed in a reused building such as the converted weaver's cottage occupied by the *Lanebottom Co-operative*, New Hey, Rochdale, in 1858 (Fig 8.6). Such co-ops are characterised by small-scale buildings and plain facades reflecting the limited scale of these local movements.

As the various societies grew in membership and capital, their range of services was extended to encompass both wholesale supply and production. This greater wealth and versatility led to the establishment of purpose-built buildings which included stores, warehouses, and offices, and which in appearance gradually changed from the purely utilitarian to the architecturally embellished. Such later 19th-century co-operative buildings might include a vernacular revival façade with gables, premises that included a butcher's and general store, and a cart entrance led to the rear workshops (*Eccles Co-operative, Barton Road, Salford*). Some complexes contained an assembly hall, where a variety of social

Figure 8.6
Lanebottom
Co-operative Stores,
Rochdale, Lancashire,
housed in a converted
weaver's cottage
(© Michael Nevell)

functions could take place, a newsroom and a library. This individualisation of a functional building is characteristic of many co-operative retail premises and in part reflected the success of many local and regional co-operatives.

A wide variety of architectural styles and building materials were used in such buildings during the late 19th century from the vernacular to the classical (*Droylsden Co-op, Tameside*) and baroque, and from stone and timber to brick and glazed tile. There was also an increasing use of architect-designed structures as can be seen in Pendleton Society's three phased buildings on *Broughton Road in Salford* which uses three architectural styles over the period 1887 to 1903.

During the early 20th century another form of co-operative retail outlet emerged: the corner shop, which was the satellite outlet of the main co-operative operation. These small grocery shops were invariably single storeyed, often rather plain box-like buildings but ones where the roof line is enlivened by the use of Dutch gables or parapets. The shop is often tiled and there is almost always an elaborate date stone.

Key elements and plan forms

Below are the key building elements to look out for on such retail co-operatives of the period 1844–1930.

Retail premises: these can have elaborate shop windows with decorative adverts and signs. They can also be premises adapted from dwellings.

Assembly halls: these are usually on the first or second floor of larger co-operative building complexes and may contain grand roof trusses, a stage and other architectural embellishments.

Libraries and newsrooms: these are usually on the first or second floor of larger co-operative building complexes and are sometimes panelled.

Manufactory structures: these are usually located to the rear of larger co-operative building complexes, although they sometimes formed separate manufacturing sites in purpose-built structures. Usually plain, functional, multi-storey structures with a loading bay, they often had an inscription naming the co-operative. Co-ops manufactured a variety of goods from furniture and clothing to shoes and metalwork. Consequently these structures have many similarities with contemporary factories of the period. The flagship factory of the CWS in Leicester, the *Wheatsheaf Works*, consisted of a quadrangle of three-storey buildings with a corner tower and a separate power house. Listed in 1994, it is subject to redevelopment.

Food process buildings: located at the rear of the larger co-operative complexes these are usually on the ground floor of larger structures or sometimes separate single-storey buildings. Processes commonly found are dairies (usually tiled rooms with road access) and bakeries (with small and medium-sized ovens).

Warehouses: these were a common element of many co-operative sites and their forms and detailing were very similar to the commercial warehouses discussed elsewhere in this section. They were commonly two-, three- or four-storey structures with open floors, often with wooden floors supported by cast-iron columns and with loading doors in at least one gable.

Further reading

Little has been published on the archaeology and buildings of the co-operative movement by comparison with the history of the movement. The historical and political background is covered in detail by two recent publications: N Robertson, *The Co-operative Movement and Communities in Britain, 1914–1960. Minding Their Own Business* (Ashgate Publishing Limited, 2010); and in a collection of essays edited by L Black & N Robertson, *Taking Stock: Consumerism and the Co-operative Movement in Modern British History* (Manchester University Press, 2009). There are, however, a number of individual, developer-funded, historic building studies of co-operative sites in the grey literature and around 83 co-operative sites are listed buildings with notable concentrations of protected buildings in Essex, Greater Manchester, and South and West Yorkshire.

8.6 Office buildings

The purpose-built office building of the 19th and early 20th century may seem somewhat removed from the archaeology of industry but such structures became the homes of firms that ran the distribution network, banks that financed the sale of raw materials and the capitalisation of industry, and the headquarters of many of the larger manufacturing concerns of the period. The larger manufacturing centres (Birmingham, Leeds, and Manchester), political centres (Cardiff and Edinburgh) and ports (Bristol, Glasgow, and Liverpool) all had substantial office districts, although that in the centre of London became, along with its docks, the biggest such complex in the world during the 19th century. Smaller market and manufacturing towns usually had office buildings close to the transport termini, in particular the railway station.

Historical development

Purpose-built office buildings have their origins in the 18th-century warehouse with ground-floor offices, but in the late 18th century the first speculative development of dedicated offices designed and fitted for brokers emerged in both Liverpool and London. Such offices were usually found around the exchange buildings. As well as the speculative office, in the mid-19th century the flagship office building for banks, insurance, and manufacturing companies arose. These tended to have elaborate facades in a variety of historical styles (gothic, palazzo and classical were very common motifs) and costly materials such as stone and marble that advertised their status. The development of new building materials in the late 19th century, such as steel beams and concrete, and the invention of the powered lift, allowed larger and taller office buildings to be constructed. These became the immediate predecessors of the modern general office structure. The development of suburban public transport, the emergence of private car ownership, and the spread of the telephone as a new means of rapid communication in the early to mid-20th century freed the office block from its city centre roots. It thus allowed such structures to be built on the outskirts of towns and cities, away from the traditional business district close to the railway station and warehouse zone.

Architectural details and interior forms

Early office buildings were usually three storeys with a cellar and attic, but the invention of the hydraulically powered lift in the 1860s, and its popularisation in the 1880s, allowed offices six to eight storeys high to be built. These 19th-century offices were often entered by a flight of steps through a decorated entrance, including the name of the building, that led to an equally impressive hall area where there might be a desk for a concierge. Stairs and corridors led to the office suites which consisted of a single room or a double office with two interconnected rooms. The latter comprised an outer general office for the clerks, which was furnished with sloping desks, possibly with a partitioned area for more senior staff. The inner, higher-status and more private room was used for the senior staff or business owner and had a single desk. There might also be a walk-in strong room and a public area. Larger businesses could rent a floor or even the whole building. Whilst washbasins might be provided within each office suite, the toilets were usually confined to the attic space, where there was a flat for a caretaker and his family. In general public access points, such as halls and corridors, and the office suites of the owner or senior staff, became more elaborate as the 19th century progressed and such plan forms were still being built into the early 20th century.

Adequate ventilation of the corridors and stairs was important and this led to the use of iron gates rather than solid doors at the main entrance. As important was the need for natural light and this led to the frequent use of a courtyard plan and light-wells with a glazed roof. Light-coloured brick or tile was often used to reflect light into the corridors of the building. Large windows were also inserted to make as much use of the natural light as possible. The adoption of electric lighting during the 1890s did not immediately affect the design of office buildings, which continued to use large windows and light-wells wherever possible.

The use of fireproofing building techniques, such as cast-iron columns supporting barrel vaulting, started to appear in office buildings during the mid-19th century, but the combination of lifts and steel framed-construction techniques encouraged the building of taller office blocks from the 1890s onwards. The use of these new building materials reached an early pinnacle in the Royal Liver Building of 1908–11 at the Pier Head in Liverpool, which was probably the largest office building in Britain at that date.

Key sites

Whilst most towns in Britain have multi-storey offices, few retain many examples of their Victorian and Edwardian predecessors. However, some of the best surviving groups of early office buildings are still to be found in the centres of the larger ports and commercial cities of Britain. These include *Glasgow*, *Leeds*, *Liverpool*, and *Manchester*, and the administrative heart of the capital, *Whitehall*.

Further reading

J Sharples & J Stonard's *Built on Commerce: Liverpool's central business district* (English Heritage, 2008) is probably the best introduction to the purpose-built office building of the period, discussing the origins and development of the building type. The newer *Pevsner Architectural Guides*, published by Yale University Press with the Buildings Book Trust, describe many fine individual Victorian and Edwardian office buildings in detail, as well as placing them in their urban context; see especially those volumes covering the Victorian city centres such as Glasgow, Leeds, Manchester, and Nottingham.

8.7 Public houses

The public house emerged as a distinct building type during the 19th century and was one of the most iconic structures of the new industrial towns and cities (Fig 8.7). It incorporated features from earlier building types which had provided drink, food, and shelter for centuries – the inn, tavern and alehouse – whilst key features of the 18th-century gin shop (and its successor, the early 19th-century gin palace) also found their way into Victorian and later public house design. Public house design was always influenced by the demands of legislation, commercial pressures, and social change.

Historical development

During the 18th century, increasing pressure from the Justices of the Peace for alehouses to be 'fit for the purpose' led to a gradual increase in size of the traditional alehouse, accompanied by increasing specialisation in the way rooms were used. Provision for meetings, in the form of club rooms, and for games, with skittle alleys, bowling greens, or even billiard rooms, became increasingly common. The term 'public house' came to describe this new, developed, alehouse. Another 18th-century influence which helped to shape the public house was the growing popularity of drinking spirits (especially gin). The gin shop (or 'dram shop') operated on a rapid turnover of customers, which was enabled by the introduction of the counter, separating the customer from the server, providing a surface for pouring drinks, and placing an onus on the customer to seek service. It was a feature of a shop rather than of the traditional alehouse, but by the 1820s it was beginning to appear in public houses as well. It facilitated the adoption of the hand-pump, or beer-engine, which had been invented in the 1790s and which reduced the labour needed to fetch drink from the cellar. By 1830 both the counter and the hand-pump were a feature of the busier urban public house.

In 1830, in an attempt to stimulate the depressed agricultural sector, to open up the pub trade, and to counteract the perceived evil of spirit drinking, the government passed the Beer Act, which allowed any ratepayer to sell beer after paying an annual excise fee of two guineas, without obtaining a Justices' licence. The result was an explosion in the number of drinking houses – by the end of the year over 24,000 of the new 'beerhouses' had opened. Most were in terraced urban dwellings, often in back streets or in cellars, and virtually impossible to police. The Wine and Beerhouse Act of 1869 gave the Justices some control over beerhouses, and set out the grounds for refusing licences. Their powers were augmented by the 1872 Licensing Act, which set out minimum accommodation standards (a minimum of two public rooms was necessary before a spirit licence could be granted) and also gave them powers to transfer licences between premises. As a result, the Justices were able to bring the number of licensed premises under control and to close the more disreputable houses. They also had a stronger bargaining position when it came to issuing licences for new pubs to serve the rapidly expanding suburbs, so that brewers (who by now owned the majority of pubs) were forced to surrender multiple licences in exchange for permission to build in new areas. Official attempts to control the sale of alcohol had increasing public support, particularly as the Temperance movement (which first appeared in England in 1830) grew in size and influence.

As a result of the 1872 Licensing Act there was a scramble by brewers to acquire public houses, which reached its peak in the 1880s and 1890s, and

Figure 8.7 The Lord Nelson public house in Manchester Road, Nelson, Lancashire (© Lynne Walker)

increasing pressure upon pub owners to improve their premises, resulting in the great late Victorian wave of pub rebuilding. The scramble for pubs peaked in the late 1890s, and the market crashed, in London at least, in 1899. A 1902 Licensing Act gave the Justices rights to approve alterations, and to insist on improvements to those pubs which they believed to be sub-standard. The Licensing Act of 1904 went much further, setting up a system under which the Justices could actively set about closing pubs, funded by an annual levy on all licence holders; as a result, 12,500 pubs had been closed by 1920. Faced with this situation, and in response to the demands of the Temperance movement for total prohibition, pub owners cut back on ostentation and display. Taking their cue from such organisations as the People's Refreshment Houses Association, an emphasis was put on the provision of food, non-alcoholic drinks, and of facilities for activities which did not involve excessive drinking. The change in emphasis was marked by the adoption of more restrained architectural styles – olde English revival, with its use of half-timbering (and all its 'merrie England' connotations), was particularly popular in the years before World War I.

On the outbreak of war, the government assumed sweeping powers over all aspects of British life. Pub opening hours were cut back, and the supply of beer restricted. In 1916 pubs and breweries in the vicinity of a number of important munitions factories were taken into state control to reduce drunkenness and the risk of accidents among the workforce. Although most were handed back at the end of the war, the pubs of Carlisle were retained until 1972, and used to test ways of reducing alcohol consumption and the disorder which resulted from excessive drinking. Restrictions on opening hours were only partially lifted by the 1921 Licensing Act, and the development of other forms of entertainment, such as radio and the cinema, also had an impact on pub attendance during the mid-20th century. The great campaigns of slum clearance in many towns and cities saw the disappearance of numerous older, smaller pubs, whose licences were extinguished or transferred to new sites in the suburbs and estates. Pub building and refurbishment effectively came to an end in 1940, and did not resume until 1950. Until the late 1960s the majority of new building and refurbishment was on traditional lines, with multi-room interiors the norm, although post-war austerity and the experimental use of new materials had an impact upon the quality of workmanship. The social revolution of the 1960s eventually impacted upon the public house, with the sweeping away of internal divisions and the creation of large unified interiors becoming almost universal after 1970, to the extent that little survives from earlier pub interiors, and much of that is fragmentary.

Architectural details and interior forms

The internal design of public houses changed steadily throughout the 19th and 20th centuries but the classic features of the public house, the counter and the hand-pump, were in place by 1830. Another set of design features was adapted from the 'gin palace' after 1820 – plate glass windows, gas lighting and lavish fittings – aimed to draw in the crowds and serve them efficiently.

As Victorian industry and transport developed, an ever wider range of decorative materials became available: cut, etched and coloured glass, mahogany and teak, polished granite, tiles and mosaics, were all applied to public houses. As pub planning developed during this period, pub interiors became increasingly subdivided, at least in the larger urban areas, with the emergence of a distinct hierarchy of spaces which reflected subtle gradations of social status. The most basically furnished space was normally the 'public bar' (also known as the 'vault' or 'dram shop'), whilst slightly superior accommodation might be found in the 'tap room' or 'smoke room', and the most comfortable in the 'lounge' or 'saloon'. Some pubs ran to a 'private bar' or 'bar parlour', typically set aside for the most long-standing customers or the licensee's particular friends. The better-quality rooms were often more tucked away, or were served by hatch or window to give their patrons more privacy. The cut-throat competition for customers resulted in the provision of facilities which would attract them in and keep them drinking – billiard rooms, club rooms, and concert rooms became features of larger urban pubs.

Local bye-laws and the 1872 Licensing Act resulted in a large growth of designed public houses towards the end of the century, with architectural practices and new planning regulations having an increasing impact on the design of the urban public house. Thus, whilst the new pubs of the mid-19th century had usually had Italianate exterior designs, particularly in London, from the 1870s an extraordinary range (and in many cases, mixture) of architectural styles was pressed into service. However, Gothic was rarely used for pubs as it was widely perceived as the appropriate style for church buildings. The subdivision of pubs was most marked in London and in major urban centres such as Birmingham and Liverpool, which also saw the most spectacular examples of the pub-designer's art erected at the end of the century. The Victorian pub came to be epitomised by huge and imposing buildings, decorated with mirrors, tiles, and etched and stained glass, divided into numerous drinking spaces by varnished wood partitions. Yet, even in the larger towns, these were the exception rather than the norm; the more humble two- or three-room establishment, with little architectural embellishment, endured in large numbers in both rural areas and less important urban streets. Regional variations are also apparent in internal planning and the provision of facilities.

The State Management Scheme of World War I closed large numbers of smaller pubs, and built or rebuilt many others on 'reformed' lines. The emphasis was again on food and non-alcoholic drinks, with facilities for games and activities as an alternative to drinking. 'Perpendicular drinking' was discouraged by the provision of relatively small counters, matched by increasing the amount of seating.

Twentieth-century urban pubs were designed to encourage visits from the increasing ranks of motorists; the enormous 'roadhouse', with its car park, bowling green, and range of facilities including dining room and games rooms, became a familiar sight of suburban estates and arterial roads after 1920. Such buildings were most often 'brewer's Tudor' (a derivative of 'olde English revival') or 'neo-Georgian' in style, although one or two brewers bravely espoused modernism; 'Moderne' or 'Art Deco' pubs were never common, however, and survivors are rare. All were characterised by the continued provision of a range of rooms offering different facilities and varying standards of accommodation. As in the later 19th century, many pubs continued to be built on more traditional lines, with limited accommodation and little embellishment.

Further reading

The best overview of the design and plan of the public house is provided by G Brandwood, A Davison & M Slaughter, *Licensed to Sell: the History and Heritage of the Public House* (2nd edn, English Heritage, 2011), whilst the historical background of the industrial period public house can be found in M Girouard, *Victorian Pubs* (Yale University Press, 1984) and P Jennings, *The Local: a History of the English Pub* (Tempus, 2007). Over 5100 public houses are listed in England alone.

CHAPTER NINE

Utility industries

9.1 Introduction

The utility industries played a pivotal part in shaping the industrial world in the 19th and 20th centuries, but their archaeology is often overlooked. In many cases, British companies pioneered the technology employed by early utility industries, as well as their business models. However, organisational developments, notably the privatisation of nationalised industries from the 1980s, together with technological change, afflicted all these industries and has rendered many important sites redundant and ripe for redevelopment, particularly in urban areas. This section highlights the key aspects of sites and structures relating to gas and electricity production and distribution, water supply, and sewage disposal.

9.2 The gas industry

Background

The gas industry grew out of a need to develop a more efficient and economical form of lighting than the oil lights which preceded it. The piped supply of gas in urban areas facilitated the lighting of streets and this form of lighting is widely considered to have had a dramatic impact on almost all aspects of life. Originally, gas was used almost exclusively for lighting; other uses, such as cooking and heating, followed later. The gas industry was the first true utility industry, with several large, vertically integrated companies, and had enormous influence on political and public attitudes, paving the way for future public utilities. The industry in Britain was nationalised in 1948 and then privatised in 1986. Gas has become a major world-wide industry and now supplies over 40% of the UK's energy.

The first buildings to be lit by gas were a number of textile mills in northern England, around 1806. These mills had their own gas works, and private gas works continued to be built at factories, mines, railway stations, and country houses in more remote locations until the last quarter of the 19th century, but most gas consumers obtained their gas by pipe from a public gas supplier. The world's first public gas works opened in 1813 in Great Peter Street, London, and within 20 years most large towns and cities in Britain, and several throughout Western Europe and North America, had their own gas companies.

The technology of gas manufacture

The technology of making gas from coal remained essentially unchanged from the birth of the industry until coal gas manufacture ceased in the 1970s. Coal was heated in enclosed horizontal vessels known as retorts and the gas given off, a mixture of hydrogen, methane, carbon monoxide, and various impurities, was passed first through a condenser to remove tar (which was a valuable by-product) and then through one or more purifiers to remove impurities. The residue left in the retorts after the coal had been distilled was coke, which was also a valuable by-product. It was both uneconomic and impractical to match the rate of gas production to the demand, so gas works invariably had one or more gas holders (often erroneously called 'gasometers'). From the late 19th century onwards, some rationalisation of gas production was achieved by the construction of larger and more efficient gas works, each replacing a number of smaller works. In the 1950s, new processes for manufacturing gas, known as 'reformer gas', at high pressure from petroleum feedstocks were introduced into Britain and then in the 1960s these were supplanted by the direct use of natural gas piped at high pressure from offshore. For a brief period after 1890 until the introduction of electricity, small self-contained plants generating acetylene or petrol vapour were a popular alternative to coal gas for lighting country houses and other buildings remote from the public supply.

Buildings of the gas industry

Where possible, gas works were sited in locations which facilitated the delivery of coal and the removal of by-products and waste. They were situated at the lowest point in an area, as the pressure of the lighter-than-air gas rose with altitude; thus, early gas works were often located alongside canals and navigable rivers. Later, gas works were frequently served by their own railway sidings.

The key structures of all gas works were:

- Retort house(s). This was generally the largest building on a gas works and varied in size depending on the size of the works (dictated by the number of retorts needed). The retort house for a small private or village gas works might have a floor area of around 20m² whereas that for a large urban works could be 20 or 30 times this size. A distinguishing feature of all retort houses was the height of the internal space, typically in excess of 5m, to accommodate the ascension pipes and associated water traps (known as hydraulic mains) which conveyed the gas from the retorts. Large urban gas works built in the later 19th century often had machinery to fill and empty the retorts (a task still done by hand in a few small works as late as the 1970s) or vertical or inclined retorts, which required more space. Retort houses generally also had ventilated roofs with raised sections (Fig 9.1), although these tended to be replaced if the building was later adapted for other uses;

Figure 9.1 Gas works buildings, Wimpole Hall, Cambridgeshire. The retort house is identifiable from its height and ventilated roof; the smaller building on the right was the purifier house (© Ian West)

+ Purifier house. Sometimes the purification equipment was located in the open or in open-sided sheds but often a separate building, generally smaller than the retort house, was provided. The chemicals used in the purification process were stored either in a dedicated building or in a separate part of the purifier house. At smaller private gas works, a single building might have combined the functions of the retort and purifier houses, in which case it was simply referred to as the 'gas house';

+ Coal store. The efficiency of the gas production process was impaired if the coal was wet so it was normal to store it in a covered yard;

+ Gas holder(s). From almost the birth of the gas industry, gas holders consisted of closed cylindrical vessels made of wrought-iron (later steel) plate, supported above a tank of water by the pressure of the gas within. Earlier examples typically had tanks 5–10m in diameter but by the early 20th century holders of 40m diameter were not uncommon. Some holder tanks were above ground, constructed of wrought iron or steel, but most were below ground, lined with brick sealed on the outside with puddled clay. By the middle of the 19th century, telescopic holders with multiple sections (known as 'lifts') which collapsed inside each other provided greater storage capacity than a single-lift holder for the same cross-sectional area. Throughout most of the 19th century, external cast- and wrought-iron guide frames were used to provide horizontal stability for the floating lifts but from *c* 1890 the cheaper spiral-guided design, which needed no external frame, became more popular. From the 1930s, a few large urban gas works built waterless gas holders, based on designs common in Germany and the US.

Larger and later gas works included a number of other specialised buildings and structures, such as:

+ exhauster and booster houses, containing machinery driven by steam or gas engines to pump the gas through the works and into the mains system;
+ meter houses;
+ rail sidings and coal handling facilities;
+ control buildings, offices, and laboratories.

As gas manufacture was a continuous process, smaller gas works usually had a house alongside to accommodate the superintendent or manager and larger gas companies sometimes built workers' housing nearby (Fig 9.2). Away from the gas works itself, gas companies built offices and showrooms and erected street furniture such as cast-iron instrument and governor kiosks; local boards or councils erected gas lamp columns. There are no significant remains of the brief era of reformer gas manufacture but consideration is already being given in Scotland and Norway to the preservation of structures associated with natural gas processing.

Key sites

A complete small town gas works dating largely from the 19th century has been preserved as a museum in *Fakenham*, Norfolk. Other similar examples exist in *Biggar*, Scotland, and *Carrickfergus*, Northern Ireland. Many smaller examples of gas works buildings such as retort and purifier houses have survived, adapted for other purposes, both on sites abandoned by public gas suppliers when they became too small, and at country houses and factories. For example:

- *Gas Street, Birmingham* – retort house and coal store;
- *Coldharbour Mill, Uffculme*, Devon – retort house;
- *Quarry Bank Mill, Styal*, Cheshire – retort house and gas holder tank;
- *Shaw Lodge Mill, Halifax* – ruins of retort house with retorts and gas holder tanks;
- *Holkham Hall*, Norfolk – gas house;
- *Wimpole Hall*, Cambridgeshire – retort and purifier houses (see Fig 9.1);
- *Culzean Castle*, Ayrshire – gas house;
- *Mount Stewart*, County Down – remains of gas house with retorts.

There are fewer recorded surviving examples of buildings associated with later and larger urban coal gas works, partly because it has generally been harder to find alternative uses for these larger structures, so many have been demolished. However, a great number of such buildings survive on sites still in operational use by the gas industry and have yet to be assessed for their historical and archaeological significance. The remains of two large purifier houses and an engine house survive at *Canon's Marsh*, Bristol, awaiting adaptive reuse, but many other buildings on this site which would have demonstrated the scale and integrity of a large urban gas works have been demolished. Some substantial buildings remain, listed Category B, at *Baltic Street, Leith*, Edinburgh. It should be noted that the presence of toxic and hazardous residues on most former gas works sites makes both archaeological investigation and redevelopment costly and difficult.

Figure 9.3 Partially infilled gas holder tank, Ascott, Buckinghamshire. The building behind housed the *c* 1890s' electricity generating plant (© Ian West)

Dozens of gas holders remain in daily use in winter by the British gas industry, although this number is now decreasing steadily as organisational and technical changes have increased the availability of cheaper forms of gas storage. Some of these holders have Grade II listing and several, particularly older examples with external guide frames, have become valued components of urban landscapes, but listing has not always ensured survival. For example, a unique set of Grade II listed conjoined gas holders dating from *c* 1880 at *St Pancras* was demolished *c* 2001, although some of the guide columns are due to be re-erected *c* 2011 on the nearby University of the Arts site. In some other European countries, including Ireland and Germany, alternative uses have been found for the outer structures of gas holders but this has not yet been attempted in Britain. The practice of placing gas holders within buildings quickly fell from favour in Britain but a pair of gas holder buildings and the associated gas company offices survive in *Warwick*, converted into apartments. When gas works sites were cleared in the past, the below-ground tanks of gas holders were often simply filled with site debris, leaving the brick or metal tanks, coping stones and foundations of support columns intact (Fig 9.3).

Original gas street lamp columns and other types of street furniture have been swept away by urban redevelopment and modern reproductions abound. One of the finest collections of original gas lamp columns is in *Beverley*, East Yorkshire, where there are many examples, made by local foundries in the 1820s or 1830s, in their original locations.

Further reading

General histories of the British gas industry and its technology include D Chandler & A D Lacey, *The Rise of the Gas Industry in Britain* (British Gas Council, 1949), and T I Williams, *A History of the British Gas Industry* (Oxford University Press, 1981). Business histories range from numerous booklets produced by local enthusiasts (eg K Golisti in Yorkshire) to more extensive regional accounts, including J F Wilson, *Lighting the Town: A study of management in the North-West gas industry 1805–1880* (Paul Chapman Publishing Ltd, 1991), and S Everard, *The History of the Gas Light and Coke Company 1812–1949* (A & C Black, 1992).

A comprehensive archaeological study of the gas industry has yet to be written. Many individual gas works sites have been subject to archaeological investigation prior to redevelopment but most results remain unpublished. Examples of some which have been published include A Francis, *Stepney Gasworks: the archaeology and history of the Commercial Gas Light and Coke Company's works at Harford Street, London E1, 1837–1946* (Museum of London Archaeological Service, 2010), and M Mills, *The Early East London Gas Industry and its Waste Products* (M Wright, 1999). A draft MPP Step 3 report for the gas industry and a supplementary report covering gas holders were produced for English Heritage in 2002 by M Trueman but not published, although such reports may become available in the future. A useful study of gas street lamps and other street furniture is G Warren, *Vanishing Street Furniture* (David & Charles, 1978).

9.3 The electricity industry

Background

Early experiments in the properties of electric currents utilised simple batteries but the key technological breakthrough was Michael Faraday's discovery of the principles behind the dynamo in 1831, which enabled mechanical power to be converted into electricity. Telegraph systems and outdoor lighting using arc lights provided the first practical uses of electricity, usually generated from batteries or by dynamos powered by steam engines or water power. The world's first electric street lighting was installed in Godalming, Surrey, in 1881 with power generated at an existing water mill. The development of the incandescent light bulb around 1880, by Swan in Britain and Edison in the USA, enabled electricity to compete with, and soon overtake, gas for indoor lighting and other uses for electricity followed quickly. In particular, the electric motor, which developed alongside the dynamo, provided compact and easily controlled mechanical power for industry and transport applications.

The majority of early electricity generating stations produced direct current (DC), which was capable of being stored in accumulators to provide power when the generators were not running but could only be distributed over very short distances. Many premises such as factories, mines, and country houses therefore had to install their own generation plant and early public supply systems were confined to the centres of urban areas, where they were often municipally owned and supplied electricity for tram systems as well as for street lighting, industrial and domestic use. By 1912 there were over 400 generating stations providing public electricity supplies and an even greater number of private generating plants. Alternating current (AC) allowed electricity to be transmitted over much greater distances by utilising transformers to increase and decrease the voltage but AC generation did not supplant DC until the 1920s, when the first national grid was created to connect local power stations, leading, after World War II, to consolidation of power generation into larger and fewer stations. The electricity industry was nationalised in 1948, with the Central Electricity Generating Board taking responsibility for generation and high-voltage transmission; it returned to the private sector in 1990.

Electricity generation

Some of the earliest generating plant used water turbines to drive the dynamos and so had to be located by a water source, often utilising the infrastructure of existing water mills. Where water power was not available, horizontal steam engines were initially favoured but oil and gas engines were widely adopted for small private generating stations, from the 1890s onwards, whilst the larger urban stations sometimes used high-speed vertical gas engines. However, the steam turbine, invented in 1884, proved to be the most efficient prime mover to produce the high shaft speeds required for alternators. Steam turbo-alternators

sites served by railways or navigable waterways to facilitate coal delivery, before the development of the National Grid led to the construction of large stations well away from centres of population.

All steam-driven power generation requires a considerable capacity for cooling the process steam. Coastal or estuarial locations have often been chosen because of their almost limitless supply of cooling water but elsewhere cooling ponds or towers were used. Early cooling towers were usually rectangular and constructed of wood or reinforced concrete until these were replaced from the 1920s onwards by the hyperbolic design still in use today (Fig 9.6). Other structures associated with electricity generating plant include coal and ash handling plants, transformer and switchgear rooms, control and administrative blocks etc.

Away from the power stations, transformers (sub-stations) were initially housed in buildings or kiosks but most are now in open enclosures. The development of the National Grid from the late 1920s saw pylons spreading across the countryside. These have grown in size as transmission voltages have increased and are often the most visible evidence of the electricity industry. The local electricity companies (later Boards) built offices and showrooms, sometimes in a style which emphasised their clean, modern image in contrast to the gas industry.

Key sites

The survival of buildings associated with the electricity industry mirrors that of the gas industry in two respects: firstly, buildings associated with the early days of small-scale generation are more likely to have been retained and adapted for other purposes than many later, larger structures. Secondly, significant buildings remain on sites still in use by the electricity industry and have yet to be assessed for their historical and archaeological significance.

There are dozens, probably hundreds, of surviving buildings built or adapted to house early private generating plants at factories, mines, and country houses; the original purpose of these is frequently not recognised. Perhaps the most well-known example is at *Cragside*, Northumberland, which is believed to have been the first house in the world to have been lighted by incandescent bulbs. The power house of 1886 contains much original hydro-electric equipment. Other examples include:

+ *Hestercombe House*, Somerset – water mill converted for hydro-electric generation in 1895, recently restored;
+ *Longford's Mill*, Minchinhampton, Gloucestershire – former water-powered woollen mill with original water- and steam-powered electricity plant dating back to 1904;
+ *Ascott*, near Wing, Buckinghamshire – generator house complex dating from before 1899 (see Fig 9.3).

Some sites of early small-scale hydro-electric generation have been returned to use, and others are under consideration, with new or original water turbines driving modern alternators, including *Chatsworth House*, Derbyshire, *Alnwick Castle*, Northumberland, and *Gayle Mill*, North Yorkshire.

Figure 9.7
Ardnacrusha power
station near Limerick,
part of the 1920s
Shannon scheme in
Ireland (© Marilyn
Palmer)

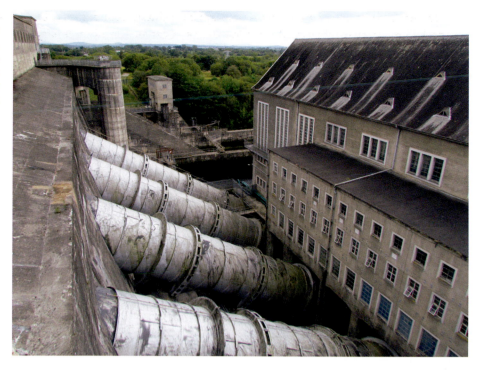

A former water mill, adjacent to *Powick Bridge* near Worcester, was converted in 1894 to become the world's first combined steam/hydro-electric power station. This ceased generating in the 1950s and has been converted to residential use. An intact example of an early public electricity generating station, built in 1903, survives as *the Southern Electricity Museum* in Christchurch, Dorset. Other significant examples of this phase of the industry's development include:

  * *Bristol Counterslip Power Station* – built 1899 for the city's tramway system (see Fig 9.5);
  * *46, Kensington Court, London* – parts of the generating station established in 1886 by one of the industry's pioneers, R E B Crompton;
  * *Electricity sub-station, St George's Place, Cheltenham*, built 1895 in Italian gothic style.

The Tavistock canal, built in the early 19th century to connect the town to *Morwelham Quay*, was purchased in 1933 by the West Devon Electricity Supply Company, which constructed a hydro-electric power plant at the Quay using the canal and tunnel as a water supply. This still feeds power to the National Grid.

Many buildings associated with hydro-electric generation remain in use in Scotland, such as the 1920s' *Falls of Clyde station*, near Lanark. In Ireland, the Shannon hydro-electric scheme was begun not long after Irish independence in 1922 and the power station at *Ardnacrusha* near Limerick retains many of the original features, including the control room (Fig 9.7). The pumped storage schemes at both *Dinorwig (Electric Mountain)* and *Cruachan (Hollow Mountain)* have visitor centres.

The turbine hall at London's *Bankside power station*, built in 1947 to a design by Sir Giles Gilbert Scott, now houses Tate Modern and provides a rare example of the adaptive reuse of a major component of a large, later power station. However, the practical difficulties of such schemes is graphically illustrated at the nearby *Battersea Power station*, the first phase of which was built in the 1930s with a similar architectural pedigree to Bankside, where successive schemes for reuse stretching back several decades have yet to ensure the long-term survival of the buildings. Large power station structures in more remote locations than central London face even greater challenges.

Alternative uses have yet to be found for redundant cooling towers, as illustrated by the pair of 1930s' hyperbolic towers at Blackburn Meadows, Sheffield, which were demolished in 2008, despite a vigorous campaign for their retention. Some power station cooling towers, like gas holders, have become highly valued components of the landscape and other such battles can be expected in the future. Any hopes of preserving parts of nuclear power stations in the future will be faced with problems of radioactive contamination as well as the scale and remote location of the buildings.

Further reading

Studies of the electricity industry have tended to focus on technical and business history, for example B Bowers, *A History of Electric Lighting and Power* (Peter Peregrinus Ltd, 1982), L Hannah, *Electricity before Nationalisation: a study of the electricity supply industry in Britain to 1948* (MacMillan, 1977), and R A S Hennessey, *The Electric Revolution* (Oriel Press, 1972).

Greater emphasis on the industry's physical remains is displayed by Historic Scotland's *Power to the People: the built heritage of Scotland's hydroelectric power* (Historic Scotland, 2010), and M Stratton, *Ironbridge and the Electric Revolution* (John Murray in association with National Power, 1994). English Heritage, too, has taken an interest in the future of nuclear power stations and W Cocroft undertook a SHIER report on nuclear power stations.

The most useful contribution to the study of the physical remains of the electricity industry in England lie in English Heritage's MPP reports, Steps 1–3 by M Trueman of Lancaster University Archaeological Unit (1994–1998) and Step 4 by Gill Chitty (2000).

9.4 Public water supply and sewage disposal

The supply of potable water to the public has a long history, which in England began with the Romans who piped water to their centres of population. Roman water-lifting devices were excavated in London in 2003; a replica built by the Museum of London which has now been relocated to the Ancient Technology Centre at Cranborne in Dorset. Elsewhere the remains of various Roman aqueducts are known, particularly at Lincoln. In the medieval period the monasteries developed supplies for themselves and the general public, directing water from source via leats, pipes, and conduits to conduit heads. Private and public conduit systems were built during the 16th and 17th centuries, known as the 'conduit age', which included the New River from Hertfordshire to north-east London in 1613. Power for these systems was gravity, water or muscle power. As the sources of the water became increasingly polluted during the industrial revolution, leading to diseases such as cholera and typhoid, the new technologies of that period were used to tackle the increasing demand for good-quality water. The Westminster doctor John Snow (d.1858) established the link between cholera and foul water in 1850 and the scale of the problem was underpinned by statistical evidence such as that collected by Edwin Chadwick (d.1890). This influenced the creation of a regulatory framework that has been in place since the 1840s. The 1875 Public Health Act empowered local authorities to provide clean water supplies, and to collect water-borne sewage and treat it before disposal. The new technologies of the industrial age were put to use to tackle the increasing demand for good-quality water.

In upland areas natural lakes were enlarged and new reservoirs created by the construction of dams across valleys, this fresh water then being piped over a considerable distance to the major cities. The dams built for impounding reservoirs were constructed of masonry until the early 20th century, since when concrete has been used, or earth embankment dams with a clay or concrete core, a technique in which Britain made a major contribution to the development of dam building. Several early examples were built in the Pennines to supply water to growing northern mill towns, and the mass concrete arch dam at Haweswater, constructed for Manchester Corporation in 1941, was the first buttress dam in Britain. In lowland areas water continued to be sourced from wells, boreholes, springs, and water courses, but when this became insufficient to meet demand, reservoirs were created behind embankment dams such as at Abberton, Essex (1930s), and Rutland Water (1976). To deliver this water to the customer required extraction from the source, storage and treatment, and further storage before it was delivered. Although gravity was used where possible, there was the need for pumping between most of these stages. The water supply system is thus a network with a number of components spread out over a large area.

Key elements and plan forms

Throughout the industrial age, the supply of fresh water and the disposal of waste water or sewage have usually been conducted by one organisation in each geographical area. This section concentrates on those structures that were constructed during the 19th and 20th centuries. During this period, architecture was used by water companies as a public expression of purity, improvement, safety, and reliability to their customers. Thus, both pumping stations and water towers were often elaborate in design, reflecting prevailing styles of architecture, with many 19th-century examples celebrating high gothic and, more recently, the modern movement, for example in Essex and Suffolk. For the water companies to create a clean impression for their customers, waterworks might be set within a designed landscape. As a number of the larger sites were built away from centres of population, housing was required for the staff of the works. These houses are an important component part of the group of structures associated with water supply and sewage treatment sites.

Water pumping stations

These were needed at a number of points within the whole supply system – to extract water from source to treatment works (known as low-lift stations), to move it from there to storage facilities (high-lift stations), and then to transport it from those to the customer. The first power to be used in pumping stations was steam – beam engines initially followed by compound vertical and horizontal engines. The pumping stations needed height to house the beam engines; light and ventilation were also required, so pumping stations have distinctive fenestration – tall, round-headed windows are common as are other types such as clerestories. Later gas, diesel and then electric pumps were introduced. These sometimes supplemented and sometimes replaced the earlier steam plant and were frequently housed within the same buildings with little external alteration. More recent electric pumping stations have become characterless, secure, vandal-proof boxes with no windows. In order to deal with the maintenance of the early heavy pumping engines gantry cranes were installed which again dictated the height of the buildings. Water pumping buildings are characterised by:

+ High buildings with tall, round-headed and other types of window providing light and air (Fig 9.8);

Figure 9.8 The South Essex Waterworks Co. developed the Stifford Pumping Station at Davy Down in 1926–27 and it housed three diesel pumps built by Sulzer to pump water from a 42m borehole. The pumping station has been restored as part of the Davy Down Riverside Park and is opened for the public to visit (© Tony Crosby)

- Other component structures, including housing for staff, boiler houses and chimneys;
- Presence or evidence of original and/or subsequent pumping engines and gantry cranes.

Water storage

Storage of the water ready for treatment or delivery to the customer was provided for in a number of different structures – open reservoirs, service reservoirs, and water towers. Covered service reservoirs survive from the early Victorian period and are structures of civil engineering interest, being elaborate underground vaulted structures of brick or concrete, covered to give the impression of a grassed field. In consequence little is visible above ground. Water towers, which

Figure 9.9
Polychromatic
brick water tower
in Finedon,
Northamptonshire,
erected 1904–05
(© Marilyn Palmer)

are inherently more visible, were placed at a high point within the area of supply in order to provide the necessary pressure to move the water by gravity and to provide a storage buffer between the pumping station and the consumer. Cast-iron tank water towers first appear in the 1820s; the early examples are normally round but later examples are rectangular. The tank is supported on a sub-structure made of various materials which changed over time from brick or stone to iron frames. In the 20th century concrete became the most common material, with the first concrete tower erected near Liverpool in 1904. Many early water towers have considerable architectural embellishment (Fig 9.9). As well as providing support for the water tank, the sub-structure could also contain a working area, pumps, access to the tank, and even accommodation for the engine-man.

Waterworks

These are sites comprising a number of component parts which, if all or most are of historical, architectural and technological significance will be of added group value. A waterworks may consist of pumping stations, open or service reservoirs, filter houses, staff houses, offices, and laboratories.

Sewage treatment

As water supply improved and flushing water closets began to be introduced, the problem of effluent disposal in cities became more pressing. Septic tanks and cess pools coupled with direct discharge into the local river or the sea were no longer acceptable. From the mid-19th century onwards most of the larger cities in the country began to construct sewerage systems. In London an act passed in 1858, after the infamous Great Stink, enabled the commencement of the construction of the great sewerage system engineered by Sir Joseph Bazalgette. As well as building sewerage systems, many towns also built large pumping stations both to help the flow of the effluent, when gravity flow was insufficient, and to discharge the sewers at their outfall. Eastney at Portsmouth (built in 1864) and Crossness (built in 1865) are outstanding examples of a type which, when built, pumped the untreated effluent into an adjacent river or the sea. In the case of inland areas, of which Leicester and Burton-on-Trent are typical, the untreated effluent would be pumped to a sewage farm some distance outside the city, for spreading on the land. Although most major cities had sewerage systems by 1900, sewage treatment works, introduced from the 1850s (the first established at Leicester in 1853), were slow in development, not being widespread until well into the 20th century. The treatment of sewage was also slow to develop, with most of the basic treatment processes having been largely developed by the beginning of World War I. With the changes in technology, treatment works have undergone steady rebuilding such that structures of historic significance, other than pumping stations, are rare and are also not isolated features, being part of a complex site. During the 20th century, further major improvements were made to the sewerage system and

Figure 9.10 Clay Mills sewage pumping station in Burton-on-Trent contains four rotative Woolf compound beam engines made by Gimson & Co. of Leicester in 1885 (by courtesy of Ian Shipley, www. isphotographic.co.uk)

to the provision of sewage treatment to reduce pollution in the major rivers, estuaries and the sea. Sewage treatment works typically consist of settling beds, filter beds, pumping stations, reservoirs, staff houses, offices, and laboratories.

Key sites

The *Ancient Technology Centre*, Cranborne, Dorset, houses a replica of a Roman water-lifting device. There are numerous preserved steam water pumping engines throughout the country, many of which are still run periodically and operate as museums. These include:

- *Ryhope Engines Museum* – two 1868 beam engines in the Sunderland waterworks (www.ryhopeengines.org.uk);
- *Papplewick Pumping Station* – two James Watt beam engines at the Nottingham waterworks (www.papplewickpumpingstation.co.uk);
- *Hereford Waterworks Museum*, which traces the history of water supply and includes working triple-expansion steam engines (http://www.waterworksmuseum.org.uk);
- *Kew Bridge Steam Museum*, which tells the story of London's water supply from Roman times and includes a large collection of different steam pumping engines (http://www.kbsm.org);

- *Blagdon Pumping Station and Visitor Centre* – dam, reservoir and pumping station built in 1890s to supply water to Bristol (http://www.bristolwater.co.uk/leisure/blagdon-info.asp).

Good examples of steam-powered sewage pumping stations survive at:

- *Abbey Pumping Station* – opened 1891 to pump Leicester's sewage to the Beaumont Leys treatment works (http://www.leicester.gov.uk/your-council-services/lc/leicester-city-museums/museums/abbey-pumping-station/);
- *Crossness Pumping Station* – opened 1865 as part of Sir Joseph Bazalgette's sewerage system for London (http://www.crossness.org.uk);
- *Eastney Beam Engine House* – contains a pair of Boulton and Watt beam engines built to pump Portsmouth's sewage to the sea (http://www.portsmouthmuseums.co.uk/EastneyBeamEngineHouse.html);
- *Clay Mills Pumping Station, Burton-on-Trent* (see Fig 9.10) – contains four Woolf compound beam engines built by Gimson's of Leicester in 1885 (http://www.claymills.org.uk/).

In recent years, many disused water towers have been converted for residential use; some examples can be seen on the web site of the British Water Tower Appreciation Society (http://bwtas.blogspot.com) (accessed 19 November 2011).

Further reading

A brief introduction is given in P Naylor, *Water Supply* (Shire, 2005), and more detail is provided by H Barty-King, *Water: The Book* (Quiller, 1992). M Lewis' article 'Our debt to Roman engineering: the water supply of Lincoln to the present day' (*Industrial Archaeology Review* 7:1, 1984, 57–73) considers the Roman aqueduct at Lincoln and its successors. The architecture of water supply is covered in J Douet, *Temples of Steam: Waterworks Architecture in the Steam Age* (Bristol Polytechnic, 1992), and a detailed study of water towers can be found in B Barton, *Water Towers of Britain* (Newcomen Society, 2003).

An excellent description of pumping stations is provided by Kew Bridge Steam Museum, 'Temples of Steam: The Art of the Pumping Station' (*Archive*, **12**, 49–64). Specific system histories include R Ward, *London's New River* (Historical Publications, 2003), and S Halliday, *The Great Stink of London* (Sutton Publishing, 2002).

There are a particularly good series of MPP reports on the water and sewage industries: J Douet, Step 1 (1995); M Trueman, Step 3 (2000); G Chitty, Step 4 (2001); M Trueman, Thematic List Review: Water Towers (2000).

CHAPTER TEN

The future for the study of industrial archaeology

10.1 Introduction

This book, written half a century after the first organised activity which was labelled as 'industrial archaeology' took place, has tried to demonstrate how the subject has been transformed from a fringe activity to an internationally recognised element of the discipline of archaeology. We have defined industrial archaeology as the study of the evidence for people at work, a type of human activity rather than just a type of site, since 'work', even after the so-called 'Industrial Revolution', could be based in domestic as well as non-domestic locations. The time frame is the classic period of industrialisation from the early modern and modern periods, mainly the early 18th to the 20th centuries, characterised by capital investment on a large scale in both buildings and equipment and the organisation of the labour force to maximise production, although not necessarily all grouped in large buildings. We have shown that industrial archaeology also deals with the wider economic and social landscape of this period, as much concerned with analysing the origins and impact of the Industrial Revolution as with charting, recording and understanding the technological innovations with which it is usually associated. Particular emphasis has been placed in the book on the housing of the labour force in both rural and urban situations, and we have included some consideration of the leisure activities of the workforce although much more could be said on this. Industrial activity has had a greater impact on the landscape than any other human intervention since the clearance of the forests and the development of farming in the prehistoric period, especially in the exploitation of mineral resources, their associated processing and the transport networks necessary for their distribution.

The day training schools in which this book had its origins were intended to acquaint delegates with the significant features of industrial buildings and structures, and thus many of the chapters have been concerned with what one might term 'above-ground' industrial archaeology. However, one aspect of the development of the discipline emphasised in Chapter One is the increasing interest in the excavated remains of industrial activity, largely because of the participation of professional archaeologists in development work on brownfield sites. We have endeavoured as much as possible to ascertain what 'below-ground' activity has taken place on industrial sites and to point readers in the direction of the grey literature in which most of the results of such work are embedded.

We have also tried to work our way through the dichotomy of industrial archaeology being regarded as both an archaeological study of the ways in which people lived and worked in the past through the physical remains which survive into the present and at the same time a conservation movement to protect and interpret those remains. The popular and even the professional conception of industrial archaeology has tended to adopt its meaning as a movement to conserve the industrial past, which would be better termed 'industrial heritage', and we hope that we have redressed the balance by showing just how much can be learnt about the way our forebears lived and worked in the industrial period through the study of its standing and excavated remains. Nevertheless, we recognise that the conservation and interpretation of the standing remains of industrial activity in the world's first industrialised nation are an important aspect of industrial archaeology, and have devoted some space to a consideration of the protection as well as the adaptive reuse of industrial structures.

The way in which this book came into being means that we have had to concentrate on industrial archaeology in the British Isles. This does not mean that we think that industrial activity in Britain was divorced from events elsewhere in the world. On the contrary, British industrial development was part of a global economy, related both to its position in the Atlantic World as well as to its widespread Empire. The vast expansion of the iron and cotton industries, for example, with the consequent effect on the buildings and landscape of much of midland and northern Britain, would never have taken place had it not been for the demands of Britain's global trading networks. Industrialisation rapidly became a world-wide phenomenon not particular to a century, or indeed country, and so it is vital for archaeologists to provide a distinct view of the origins, course and consequence of this process of technological change at a regional, national and international level. We are also fully aware that the discipline of industrial archaeology, especially in its concomitant sense as an industrial heritage movement, is very active in Europe, America and Australasia and would very much have liked to explore this too – but that is another book!

10.2 The resource

One of the chief problems faced by any archaeologist studying the industrial period is the mass of data available, both physical evidence such as standing buildings, machinery, industrial landscapes, written documents, maps and drawings and more recently the growing amount of excavated evidence revealed by developer-funded work undertaken on sites of this period. We have tried to suggest some approaches to making sense of this data, including methodologies charting archaeologically the impact of new industrial-period monument types on a given piece of landscape; exploring the relationship of these new monuments to contemporary local social groups; and undertaking historic landscape characterisation to help understand change at the county or regional level. The growth of the desk-based assessment as one of the most important archaeological planning tools of the last twenty years has meant that the idea of studying a wide range of documentary material, familiar to the first industrial archaeologists of the 1950s and 1960s, has also become embedded in developer-funded archaeological projects, and we have explored the value of historic map regression for the industrial period.

We have very much welcomed the increasing participation of professional curatorial and contract archaeologists in the practice of industrial archaeology in the last two decades. Nevertheless, the most valuable resource for industrial archaeology remains the large number of volunteers who are prepared to deploy skills often derived from their own professional lives on, for example, recording and preserving machinery or conserving and interpreting industrial structures. Most British counties have a group of people interested in industrial archaeology who usually undertake a variety of activities ranging from documentary research, recording industrial buildings in considerable detail, maintaining industrial sites and displaying them to the public and, in some cases, undertaking specific excavation projects. As pointed out in Chapter One, all the early county surveys of what industrial structures had survived into the 20th century were, with the exception of Northern Ireland, undertaken by voluntary groups. Industrial archaeology has been very fortunate in the quality of its volunteer participation, and the provision of some funding and direction to channel this volunteer enthusiasm remains very important, given cuts to professional staff in curatorial and contract archaeology.

One major concern is the provision of new blood into work on the industrial heritage that is generally recognised as a key element of Britain's contribution to world culture. Many university-based archaeology courses now include some industrial archaeology, usually under the broader category of historical archaeology, but there are few staff who have the necessary knowledge to acquaint students with the fundamental principles of the discipline. Of equal concern is the perceived discontinuity between the undergraduate archaeology curriculum, which lecturers feel should impart understanding of the past within a theoretical and methodological framework, since few of their students will actually continue in archaeology, and the practical needs of archaeological employers from those who do join the profession – a disjunction that has been repeatedly stressed by the Archaeology Training Forum. Yet urban development, until very recently, has led to a massive increase in the amount of archaeological work being undertaken on brownfield sites, requiring practitioners who can both draw upon the necessary briefs on the curatorial side and fieldworkers who can recognise the remains of different types of power sources or industrial processes and understand the human context of industry in terms of workers' housing and social institutions. Given changes to university funding, it may well be that the necessary skills have to be acquired through postgraduate training, often by Distance Learning or Continuous Professional Development courses which can supply training without loss of salary, something that applies not just to archaeological activity or building recording but also to the management of Britain's internationally important industrial heritage.

10.3 Research agendas

Although a great deal has been achieved to ensure recognition that the material evidence of the industrial period, whether standing remains or below-ground archaeology, contributes to debates on important questions like the impact of industrialisation on both the countryside and townscapes or the ways in which technological change in the processes of production was reflected in patterns of consumption, we need to continue to work to convince planners, developers and others involved in the conservation and restoration of sites of the value of industrial archaeology. We have, therefore, to establish priorities on particular sites which come up for development by drawing up, and publicising, good typologies of standing industrial buildings; remaining alert to new field and analytical techniques which can expand the range available on complex industrial sites; and continuing to promote contact and dialogue between all parts of the archaeological community, whether academic, professional or volunteer. As the current economic and legislative climates make both planners and developers more cautious, it is increasingly important for archaeological curators to be able to justify their recommendations. A competently prepared Research Agenda, coupled with site-specific information gleaned from a desk-based assessment and fabric appraisal, permits a fairly good degree of predictive modelling on most sites and allows even a non-specialist curator both to make confident recommendations and to justify them to a potentially hostile third party. We hope that this book, together with the national and regional research agendas already available in the UK, will go some way towards enabling this process to work more smoothly.

10.4 The industrial heritage

English Heritage identified our industrial heritage as the theme for its 2011 Heritage at Risk programme. As its Project Officer Shane Gould pointed out, the large-scale economic changes in recent decades have led to the loss of entire landscapes associated with England's unique industrial heritage, notably, of course, coal mining and the textile industries. The Heritage at Risk programme presented an opportunity to take stock of the risks to what remained and to assess the effectiveness of possible solutions. This would be done, to quote English Heritage's own website, by getting 'owners, developers, local people, voluntary bodies, academics, professionals and politicians debating the future of our industrial heritage before it is too late' (see http://www.english-heritage. org.uk/caring/heritage-at-risk/industrial-heritage-at-risk/). Nearly 11% of Grade

I and II* industrial buildings are at risk, far higher than the 3% of Grade I and II* buildings of other types which are at risk in England. The sheer scale of some historic industrial processes, such as mining, quarrying and mass production, can be a conservation challenge in itself, while large industrial buildings present particular problems in reuse.

Sir Neil Cossons has drawn up a challenging programme for English Heritage in Issue 67 of English Heritage's *Conservation Bulletin*, which was devoted to the industrial heritage (available as a free download from English Heritage – http://www.english-heritage.org.uk/publications/conservation-bulletin-67/). He suggests that there are six priorities for English Heritage in helping to ensure the future of the industrial heritage. These comprise: powerful advocacy in promoting the cause of industrial places; working with voluntary advocacy organisations; securing the future of those sites preserved by the voluntary sector; securing the future of key industrial buildings at risk; a determined programme to ensure the future of the more 'invisible' industrial heritage, such as workers' housing; and pressing the case for the designation of post-war industrial buildings – industrial activity is a continuous one, not just a product of the 18th and 19th centuries. Sir Neil has worked tirelessly in the cause of the industrial heritage throughout his career, and we hope that his challenges can be met as a result of English Heritage's well-publicised Industrial Heritage at Risk initiative.

Adaptive reuse has proved to be the salvation for many redundant industrial buildings, as demonstrated in Section 1.4 of this book, but the high costs of conversion and, in some cases, decontamination, remain a deterrent to many developers, particularly if the building is in an area of low property values. Industrial sites which survive as unroofed structures pose particularly difficult conservation challenges, although the Heritage Lottery Fund, founded in 1994, has enabled many local groups to form charitable trusts to save them. However, the recurrent costs of maintenance as well as succession planning in the trusts have raised concern about the long-term future of the UK's preserved industrial sites, as was outlined in a report to English Heritage by Sir Neil Cossons in 2008 (available as a free download – see http://www.english-heritage.org.uk/content/publications/docs/sustaining-englands-ind-heritage.pdf). The Industrial Heritage at Risk initiative has, however, made advice and guidance on the conservation of industrial sites more easily accessible: there is guidance for owners and developers on its website – (www.english-heritage.org.uk/developers); the Architectural Heritage Fund (www.ahfund.org.uk) has established a three-year grant scheme to encourage local groups to take on industrial buildings; and an Industrial Heritage Support Officer is to be appointed within an outside organisation to provide help to those preserving historic industrial sites for public access.

Yet, industrial archaeology and heritage is at risk from many quarters, not just neglect and redevelopment. Further threats of cuts to the funding of local planning archaeology services continue as British archaeology undergoes its biggest structural change since the early 1990s, when the principle of 'the developer pays' was introduced into planning guidance and regulations. Furthermore, it is not clear whether the new National Planning Policy Framework proposed for England will maintain the current level of protection for archaeological sites within the planning process, especially currently unprotected sites, many of which are industrial in origin. Continual vigilance will be needed on the part of all those who work in, or care about, industrial archaeology and heritage, just as was the case over 50 years ago when the discipline was first launched. The Council for British Archaeology was one of its staunchest advocates back in the 1960s and continues to promote the discipline, as can be seen from the publication of this book. They were joined later by the Association for Industrial Archaeology and its many affiliated societies which represent the thousands of volunteers prepared to work for the future of industrial archaeology and heritage, as well as publishing the results of professional and volunteer research. This book is intended to be of assistance to all sectors, professional and voluntary, which care about the future of Britain's internationally important industrial heritage.

Index

Entries in bold refer to Figures

clay industry
 brickworks 116–17
 buildings associated with 117
 kilns 117–18, **117**
 uses of products 116
bridges 240–41, **241**, 250–51, 259
 building materials 240, 241, 250, 259
Brindley, James 248, 252
Bristol 76, 142, 157, 174, 175, 178, 272, 276,
 283, 301, 308
Bristol Industrial Archaeology Society 4
British Waterways 249, 250
brownfield development 32, 36
brownfield sites 1, 7, 164, 309, 311
Brunel, I K 226, 240, 256, 259, 261
Buchanan, Angus 3, 4, 5, **5**
Buck, George Watson 261
building materials 37, 57, 61, 62, 161, 170,
 172, 193
buildings
 changes of use 20 *see also* adaptive
  reuse of industrial buildings
 demolition of 26
 fixtures and fittings, recording of 19
 form of following function 61, 158, 185,
  200
 place in work-flow 20
 recording of 18–20
 siting in landscape 21 *see also*
  industrial archaeology, landscape
  context
Buildings at Risk Register 40
bye-laws 224, 227, 288

Cadw 23, 25, 32, 33
canals 12, 235, 244, 247–9, 267 *see also*
 bridges; river navigations
 adaptive reuse of 254
 aqueducts 252–3, **252**
 buildings associated with 250 *see also*
  warehouses
 'canal mania' 247
 canalside furniture 253–4
 decline of 248–9
 effects of 248
 further reading 254–5
 key sites 254
 landscape context 249–50
 leisure use 249

lifts and inclined places 252
locks 251
restoration of 249, 254
tunnels 253
water supply 253, **253**
charcoal production 154–6, 157–8
Cheshire 6, 143, 173, 185, 214, 219, 220
chimneys 102, 196, 199, **202**
cider manufacture 71–2
cider mills 71–2, **71**
Civic Voice 33
civil engineering 235
clay industry 111, 118–19 *see also* brick and
 tile making; pottery making
 assessment of sites 119
 extraction 111–12
 further reading 119–20
 key sites 112, 115, 118
 kilns 112–13
 mechanisation of 112
 processing 112–13
 raw material 111–12
coal industry 99, 128–32, **130**, 233
 assessment of sites 132
 by-products 131, **131**
 drainage *see* drainage, of mines
 extraction 128–9
 further reading 133–4
 key sites 133
 power sources 129–30
 processing 131
 recording of 132
 ventilation 130–31
 workforce 132
coastwise shipping 72, 126, 131, 235, 247
Conservation Areas 27–8, 34, 262
contamination of sites 18, 36, 138, 159, 295,
 302 *see also* pollution
co-operative movement, the 73, 280–83
 agricultural production 281
 assembly halls 282
 food process buildings 283
 further reading 283
 libraries 282
 manufacturing premises 283
 mass production of goods 281
 retail premises 281, **282**, 282
 wholesale buying 281 *see also*
  warehouses

impact on environment 22 *see also*
    contamination of sites
impact on landscape of 10, 11, 310
social impact of 11, 12, 311
speed of 10, 162
technology and science of 9, 12
industry
    change in 33
    classification of 26
    decline of 5–6, 20, 162
Inland Waterways Association 249
internal combustion engines 79, 80
Ireland 56, 69, 70, 90, 101, 141, 143, 175,
    191, 234–5, 248, 301 *see also* Northern
    Ireland
iron and steel industry 85, 149, 155
    assessment of sites 152
    extraction and calcining 150
    fuel 150–51
    furnaces 150, 151, **151**, **152**
    further reading 153–4
    key sites 152–3
    locations of 150
    smelting 150
    steel manufacture 151–2
Ironbridge Institute 13

jenny shops 194, 195
Jessop, William 241, 248, 252
Journal of Industrial Archaeology, The 5

Kay, James 191
Kay, John 186

lace industry 209–10, 211
    domestic production 209–10, 219
    factories **209**, 210, **211**
    machinery 209–10
    mechanisation of 210
Lancashire 39, 163, 196, 200, 201, 214, 215,
    216, 218, 220, 234, 281
    Bank Top 224
    Burnley 201, 230
    Chorley 158, 227
    Egerton 224, 230
    Fylde, the 93
    textile mills in 39, 101, 103, 185, 192,
        197, 198, 199, 201
    Warton 173
land management 27, 28, 31

land values 223, 228, 277
LEADER programmes 31
leather industry
    boot and shoe manufacture 181–3, 211,
        219, 220, 281
    decline of 180
    development of 180
    further reading 183–4
    key sites 183
    locations 180, 183
    mechanisation of 180, 182, 183
    regulation of 180
    requirements of 180–81
    structures associated with 181, **182**, 183
    tanning 179–80
    working systems 181–2, 183
leats 85, 139, 157, 201, 303
Lee, Edmund 95
legislation 21 *see also* Corn Laws
    Ancient Monuments and
        Archaeological Areas Act (1979) 24
    Ancient Monuments Protection Act
        (1882) 24
    Beer Act (1830) 286
    Education Acts 208
    Explosives Act (1875) 157
    Heritage Protection Bill (2009) 27
    housing acts 227
    licensing acts 286, 287, 288
    Planning (Listed Buildings and
        Conservation Areas) Act (1990) 25
    Stannary Law 144, 147
    Wildlife and Countryside Act (1983)
        29
Leicestershire 183, 205, 206, 208, 209, 211,
    218, 220
Lever, William Hesketh 222
lime burning 120
    further reading 122–3
    key sites 122
    kilns 120–21, **121**, 122
    location of 121
linear monuments 12, 18
linen industry 185, 187–8, 200
    mechanisation of 185–6
listing, of buildings 24–5, 26, 27, 30, 262,
    263, 268, 296, 313
Liverpool 65, 76, 105, 268, 276, 283, 284,
    285, 288
    Albert Dock **35**, 36, 273, 279